Cuban Economists on the Cuban Economy

CONTEMPORARY CUBA

UNIVERSITY PRESS OF FLORIDA

Printed in the United States of America. This book is printed on Glatfelter Natures Book, a paper certified under the standards of the Forestry Stewardship Council (FSC). It is a recycled stock that contains 30 percent post-consumer waste and is acid-free.

This book may be available in an electronic edition.

18 17 16 15 14 13 6 5 4 3 2 1

Library of Congress Cataloging-in-Publication Data
Cuban economists on the Cuban economy / edited by Al Campbell.
p. cm. — (Contemporary Cuba)
Includes bibliographical references and index.
Summary: Brings together some of Cuba's most prominent economists to examine Cuba's economic history and analyze changes in policy during the years since the collapse of the Soviet Union.
ISBN 978-0-8130-4423-1 (alk. paper)
1. Cuba—Economic conditions. 2. Cuba—Economic policy. 3. Cuba—Social conditions.
I.Campbell, Al. II. Series: Contemporary Cuba.
HC152.5.C835 2013
330.97291—dc23 2013007065

The University Press of Florida is the scholarly publishing agency for the State University System of Florida, comprising Florida A&M University, Florida Atlantic University, Florida Gulf Coast University, Florida International University, Florida State University, New College of Florida, University of Central Florida, University of Florida, University of North Florida, University of South Florida, and University of West Florida.

University Press of Florida
15 Northwest 15th Street
Gainesville, FL 32611-2079
http://www.upf.com

Cuban Economists on the Cuban Economy

Edited by Al Campbell

John M. Kirk, Series Editor

UNIVERSITY PRESS OF FLORIDA

Gainesville / Tallahassee / Tampa / Boca Raton

Pensacola / Orlando / Miami / Jacksonville / Ft. Myers / Sarasota

For Ángela Ferriol (1953–2011), the midwife of this book, without whom it would not have seen the light of day, who treated its birth with the same responsibility and care that characterized all her social and personal work.

For Alfredo Morales Cartaya (1948–2010), who dedicated his life to serving the working people of Cuba.

Contents

Tables

Figures

Acknowledgments

My greatest gratitude for their perseverance despite the always present difficulties in communication caused above all by the U.S. blockade of Cuba of course goes to the thirteen contributing authors. Anyone who has been involved in collaborative work between academics in Cuba and the United States knows of the difficulties and delays this causes and the significant extra efforts required to carry out what should be normal academic work. A major hope of all of us is that this work will make a small contribution to weakening one important part of the blockade, the various limitations on the presentation in the United States of Cuban views on the many aspects of Cuba's reality.

While any book receives important support throughout its gestation from too many people to list, the following seven must be singled out for their particularly important contributions, presented here in chronological order.

The fundamental idea of the value for English-language readers of a book like this in which Cuban economists expressed their understanding of the Cuban economy came out of a series of discussions between myself and Ángela Ferriol. She then played the central role in assembling the thirteen contributing authors and in maintaining contact between myself and them over the period of the writing and revision of the chapters.

Translating this much material from Spanish to English was a major part of the creation of this book. And while in the end all final decisions on the translation are mine, Ángel Ramón Milán did the initial translation of the large majority of the material.

John Kirk from Dalhousie University is the academic editor of the Contemporary Cuba series of the University Press of Florida. His long experience publishing books on Cuba enabled him to see value in the original proposal long before its initial efforts had congealed into anything approaching academic acceptability. He cannot be sufficiently thanked for his unflinching encouragement from the manuscript's beginnings through the several revisions right up to its acceptance.

Amy Gorelick is acquiring editor at the University Press of Florida. Her editorial guidance was both amicable and precise. It took significant work over an extended period of time to steer me through the detailed requirements of preparing and submitting a manuscript, a type of work that is not one of my loves or strengths.

The outside reviews of the manuscript by an anonymous reviewer and Professor Eloise Linger of SUNY Old Westbury were done both very thoroughly and well and were therefore extremely helpful.

Kirsteen E. Anderson worked her magic on both the formatting and the language, transforming both significantly to produce the almost-final form of this work.

Finally, there was the task of converting the many graphs from the sort that academics use in papers to the kind required in such a book, a task beyond my technical abilities that was carried out artistically as well as technically by Regula Bürki.

To recognize the extent of their efforts would, for this book, be inadequate. It must be acknowledged that without their various profound contributions, this book would never have seen the light of day.

Abbreviations

ACT	Actividad Científica y Tecnológica (Scientific and Technological Activity)
AIDS	acquired immunodeficiency syndrome
ALBA	Alianza Bolivariana para los Pueblos de Nuestra América (Bolivarian Alternative for the Americas)
ANIR	Asociación Nacional de Innovadores y Racionalizadores (National Association of Innovators and Rationalizers)
BTJ	Brigada Técnica Juvenil (Technical Youth Brigade)
CADECA	casa de cambio (currency exchange house)
CARICOM	Caribbean Community
CCS	Cooperativa de Créditos y Servicios (Cooperative for Credits and Services)
CDR	Comités de Defensa de la Revolución (Committees for Defense of the Revolution)
CEE	Comité Estatal de Estadística (State Committee for Statistics)
CEPAL	Comisión Económica para América Latina y el Caribe (Economic Commission for Latin America and the Caribbean)
CIGB	Centro de Ingeniería Genética y Biotecnología (Center for Genetic Engineering and Biotechnology)
CIS	Commonwealth of Independent States (former Soviet republics)
CITMA	Ministerio de Ciencia, Tecnología y Medio Ambiente (Ministry of Science, Technology, and the Environment)
CMEA	Council for Mutual Economic Assistance, alternatively referred to in English as COMECON
COMECON	Council for Mutual Economic Assistance, also referred to in English as CMEA
CPA	Cooperativa de Producción Agropecuaria (Agricultural Production Cooperative)

CTC	Confederación de Trabajadores de Cuba (Confederation of Cuban Workers)
CUC	convertible Cuban peso
CUP	Cuban peso (nonconvertible)
ECA	economic complementation agreement
ECLAC	Economic Commission for Latin America and the Caribbean
FCT	Fórum de Ciencia y Técnica (Science and Technology Forum)
FDI	foreign direct investment
FEU	Federación Estudiantil Universitaria (Federation of University Students)
G8	Group of 8, eight countries among the world's largest economies
GDP	gross domestic product
GOSPLAN	State Planning Committee of the former Soviet Union
HDI	Human Development Index
IEA	international economic association
ILO	International Labor Organization
IMF	International Monetary Fund
INIE	Instituto Nacional de Investigaciones Económicas (National Institute for Economic Research)
INIT	Instituto Nacional de la Industria Turística (National Institute of the Tourism Industry)
IT	information technology
JUCEPLAN	Junta Central de Planificación (Central Planning Board)
LAIA	Latin American Integration Association
MEP	Ministerio de Economía y Planificación (Ministry of Economy and Planning)
MINCEX	Ministerio del Comercio Exterior (Ministry of Foreign Trade) from 1961 to 2009, thereafter Ministerio del Comercio Exterior y la Inversión Extranjera (Ministry of Foreign Trade and Investment)
MINREX	Ministerio de Relaciones Exteriores (Ministry of Foreign Affairs)
MINTUR	Ministerio de Turismo (Ministry of Tourism)
MINVEC	Ministerio de la Inversión Extranjera y la Colaboración (Ministry of Foreign Investment and Economic Cooperation), fused into the new MINCEX in the reorganization of 2009

NEES	National Electrical Energy System
OACE	Organismo de la Administración Central del Estado (Body of the Central State Administration)
OECD	Organization for Economic Cooperation and Development
ONE	Oficina Nacional de Estadísticas (National Office of Statistics)
PAHO	Pan-American Health Organization
PNUD	Programa de las Naciones Unidas para el Desarrollo (United Nations Development Programme)
Project SABE	Proyecto Salud, Bienestar y Envejecimiento (Research Project on Health, Welfare and Aging)
SCIT	Sistema de Ciencia e Innovación Tecnológica (System of Science and Technological Innovation)
TFR	total fertility rate
UBPC	Unidad Básica de Producción Cooperativa (Basic Unit of Cooperative Production)
USITC	U.S. International Trade Commission
WTO	World Trade Organization

Introduction

Finding a New Road (Again) to a Socialist Economy and Economic Well-Being in Cuba

AL CAMPBELL

Since Cuba announced to the world on April 16, 1961, that it was embarking on the construction of a socialist state, the history of its economic policies has been one of constant change within continuity. Its evolving economic policies can be divided into a somewhat standard periodization as follows: 1961–65, the Great Debate; 1966–70, the Revolutionary Offensive;[1] 1971–75, transition to a modified Soviet economy; 1976–85, modified Soviet economy; 1986–89, Rectification Process; and 1990–present, the Special Period (see chapters 1 and 2 for somewhat different variants on this periodization). Sometimes the transition from one period to the next involved fundamentally different reconceptualizations of what was actually central to socialism. In all cases, the policies of successive periods implemented significant changes in emphasis to achieve what was necessary at that moment to promote a socialist economy in Cuba. The continuity through all the changes has been exactly that commitment to building a socialist economy, even though discussions have never ceased in Cuba about exactly what that means and how best to do it.

This continuous commitment to creating a socialist society has guided Cuba's choices in building its economy, and its importance must not be underestimated. The dominant (though not exclusive) premise taught to economists in capitalist countries is that there is only one "real economic problem": to make the "pie" (the GDP) grow as fast as possible.[2] Conservative-leaning economists consider the distribution of the social product to be automatically just, because they hold that the market returns to "factors of production" (which includes working people) what those factors contribute to production. More liberal economists recognize that the government could always step in and redistribute the market's resources in accordance with any desired results; therefore, in their view social redistribution is a political issue, not an economic one with which they should concern themselves. Hence, both conservative and liberal capitalist economists in general find distribution of wealth to be an inappropriate issue for economic consideration.

In contrast, as the chapter authors will note repeatedly, a socialist economy has a different goal: it directly targets the well-being of the population. Societal well-being is a much more difficult concept to measure than GDP, a topic addressed in chapter 5. It is, however, essential to understand that Cuba's economic policies have this fundamental goal in order to consider its economic performance in any meaningful way. Of course, Cuban policymakers hold that GDP growth and improved economic efficiency are necessary for improved societal well-being. But the important difference is that for them economic growth alone is not sufficient and is not identical with workers' well-being. Certain means of improving efficiency or GDP can be harmful to the well-being of the majority of the population. This different goal clearly has the potential to cause Cuban policymakers to act differently than their capitalist counterparts would. Economists who cling to the beliefs that all economic policies are based on GDP growth, and that Cuba's declarations of socialism are either irrelevant or harmful to good growth policies,[3] will necessarily fail to understand why Cuba's economic policies have been what they are.

When in the 1990s Cuba entered its worst economic downturn since the triumph of the Revolution, it acted in ways counter to capitalist economic policies. It chose to borrow as heavily as it could despite the negative consequences to its debt and credit rating. It chose to allow an excessive buildup of domestic liquidity by keeping people on payrolls to prevent widespread unemployment, even when factories did not have the inputs to carry out production. As almost all the contributing authors note, Cuba did this to defend, to the maximum extent its problematic economic situation allowed, the important gains in human well-being it had achieved in terms of health care, education, and the elimination of poverty and clinical hunger.

These steps are directly opposite to the adjustment programs that the International Monetary Fund (IMF) has imposed on many third-world countries since the 1980s in the name of (restoring) economic growth and long-term efficiency. Most of the IMF austerity programs failed to restore healthy growth, but that is not the issue here. Rather, the important point is that Cuba ruled out severe austerity measures precisely because its basic economic goal was human well-being, not GDP growth. Cuban leaders understood that policies of consuming more than was produced were unsustainable, and that eventually excess liquidity and hidden unemployment would have to be eliminated. But their goal of maximizing human well-being caused them to incur costs that would have to be repaid in the future, in order to cushion the shock to the country's weakest and most vulnerable people, sparing them the fate of the weak and vulnerable during economic crises throughout capitalist Latin America and the third world. Again, the point in relation to this volume is that Cuba's economic behavior cannot be understood unless one recognizes that Cuba's commitment to building socialism entails some different economic goals, as chapters 5, 6, and 8 in particular illustrate.[4]

Opponents of the Revolution frequently argue that the thread of continuity that has run through Cuba's economic policies over the decades—namely, its commitment to building socialism—has been a project of the government and the Cuban Communist Party, imposed on the population without any broad support. There are almost no independent public-opinion polls that can provide evidence either for or against this assertion. There was, however, one such poll and, given its uniqueness, I find it somewhat surprising that it has rarely been cited in the ongoing debate outside of Cuba.

In November 1994, near the worst time in the Special Period, the *Miami Herald* commissioned the Costa Rican firm CID-Gallup, which is associated with the Gallup Organization, to conduct a standard independent poll in Cuba on the population's attitudes toward various aspects of the Revolution and their lives. The large sample size of 1,002 adults interviewed would predict statistically that their answers would match the average attitudes of the entire population to within +3 percentage points. Of the forty-six questions, two specifically addressed popular support for the Revolution and its policies. With regard to political outlook, 10 percent of respondents identified themselves as Communists, 10 percent as Socialists, and 48 percent as Revolutionaries (24 percent said they were not integrated into the Revolution). Given that in Cuba the word *socialist* has been used to mean "social democratic," and *communist* until recently denoted the policies of the Soviet Union, this result clearly shows broad (but equally clearly not universal) popular support for the policies of the Revolution. A second question directly posed this issue by asking the respondent, taking into account both the achievements and failures of the Revolution, which he or she felt on balance was greater. Fifty-eight percent said there were more achievements than failures, while 31 percent said the opposite.[5]

Many opponents of the Revolution outside of Cuba hoped that when Raúl Castro replaced Fidel as the leading figure in the government in the summer of 2006,[6] his "pragmatism" would lead to the termination of Cuba's socialist project and a restoration of capitalism. Raúl's reputation for pragmatism is indeed well deserved, but he has made clear in statement after statement from the day he assumed power that his goal is to pragmatically address and resolve the specific problems in Cuba's economic and social model for building socialism, while maintaining its strengths. A particularly well-known statement of his intentions, and his understanding of the popular sentiment, is the following:

> They did not elect me president to restore capitalism in Cuba or to surrender the Revolution. I was elected to defend, maintain, and continue perfecting socialism, not to destroy it.... [I]n the year 2002—specifically between June 15 and 18—8,198,237 citizens, almost the entire voting-age population, signed the request to this Assembly to promote the constitutional reform that ratified the Constitution of the Republic in all its parts, and declared irrevocable the socialist nature and the political and social system contained within our fundamental law, which was approved unanimously by the deputies of the National Assembly in the special session held on June 24, 25, and 26 of the same year.[7]

The concrete economic policies described in the following chapters can only be understood as Cuba's attempts to find a new road to the same popularly (but not universally) supported goal that it has pursued since 1961, the construction of a socialist economy.

Origin and Purpose of This Volume

This book originated in a conversation about the Cuban economy between the editor and one of the contributors, Ángela Ferriol. It seemed to both of us that many of the same issues about the Cuban political economy that constantly appeared in both the press and academic papers outside of Cuba were also being extensively written about by a large body of Cuban researchers. Yet although these works inside and outside of Cuba generally addressed the same issues, they often did so from different perspectives—looking at the same questions within different frames. The standard concept in science that studying the same issues from different perspectives deepens understanding argues for a wide dissemination of the studies from the Island among both researchers and the general population outside of Cuba.

Politicians and the media outside of Cuba often argue that both academic economists and policymakers on the Island are divided into two camps: those who seek reform versus those who oppose it. That is simply false. Not only essentially all Cuban economists, but also essentially the entire population of Cuba, favor significant economic transformations. Almost no one "opposes economic reform." What does exist, however, is a broad spectrum of opinions on what types of changes and what exact changes are needed or would be best.

So the difference in the frame of Cuban economists versus those outside of

Cuba does not revolve around the need for economic reform, which all agree on. What it does concern is how to continue Cuba's five decades of working to build socialism: how to design economic policies not only for growth and efficiency but at the same time directly for human well-being. The majority of economists outside of Cuba advocate ending socialism as the key to Cuba's growth and development.[8] The majority (though not all) of economists within Cuba advocate continuing the five-decade-long project of building socialism, while making important changes in the way this is done. As the chapters in this collection illustrate, Cuban political economists do not downplay the economic problems Cuba faces—after all, it is their job to uncover and correct them—but they tend to see and present the problems within the context of the Island's overall economic, political, and social processes, which have also achieved important successes. What they mostly advocate, then, are proposals that they believe will maintain the social gains at the same time that they overcome the economic problems. Even when they call for major reforms, as many Cuban political economists do, they tend to view these as a major tune-up of a system that needs extensive refurbishing and renovation, not as abandonment of the system that has brought them important gains.

Cuban research and information on the Island's economy is extensive, but several factors have consistently limited the amount that is disseminated abroad. The most immediate reason is the language barrier. Almost all Cuban research, and even statistical compilations, is written in Spanish, and only a small (though important) part of that gets translated into other languages. This, of course, is a minor barrier to academic specialists on Cuba and to the international press. It is, however, a major impediment to, for example, the many people in the world who are interested in socialism but are not Cuban specialists. For example, *Cuba Socialista,* the theoretical and applied journal of the Central Committee of the Communist Party of Cuba, runs many articles on the economic situation in Cuba and on how to improve it, but the articles appear only in Spanish. The same is true of all of Cuba's specialized economics journals.

A second problem is the nature of an important part of Cuban research. Much research is done directly for Cuban agencies that use the results to intelligently carry out the nation's programs and policies and is not conducted for the purpose of publication and distribution to the entire Cuban political economy community. These research results are largely inaccessible to anyone outside or inside Cuba who is not involved in the particular project or has not built a network of contacts that includes people involved in such work. This is not primarily a matter of secrecy; it is simply that only people involved in the work know what research has been produced. Such activity constitutes only one part of Cuban economic research, but it does include important work that would deepen and enrich foreign academic studies of the Cuban economy were it, or research derived from it, readily available. The present collection is unique and important because many of the chapters do draw on practical studies of this type.

A third limitation to dissemination of published research outside the Island is a straightforward problem of the absence of a mechanism for distribution. People outside the Island can fairly easily subscribe to a few journals of economic interest, such as *Cuba Socialista.* There are a few others, such as *Revista Bimestre Cubana de la Sociedad Económica de Amigos del País,* that visitors can fairly easily subscribe to on the Island and have mailed out, but these do not have foreign distributors in places like North America and most of Europe. This, of course, greatly reduces possibilities for their dissemination. Other journals, like *Cuba: Investigación Económica,* a particularly important economic journal that is referenced repeatedly in many of the chapters herein, simply do not have the infrastructure for foreign subscriptions. Their dissemination outside Cuba is essentially nonexistent.

In light of the paucity of foreign dissemination of Cuban research on the Cuban economy, the procedure that seemed obvious to our minds was to invite a number of domestic economic experts to write overview pieces on their specialties, have these translated, and then publish them as a book. With that decision made, the next most immediate question was what areas to solicit works on. As with any modern economy, there are far more aspects to the Cuban economy than we could present in a single book. It was easy to find important ideas to present, and this volume does that, but it makes no claim to be a comprehensive treatment of the Cuban economic system.

The Content of This Book

This collection of studies is focused on the Cuban economy during the Special Period, 1990–2010. While change has been a constant throughout the history of Cuba's economic policies, the changes in this period have clearly been the most momentous since the transition five decades ago that ended capitalism and began building socialism. To understand not only the scope of these changes but also their very nature, one must understand something about the preexisting condition. Every author was asked to discuss to some extent—in accord with his or her topic and how he or she chose to approach it—relevant features of Cuba's economic history from 1959 to 1990. These historical reviews are necessarily brief and must not be misunderstood as attempts to review the Revolution's full five-decade economic history, even pertaining to a particular topic, a task that would require a series of book-length studies. Rather, the historical background establishes the necessary context for understanding the changes of the Special Period.

The contributors to this volume are all well-known and extensively published political economists in Cuba. They represent the three types of institutions where Cuban economists are found: government agencies, universities, and think tanks associated with a particular government agency or university. A given economist might move from one employment setting to another throughout his or her career, and some members of think tanks have dual appointments at universities.

We requested that the contributors focus on the major changes in Cuba's strategies to develop a socialist economy over the whole course of the Special Period, not specifically on what is happening in Cuba now. The majority of chapters were written in the first half of 2010, prior to the release of most 2009 data (in addition, not all published data are updated yearly), so many articles use the two decades of data up to 2007 or 2008 to illustrate some of their arguments. Much of the data for 2009—and, in particular, the data-rich *Anuario Estadístico de Cuba,* published every year by the National Office of Statistics (ONE)—were released a few months later than in previous years, in the fall of 2010. Where possible and appropriate, the chapters were updated in early 2011 to include 2009 data while I was translating them. At that time a very small amount of 2010 data were available, and where possible this was incorporated.

In September 2010 Raúl Castro made the long-anticipated announcement that the four-year study/popular consultation[9] on creating a new economic model for Cuba would soon be presented to, and formally discussed by, the population, then voted on at the next Party Congress in April 2011. This announcement required that specific decisions be made concerning these essays. The authors were specifically asked not to comment on the proposed reforms in their final chapter revisions for three reasons. The first and most obvious reason is that what is being circulated in Cuba as I write this introduction in early 2011 is a draft. To be sure, this draft is the result of many socially broad discussions and a very lengthy study, so it is almost certain that the final version adopted will strongly resemble the draft. There will, however, be numerous changes in details, and these details can be important signals for what the reforms will really mean.

A deeper reason for not discussing the effects of the proposed reforms is that, as indicated previously, the intent of this volume is to present the way Cuban economists see the changes in their economy over the Special Period, based on current data. Clearly, anything they write concerning specific effects of the proposed reforms must be speculative. And further, the reforms target medium- and long-term structural changes. It will be several years before one can even begin to meaningfully evaluate from the data whether the reforms are starting to yield the desired results. In fact, given the immediate disruptions in "business as usual" entailed by the large structural changes being proposed, one would expect many empirical measures to worsen for a year or two before beginning to improve, even if they are eventually successful. The Cuban economist Joaquín Infante recently made this point, which all Cuban economists understand, in an interview with *Juventud Rebelde*: "Yes, there are going to be negative effects in 2011 and 2012, in my opinion. But we have no alternative but to straighten out certain things. If we don't do it, we will lose the socialism that has cost us so much, and has given us so much. But then, in 2013, we will begin to see the benefits, I have no doubt."[10]

The third reason for not writing in this collection about the upcoming reforms is that, as concepts, they contain nothing new, nothing that has not been under continuous discussion for at least the two decades of the Special Period. Hence, all the ideas behind the post-2011 proposed reforms are already discussed throughout this collection. As a concrete example, one of the largest (and most surprising to people outside Cuba) changes is the proposal to cut 500,000 people from the state sector of the economy in the near term, roughly one-tenth of the workforce, and an additional 500,000 over coming years. The need to eliminate hidden unemployment (or underemployment) in order to increase the efficiency of the economy, and hence allow an increase in the population's standard of living, is discussed in general in many of the articles in this collection. Even the fact that cuts of such magnitude are required to reduce the significant level of hidden unemployment in the state sector has long been understood. An in-depth study of the Cuban economy published in 2000 by the Economic Commission for Latin America and the Caribbean (CEPAL) indicated that the additional hidden unemployment in the state sector in 1998 compared to 1989, which resulted from limiting employment reductions in the face of the economic crisis, was more than 700,000.[11]

Cuba in fact has already had real-world experience in grappling with this problem in the past decade, having reduced the sugar production workforce by 100,000 and successfully redeployed those workers throughout the economy between 2002 and 2004.[12] Of course, success under Cuba's conditions in 2004 does not guarantee success of a program whose immediate phase is five times larger under the different conditions of today's world economy, which seems likely for at least a number of years to be marked by various manifestations of the ongoing Great Recession. As repeated throughout the chapters, however, the declared intention in implementing the program is that, as in 2002–4, "no one will be abandoned to his individual fate." The immediate point for my purposes is only that the considerations of the last two decades of the Cuban economy covered in these chapters already pose the issues involved in the post-2011 proposed reforms. In fact, analysis of the last two decades of economic policies and performance is the only way to understand what the next proposed reforms hope to achieve, and why.

The same point applies to the other "major issues" in the proposed reforms, among which are these:

- Opening more work to small-scale self-employment (while maintaining state ownership as "the principal form of the national economy")[13]
- Accelerating the import-substitution drive, most immediately in food production, and building productive chains for domestic products
- Shifting production of all goods, but exports in particular, toward higher-value-added products, and in particular toward those with high scientific knowledge content
- Refocusing the safety net so that it efficiently delivers support to those in need, thereby maintaining the commitment not to abandon anyone, while eliminating the costly support systems that have delivered goods to those who do not really need special support, at a cost to all of society in the form of lower wages for those who are working

Again, in relation to the contents of this book, the important point is that all of these issues are exactly the same ones that have dominated the economic discussions in Cuba for the last two decades. The concrete meaning for Cuba of the reforms presently being considered can be understood only in terms of the theoretical discussions and practical experiences of the last two decades. The proposed reforms are not a "new road" for Cuba's project of building socialism: that new road has been under construction since the onset of the Special Period. The proposed reforms are clarifications and systemizations of the road that Cuba has been working to discover and to build for the last twenty years.

But the fact that the coming reforms share a theoretical continuity with the last two decades of economic policies does not downplay the importance of the social-political-economic act of debating, adopting, and implementing the reforms as a new consistent model for the Cuban economy. To the contrary, in all their discussions the Cubans refer to this as a life-and-death issue for their socialism and their Revolution. I would argue that the extension, coordination, and systemization of these policies will after the fact be seen to establish the year 2010 as the end of the Special Period and 2011 as the beginning of a new period in the Cuban Revolution's economic history.

We decided to frame this book around four areas that are important for understanding the Cuban economy. First, it is impossible to understand the concrete performance of various branches of goods and services without understanding the macroeconomic framework they exist in. Second, the economic policies have direct human well-being goals that must be specifically considered to understand Cuba's economic system. Third, with the macroeconomic and human well-being context in place, the concrete specifics of individual sectors of production then become relevant. And finally, Cuba's commitment to building a socialist economy as part of a socialist society is a constant factor. Therefore, we solicited twelve chapters, four on each of the first three areas. As the reader will see, however, all four of these aspects appear to a greater or lesser extent in every chapter. Accordingly, this book is divided into three parts: the macroeconomy, socioeconomic issues, and specific branches of production.

The Macroeconomy

The term *macroeconomy* refers to the sum of the effects in all the branches of the economy. A complete understanding of the changes in the Cuban economy over the twenty-one years from 1990 to 2010 is served by an analysis of the macroeconomy in two ways. First, given the impossibility of addressing each branch of production in the entire economy in a single book, changes in the macroeconomy can serve as an abbreviated proxy for such a massive presentation. Beyond serving as an abbreviated proxy for a comprehensive branch-specific study, the macroeconomy serves as a frame for the changes in each branch, and for socioeconomic changes. Whether the macroeconomy grows quickly or slowly, has a binding foreign-exchange constraint or does not face that growth limitation, has or does not have excess liquidity and inflationary pressures, has or does not have idle productive capacity and labor (unemployment), and so on, determines the types of policies that are possible for improving performance in all branches of the economy and the social economy.

Chapter 1, by José Luis Rodríguez, and chapter 2, by Oscar U-Echevarría Vallejo, both provide broad overviews of the major macroeconomic changes since 1990. Methodologically, they take a similar historical approach, whereas their content is complementary. Both authors recognize the need for a substantial review of Cuba's macroeconomy before 1990 in order to understand the starting point that was so important in determining what types of changes were both possible and necessary during the Special Period.

The capitalist prerevolutionary period created numerous economic problems and distortions that, while generally mitigated, still existed in 1990 and still exist today. Two among many of these are an unbalanced (and hence dependent)[14] production and trade spectrum and poorly qualified (and hence underproductive) labor. Notwithstanding important progress made over the years in regard to the latter, both of these have been significant obstacles for five decades to Cuba's socioeconomic development. The frenzied efforts in the 1960s to overcome simultaneously and almost immediately all the manifestations of capitalist underdevelopment were unsustainable, notwithstanding important achievements in industrialization, planning, and social services. The unsustainability of this "revolutionary offensive" led to a change in the approach to building socialism and to a period of growth and development as part of the Council for Mutual Economic Assistance (CMEA, an organization for economic cooperation among Soviet allies) and its international "socialist division of labor." And while growth and development yielded gains, particularly in industrialization and improved standard of living, they also created problems. The growth and development model did not develop internal productive chains, which increased Cuba's external dependence and its foreign-exchange problems. Not only was the development model too "automatic" to be consistent with Cuba's socialist goal of developing humans as conscious agents for building a better society for themselves, but also in narrow economic terms its potential was becoming exhausted over time. To counteract the slowing economic progress, it would have been necessary for Cuba to switch from extensive to intensive growth and development, which was not part of the model. The Rectification Process launched in the mid-1980s aimed to correct these problems without losing the previous model's strengths, but it was cut off while still being initiated due to the political collapse of the CMEA countries and the consequent 85 percent drop in Cuba's essential foreign trade. Rodríguez's and Echevarría's historical approach argues that the policies and the results of the Special Period can be understood only in light of both the successes and the never-resolved problems from all these previous economic periods.

Both chapters review chronologically the problems and constantly changing policies that Cuba adopted to survive and then to recover economically during the Special Period, as well as during the subsequent structural changes that were necessary. Rodríguez presents somewhat more data revealing the constant dialectic of problem–policy response–new problem emerging as the old problem is mitigated, whereas Echevarría focuses rather more on the resulting structural changes. Like all authors in this collection, these two both conclude by identifying the issues on the table today that must be addressed in order to move forward, but Rodríguez devotes a lengthier section to these issues. This balance lends complementarity to the two opening chapters.

Any discussion of Cuba's macroeconomy must fairly early bring up a fundamental problem common to the majority of third-world economies: its foreign-exchange constraint. One option to relax this constraint is foreign investment, but such investment must always be monitored to ensure it provides more help to the recipient economy than harm. The other option is to try to increase its generation of foreign exchange by reducing its imports (import substitution) or increasing its exports (export promotion). The high import coefficient for much of Cuban production reinforces the problem of imports, since the desired goal of increased growth itself rapidly increases imports, making the reduction of its import coefficient a contributory economic goal. All four of the chapters in the "Macroeconomy" section, along with a number of other chapters in this book, bring up this fundamental issue. Chapter 3, by Nancy A. Quiñones Chang, is directed to Cuba's changing trade and foreign investment behavior and patterns connected to its insertion in the international economy since 1990.

Borrowing can effect a short- and even medium-term resolution of an unfavorable foreign-exchange gap. If things go well, borrowing can be a "free lunch." Borrowed money can put to work unutilized capital or labor resources (which Cuba certainly has had during the Special Period). If the country can then sell the output internationally, it can pay off the loan with revenue left over. This scenario entails several problems for any third-world country, but Cuba has suffered disproportionately in this regard due to the unremitting economic aggression of the United States. Over the last thirty years, the majority of lending to third-world countries has shifted from relatively low-rate governmental bilateral or multilateral lending to higher-rate private lending. This shift in itself has raised the cost to Cuba of this type of borrowing. But in addition the United States has consistently pressured or prevented official lending bodies from making loans to Cuba. By (among other things) making it more difficult for Cuba to sell its production internationally, the United States has directly and indirectly discouraged lending from private sources, or made what private lending Cuba could secure more expensive. So a first concern for Cuba—especially in the very short run when their existing financing arrangements with CMEA and in particular the USSR were abruptly canceled—was to reinsert itself into the circuits of international private finance or, where possible, official multilateral or bilateral public lending. The Special Period as a whole has been particularly difficult for Cuba in this regard. Although some increased bilateral lending from Venezuela and China in the first decade of this century has improved the situation a little, financing remains a major problem.

Over the medium to long term the fundamental solution to this problem is to increase exports of goods and services and decrease imports to achieve a balance of trade. The Special Period has been marked by structural changes in both exports and imports, in regard to both geography and products. The chapter ends with a section on "looking ahead" in light of the major current problems in this area.

There is one part of the Island's macroeconomic policies that Cuba does not share with the large majority of the countries of the world, which have capitalist economies: planning. Elena Álvarez González opens chapter 4 by presenting planning not as a matter of increasing macroeconomic efficiency (which Cuba believes planning in fact does) but rather, in the words of Che Guevara, as "the way of being of a socialist society." As I argued earlier in the introduction, Cuba's commitment to building socialism has been the element of continuity underlying all the shifts in its economic policies. Hence, it follows that Cuba will continue to use planning to manage its macroeconomy. On the other hand, given the universal agreement in Cuba that the roads to socialism tried before 1990 are no longer even options, it follows that a new planning process has had to be developed over the course of the Special Period.

Again, to understand the current planning process one has to understand Cuba's history of planning in the 1960s and in the CMEA era. That provides the foundation for understanding how the present changes in many economic mechanisms have generated the need for changed planning to address the new ways they function. Álvarez describes the planning process that has developed as of today, but given that the new model for building socialism has not yet been fully elaborated, we can expect ongoing changes in planning procedures. The chapter ends on exactly this note, by describing the primary challenges that planning must likely address, given the salient problems in Cuba's economy today.

Socioeconomic Issues

With the macroeconomic framework established, the book next turns to the heart and soul of Cuba's economy and economic policies: socioeconomic issues, that is, the direct impact of the economy on the quality and nature of the lives of the Cuban population. While the goal of building a socialist economy influences all of Cuba's policies and practices for promoting economic growth (in theory an objective common to all economies), this impact is particularly evident in Cuba's ideas on what socioeconomic development entails.

Rita Castiñeiras García provides an overview of this issue in chapter 5. After a general discussion of the difficult issue of measuring well-being and a historical description of what the Revolution faced when it began in 1959, she then outlines the orientation and achievements of Cuba's socioeconomic policies to date. Castiñeiras then turns to the main task of her essay, a brief consideration of thirteen specific dimensions of Cuba's socioeconomic policies and their results: the changing demographic characteristics of the population (elaborated further in chapter 7), human development, inequality, employment, social security and welfare, women's role in society, food, public health, education, culture and art, sports, housing, and the environment. She next considers the additional set of socioeconomic policies introduced as part of the "Battle of Ideas" at the beginning of the twenty-first century, the multidimensional social, ideological, and cultural counterattack launched against the consumerist vision of a good society that the United States epitomizes. The chapter ends with consideration of the question, How much of its scarce material resources does Cuba really invest in its verbally attractive commitment to socioeconomic development?

Poverty, extremely widespread throughout the third world and significant even in much of the wealthy first world because of its inegalitarian societies, is an extreme expression of overall low well-being. Given the Revolution's central goal of continually improving human well-being, the elimination of poverty was on its agenda from day one. As Ángela Ferriol notes in chapter 6, by the 1980s Cuba had been so successful in this arena that the issue had disappeared as a topic for study. The 1983 book *La erradicación de la pobreza en Cuba,* by J. L. Rodríguez and G. Carriazo, carefully details the policies that had achieved this goal, and their results.

The 1990–93 economic disaster that initiated the focal period of this book, however, certainly left many Cubans, in Ferriol's words, with "insufficient monetary income" to meet all their basic needs. At the same time, unlike the poor in most of the world, a number of their basic needs were met in full (for example, education, health care, and social security) or in part (for example, food and housing)[15] despite their inadequate incomes. Ferriol opens by discussing the historical background of the situation the Revolution inherited in 1959 and what it achieved in the next thirty years, then chronicles the reemergence in the 1990s of people who lacked the income to meet all their basic needs. To emphasize the severity of the problems this group faced and simultaneously how their situation differs from standard poverty, many Cuba scholars have adopted the term "at-risk population" for them.

While it is important to recognize and understand the differences in this group's well-being from traditional poverty, their condition is in no way acceptable to the Revolution's central goal of continually improved human well-being. Hence from the moment in 1994 when the economy's free fall was stopped and the long process of recovery began, government resources have been directed to improving this group's well-being, even at the expense of necessary productive investment. These efforts were qualitatively increased in the 2000s. But as Ferriol discusses, Cuba must undertake these efforts while simultaneously redesigning the basic model for building socialism to accommodate the post-1990 economic environment. This means that the structures and practices for socioeconomic improvement must be made consistent with the structures and policies of the whole economy, even though these latter structures and policies in fact have not yet been fully worked out. Cuba's degree of success in addressing this problem—albeit that it has not yet achieved its goal—is sufficient to suggest a number of lessons. Ferriol ends her essay with these lessons, which some other countries might apply in their fight against poverty.

A strong indicator of the significant success of Cuba's socioeconomic policies over the last fifty years is its first-world demographic profile resting on its third-world per capita GDP. Cubans live much longer now than they did at the beginning of the Revolution, and longer than people in other countries with similar levels of per capita GDP. Cuba also has experienced a first-world fall in its total fertility rate. In chapter 7 Juan Carlos Alfonso Fraga discusses in detail the major prospective economic problems this "aging population" portends for Cuba over the coming decades.

Among a number of consequences, the two most problematic are the following. First, the demographic shift implies a continually decreasing number of working people supporting an increasing number of dependent people. Until now the increased percentage of the population over age fifty-nine has been offset by a declining percentage of the population under age sixteen. But that offset will now cease, and hence Cuba will face a continually increasing dependency ratio over the coming decades. The second problem that Alfonso discusses at length is the numerous different costs associated with meeting Cuba's commitment to provide for the well-being of elderly people in accordance with their increased needs. The first cost that comes to mind is increased medical care, but as Alfonso argues, there are many other expenses if these people are to be supported in maintaining a dignified life. The aging population is a much greater economic problem for Cuba than for first-world countries because of its lower per capita GDP and labor productivity. It is a much greater problem for Cuba than for typical third-world capitalist countries because of Cuba's ideological commitment to ensuring state-supported well-being for anyone with inadequate personal means or family support.

Socialist ideology has always held that under capitalism the well-being of working people at their workplaces must necessarily be low,[16] and a central reason for transcending capitalism is to achieve continual improvement in human well-being. Hence from day one of the Revolution, labor policies have been an extremely important part of building a new society and have been given great attention. Alfredo Morales Cartaya opens chapter 8 with a review of the working conditions before the Revolution and the important, radical changes in the first decade of the Revolution. The bulk of the essay then addresses eleven dimensions of working conditions and labor relations today: general conditions of work including safety and health, labor conditions and protection for women and adolescents, labor contracts and collective labor agreements, resolution of labor conflicts, salaries, increased efficiency and labor productivity, social security and pensions, unemployment, self-employment, international labor agreements, and trade unions.

Between the time Morales finished his chapter in mid-2010 and the time I am finishing this introduction in early 2011, the topic of his short "Challenges Ahead" concluding section has moved to the center of all political debate in Cuba. The sought-after and promised improvements in human well-being cannot be reduced to material standard of living alone, but that is an essential component. As many of these chapters allude to, there is a broad consensus in Cuba that the population's material standard of living needs to improve and that the key to accomplishing this is increased labor productivity and general productive efficiency. But exactly at this point Cuba's chosen commitment to building socialism takes center stage, particularly in relation to the treatment of labor in this process. Improving labor productivity and general productive efficiency will require further changes in labor conditions and relations beyond those already instituted over the last twenty years. But whereas today first-world countries and most of the third world are attacking labor's rights and previous gains, Cuba's socialist commitment precludes that path. Rather, as Morales argues,

> Cuba must improve its efficiency and labor productivity while maintaining its many labor rights and positive labor relations . . . extending them, and maintaining and extending the many other achievements of the Revolution for its working people. Its new labor relations, just like the previous ones, must be created and understood as a central part of its project of building socialism, but now under changed world conditions.

Specific Branches of Production

Within the context established by the first two sections of the book, the final section looks more closely at the economics of a number of specific areas: tourism (a branch of production) and agriculture and knowledge-based sectors (which are aggregations of a number of related specific branches of production). These topics are particularly important to the Cuban economy. Tourism has been essential to Cuba's short-term survival during the Special Period, and it will continue to be an important branch of the economy in the long run, even though its relative importance is already declining. Agriculture (including food sovereignty) and knowledge-based sectors are two aggregates of production that will be central to Cuba's long-term development; they are already making contributions in the short term, albeit so far fulfilling only a small part of their potential.

Tourism has been the most important single industry of the last two decades, the "ersatz sugar industry."[17] But that observation greatly understates its importance to the Cuban economy over the period that is the focus of this book. It is hard to imagine how a complete economic collapse—and, with that, an end to Cuba's fifty-year experiment in building socialism—could have been avoided without the remarkable performance of the tourist industry during the Special Period.

As Miguel Alejandro Figueras and Alfredo García Jiménez present in their chapters, the tourist industry has three very specific aspects that differentiate it from other branches of production in Cuba. The first is fairly narrowly economic. The starting point for Cuba's commitment to build its international tourist industry in the Special Period almost de novo was that this industry could generate rapid returns on investment; generate foreign-exchange earnings; and given its potential profitability, attract foreign capital to build the industry more rapidly than Cuba's capital resources would allow.

A second important consideration for Cuba concerning tourism is, however, ideological. There are two aspects to this, one historical, the other related to socialist consciousness. First, Havana had a booming tourism industry for the first half of the twentieth century, particularly in the 1950s. But this was a tourism oriented toward gambling, prostitution, and associated activities, and brought with it governmental corruption. It was a point of national pride that the Revolution eliminated this black mark on the reputation of the Cuban people. While the "simple solution," of course, was to remake the new tourism with a different nature, this history still presented an issue that had to be addressed with the reintroduction of international tourism. It is relatively easy to severely limit gambling and organized prostitution, but preventing the nationally insulting emergence of informal prostitution is extremely difficult without severely limiting the rights of Cubans to mingle with foreign tourists. Organized campaigns by the Federation of Cuban Woman and other organizations, particularly in the 1990s, ideologically addressed this issue with some (far from complete) success, and that success has made it much less of a point of discussion in Cuba today than it was in the 1990s. The broader ideological issue has to do with conflict between the impact of large numbers of foreigners coming to Cuba to consume (often conspicuously, and being encouraged to do so for the success of the industry) and the continuous process of developing in the Cuban population a socialist consciousness oriented toward human development as opposed to materialist consumption.

A third consideration, and one that is particularly salient for natural resources–based tourism everywhere, is its interaction with the environment. To begin with, in a narrow business sense Cuba would be killing the goose that lays the golden eggs if its tourism development were to pollute or overdevelop the environmental attractions that tourists are coming to enjoy. More broadly, given the importance to human well-being of a healthy environment, protecting and preserving the environment is a goal in itself for Cuba.

Agriculture has historically been a vital component of the Cuban economy, but in the form of commercial export crops, above all sugar. As Ángel Bu Won and Pablo Fernández Domínguez argue in chapter 11, this sector of production still has underutilized export potential that is important to exploit as one part of building the foreign-exchange balance that Cuba needs. Much more important today, however, particularly in the short term,[18] is agricultural production for the domestic market. Above all this means food, whose importance is expected to be reinforced in both the near and distant future as international food prices continue to rise. Food security is important for three reasons. First, Cuba still imports a large amount of the food it consumes, which limits the foreign exchange available for developing the Cuban economy. Second, food is increasingly being used internationally as a political weapon, and hence the issue of food sovereignty (the ability of a country to meet its own food needs) as a necessary component of national sovereignty has become a topic of international discussion in recent years. Third, and in the final analysis the most important for Cuba, increased domestic food production is important for Cuba's central goal of constantly improving its population's well-being, especially given rising costs and other problems in international food markets.

Turning to the final area of production highlighted in this book, further development of knowledge-based sectors is seen as of central importance to Cuba's medium- and long-term economic growth and development. Cuba has already achieved some impressive results, both domestically and internationally, with a few of these products, typically considered to lie outside the purview of third world countries. Vito N. Quevedo Rodríguez argues that Cuba's commitment to socialism and its world-recognized achievements in education over the entire course of the Revolution (itself part of Cuba's commitment to socialism) together have given the Island an advantage over other third-world countries, and in some cases have made it competitive with first-world countries. Quevedo details how Cuba built a general institutional structure and accompanying culture that promotes science, technology, and innovation. He then examines four knowledge-based products with which Cuba has had important successes: biotechnology, information technology and communications, energy production, and environmental protection. Such knowledge-based advancements place Cuba among the vanguard in what many scholars regard as key sectors of future human economies throughout the world.

Conclusions

It is not very surprising that Cuban economists continually produce a large amount of quality research on their own economy, research that Cuban policymakers rely on heavily. Notwithstanding Cuba's relative isolation, however, it is somewhat surprising how little of this research is translated into foreign languages, and hence how few of the details of Cuban economic thinking and debates are known to both supporters and opponents of the Cuban Revolution outside the Island. This book aims to make a small contribution to addressing that problem.

In 1990, in the first instance because of the collapse of the trading partners with whom its economy was extremely integrated, Cuba suddenly entered the most severe economic crisis in the history of the Revolution. Not only did Cuba face a decline similar in depth and length to the 1929–33 Great Depression in the United States, but it also was limited by several barriers to economic recovery that the United States did not face during the Depression. The fundamental one was that it could not simply reactivate its previous economy, but rather simultaneously had to profoundly restructure its economy with dramatically reduced resources. In addition, it was a small open economy in a world dominated by a neoliberal capitalist system antagonistic to Cuba's primary goal of building socialism. While this generalized antagonism would and did make Cuba's recovery more difficult, by far the major deliberate external damage came from the U.S. blockade and intense general economic aggression against Cuba over the entire Special Period.

As the following chapters make clear, the Special Period has been both a time of economic recovery and, more fundamentally, of the deepest changes in the Cuban economy since its declaration of socialism in 1961. As I write this, Cuba is engaged in a popular consultation and debate on what its new economic model should look like, which will culminate in April 2011. However, exactly how the ideas in the resulting model will be put into practice and what their results will be will only unfold slowly over the coming years. The one thing that is certain is that Cuba is traveling a new road for building socialism that began at the onset of the Special Period in 1990, with the experiences presented in this book.

Notes

1. Outside of Cuba this period is often considered to be the application of the ideas that Che Guevara argued for in the Great Debate. Although he did indeed champion the importance of moral incentives, and moral incentives have been one factor in Cuban

economic policies over their entire history since the triumph of the Revolution, scholars both inside and outside Cuba have carefully documented that this period was not consistent with Che's economic ideas. See, for example, Robert Bernardo, *The Theory of Moral Incentives in Cuba* (Alabama: University of Alabama Press, 1971); Carlos Tablada, *Economics and Politics in the Transition to Socialism* (Sydney: Pathfinder/Pacific and Asia, 1989); and Helen Yaffe, *Che Guevara: The Economics of Revolution* (New York: Palgrave Macmillan, 2009).

2. The behavior of the financial sector in the current crisis in the United States demonstrates that in fact powerful economic actors in capitalist countries are really interested in their individual profits and will act to enhance those even if doing so slows national economic growth. The issue of concern here, however, is what economists outside of Cuba think and say about the Cuban economy. Notwithstanding its minor importance to capitalist businesspeople, almost all mainstream economists cite growth of the GDP as the only metric for social well-being they need to consider, because it is an article of their faith that "a rising tide raises all boats."

3. In fact, Cuba has experienced a healthy though not exceptional rate of economic growth over the entire course of the Revolution. The 1960s were lackluster, the 1970s were healthy, and the first half of the 1980s was strong. For the quarter century from 1960 to 1985, Cuba had the second-highest rate of growth of real GDP in Latin America. See Andrew Zimbalist and Claes Brundenius, *The Cuban Economy* (Baltimore: Johns Hopkins University Press, 1989), 165. Even including the economic implosion in the early 1990s, which had fundamentally external causes, Cuba's rate of growth of real GDP from 1959 to 2008 matched the average for Latin America. See chapters 1 and 2 in this collection for discussions of Cuba's growth throughout the various periods of the Revolution.

4. As chapter 8 discusses, increasing enterprise efficiency is a central economic policy in Cuba today. Because of the goal of the Revolution, however, employers are barred from accomplishing this by lowering workers' wages.

5. A report on the poll is given in the then-bimonthly magazine of the Center for Cuban Studies in New York, *Cuba Update,* February 1995, 9.

6. After giving two long speeches on July 26, 2006, Fidel became seriously ill. Fidel held the office of president of the Council of State as well as president of the Council of Ministers (sometimes referred to as prime minister). Raúl was first vice-president of both bodies. All these positions are voted on by Cuba's popularly elected legislature, the National Assembly of People's Power. In line with Article 94 of the Cuban Constitution, when Fidel became ill, power passed to the next highest person in the government, Raúl Castro. Given the uncertainty concerning the nature of the illness and the time necessary for Fidel's recovery, no official changes in government titles were effected at that time: Raúl became acting president by vote of the National Assembly of People's Power on July 31, 2006. He was subsequently elected president on February 24, 2008.

7. Raúl Castro, speech to the National Assembly on August 1, 2009, available in the archives of Juventud Rebelde at www.juventudrebelde.cu. All translations are mine.

8. I argue here that the reason it is important to read the works of Cuban economists is the pro-socialist frame that most of them operate in (as well as their perspective from

daily life in that system). At the same time, it is worthwhile to note that there are two very different currents among the anti-socialist economists outside of Cuba. Very briefly, one current is strongly opposed to all the policies of the Cuban government and sees a neoliberal situation where "unfettered markets" reign as optimal for a post-socialist Cuba. Well-known authors in this camp who do serious work on Cuba include Jorge Pérez-López and, slightly less stridently, Carmelo Mesa-Lago. The other, very different group supports many of the obvious accomplishments of the Revolution and almost all favor having a relatively active and progressive government that does play an important (though reduced) role in the economy and maintains some sort of social safety net. They usually present their proposals as a combination of "more markets" and "privatizing the state's assets." All of these together would constitute a restoration of a somewhat social democratic or welfare capitalism, though these authors never use that term in their proposals. Well-known authors of this orientation are Claes Brundenius, Manuel Pastor, and Andrew Zimbalist. See, for example, Pastor and Zimbalist's proposal for privatizing the Cuban state's assets using the sort of coupon programs designed for and used in several Eastern European countries to effect their return to capitalism. Manuel Pastor and Andrew Zimbalist, "Waiting for Change: Adjustment and Reform in Cuba," *World Development* 23, no. 5 (1995).

9. Almost immediately after being elected acting president by the National Assembly of People's Power on July 31, 2006, Raúl launched a broad, ongoing process of popular consultation on Cuba's economic (and social) problems. He went first to a number of organizations and institutions. In September he called for input from the trade unions, and in October from the newspapers, a call particularly picked up by *Juventud Rebelde.* In December Raúl appealed to students in the Federation of University Students (FEU) and to the delegates to the National Assembly, and in June 2007 a nationwide survey of all members of the Communist Party asked for ideas on how state-run businesses could be run more efficiently. Finally, the process took its biggest step forward following Raúl's speech on July 26, 2007, starting in August and accelerating in September. For three months, meetings were held in Communist Party cells, Committees for the Defense of the Revolution (neighborhoods), and in workplaces to air whatever social and economic concerns people had. A vast discussion unfolded about everything from salaries, food prices, housing, transportation, restrictions on travel, the two-tiered money system, and the lack of resources at the once academically outstanding schools in the countryside to opposition to police interference with retirees who sell whatever they can in the street (for example, roasted peanuts) to increase their inadequate income. (See Al Campbell, "The Cuban Economy: Data on Today's Performance and Information on Tomorrow's Projected Changes," University of Utah Working Paper 2008-08, 2008, at http://economics.utah.edu/publications/2008_08.pdf.) The results from all the meetings in this national consultation were collected and used as input, along with numerous other inputs, for continued study over the next three years. The resulting proposals were printed and distributed to the entire population in November 2010 (see http://links.org.au/node/2037 for an English translation). A comprehensive national discussion like the previous ones took place from December to February, which will be followed by a vote

on the new economic model (including modifications from the national consultation) at the upcoming April 2011 Congress of the Communist Party.

10. See http://www.juventudrebelde.cu/cuba/2010-12-12/economia-cubana-de-mandatos-o-de-utilidades.

11. See CEPAL, *La economía Cubana: Reformas estructurales y desempeño en los noventa* (Mexico City: CEPAL, 2000), 253. In round numbers, in 1998 the economically active population was 4.5 million, of which 80 percent (3.6 million) were employed by the state. Productivity per worker was 20 percent lower in 1998 than in 1989, so cutting 20 percent of the workforce and keeping output the same would eliminate this hidden unemployment (to the 1989 level). That would be 720,000 workers.

12. Brian Pollitt, "Crisis and Reform in Cuba's Sugar Economy," in *The Cuban Economy*, ed. Archibald Ritter (Pittsburgh: University of Pittsburgh Press, 2004).

13. Point 2 in the proposed reforms.

14. The frequent argument that because of its small size the Cuban economy necessarily must have dependent, unbalanced production is false. One among many counterexamples is Switzerland, a country two-thirds Cuba's size that exports roughly 50 percent of its GDP. It is true that due to its size the Cuban economy could not be efficient if it was autarkic, but it cannot be said that its size must cause an unbalanced or dependent productive structure.

15. No one suffered to the extent of being clinically malnourished during the Special Period, but a small number of people would have been popularly considered to be malnourished, and for a few years a significant number of people experienced chronic hunger. No one lost his or her home and had to live on the street. These were both important achievements of Cuba in these extremely difficult times. Relevant to Ferriol's essay, without minimizing the seriousness of Cuba's social problems, these facts underline the difference between inadequate income in Cuba and poverty in other countries.

16. Independent of their income, the reasons for lack of well-being include alienation, lack of collective democratic control of the workplace that they are part of, and more simply, their subaltern role and corresponding treatment at work, which is inconsistent with human dignity.

17. Specifically, tourism replaced sugar as the main source of foreign exchange, as a major object for foreign investment, and as an important source of employment. These had all been major roles of the sugar industry before its dramatic decline during the Special Period.

18. Developing an industry capable of successful, large-scale exports to highly competitive international food markets requires significant time to establish quality and reduce production costs.

Part I

The Macroeconomy

1

Fifty Years of Revolution in the Cuban Economy

A Brief Overview

JOSÉ LUIS RODRÍGUEZ

The triumph of the Cuban Revolution initiated a profound process of social and economic development. Achieving this growth from the starting conditions in 1959 was, however, a particularly difficult and complex process. All three of the essential characteristics of underdevelopment were highly salient in the Cuban economy: a structurally unbalanced economy, serious social problems, and absolute political subordination to the interests of American monopolies.

Initial Conditions: The Cuban Economy in 1958

Immediately prior to the Revolution, Cuba's overall economic situation can be characterized as fundamentally agrarian with a very backward agricultural system that was subordinate to the interests of American corporate capital.[1] The defining activity was the production and export of sugar, based in a landownership system of large plantations (*latifundios*). Industry was only marginally present and was largely restricted to sugar processing. Workers suffered extremely high rates of unemployment, underemployment, and seasonally limited employment. The social dimension of Cuba's underdevelopment was manifested in a number of socioeconomic indexes: a high rate of infant mortality, low life expectancy, poor sanitary conditions, a lack of health-care facilities, high rates of illiteracy, extremely unequal distribution of income, and very inadequate social assistance and pension systems.[2] Although Cuba was not among the least developed Latin American countries, it was arguably the most dependent on and subordinate to foreign interests. These were, of course, opposed to any attempts at endogenous national development, even within a capitalist framework.[3] All of these considerations together necessitated basic structural transformations in the Cuban economy, not only for any attempt to pursue social justice, but even for any attempt to promote true economic development.

Postrevolution Economic Development Strategies, 1959–1975

Even before it triumphed, the Cuban Revolution adopted the position that economic and social development are intrinsically connected. Not only is the purpose of economic growth to promote social development and human well-being, but also social development promotes economic growth. Furthermore, any process of authentic social and economic transformation requires active participation by the population.

Changing the conditions that prevailed pre-1959 in order to enable true development demanded fundamental economic and social transformations. Because of its economic and political subordination to U.S. corporations, Cuba had no endogenous capitalism or national business class that could conceivably promote such changes. Hence only the state, guided by a socialist orientation to economic and social development, could be in the position and have the authority to direct the necessary material and financial resources to facilitate economic growth and social well-being. However, it would need to accomplish this in the face of continual active opposition from foreign capital and its internal agents and allies.

The first steps in establishing a state-directed socialist development strategy that promoted the interests of the majority were to improve the distribution of income and to expand state ownership of property tied to the major means of production.[4] The most important structural transformations in property ownership took place between 1959 and 1963. The Agrarian Reform Law approved in May 1959 changed the nature of Cuba's economy. It gave about 40 percent of the arable land to the state and to small farmers. A second Agrarian Reform Law in 1963 eliminated capitalism in Cuban agriculture.

Another decision with major consequences was the nationalization of all properties belonging to U.S. companies in the summer of 1960. This move was a response to the Eisenhower administration's attempt in July of that year to bring down the revolutionary government by cutting off Cuban sugar exports to the United States. Between September and October 1960, the process of nationalization was then extended to industries and property owned by major Cuban capitalists, who were actively opposing all the ongoing changes.[5] The result of these changes in property ownership was that by the end of 1960, foreign trade, banking, and wholesale trade were 100 percent state-owned, while construction and industry were each 85 percent, transportation was 80 percent, retail trade was 52 percent, and agriculture was 37 percent nationalized.

By 1968 all of these branches were entirely state property, except for agriculture, which was about 70 percent state-owned.[6]

By October 1960, these fundamental reductions in private ownership of the means of production, plus many of the commitments of the Moncada Program,[7] were either accomplished or being addressed by social programs. The Cuban society could thus be considered to have embarked on the path to constructing socialism.[8] To accomplish this aim required a strategy of development. The two pillars of the original plan for transforming the economy were industrialization and diversification of agriculture. The intent was to achieve both objectives very rapidly and to finance them mainly with domestic assets.[9] This initial effort quickly ran into a combination of external and internal barriers, however, among which some of the most important were

- the precipitous fall in sugar exports due to the loss of Cuba's overwhelmingly preeminent market, the United States;
- the resulting lack of any assured market for Cuba's sugar exports;
- the resulting foreign-exchange imbalance, which impeded all of Cuba's development programs;
- the low level of education among the Cuban labor force;
- the low level of managerial skills among the new revolutionary managers; and
- the U.S. economic blockade and military aggression, particularly between 1960 and 1965.[10]

Some of these issues could be addressed immediately, others required the initiation of ongoing development programs, and of course, the U.S. blockade and economic aggression continues to this day.

By the middle of 1963 it was clear that the initial approach was not working, necessitating a major change. Faced with the U.S. sugar boycott, Cuba had elected immediately to shift land that for decades had been devoted to sugar into diversified agricultural production for internal consumption in order to substitute for food imports. This shift, however, left Cuba with a severe shortage of foreign exchange, which crippled its state industrialization efforts, its ability to build the infrastructure necessary for national development, and even its efforts to develop the required competencies in the labor force. Therefore, Cuba elected to return to producing and exporting the crop it already had the infrastructure and skills to produce: sugar. Sugar revenues, it was reasoned, could generate the necessary foreign exchange to support a gradual, ongoing process of industrialization and balanced economic development. For this strategy to succeed, however, Cuba needed a large and secure market offering stable prices for its sugar. This was achieved via an agreement with the Soviet

Union to export 24.1 million tons between 1965 and 1970 at what was then a favorable price: 6.11 cents per pound.[11] This strategy was pursued until 1975, but its implementation varied in accordance with changes in Cuba's overall economic policies.

There were three different overall economic policies during those years. The first period, in 1963–64, was characterized by a deep and wide-ranging discussion on how to organize the economy, and specifically on how individual productive enterprises should relate to the national agencies responsible for regulating the economy.[12] Two different approaches were debated. One, whose best-known proponent was Ernesto "Che" Guevara, advocated a centrally financed system for all state enterprises. The other proposal, advocated by Carlos Rafael Rodríguez, was enterprise self-financing, similar to the practice in the USSR and socialist Europe.[13] The discussions were not only—in fact, not even primarily—about economic mechanisms. Rather, the debates addressed conceptual issues central to the nature of socialism, in particular those related to markets and monetary relations,[14] discussions that are again very much on the economic and political agenda in Cuba today.

This debate was never completely resolved before a new system was initiated in 1965. Some conceived of it as a hybrid of the Guevara and Rodríguez systems, in that it drew some elements from each. In fact, however, it ended up lacking the internal logical consistency of either approach. It is not much of an exaggeration to say that, instead of regulating, controlling, or seeking to build alternatives to market relations, this system largely just declared market relations transcended and ignored the market conditions that actually existed. This thoroughly idealistic approach to building socialism naturally led in a fairly short time to a sharp decline of productive efficiency and economic performance in general that affected the economic development strategy.[15]

A target was set of producing ten million tons of sugar in 1970, a goal that was elevated to a national test of existing policies and whose implementation seriously disrupted the rest of the economy. The failure to achieve this target led to a proposal to thoroughly review Cuba's economic policies, a process that began in the second half of 1970. The outcome was the third set of policies in this period: the gradual adoption and development of a system similar to that of the USSR and the other socialist countries of Europe, though with a number of endogenous modifications. In particular, and pertinent to the unresolved debate of 1963–64, Cuba basically adopted a classical self-financing system. A particularly important result of this structural change was that it enabled Cuba to become a full member of the Council for Mutual Economic Assistance (CMEA) in 1972.

When the First Congress of the Cuban Communist Party met at the end of

1975, attendees evaluated the first fifteen years of the Cuban Revolution. This assessment produced the following important conclusions concerning growth, development, and social transformation:

- GDP growth fluctuated greatly over the first decade (1959–69), but averaged only 2.8 percent. The subsequent close economic cooperation with the socialist community, however, raised the average rate of growth to 4.7 percent for 1959 to 1975. On the other hand, the rate of investment and annual productivity growth were both low, measuring only 13.1 percent of GDP and 0.5 percent, respectively. An important point regarding the modest rate of growth in the first decade, however, is that a large portion of both the country's financial and material resources and the government's attention were directed to the issue of defense. The U.S. blockade was particularly disruptive and costly until Cuba deepened its relationship with the socialist community.
- Whereas in 1958 the primary, secondary, and tertiary sectors constituted 22 percent, 29 percent, and 49 percent of the GDP, respectively, by 1975 these proportions had changed to 14 percent, 31 percent, and 55 percent.[16]
- The development strategies of the first fifteen years had partially accomplished their intended goals. The necessary infrastructure for agricultural development had been created. Industrial sectors had increased their contribution to the GDP. Basic utilities, such as electricity, transportation, and water supply, had been developed to the levels required for the initial transformation of the economy. The general educational level of the population and the skills of the labor force had risen sufficiently to meet the requirements of the immediate goals for industrialization.[17]
- One of the most remarkable achievements of Cuba in this period was its significant progress in widespread socioeconomic transformation. Education, health care, and social security were established as basic human rights and universally provided free of charge. Practically all the most important social indexes improved. The result was a higher standard of living and improved quality of life, especially for those who had limited opportunities before 1959.
- Finally, there were, of course, many economic and social problems which remained to be addressed. An important lesson was how complex the process of constructing socialism is, particularly in a poor country lacking experience in managing a non-capitalist process of development, and one that was forced to direct significant effort and

resources to defending its sovereignty. A still broader lesson was that there are limits on how fast humans can fundamentally alter their behavior. But in spite of these failures and shortcomings, the socialist project had accomplished enough successes to obtain the necessary political support of the majority of the population.

Cuban Development under the Socialist Economic System, 1976–1989

With the preconditions for further industrialization of the country in place, the Cuban economy entered a new stage of industrial development in the framework of CMEA. Implementing this new stage, however, required new strategies that entailed major changes in both finance and economic organization.

With regard to finance, two developments were particularly important. First, since the early 1970s, Cuba had received from the USSR soft credits amounting to about 3 billion pesos to cover the commercial imbalances of the 1960s plus investment credits agreed to between 1972 and 1974.[18] Second, in 1976 Cuba and the USSR reached a historic agreement that aimed at establishing an indexation of exports with import prices in order to end the deterioration in the terms of trade.[19] This gave Cuba fair treatment for the first time in the history of its foreign trade. The result was about a 50 percent growth in the country's purchasing power compared with world market prices.[20]

Opponents of the Revolution maintain that at this time Cuba had a subsidized economy, but it is important to note that this perception is inaccurate for several reasons. First, when the higher-than-world-market prices are considered in light of what they were intended to be—a maintenance of previously existing exchange prices in the face of a world system that discriminated against the third world—they did not constitute additional subsidies. Second, the higher prices only partially offset the economic damage to Cuba caused by the U.S. blockade, losses that amounted to $30 billion by 1990, so again one cannot speak of Cuba having on net a subsidized economy. Finally, the prices the USSR paid for Cuban exports such as sugar or citrus were also favorable for the Soviets, if one takes into account the opportunity costs of producing those products internally, or of importing them on the global market, which would have resulted in a dramatic spike in world market prices.[21]

The rapid dynamism of Cuban economic development in this period demanded extensive financial resources, and as noted, most loans were obtained on favorable terms from the socialist community. With the push to recycle petrodollars in the 1970s, however, Cuba was also able to obtain significant financing from capitalist countries. Thereby, Cuba's external debt in convertible currency rose from $291 million in 1969 to $2,913.8 million by August 1982. At that time Cuba proposed, and its creditors accepted, a renegotiation of 36 percent of its convertible currency debt in a multiyear repayment plan. However, Cuba's partners imposed additional and unacceptable demands in 1986, causing the repayment plan to be suspended. By 1989 the debt in convertible currency had risen to $6,165.2 million for three main reasons: the devaluation of the Cuban peso against the U.S. dollar in 1986, the very high interest rates (and priority repayment terms) Cuba had to pay for the small amounts of credit in convertible currency that it still needed and obtained, and the relatively weak performance of the Cuban economy in the second half of the 1980s.[22]

Cuba's debts to the Soviet Union also became problematic during the 1980s due to the changes in the economic policy that occurred with the perestroika. The 1975 agreement freezing the terms of trade began to unravel, and as a result Cuba suffered a 21 percent decrease in its terms of trade with the USSR. This in turn led to a sharp increase in the convertible ruble debt between 1980 and 1990.[23] Furthermore, Cuba's economic relations with all the CMEA countries began to deteriorate after 1986 due to the internal and external economic and political upheaval in those countries. Although CMEA was not formally disbanded until 1991, by 1989 its Eastern European member nations had reduced their trade with Cuba, at a great cost to the Island given its productive integration into CMEA. By then Cuba's only significant economic relations with CMEA countries were with the USSR, and these too soon broke down. In light of all these issues, and the fact that its ruble debt now had to be repaid in convertible currency, Cuba considered its Russian debt a matter for discussion and renegotiation. It therefore repudiated Russia's non-negotiated 1990 edict on what Cuba owed in convertible currency.[24]

With regard to the organization of the economy, the biggest changes in this period occurred in the early 1970s and related to its insertion into the international socialist division of labor that prevailed in CMEA. Above all, these changes involved redesigning Cuba's economic structure to complement the rest of CMEA's production. Under any conditions, making room for such new developments in an existing industrial division of labor would not be an easy task economically or politically. But two absolutely necessary prerequisites required particular development. As discussed in chapter 4, Cuba had developed various basic planning capabilities, but they needed to be both expanded and redesigned to match standard CMEA procedures, especially in terms of medium- and long-range planning. More problematic was that integration required a well-designed economic management system, something that was practically nonexistent in Cuba at that time. While partial agreements on integration were implemented over the first half of the 1970s, it was not until 1975 that Cuba developed all the prerequisites to enter into a full normal agreement with CMEA. Even then, given the complexity of planning and the institutional difficulties of carrying out such a transformation for both Cuban planners and their counterparts in other countries, the short-term changes in Cuba's economic structure and performance were necessarily more modest than the ambitious Cuban plans.[25]

To establish all the prerequisites for integrated long-range planning beyond the annual and five-year plans took even longer, of course. In 1978 Cuba developed projections to the year 2000. However, the coordination and agreements with the Soviet Union and other CMEA members corresponding to these long-range plans were not completed until several years later (and in many cases were only partially completed).[26] By the time they were in place, of course, it was only a few years before the effective demise of CMEA in 1989.

Cuba's initial specialized niche in CMEA's socialist division of labor involved both export promotion and import substitution. The process began with both utilizing its existing traditional exports and developing the capability to produce commodities that were imported in large quantities but for which clear domestic production capability existed (for example, much of the food consumed in Cuba). Hence the initial specialization plan aimed to expand the sugar and nickel industries as two of the most important exports. At the same time, large import-substitution projects were initiated for food and textiles. In addition, the goal was to develop productive chains whenever possible. Hence, for example, the chemical, machinery, and construction industries were all directed more toward producing necessary inputs for domestic production chains than to producing exports.[27] The intensification of development linked to Cuba's new phase of industrialization manifested in the increased rate of investment. This percentage grew from 11.8 percent of GDP in 1970 to 23.3 percent in 1980 and to 26.8 percent in 1989. This process ran into serious economic problems after 1980, however, as the investment yield stagnated or declined, indicating decreasing investment efficiency.[28]

The other major change in the structure of the Cuban economy by 1975 was the introduction of a self-financing model of management that resembled what existed in the Soviet Union prior to the reforms there in the 1960s. This policy was based on material interest, enterprise autonomy, and monetary control of the economy. It was a very different model of economic organization and operation than Cuba had used in its first decade. The change made good sense considering Cuba's very poor economic performance in the late 1960s,[29] the apparent success of the reforms then taking place in other socialist countries, and the absence of other feasible alternatives. Nevertheless, Fidel Castro warned in 1975 that in socialism, no mechanical, impersonal system or automatic set of rules could substitute for human consciousness, ideology, and organized popular participation, because the factors that generate economic efficiency and efficacy in capitalism (at a very high human cost) no longer exist in socialism. Subsequently, additional important changes were introduced, including opening room for private self-employment among workers in 1978, a market with unregulated prices for agriculture products in 1980, a new openness to foreign investment in 1982, and a new law governing agricultural cooperatives. A more decentralized management system for enterprises was also introduced in 1982.

Many of these aspects were present in the Soviet model, yet they led to a number of problems in Cuba's economy. By the early 1980s several macro- and micro-level economic imbalances appeared, and these were aggravated by a number of political mistakes at the time. During the early and mid-1980s Fidel and Raúl Castro gave a number of major speeches calling for a critical reevaluation of the overall economic policy. Subsequently, in November 1984 the Central Group was established with responsibility for reshaping the management of the macroeconomy. Thereby, the responsibility for supervising the economic planning and control of the economy and for instituting necessary changes was placed more immediately and directly in the hands of top government and party leaders.[30]

The process of reevaluating economic policies continued throughout 1985 and 1986. The outcome was the launching of what was called the "rectification process of mistakes and negative tendencies" at the Third Congress of the Cuban Communist Party in 1986.[31] The rectification approach involved two types of policies. On one hand were traditional economic policies aimed to address Cuba's imbalances. For example, a high priority was given to increasing exports and substituting for imports in order to achieve a better foreign trade balance to accommodate Cuba's difficulties in servicing its foreign debt in convertible currency and its diminishing financing from the socialist bloc. At this time, the government took the first steps to develop two aspects that were to become important to Cuba's economic survival in the 1990s: attracting foreign tourism and investment. But at the same time an important component of the rectification process—following from Fidel's 1975 warning—was to develop policies that addressed the deeper issue of searching for a more balanced means of managing the economy that combined economic mechanisms with appropriate political mobilization of workers.

Despite the difficulties during the 1976–89 period, Cuba achieved important advances in macroeconomic development, which included the following:

- GDP grew at an annual rate of 3.8 percent despite a sharp decline between 1986 and 1990, when the economy was practically stagnant. Productivity grew at 2.2 percent annually. The rate of investment was estimated at 26 percent in the 1980s, and there was a modest increase in the weight of the industrial sector, from 31 percent to 35 percent of the GDP.[32]
- The process of industrialization continued to make important advances. The branches of industry electronics, nonelectric machinery, electricity generation, fisheries, and metallurgy together grew at 8.3 percent per year from 1975 to 1989. The growth of the other nine branches of industry averaged 3.2 percent.[33] These gains, though important, fell short of Cuba's projected industrialization goals. Furthermore, the industrial development contrasted sharply with the shortfalls in agriculture. Not only did agriculture not meet its projected goals to the extent that there was almost no progress in this major sector of the economy, but that failure came despite the allocation of significant resources to the sector.
- Socioeconomic advances continued during this period. The public health and education indexes continued to improve, achieving first-world levels by the end of the period. Improvements in social security, standard of living, and housing were particularly notable.

Notwithstanding these advances in growth, industrialization, and socioeconomic development, Cuba faced a number of major economic problems by the late 1980s. The four main problems were the nature of its economic policies, as discussed previously, particularly between 1980 and 1985; constraints resulting from a shortage of convertible currency earnings and foreign financing; problems with its economic integration and in particular with its foreign trade with the socialist countries after 1986; and damage caused by the U.S. blockade. These conditions produced several difficulties, the four greatest being minimal success at increasing exports and import substitution, inefficiency of investment, rapid growth of foreign debt, and inflationary pressures. All these issues together created the need for accelerated change toward a more effective economic policy, a process that was ongoing by the end of the decade.

The Decisive Battle in the Special Period and the Prelude to Today's Ongoing Changes, 1990–2009

On August 29, 1990, the Cuban press published a notice announcing that due to the Soviet failure to deliver a number of essential contracted imports, especially oil, a special period of extraordinary measures would be implemented to face the pending crisis.[34] The fundamental reason for these missed deliveries was the breakdown of the Soviet bloc in Europe. So-called reformists in the socialist governments of those countries had been promoting the acceleration of market-oriented reforms since 1985–86, and their failure led eventually to abrupt transitions to capitalism. This occurred in the European socialist countries in 1989 and culminated in the dissolution of the Soviet Union in December 1991.[35]

The Cuban economy was extensively integrated with the socialist countries in the crucial areas of trade and investment. These nations supplied 85 percent of Cuba's imports, received nearly 80 percent of its exports, and provided 80 percent of its investments.[36] The very sudden, near-total disruption of all these relations was the major reason for the depth of Cuba's economic crisis in the early 1990s. As always, the comprehensive U.S. blockade was an important secondary cause. In October 1992 the United States further tightened its blockade with the Torricelli Act, intended to bring down the Cuban government in the wake of its economic crisis. By 1995 the accumulated losses due to the blockade were estimated at $45 billion, $15 billion of which came in the previous five years. That is an average annual cost of $3 billion per year to an economy that at its low point in 1993 had a GDP of about 13 billion pesos. Depending on the exchange rate one uses, that translates into a loss of at least 20 percent of GDP.[37]

The economic crisis was extreme. The GDP fell almost 35 percent between 1989 and 1993. Imports at current prices fell 75 percent in those four years. The fiscal deficit rose to about 33 percent of GDP by 1993. The standard of living of the population deteriorated sharply. For example, the daily intake of calories and protein fell by more than 30 percent, and nutritional inadequacies even led to the appearance of optical neuritis and neuropathic epidemics in 1993.[38]

At this time of economic crisis, when nearly all the former socialist community had just converted to capitalism, and neoliberalism and its structural adjustment programs were dominating the capitalist world, many people believed the disappearance of the socialist system in Cuba was inevitable. Yet Cuba chose to defend its socialist model, while still making whatever changes were necessary to adapt to the new world conditions. Cuba remained convinced that only socialism could provide economic and social equity and that it was possible to achieve economic efficiency without making the transition to a market economy.

As the crisis unfolded, an emergency economic program was put into effect. Its fundamental objectives were to combat the crisis, to limit its negative effects as much as possible, and subsequently to recover from it. Two key concerns arising from Cuba's commitment to socialism were to accomplish this both with as little social cost as possible and with the necessary political support to carry out the economic measures. Specifically, this concern meant rejecting the neoliberal recovery strategy being imposed at that time on many other economically troubled third-world countries, because in such a recovery strategy the sacrifices fall disproportionately on the poor.

Given the origin of Cuba's crisis, the first task was to effect sweeping changes in the organization of both its domestic economy and foreign trade in ways that would enable its reinsertion into a very different global economy. To carry out such major reforms in the midst of a severe economic crisis, and in keeping with the tradition of popular participation in the Revolution, it was considered appropriate to achieve as strong a political consensus as possible. Hence, a massive consultation with the populace was carried out between May and October 1991 to discuss the fundamental issues to be presented to the assembly of the Fourth Congress of the Cuban Communist Party, which was held in October 1991. Of the 3.5 million citizens who participated in the discussions, only 0.1 percent questioned whether socialism was desirable and necessary for combating and overcoming the crisis, while an even smaller 0.005 percent specifically proposed a market economy.

Broadly speaking, a number of the specific measures in the emergency economic program of 1990–93 significantly changed the economic paradigm in that, without renouncing the socialist essence of the economy, they opened up considerable space for market mechanisms designed to reactivate production and services. A number of the measures that outsiders most frequently comment on were not implemented until 1993–94, but Cuba's intention to go in that direction was already clearly evident at the Fourth Congress. These emergency measures had their intended effects: to avoid malnutrition; to maintain important socioeconomic services such as health care and education; and beyond that, to prevent any further reduction in the population's standard of living.[39]

All these emergency measures had clearly defined economic and political objectives that constrained their application: they would meet those objectives and go no further. Cuba's leaders were always very open about the fact that they were adopting elements of capitalism and that the existing world situation forced them to do so to secure the immediate well-being of the population and the survival of the Revolution. The measures were not what they would have preferred to adopt had other options been viable. Furthermore, the measures were always to be controlled so that they would not develop a momentum of their own that would gradually reintroduce capitalism, as opponents of the Revolution hoped. In 1995 Fidel Castro explained, "We cannot guide ourselves by the criterion of what we like or dislike, but rather by what is and is not useful for the nation and the people in these very decisive moments in the history of our country." He added, "We have said that we are introducing elements of capitalism in our system, in our economy; that is a fact. We have talked even of the consequences that we see from the use of such mechanisms. Yes, we are doing it."[40]

The persistence of mercantile-market relationships in socialism has been the subject of important debates for many years. However, the objective reason for these relations was scientifically explained only at the end of the 1960s. At that time economists demonstrated that the direct social characteristics of labor could not attain sufficiently unmediated expression in socialism because the productive forces of society remained underdeveloped. This situation manifested in a relative separation between personal economic interest and the collective interest. Within the context of the social division of labor, this separation requires that market categories measure each person's contribution to the collective interest, even when the means of production is collectively owned.[41]

This economic situation is apparent in the contradictory relationship between the market and a planned economy in socialism. Understanding this fact has had a strategic importance for the survival of the Cuban revolutionary project. Truly free markets are contrary to socialism's social and political goals. Adopting market mechanisms while failing to understand that they contradict socialism would propel Cuba toward capitalism, and hence end its revolutionary project. At the same time, market mechanisms are necessary in socialism as long as the forces of production are insufficient for the collective nature of labor to express itself without mediation. Failure to understand this, particularly in the specific context of a small open economy in crisis in a world thoroughly dominated by capitalism, would have led Cuba to reject the market mechanisms necessary to survive its economic crisis and hence also would have brought about the end of its revolutionary project.[42]

I turn now to a more detailed consideration of the almost twenty years of the Special Period and how it transformed the Cuban economy. It is necessary first to identify the economic and social conditions at the onset. I then divide its twenty years into several stages.

The Cuban Economy in 1990

During the first thirty years of the Revolution, Cuba created important reserves of revolutionary consciousness, human capital, political leadership, and material resources. These were to be crucial assets in surviving the crisis. The most important factor was the popular political consciousness, consisting of a combination of a strong commitment to national sovereignty with an understanding of the benefits thirty years of the socialist Revolution had brought to Cuba in comparison with neighboring third-world countries. This awareness was at the heart of the population's ability to tolerate extremely difficult economic conditions while remaining committed to building socialism, which they saw both as the only road to authentic economic and social development in a world dominated by large capitalist powers and as necessary to maintain real national sovereignty.

Since the Revolution, the Cuban government had applied a concept of development that viewed economic growth as indivisible from social development and progress in basic social services. This was important to the nature of Cuba in 1990 for two reasons. First, it was an important contribution to the development of the aforementioned revolutionary consciousness. In terms of socioeconomic development there was a significant improvement on all indexes, including a rise in the average level of education to 6.4 years, a first-world level of health, the disappearance of chronic unemployment, a highly equitable distribution of income, and a general improvement in the standard of living of all citizens.[43] Second, the advances achieved in education, public health, social security, culture, and sports led to a large accumulation of human capital. This human capital was not only invaluable in implementing the emergency measures for confronting the crisis, but by the turn of the twenty-first century it was to become a central component of Cuba's strategy for post-crisis long-range development.

The life-and-death issue of Cuba's ability to respond rapidly to each new aspect of the unfolding crisis and subsequently to chart a path for recovery depended on the quality of its political leadership. It had to be able to understand the ramifications of each new event, identify the economic and social contradictions the events would unleash, and at times predict impending changes in order to begin preparing for them.

With regard to material resources, between 1959 and 1989 Cuba's GDP had grown at an annual rate of 4.4 percent, investment at 8.3 percent, labor productivity at 3.4 percent, industrial production at 4.5 percent, and agriculture at 2.5 percent. The basic infrastructure of the country was expanded and transformed, leading to a positive change in the structure of the GDP, particularly in the greater relative contributions of industry and services.[44]

In summary, in 1990 Cuba was in a position to accelerate its development process significantly. This readiness rested primarily on the human capital it had accumulated over three decades and the gradual transformation of its economic structure in the framework of the international socialist division of labor. Important structural and organizational problems remained to be resolved, however. Especially important were those related to the foreign debt, the financing of the investment process, the expansion of exports, the substitution of imports, and food security. Each of these issues had to be resolved in a way that was economically, socially, and politically consistent with the Cuban socialist paradigm.

Thus, in 1990 Cuba faced a contradictory situation: good potential for accelerated development and a set of economic barriers it had to remove in order to realize that potential. How that situation would have evolved was never tested by history. The sudden disappearance of the Eastern European socialist countries and the Soviet Union created an emergency that obliged Cuba to rapidly change its economic strategy in order to guarantee the survival of the Revolution, and subsequently to find a new path for building socialism.[45]

The Breakdown of Socialist Europe and the Initial Perception, 1990–1991

At the beginning of the Special Period the initial prediction was that there would be a sudden drop in the GDP but a relatively rapid recovery, due to the maturity of several economic programs in progress and the maintenance of relatively stable international economic relations. Supporting that perception was the existence of stockpiles of several important products, the reduced but still existing economic agreements with the USSR,[46] the expected rapid development of the Food Program approved by the National Assembly in December of 1990,[47] and the rapidly growing tourism and biotechnology sectors. The international economy was doing relatively well, and the Torricelli bill had not yet been proposed to strengthen the long-standing U.S. blockade.

The economic situation continued to worsen through 1990, however, leading to the declaration of the Special Period at the end of August; by the end of December the GDP had fallen 2.9 percent for the year. The situation continued to worsen rapidly in 1991, when GDP declined by 10.7 percent and many important stockpiles were exhausted. The Soviet Union fell at the end of December, and the majority of the Commonwealth of Independent States (CIS) that emerged in its place broke most of their economic ties with Cuba.[48]

Hence by the end of 1991 the expectation of a rapid recovery had disappeared. The Economic Resolution of the Fourth Congress of the Cuban Communist Party, which took place in October 1991, projected a deep and prolonged crisis. As indicated, 1991 had already been a bad year by that time, and the sudden termination of most of Cuba's external trade and financial flows on the eve of 1992 ensured that this scenario would be deep and prolonged.

The Sudden Downfall, 1992–1994

The massive and abrupt rupture of Cuba's international economic relations triggered a crisis that threatened a national economic collapse. In response, the

Cuban government acted decisively to thoroughly reshape its foreign trade structures as quickly as possible in order to permit effective interaction with the capitalist world markets.[49] The most important change was the elimination of the centralized monopoly on foreign trade. Export enterprises became self-financing, paying for their imports using their export earnings. The government still used any excess foreign-exchange earnings these enterprises generated to support social services as well as to pay for imports of necessary inputs for non-exporting productive enterprises. New public stockholding companies were set up in order to circumvent the U.S. blockade, contributing further to decentralization. At the same time, while foreign investment in joint ventures had been legal since 1982, it had been virtually nonexistent. Now a high-priority campaign was launched to attract the types of foreign investment that would benefit the Cuban economy, focusing on three specific channels: restarting idled Cuban productive capacity, providing foreign markets for Cuban production, and transferring technology and management practices that would ready additional branches of Cuban production for international competition.

All these transformations required changes in the Cuban Constitution. These issues had been among the many discussed in the national popular consultation during 1991, and the necessary constitutional changes were then ratified by the National Assembly in the summer of 1992. Two of the most significant constitutional changes for the economy were eliminating the state monopoly on foreign trade and recognizing mixed property.

Despite these rapid changes in the foreign trade and investment structures, Cuba's GDP fell by another 11.6 percent in 1992. The need for major organizational and institutional changes in the domestic economy therefore became apparent. Optimally, such changes would follow a broad popular discussion to solicit public consensus. This was partially accomplished during the widespread consultations held throughout much of 1991 leading up to the Fourth Party Congress, but by 1992 the situation had changed so much and so many new issues had arisen that further popular discussion was warranted. Unfortunately, however, by mid-1993 the economic decline was so severe that immediate action to restructure the domestic economy was vital to prevent collapse.[50] Three problems required immediate attention: the lack of foreign-exchange earnings was choking the domestic economy, food shortages were acute, and unemployment and underemployment were rising;[51] the last two problems were, of course, a direct result of the dramatic economic contraction.

In his speech delivered at the 26th of July celebration in 1993, Fidel Castro publicly announced that major transformations had to be made in the Cuban economy. The most surprising announcement was that whereas previously possession of foreign currency had been illegal, the government would now establish a dual monetary economy.[52] Most basic necessities would be purchasable with Cuban pesos, and other goods would be purchasable only with convertible currencies.[53] Enterprises that conducted transactions in convertible currency had to keep separate Cuban peso and convertible currency accounts.[54] Furthermore, the government introduced the Foreign Currency Incentive System. This system allowed workers in certain key sectors of the economy to receive a portion of their incomes in convertible currency as an incentive to increase their productivity.

These reforms were implemented only after considering all the usual alternatives. Currency devaluation was rejected because of the problems it would cause for the already crippled productive sectors and because, given Cuba's isolation from the capitalist world market at that time, it would have had only minimal effects in stimulating exports or reducing imports. Transition from the Cuban peso to another devalued national currency—as Argentina had done—was considered even more drastic and suffered from the same inefficacies as simple devaluation.

The introduction of foreign currencies into the Cuban economy had positive and negative impacts. Its greatest positive effect was that it allowed individuals to spend foreign remittances and convertible currency incomes inside Cuba. As a result they soon became one of the largest sources of the critically necessary foreign exchange. Cuba set up a network of convertible currency stores where luxury goods and supplementary basic goods could be bought at prices that included steep taxes. Those people who received hard currency from abroad or for their work in Cuba could thereby improve their individual level of consumption, but at the same time the state was able to obtain the convertible currency it needed to bolster domestic production as well as to provide a basic level of goods and services to the entire population. Second, convertible currency supported foreign investment. Third, direct government attention to convertible currency promoted more effective management of both convertible currency and foreign financing, serving to direct the scarce convertible currency to the most dynamic branches of the Cuban economy where it would generate the greatest returns. Finally, the Foreign Currency Incentive System was effective in stimulating increased productivity with minimal expenditure of resources. Eventually, between 25 and 30 percent of the workers employed in state enterprises were covered by the incentive system.

This decriminalization of possessing and spending convertible currency in Cuba had two major and interrelated negative effects that were incompatible with socialist principles. The first was a growing inequality in material standards of living simulating what exists in capitalism. The second was the delinking of workers' income (and hence standard of living) from the quantity and quality of the work they performed. Instead, the primary factor became the receipt of remittances from abroad. These two problems are very much under discussion in Cuba as I write this chapter.

Still, not all convertible currency was available to the Cuban government for productive or social uses. Any funds (at that time primarily U.S. dollars) that were circulating in the convertible currency market, or that people were saving for future use, were essentially tied up. Therefore, in 1994 the Cuban government effectively started printing its own convertible currency for use only in Cuba. These so-called convertible Cuban pesos (CUCs) were at the time exchangeable for U.S. dollars at a one-to-one rate and were accepted exactly like dollars in the convertible currency stores. Dollars and other currencies were allowed to circulate, but the government pulled as much as possible out of circulation and redirected it to social ends. The majority of the circulation in the convertible currency market in Cuba gradually became Cuban-printed CUCs.

On balance the partial dollarization of the Cuban economy was a successful catalyst in Cuba's economic recovery. Given the two aforementioned important social costs plus certain technical economic costs, however, this measure was always intended to be temporary. By 2003 a number of the downsides of the system were becoming more problematic, including in particular macro- and microeconomic imbalances, as Fidel Castro discussed in a critical appraisal of dollarization.[55] A first step toward reversing dollarization was to ban the legal circulation of convertible currency in 2004. Anyone receiving foreign currency had to convert it into CUCs in order to make purchases in Cuba. As Cuban leaders have frequently stated, the final goal is to resolve the problem through the return to a single Cuban currency. This transition will likely take place through gradual adjustments of the exchange rate between Cuba's two currencies until the CUC can disappear and the Cuban peso will exchange with convertible currencies in accordance with free-market conditions (perhaps influenced by government interventions, technically referred to as a "dirty float"). These issues continue to be topics of discussion at present in Cuba.[56]

A second monetary problem that was crippling the real economy and had to be resolved quickly was inflationary pressure. The need to restore a domestic financial balance led the National Assembly to adopt a set of measures approved on May 1, 1994. The main measures to reduce the fiscal budget deficit were a reduction of subsidies to unprofitable enterprises, an increase in prices of and tariffs on certain nonessential goods and services, and the introduction of a new tax system.[57] These measures enabled the state to reduce the national liquidity by 17.7 percent between 1994 and 1999 and to achieve a dramatic reduction of the budget deficit, from 33 percent to 2.4 percent of the GDP. It also ended the continual fall of the value of the peso against the

U.S. dollar and created the conditions for the peso's strong revaluation in the following period.

Particularly important was the fact that all these measures were widely discussed with the population before being enacted, unlike the neoliberal monetary reforms being imposed all over the rest of the world at that time. Between January and March 1994, three million workers (85 percent of the workforce) met in multiple sessions in eighty thousand workplaces to discuss the issues that the National Assembly later decided on. The extensive popular input from these meetings, which became known as "workers' parliaments," significantly influenced the timing and content of the draft proposals.

Such extensive monetary and financial foreign and domestic transformations merely laid the groundwork for further fundamental changes in the real economy. Major decisions and transformations were necessary in the organization of agriculture, the private sector, enterprises, and state agencies in order to expedite recovery and promote the strongest possible long-term growth of the economy.[58] Two problems in the real economy requiring immediate attention were food security and unemployment/underemployment resulting from the national economic depression.

To increase food production, state farms were converted into a new type of cooperative known as a Basic Unit of Cooperative Production (UBPC), reducing the percentage of arable land in state farms from 75 percent to 33 percent.[59] This transformation was motivated by the facts that UBPCs required much lower inputs of imported material resources and instead relied more heavily on domestic natural and human resources and that state farms were highly unprofitable and heavily subsidized.

The cooperative option provides individual or group incentives for the producer or producers because they directly participate in the distribution of profits. It was hoped this incentive would significantly raise the problematically low productivity of agricultural labor. However, because of the low level of capitalization and also precisely because of the history of low productivity in agriculture, the new cooperatives have faced many challenges, and the hoped-for improvements in productivity and output have been very slow to develop. They have succeeded in the important respect of sharply reducing agricultural subsidies, but despite some improvements, the anticipated significant increase in food production has not materialized to date, and the problematically high dependence on food imports continues.

A related policy to promote increased agricultural productivity was to reintroduce farmers' markets where prices were determined entirely by supply and demand. Once they met their state contracts, private farmers and cooperatives could sell their surplus produce in these venues. These markets immediately provided very significant amounts of total income. The government instituted certain measures to avoid some of the problems with the similar agricultural markets of the early 1980s, such as the large markup by middlemen who were not producers, which had greatly reduced the farmers' profits and hence their incentives.

With the severe economic contraction in the early 1990s, many state enterprises, the overwhelming majority of the non-agricultural sectors, no longer had productive work for many of their employees. Large numbers of workers were retained, albeit very underemployed, while others left their jobs to seek alternative means of obtaining income or goods. Cuba had always had a few tens of thousands of self-employed workers outside the agricultural sector, but this sector rapidly expanded after September 1993, when the government opened more than one hundred mostly service occupations to legal self-employment. This served two purposes. First, it gainfully employed a significant number of people whom the state was no longer in a position to employ productively because of the crisis. Second, it provided the population with a number of goods and especially services that again, in light of the crisis, the state was no longer able to provide. Further, a significant proportion of these private workers were already working underground. Hence, legalizing, regulating, and taxing their employment meant that instead of these individuals being the only beneficiaries of their illegal economic activity, all of society would benefit. Under the conditions of the Special Period—a crippled state sector, limited availability of goods and services, and excess cash—expanding self-employment was a win-win proposition. As part of the same policy there was a concurrent legalization in 1994 of similar markets in handicrafts and some small-scale industries.

Albeit important, the effects of the emergency self-employment measure must not be overestimated. The number of self-employed workers peaked at about 208,000 in 1996, then soon fell to about 150,000 and remained at about that level, registering 141,600 in 2008. Although these workers earn about two or three times the average salary, they constitute only about 3 percent of the labor force.[60] Thus, although an important policy of the Special Period, there was never any illusion that this magnitude of reemployment would be the solution to Cuba's economic difficulties.

The Beginning of the Recovery: Facing the Great Challenges, 1995–1999

After a decline in the GDP of 14.9% in 1993, by the middle of 1994 the contraction had stopped and limited growth had begun, yielding a 0.7 percent increase for the year. In 1995 GDP growth increased to 2.5 percent, marking the beginning of economic recovery. For the rest of the decade, growth in GDP averaged 4 percent annually.[61]

The government carried out a number of important economic measures in this period, building on the emergency measures of the previous few years. First, the use of hard currency in state enterprises was expanded in 1995. Second, the pursuit of joint ventures, which had become a focus several years earlier, bore their first major fruits. Third, modest foreign credit was obtained.[62] Fourth, in 1994 the first steps were taken toward reducing the seriously inflated workforce in the state's huge ministerial structure. The state's central administrative bodies were cut from fifty to thirty, with a corresponding reduction in personnel. Fifth, the banking and finance system was restructured to meet the new needs for extensive interaction with capitalist world markets and the expansion of market mechanisms in Cuba. The previous single bank was divided into the Central Bank and a commercial banking system.

In order to achieve medium- and long-term economic growth and improvements in standard of living, Cuba urgently required improved labor productivity and consequent competitiveness in its enterprises, particularly for increased international trade. Accomplishing this goal entailed changes in many dimensions of commercial operations, including their management (especially what decisions enterprise managers were authorized to make), their financial and accounting systems, and their worker incentive programs. The Cuban armed forces had already been fundamentally overhauling their industrial enterprises since the late 1980s, instituting these types of changes. Over the 1990s, the government had adapted that restructuring model for application to the scale and complexity of the entire economy, and in 1996 implemented a number of further changes in several branches of industry, including the sugar industry, actions endorsed at the Fifth Party Congress in 1997. The following year the Enterprise Improvement System (Perfeccionamiento Empresarial) was created by Decree-Law 187. The eventual goal is to convert all of Cuba's enterprises to this system, which requires them to meet a lengthy checklist of specific modern operational criteria and also offers them greater autonomy in decision making. Ten years into the conversion process, the results have been positive. Of the roughly three thousand enterprises in Cuba, the 28 percent that have been accepted into the program generate 20 percent of all sales, account for 51 percent of all profits and 72 percent of all foreign-exchange earnings, and are 50 percent more productive than their traditional counterparts.[63]

This period witnessed several improvements in other important macroeconomic indicators besides growth. Domestic financial imbalances sharply declined, with the fiscal deficit dropping to 2.4 percent of the GDP and cash liquidity to 38.5 percent. The Cuban peso appreciated strongly from its low point of 150 pesos to the U.S. dollar in February 1994 to 21 per dollar in 1999. Productivity increased by 3.3 percent per year; energy use per unit of national output decreased by 7.7 percent per year; and investment efficiency improved by 74 percent.[64]

Reduction in Social Cost and Adjustment of Economic Policies, 2000–2003

The impact of the crisis of the 1990s was particularly visible in the critical deterioration of the standard of living of the most vulnerable social groups: at-risk children and low-income elderly people. In addition, other social indicators continued showing declines—for example, university enrollments dropped, health-care services deteriorated, unemployment grew, and income distribution worsened.[65]

By 2000 the Cuban government commanded minimally sufficient resources to begin addressing the social costs of the crisis, which it did by launching a multifaceted economic, social, and even cultural program known as the Battle of Ideas. The program was particularly (though not exclusively) targeted at the highest-risk populations. Given the ongoing scarcity of resources, an important aspect of its design was to achieve the highest economic and social outcomes possible at the lowest cost. Therefore, it incorporated a new concept into Cuban social services: personalized and highly differentiated service provision dependent on each recipient's specific needs.

The Battle of Ideas evolved through several stages in response to emerging social priorities and progress on the initial basic objectives. The largest initiative in the first stage was a redesign of Cuba's social assistance programs around a large number of mostly young people who were trained in a new model of social work. The second stage focused on redesigning parts of Cuba's education system, including the expansion and decentralization of university education (dubbed "universities in the communities"). More recently the government has made huge investments to increase the coverage and quality of public health-care services. The Battle of Ideas has always contained many additional smaller projects in addition to the main ones being implemented at any given time (see chapters 5 and 6 for further information).

Adjustment of the Economic Policy and Recentralization of Foreign Currency Allocation, 2003–2005

As discussed, the dollarization of the economy and the extensive decentralization of the circulation of convertible currency had several positive economic effects in the 1990s, but by 2003 the policy was manifesting clear problems. Many enterprises whose products were generating sufficient foreign currency for their own needs were failing to act with the financial discipline necessary to ease Cuba's binding foreign-exchange constraint and contribute to its domestic production and social programs. Convertible currency tensions were once again increasing to a critical level. These were exacerbated by the fall in hard-currency earnings following September 11, 2001, particularly in the tourism sector; the tightening of the U.S. blockade, particularly concerning all Cuba's hard-currency transactions, following passage of the Torricelli Act in 1992 and the Helms-Burton Act in 1996; and an energy shortage emergency that arose in the second half of 2004, when the major electricity generation plants broke down due to age and deferred maintenance. This situation required massive hard-currency investments to rebuild the power grid.

Cuba responded with a series of new regulations, including some that to a large degree reestablished Central Bank control over convertible currency. First, the number of enterprises authorized to operate in convertible currency was sharply reduced. Next, in July 2003, operating bank accounts for enterprises doing business abroad were converted from dollars to CUCs. The Central Bank then assumed control of foreign currency exchange. Instead of currency exchanges being automatic, enterprises seeking to convert CUCs (or Cuban pesos) to convertible currency in order to buy foreign inputs had to submit requests that the Central Bank reviewed and prioritized in accordance with Cuba's overall economic needs. This gave the Central Bank the authority to reduce Cuba's foreign-exchange tensions. In November 2004 convertible currency was withdrawn from circulation in Cuba and CUCs became the only currency accepted at the network of convertible currency stores. In order to make purchases there, one now must convert hard currency into CUCs. Resolution no. 92 of December 29, 2004, enacted all these changes and almost completely centralized all foreign currency transactions in the Central Bank.

At the same time, Cuba made significant efforts to repay its overdue debts with several major creditor nations in order to qualify for fresh financial inflows.[66] The resulting possibilities for renewed credit supported additional joint venture investments. An important agreement was signed with Venezuela that enabled Cuba to import oil and pay for it with medical and educational services.[67] In 2005 the CUC was revalued against the U.S. dollar and the Cuban peso was revalued against the CUC.[68] To assist the at-risk population, cost-of-living adjustments were made in the minimum wage and pensions.

By the end of 2004 the preconditions for strong growth existed throughout the Cuban economy. GDP grew by 11.2 percent in 2005 and 12.1 percent in 2006. Cuba's current account and balance of payments were positive in 2004 and 2005.[69] With this economic surge, Cuba began in 2005 to launch a number of strategic investment programs targeted at improving the population's welfare. The Energy Revolution was introduced to address the electricity crisis and high oil prices through both energy conservation and the construction of a modern generation network. Other programs aimed to recapitalize the public transportation network, refurbish and expand the water supply infrastructure, expand and repair the housing stock, and reinforce national defense. New projects were undertaken to increase domestic agricultural production and reduce food imports. All of these projects were conducted on top of the ongoing and expanded social and economic programs in the Battle of Ideas.

Additional Urgently Needed Changes in Economic Policy, 2006–2009

Notwithstanding the exceptionally strong performance of the Cuban economy in 2005 and 2006, convertible currency shortages remained a limiting factor, particularly relative to the trade balance on goods. In 2005 the economy ran a deficit of 5.23 billion pesos on goods but a surplus of 6.38 billion pesos on services, yielding a net surplus of 1.14 billion on goods and services. Despite negative balances on net current transfers and rent, Cuba still ended up with a surplus of 140 million pesos in its current account.

Then in 2006 and 2007 the historical convertible currency constraint appeared again. In 2006 the surplus on services stayed about the same while the balance on goods deteriorated by a little more than one billion pesos due to the social and infrastructural reinvestment programs and the rising prices of oil and food. Thus, the current account dropped to a deficit of 215 million pesos and would have been worse but for a major improvement in current transfers, totaling a half billion pesos. In 2007 the surplus on services rose to 1.5 billion pesos above its 2005 level, allowing it to support roughly the same level of deficits on goods as in 2006 and once again yield a current account surplus of 489 million pesos. Higher prices for food, oil, and other imports in 2007 were partially offset by very high prices for Cuba's nickel exports, but such exceptionally high prices on that one export good could not be expected to last. By the early twenty-first century, Cuba's convertible currency constraint on the goods it needed to import for production and popular welfare was clear. It could support large deficits on its trade in goods only as long as it could sustain a large surplus on services.[70]

At the start of 2008, prices for imports of food, oil, and other goods remained high, while the price of nickel—though still healthy at around $13,000 per ton—dropped to almost half of its 2007 peak. Later in the year, as the U.S. financial crisis spread to Europe and the third world and transformed into an economic crisis, nickel prices fell further to an extreme low of $5,000 per ton before beginning a slow recovery. On balance, in 2008 Cuba paid $840 million more for its food imports than it would have had prices remained stable, while the value of its exports remained fairly stable. Moreover, three major hurricanes hit Cuba that year, causing the most monetary damage ever in a single year: $9.7 billion, roughly one-sixth of Cuba's GDP. The response to these natural disasters drove imports of goods up from roughly $10 billion to $14 billion;[71] therefore, the current account and balance of payments deficit worsened. The Cuban economy, which had fallen from its record double-digit growth of 2005–6 to a still strong 7.3 percent in 2007, fell further under its hard-currency constraint to 4.1 percent in 2008, a level exactly matching the average for Latin America and the Caribbean.[72]

In the face of the growing convertible currency deficit, Cuba instituted an import substitution program by 2008. In 2008–9 this program saved about $535 million. Import spending still rose in 2008, due to the hurricanes among other reasons. But the effects of import substitution became apparent in 2009, when imports dropped below 9 billion pesos compared to 14 billion the year before and 10 billion in 2007.

In addition to these reductions in hard-currency expenditures, Cuba carried out several other complementary cost-cutting efforts in 2008 and 2009. The social and infrastructural reinvestment plans were revisited and recalculated in light of slumping economic growth. Food allotments on the ration cards, and later at many workplace cafeterias, were cut. Quotas for a number of other items on the ration card were reduced or eliminated, and popular discussion continues about eliminating the ration card system as soon as this can be done with minimal social harm. Planned energy consumption was reduced while the search for import substitutes continued. The levels of national stockpiles were examined, and excesses were used up. The government also adjusted the retail sales plan and reduced budget expenditures in order to maintain an appropriate domestic financial balance, making spending cuts in social services that were deemed unnecessary. Furthermore, it pursued debt repayment negotiations in order to reduce Cuba's outstanding debt and open up new lines of credit.[73]

At the beginning of 2009, with the emergencies of 2008 in the past (though certainly their economic fallout continued), Cuba initially projected a return to a 6 percent rate of economic growth. But the deepening world economic crisis had negative effects on tourism, demand for exports, and prices, causing Cuba—like the rest of Latin America—to progressively downgrade its growth estimates over the course of the year. Growth projections were reduced to 2.5 percent in March and to 1.7 percent in June. The actual rate of growth for 2009 came in at 1.4 percent. Such a slow growth rate poses a serious problem for Cuba—though the Island fared well relative to the average economic decline of 1.8 percent for Latin America and the Caribbean in 2009.[74] Given the predicted slow recovery from the global Great Recession, the 2010 economic projections were only marginally higher than 2009, at 1.9 percent. The actual annual rate of growth was 2.1 percent, leading to a 2011 projection of 3.1 percent.

As has always been the case in Cuba, the 2006–9 period witnessed a continual stream of changes. Among these are the small but symbolically important changes allowing the public increased ability to purchase computers and cell phones and to use international tourist facilities in the country. A bigger change is the multiyear process of reorganizing the Council of Ministers to increase its administrative efficiency. Perhaps the change that will have the greatest long-range effect on the population is the multiyear program to return the large amount of idle arable land back into production, particularly for growing food. Formerly idle land is being leased to any citizen or entity who will contract to make it productive. State farms, all types of co-ops, and private farmers are allowed to obtain plots, but the overwhelming majority of leases have gone to private farmers (many of them new to farming). Putting unused land into production under contract, with the potential for the farmer to earn an attractive income, should raise Cuba's domestic food production.[75] By the end of 2010 farmers had leased 57 percent of the idle land, and at the present rate of distribution it is expected that slightly over 20 percent more will be distributed in 2011.[76]

All indications are that further dramatic changes in Cuba's path to socialism will unfold over the coming years, and therefore between 2006 and 2009 the leadership consulted extensively with the people to obtain their input. In his speech on the 26th of July 2007, Raúl Castro said (quoting Fidel from 2001), "Revolution means a sense of our moment in history, it means changing all that ought to be changed." He continued that every Cuban is "duty bound to accurately identify and analyze in depth every problem." These were not empty words. Starting in August and accelerating through September and October 2007, a national discussion with the entire population was organized in Communist Party cells, Committees for the Defense of the Revolution (neighborhoods), and workplaces to air whatever social and economic concerns the people had. These ran the gamut from salaries, food prices, housing, transportation, restrictions on travel, the dual monetary system, and the lack of resources at the once academically outstanding schools in the countryside, to opposition to interference with low-income retirees who peddle whatever they can on the streets without a license. Many more meetings and consultations have taken place with specific groups over the following years.

The Sixth Congress of the Communist Party, slated for April 2011, is dedicated exclusively to updating Cuba's economic and social model in light of a combination of current global realities and fifty years of experience building socialism under a variety of conditions. As of this writing in December 2010, a 291-point first draft titled "The Economic and Social Policy Development Project" has been distributed to the entire population, and a second three-month nationwide consultation on the way forward for Cuba's socialist economy is ongoing in Cuban workplaces. The resulting, significantly modified document will be debated and voted on at the Congress. The main short-term obstacles of the Cuban economy described in the draft are the deficit of the balance of payments and the lack of efficiency throughout the economy. The decisions taken will lead to a new strategy of development to confront these and other challenges, whose main goal is to create in the next five years conditions for a sustainable economic growth. A point that needs to be stressed is the profound involvement of the entire populace in not only the execution but also the design of the new form of Cuban socialism that is emerging as the Special Period finally comes to an end.

Summary and the Challenges Ahead

Cuba has achieved respectable economic performance over the last fifty years at the same time as it has succeeded in elevating its social indexes remarkably, ranking among the very highest in the third world and in some areas on par with the first world. Between 1959 and 2009, even factoring in the lengthy period of acute crisis and fifteen-year recovery, the GDP still grew at an annual average of 3.2 percent. This is close to the average of 3.8 percent for all of Latin America, which faced much less difficult conditions. The Cuban people have made great efforts and sacrifices to accomplish these achievements of the Cuban Revolution despite three primary barriers: first, the economic and social underdevelopment of Cuba in 1958; second, the complexities of constructing socialism, particularly in the face of the global hegemony of neoliberal capitalism over the past twenty years; and third, the consistently aggressive U.S. policies toward Cuba since 1959. The blockade, for example, has so far cost Cuba more than $100 billion at current prices, which is more than $239 billion in 2008 U.S. prices.

The investment effort over the course of the Revolution has involved about 118 billion pesos with a yearly growth rate of 5.7 percent: 50 percent of that was directed to infrastructure and socially oriented investments, 31 percent to industry, and 19 percent to agriculture. The structure of the Cuban GDP has changed, with the service sector increasing from 49 percent to 76 percent while the primary sector declined from 22 percent to 5 percent, and the secondary sector from 29 percent to 19 percent.[77] Exports of goods have grown at a yearly rate of 3.5 percent whereas imports have grown at 6 percent, causing a continuous foreign-exchange deficit. In the last five years a large surplus of service exports has partially relaxed, but certainly not eliminated, this hard-currency constraint. In terms of social development, an important feature of the Cuban reality today is that the Island has the highest numbers of physicians and teachers per capita in the world, and one of the lowest unemployment rates.

To understand Cuba it is important to recognize that between 1960 and 2008 it has shared its modest achievements with 160 countries: 270,743 civilian workers have extended their solidarity to improve the living conditions of the third world, mainly in the fields of education and health.[78] Recent estimates are that Cuba has devoted about 2 percent of its GDP to official foreign aid, compared to less than 1 percent among developed nations and 0.2 percent for the United States.[79]

As I have argued in this chapter, moving forward beyond the Special Period is a highly complex, multifaceted project. Among the many issues that must be addressed and resolved, three critical economic imbalances are particularly pressing in the short term. First, the perpetual balance of payments deficit and related convertible currency constraint needs to be resolved. This requires addressing both sides of the coin: sharply reducing hard-currency expenditures through import substitution while both expanding exports and continually shifting to more technologically intensive and higher-value-added exports. A related need is to gradually resolve the external debt problem, and thereby secure credit sources for the standard credit needs of a developing third-world country.

Second, the domestic financial balance must be maintained to control inflationary pressures. Related to this is the need to develop new incentives for workers to increase their productivity. These factors are bidirectionally correlated: major inflation reduces the motivation to work for a given salary, while increased labor productivity works to reduce inflation. Increased production of food for domestic consumption is particularly important in this regard and relates to the first point because food remains a major import and hence a target for import substitution. Also related to the issue of incentives is the currently heavily debated issue of linking income more directly to the quantity and quality of goods and services a worker produces. This is directed above all at minimizing social inequality and the social problems connected to remittances, which give very high incomes to a small number of people; however, for the majority of those Cubans who receive remittances, they merely supplement their regular income.

Finally, priority must be given to investments that strengthen the productive infrastructure required to reshape the Cuban economy. The immediate concerns are electricity generation, transportation, and water supply. Beyond that, an intensified program of industrialization must be relaunched.

The strong recovery in the first years of this century that was interrupted by the worldwide Great Recession must be restarted as quickly as possible. Cuba estimates that it must return to an annual growth rate of about 5 or 6 percent in the short term to resume its developmental and social progress. The Economist Intelligence Unit predicts that Cuba will decrease its budget and current-account deficits over the next four years, but given the expected slow recovery of the world economy it is forecasting a rate of growth between 3.7 percent and 4.4 percent for the same period.[80]

A new socialist development path for the near future demands further adjustments and changes to Cuba's economic strategy and policies. A number of these changes have been debated extensively over the last four years and are now appearing more frequently in recent speeches and documents, including the 2011–15 economic plan, whose first draft was approved in 2010. Central is the issue of increasing Cuba's economic efficiency and labor productivity, which in a socialist setting are crucial to supporting improvements in standard of living and social well-being.

There are four central efficiency issues. First is the elimination of underemployment in state enterprises through the reduction of inflated payrolls. Given the inability of the state to provide all the alternative productive employment needed for these workers, it must open up spaces for private employment to do so. It must create incentives for many of these workers to go into agriculture as cooperative or private farmers, because Cuba needs to boost its domestic production of food for improved nutritional well-being, reduce its hard-currency imports, and assert its national sovereignty (food security). Smaller numbers of laid-off workers will be absorbed into an expanded self-employment system, primarily in the cities, again increasing the supply of small-scale services while simultaneously ensuring that no one is allowed to fall through the cracks during the necessary downsizing of state productive units and government agencies. The second central efficiency issue is the continuation and expansion of the Enterprise Improvement System, particularly the management system. An essential component of the enterprise transformation will be to increase the active participation of workers in economic decision making, as participation creates the sense of social ownership that is fundamental to socialism.

The third central efficiency issue concerns the inability to accurately measure the total value produced by the Cuban economy because of the dual monetary system. The corollary is an inability to determine the efficacy of policies designed to improve efficiency, and hence an inability to effectively plan for further improvements. As soon as possible the necessary conditions must be created to return the Cuban peso as the sole national currency. The final central efficiency issue is to accelerate the ongoing spinoff of scientific technologies into commercial production, in an effort to transform the Cuban economy into a knowledge economy (see chapter 12).

The fifty years of Revolution in Cuba have seen five decades of changes and transformations. In that sense, notwithstanding the magnitude and importance of the pending economic changes and transformations in the next ten years, they will be just another decade of the Revolution. Three factors have been crucial to Cuba's successful development over the course of its Revolution. First is the conception of development as a process whose social and economic dimensions are intrinsically linked such that one cannot be developed without the other. Second is the principle that over the long term political factors and social consciousness take priority over economic measures. Finally, one must not underestimate the unceasing efforts of the revolutionary leadership, headed by Fidel Castro, not to better their own individual situation but to direct the nationwide effort to build a better Cuba. All three of these factors will remain crucial keys to Cuba's socialist development beyond the Special Period.

Notes

1. See Carlos Rafael Rodríguez, "Cuba en el tránsito al socialismo (1959–1963)," in *Letra con Filo*, vol. 2 (Havana: Editorial de Ciencias Sociales, 1983), and José Luis Rodríguez, *Estrategia del desarrollo económico de Cuba* (Havana: Editorial de Ciencias Sociales, 1990), chap. 1.

2. For extensive, detailed statistics, see José Luis Rodríguez and George Carriazo, *Erradicación de la pobreza en Cuba* (Havana: Editorial de Ciencias Sociales, 1990), chap. 1.

3. See José Luis Rodríguez, "La economía neocolonial cubana," *Cuba Socialista* 37 (1989).

4. Workers received about 20 percent of the national income between 1959 and 1960. See José Luis Rodríguez et al., *Cuba: Revolución y economía, 1959–1960* (Havana: Editorial de Ciencias Sociales, 1985).

5. Contrary to what many people believe due to U.S. propaganda, both foreign and Cuban property owners were offered financial compensation, in most cases based upon the value they had declared for their property in previous tax filings. Many Cuban property owners decided to leave for the United States and forgo the compensation at that time, but subsequently they—like, for example, the Canadian banks and owners of residential property—collected the money over several years. U.S. corporations were not able to seek any compensation after the United States broke off diplomatic relations in January 1961. See Rodríguez et al., *Cuba: Revolución y economía, 1959–1960*, chap. 3,

and Olga Miranda, "El proceso de nacionalización en Cuba: Nacionalización e indemnización" (presented at the International Seminar about the Helms-Burton Law, Havana, September 17, 1996).

6. See Rodríguez, *Estrategia del desarrollo económico de Cuba.*

7. The Moncada Program refers to the demands for social change of the rebels led by Fidel Castro who attacked the soldiers of the Batista dictatorship at the Moncada garrison on July 26, 1953.

8. October 1960 is the most appropriate beginning date for the construction of socialism in Cuba, albeit that its beginning is often dated to the public proclamation of a socialist state in April 1961, on the eve of the invasion of Playa Girón (referred to in the United States as the Bay of Pigs).

9. See Rodríguez, *Estrategia del desarrollo económico de Cuba*, chap. 3, para. 3.

10. Scholars analyzing this period frequently ignore the complexity of the Cuban revolutionary process, especially with regard to the effects of the aggressive U.S. stance, particularly in the first decade of the Revolution. See Jesús Arboleya, *La contrarrevolución Cubana* (Havana: Editorial de Ciencias Sociales, 2000), chaps. 3–5, and Andrés Zaldivar, *Bloqueo: El asedio más prolongado de la historia* (Havana: Editorial Capitán San Luis, 2003).

11. See Rodríguez, *Estrategia del desarrollo económico de Cuba*, chap. 3, para. 4.

12. See Ernesto Che Guevara, *El gran debate sobre la economía en Cuba, 1963–1964* (Havana: Editorial de Ciencias Sociales, 2004).

13. See Carlos Rafael Rodríguez, "Sobre la contribución del Che al desarrollo de la economía cubana," *Cuba Socialista* 33 (1988). See also Ernesto Che Guevara, *Apuntes críticos a la economía política* (Havana: Editorial de Ciencias Sociales, 2006).

14. Among other strategic mistakes, the misinterpretation of the role of the market and monetary relations in socialism contributed to the failure of the systems in Europe and the Soviet Union. In this author's view, those systems failed not because of the exhaustion of socialism but because of their distortions. See José Luis Rodríguez "La perestroika en la economía soviética (1985–1991)," in *El Libro Blanco: Las reformas neoliberales en Rusia 1991–2000*, edited by S. Glasov, S. Kara-Murza, and S. Batchikov (Havana: Editorial de Ciencias Sociales, 2007).

15. See Fidel Castro, *Informe del Comité Central del Partido Comunista de Cuba al Primer Congress* (Havana: Editora Departamento de Orientación Revolucionaria, Comité Central del Partido Comunista de Cuba, 1976).

16. See Miguel Figueras, *Aspectos estructurales de la economía cubana* (Havana: Editorial de Ciencias Sociales, 1994), chap. 2, and José Luis Rodríguez, "Cincuenta años de Revolución en la economía" (Conference of the Ministry of Economy and Planning, unpublished, December 29, 2008).

17. See Rodríguez, *Estrategia del desarrollo económico de Cuba*, chap. 3, para. 4.

18. See Hector Rodríguez Llompart, "Relaciones con los países socialistas," in *Memorias de la Revolución*, vol. 2 (Havana: Editorial Imagen Contemporánea, 2008); Germán Amado Blanco, "Tres décadas de comercio Cuba-URSS (1960–1990)," *Cuba Foreign Trade* 3 (2006); and Andrew Zimbalist and Claes Brundenius, *The Cuban Economy:*

Measurement and Analysis of Socialist Performance (Baltimore: Johns Hopkins University Press, 1989). The extent of the credits and grants Cuba received is a matter of discussion. Some authors have claimed that the USSR gave Cuba 63 billion rubles in investment credits between 1972 and 1990, a clear exaggeration. See Julio Díaz Vázquez, "Cuba y el Came," *Temas* 55 (2008). Carmelo Mesa-Lago states that Cuba received 65 billion pesos from the USSR between 1960 and 1990 and paid back only 41 billion. See Carmelo Mesa-Lago, "Una economía ineficaz y dependiente," *El Nuevo Herald*, December 24, 2008.

19. Development literature throughout the 1960s and 1970s noted the continual deterioration of the purchasing power of the third world as the value of its primary exports, agricultural and mining products, declined relative to the manufactured goods it imported from the first and second worlds. This agreement was designed to be ethically fair by ending this deterioration. Essentially, it fixed the ratio of the prices of Cuba's exports to the USSR to those of its imports at the existing level. This agreement had its intended effect: as world markets continued the trend of an increasing gap between the prices of the exports of the developed and developing worlds, Cuban goods came to have greater purchasing power from the USSR than on the world markets.

20. See Llompart, "Relaciones con los países socialistas," and Alfonso Casanova, ed., *Estructura económica de Cuba*, vol. 1 (Havana: Editorial Félix Varela, 2002), chap. 4.

21. The so-called world market price of sugar, for example, is a "dumping market" price. At that time this market involved less than 10 percent of traded sugar, with most traded sugar being produced and sold under contracts at prices well above the world market price. Once a country had fulfilled its contracts, it would dump any excess production onto the world market at whatever price was offered. Given the small size of the world sugar market, if the USSR had tried to buy all its sugar on that market, this would have caused a price spike that would have multiplied the existing world price many times over. See José Luis Rodríguez, "Las relaciones económicas entre Cuba y la antigua URSS: 1959–1990," *CIEM, Boletín de Información sobre Economía Cubana* 7 (July 1992). See also Llompart, "Relaciones con los países socialistas," and Zimbalist and Brundenius, *The Cuban Economy: Measurement and Analysis of Socialist Performance*.

22. See Banco Nacional de Cuba, "Informe Económico," August 1982; "Informe Económico," June 1990; and "Informe Económico 1994," August 1995, chap. 8. See also Rodríguez, "Las relaciones económicas entre Cuba y la antigua URSS: 1959–1990."

23. This decline accounts for about 60 percent of the outstanding Cuban debt to the USSR, which the Soviet government placed at 15,490 million rubles in November 1989. See "¿A quién hemos prestado 85,800,000 rublos?" *Isveztia*, March 2, 1990, and Rodríguez, "Las relaciones económicas entre Cuba y la antigua URSS: 1959–1990."

24. Since the Putin government was elected, Cuba and post-Soviet Russia have moved closer in their positions on this issue. Russia has agreed that the negotiations should consider Cuba's concerns regarding the doubtful origin of at least part of the debt and its claim for damages incurred by the sudden termination of existing Soviet agreements without compensation. In this regard Cuba claimed that its debt to Russia as of 1998 was $36.2 billion. See *Granma*, October 27, 2001.

25. See *Plataforma Programática del Partido Comunista de Cuba* (Havana: Editorial Departamento de Orientación Revolucionaria, Comité Central del Partido Comunista de Cuba, 1976).

26. See Francisco Martínez Soler, "Hacia una estrategia de desarrollo económico y social en Cuba hasta el año 2000," *Cuestiones de la Economía Planificada* 8 (1981). Long-term bilateral plans were signed only with the USSR (1984), Poland (1985), and Bulgaria (1986). See also Rodríguez, *Estrategia del desarrollo económico de Cuba*, and Vázquez, "Cuba y el Came."

27. See the guidelines of the five-year plans for 1976–80, 1981–85, and 1986–90 in Rodríguez, *Estrategia del desarrollo económico de Cuba*, chap. 3, para. 5.

28. See Figueras, *Aspectos estructurales de la economía cubana*, chap. 2, and ONE, *Anuario Estadístico de Cuba 1989*.

29. A very critical analysis of the economic failures occurred at the First Congress of the Cuban Communist Party. See Castro, *Informe del Comité Central del Partido Comunista de Cuba al Primer Congreso*.

30. The Central Group functioned until September 1988. See Rodríguez, *Estrategia del desarrollo económico de Cuba*.

31. The rectification process was officially launched in April 1986. See Fidel Castro, *Informe Central: Tercer Congreso del Partido Comunista de Cuba* (Havana: Editora Política, 1986), and "Discurso en la clausura de la sesión diferida del Tercer Congreso del Partido, 2 de diciembre de 1986," *Granma*, December 8, 1986.

32. Figueras, *Aspectos estructurales de la economía cubana;* Rodríguez, "Cincuenta años de Revolución en la economía."

33. See Figueras, *Aspectos estructurales de la economía cubana*, chap. 5.

34. See *Granma*, August 29, 1990. Also see "Información a la población," *Granma*, September 26, 1990, and "Información a la población sobre medidas adicionales con motivo a la escasez de combustible y otras importaciones," *Granma*, December 20, 1991.

35. See Rodríguez, "La perestroika en la economía soviética (1985–1991)"; David Kotz and Fred Weir, *Russia's Path from Gorbachev to Putin* (London: Routledge, 2007), part 2; and F. Brown, C. Ferrer, F. Florentino, and R. Oroza, *Europa del Este: El colapso* (Havana: Editorial de Ciencias Sociales, 2002).

36. See Elena Alvarez, "Planificación a mediano plazo y largo plazo: Notas para un debate," *Cuba: Investigación Económica* 6 no. 3 (2000).

37. The official exchange rate between pesos and dollars was 1 to 1. The Cuban peso was not a convertible currency, and there was much debate on what a meaningful exchange rate would be because many commodities like food were highly subsidized, housing rents were capped, and health care and education were free. But to give an idea of the impact of the $3-billion-per-year loss from the blockade, using the 1-to-1 exchange rate yields a loss of more than 20 percent of Cuba's 13-billion-peso GDP in 1993. If one argues the real exchange rate was lower, as many people do, then of course the percentage loss of GDP would go up accordingly.

38. See José Luis Rodríguez, "Cuba: El camino de la recuperación económica," *Cuba*

Socialista 16 (1999); "Panorama actual de la economía cubana" (IX Encuentro Internacional de Economistas sobre Globalización y Problemas del Desarrollo, Havana, February 9, 2007); and the conferences "Cincuenta años de Revolución en la economía" (see note 16 above) and "Elementos de historia de la Revolución cubana," *CIEM* (unpublished, July–October 2009).

39. See "Resolution on the Economic Development of the Country," *IV Congreso del Partido Comunista de Cuba: Discursos y documentos* (Havana: Editora Política, 1992).

40. See Fidel Castro, "Mientras el pueblo tenga el poder lo tiene todo," *Speeches at the International Festival "Cuba Lives," August 5 and 6 of 1995* (Havana: Editora Política, 1995), pp. 31 and 45.

41. A brief summary of many important contributions to this debate can be found in W. Brus, *El funcionamiento de la economía socialista* (Barcelona: Oikos-Tau Ediciones, 1969), chap. 4, and Guevara, *El gran debate sobre la economía en Cuba, 1963–1964.*

42. This interpretation is very different from the theory of market socialism. See Andrew Zimbalist, Howard Sherman and Stuart Brown, *Comparing Economic Systems* (New York: Harcourt, Brace, Jovanovich, 1989), chap. 13.

43. See José Luis Rodríguez, "El desarrollo económico y social de Cuba: Resultados de 30 años de Revolución," *Cuba Socialista* 39 (1989).

44. Ibid.

45. Some steps taken before the onset of the crisis were very important in mitigating its effects, but nobody could have foreseen the extent of the global changes. Fidel Castro did, however, mention the possibility of the disappearance of the USSR two and a half years before the event in his speech of July 26, 1989; at that time he stated what the Cuban position would be if that occurred. See *Granma*, July 28, 1989.

46. As late as April 1990 a trade agreement was signed between Cuba and the USSR for trade of 9.2 billion rubles, a figure higher than 1989.

47. See the report presented by the Executive Committee of the Council of Ministers to the National Assembly of People's Power, Rule VI-116 (December 1990).

48. Soviet oil imports reached 13.3 million tons in 1989, declined to 8.1 million tons in 1991, and were only 1.2 million tons in the first half of 1992. The cost of the sudden breakoff of economic relations with the socialist countries was estimated at $5.6 billion. See Carlos M. García and Gerardo Gómez, *Economía cubana: Del trauma a la recuperación* (Havana: Editorial Pueblo y Educación, 1998).

49. This transition also required fundamental changes in Cuba's foreign policy. While these were essential to the economic reorientation, they are a major topic in themselves and so are beyond the scope of this chapter except to point out their importance to the entire process of economic change.

50. Among important indicators were that the state budget deficit reached about 33 percent of the GDP; the liquidity of pesos in the population was around 66 percent of the GDP; the official exchange rate of pesos to dollars was still officially 1 to 1 but in the informal economy it reached 120 to 1 in 1994; about 60 percent of the enterprises were unprofitable; and the GDP continued to shrink as unemployment grew. An overview of this crucial stage of the Cuban economy can be found in Silvia M. Domenech, *Cuba*

economía en periodo especial (Havana: Editora Política, 1996), and García and Gómez, *Economía cubana*.

51. Many workers continued to receive their salaries even though they were laid off, a policy implemented on a massive scale as a short-term way to ensure that no one was abandoned.

52. See Decree-Law No. 140, "Concerning Depenalization of the Possession of Freely Convertible Currency" (August 1993).

53. These goods were mostly luxury items, but also some basics, including food, particularly for amounts purchased in excess of the ration card allotment.

54. See Fidel Castro, "Speech of July 27th of 1993," *Granma*, July 28, 1993.

55. See Fidel Castro, "Speech in the National Assembly of People's Power," available at www.cuba.cu/gobierno/discursos (March 6, 2003).

56. See Raúl Castro, "Speech in the National Assembly of People's Power" (December 28, 2007). See also Vilma Hidalgo, "De la dolarización a la unificación monetaria en Cuba," *Cuba: Investigación Económica* 14, no. 2 (2008).

57. See "Report of the Discussion in the National Assembly of People's Power," *Granma*, May 2, 1994, and August 4, 1994, and "First Positive Signs at the Beginning of the Financial and Monetary Recovery of the Country," *Granma*, November 22, 1994. A politically important legal measure against the speculation that the serious financial imbalance was permitting was approved at the same time to confiscate the goods obtained by illegal means. See Decree-Law No. 149 and "Concerning Confiscation of the Goods and Earnings Obtained through Unlawful Enrichment," *Granma*, May 5, 1994.

58. These measures were implemented very carefully in stages, but they did not constitute a planned "economic reform program." For an analysis of the strategic options possible for the Cuban economy, see Pedro Monreal, "La globalización y los dilemas de las trayectorias económicas de Cuba," in *Reflexiones sobre economía cubana*, ed. Omar Everleny (Havana: Editorial de Ciencias Sociales, 2004), and Alfredo González, "Economía y sociedad: Los retos del modelo económico," *Temas* 11 (1997).

59. Two other types of agricultural cooperatives, Agricultural Production Cooperatives (CPAs, in which members pooled their lands) and Cooperatives for Credits and Services (CCSs, in which individual owners jointly financed purchases), already existed in Cuba at that time. The latter and forerunners of the former go back to the 1960s. At the time UBPCs were formed, CPAs and CCSs together accounted for about 10 percent of the arable land, while peasants privately farmed about 15 percent. Subsequently, the share of arable land farmed by cooperatives grew from 10 percent to about 50 percent while the percentage of private farms remained stable. See also chap. 11 in this volume.

60. See Victoria Pérez et al., "Self-employment in Cuba," *Cuba: Investigación Económica* 14, no. 2 (2008).

61. Since then growth has occurred in every year, with an average of 4.7 percent for 1995–2009.

62. See Omar Everleny, "El papel de la inversión extranjera directa en el desarrollo económico: La experiencia cubana," in Everleny, *Reflexiones sobre economía cubana*.

63. Decree-Law No. 252 of 2007 updated the framework of the Enterprise Improve-

ment System. By 2009 nearly nine hundred of the most important enterprises were participating.

64. For more on this subperiod, see José Luis Rodríguez, "The Road to Economic Recovery," in *Cuban Socialism in a New Century: Adversity, Survival and Renewal*, ed. Max Azicri and Elsie Deal (Gainesville: University of Florida Press, 2004), chap. 7.

65. According to Claes Brundenius in "Revolutionary Cuba at 50: Growth and Equity Revisited," *Latin American Perspectives* 36 (March 2009), the estimated Gini coefficient grew from 0.22 to 0.40 in the 1990s, then remained at about that level, registering 0.38 in 2005.

66. In 2003–4 Cuba reached new payment agreements with China, Japan, and Vietnam, among other countries.

67. Between 2000 and 2004 Cuba paid for its imports of Venezuelan oil in U.S. dollars, according to the terms of the 2000 credit agreements. The new trade agreement with Venezuela was signed on December 14, 2004.

68. The U.S. dollar was devalued 8 percent; the Cuban peso was revalued 7 percent. See Monetary Policy Board of the Cuban Central Bank, Accords Nos. 13 and 15 (2005). See also Banco Central de Cuba, *La economía cubana, 1996–2006* (Havana: BCC, 2007).

69. The current account recorded a surplus of 0.3 percent of the GDP in 2004 and 0.5 percent in 2005 (ONE, *Anuario Estadístico de Cuba 2009,* Habana: ONE, 2010, table 8.1).

Beginning in 2004 Cuba modified the method of computing its GDP to include the actual economic value of its free social services. Cuban representatives discussed this new methodology with numerous international experts for several years prior to its implementation, in particular with the Economic Commission for Latin America and the Caribbean (ECLAC). The modifications took into account the 1993 United Nations guidelines for the National Accounts System.

70. Ibid.

71. Unfortunately, the 2009 *Anuario Estadístico* lists data on the balance on services only up to 2007 (see ibid., table 8.1). Table 8.3 in the 2009 *Anuario* gives data for exports and imports of goods through 2009. The figures in tables 8.1 and 8.3 differ somewhat because of minor differences in how they are calculated, but they are qualitatively the same and indicate the same changes.

72. ECLAC, *Statistical Yearbook for Latin America and the Caribbean, 2009* (Santiago de Chile: United Nations Publications).

73. See Raúl Castro, "Speech at the National Assembly of the People's Power on August 1, 2009," *Granma*, August 3, 2009.

74. ECLAC, *Statistical Yearbook for Latin America and the Caribbean, 2009.*

75. See Decree-Law No. 259 of 2008 and Raúl Castro, "Speech at the National Assembly of People's Power on August 1, 2009," *Granma*, August 3, 2009.

76. At present this involves approximately 2–3 percent of the workforce. By the end of the first half of 2009, when 39 percent of the idle land was distributed, it was delivered

in usufruct to 82,000 farmers. See Raúl Castro, "Speech on July 26, 2009," *Granma*, July 27, 2009.

77. See Figueras, *Aspectos estructurales de la economía cubana*, and Rodríguez's presentation at the conference "Cincuenta años de la Revolución cubana en la economía."

78. See Julie Feinsilver, "Cuban Medical Diplomacy: When the Left Has Got It Right," *Foreign Affairs* 6 (2006), and John Kirk and Michael Erisman, *Cuban Medical Internationalism* (New York: Palgrave Macmillan, 2009).

79. This estimation was based on calculations of the Directorate of Macroeconomic Planning of the Ministry of Economy and Planning. This percentage stands in contrast with the 1970 UN General Assembly Resolution by the rich countries of the world to commit 0.7 percent of their GNPs to official development assistance. This commitment has now been recast in terms of the millennium development goals slated for 2015. Only a few rich countries have met this commitment, none gives 1 percent, and the largest economy in the world, that of the United States, contributes at the lowest rate among the wealthy nations: less than 0.2 percent, one-tenth the estimated rate for Cuba. See www.unmillenniumproject.org/press/07.htm#04.

80. Economist Intelligence Unit Viewswire, Cuba (December 7, 2010).

2

The Evolution of Cuba's Macroeconomy

From the Triumph of the Revolution through the Special Period

OSCAR U-ECHEVARRÍA VALLEJO

A historical perspective is necessary for understanding the nature of the Cuban macroeconomy at present, as well as the scope of the adjustments and transformations of the last few years and certain important features of its recent evolution. The system of economic and political foreign dependence that prevailed in the first half of the last century created a comprehensive structural deformation in the Cuban economy. Carlos Rafael Rodríguez summarized the situation by listing seven negative characteristics of the Cuban national economy:[1]

1. Overdependence on agriculture, leaving the economy underdeveloped and subordinate to foreign interests
2. Deterioration in social aspects of the economy
3. Endemic unemployment and underemployment
4. An open and dependent economy
5. Dependence on a single export and single product, making the economy highly vulnerable to external impacts
6. Unilateral trading relations, highly dependent on a single market
7. Foreign ownership of key areas of the national economy

Through maximizing its natural comparative advantages, Cuba had become heavily dependent on a single export, sugar.[2] The resulting reliance on one product enabled foreign events to wreak havoc on the domestic economy.[3] The fundamental weaknesses in the preceding list made Cuba very vulnerable to economic crises, and it had to face three major ones during the twentieth century.[4] Two of these came after the triumph of the Revolution and therefore contained notable political nuances and features. Cuba's current economic situation is still very strongly marked by the last of these crises, namely, the Special Period, and by the major economic transformations adopted to overcome it.

After 1972 Cuba was able to mitigate to a certain extent some of the structural weaknesses in its economy through the pattern of economic relations and linkages it established in the context of its integration into CMEA.[5] For example, such relations guaranteed stable supplies of productive inputs, markets for exports, and access to financing, which were necessary conditions for the productive transformations Cuba undertook as part of its policies aimed at restructuring the economy.[6] In addition, they offset to some degree the negative impacts of the blockade that the United States imposed on Cuba in the early 1960s.

However, integration into CMEA was not able to prevent the emergence of some economic distortions, such as in the relative prices for and therefore distribution of inputs for production, which contributed to problems in completing the productive chains for some core resources.[7] Of central importance was the fact that despite Cuba's relations with CMEA, the traditional structural deformation of its economy resulting from its overdependence on a single product was not substantially modified after 1959. As a result, the Cuban economy remained acutely vulnerable to external pressures,[8] which laid the foundation for the crisis that the country underwent at the end of the century when the imports of goods and expertise that it relied on disappeared.[9]

Thirty Years of Transformations: 1959–1989

In light of the historical situation just outlined, after 1959 Cuba undertook economic transformations aimed directly at overcoming the obstacles and bottlenecks created by the severely deformed structure of the economy. With regard to macroeconomic management, Cuba was faced with two essential objectives: achieving economic development and building an equitable society. From its inception the Cuban Revolution has recognized as a central tenet of its development strategy that there is a close relationship between the economic base and social welfare. Economic growth is a necessary but not a sufficient condition for social development. It is necessary to directly consider how the nature of economic growth influences the well-being of the population. Therefore, functional as well as structural aspects have to receive careful attention. Development policies are designed to simultaneously address economic and social problems, with each being an integral part of the other. In brief, this principle requires that the country's development must be comprehensively evaluated on both economic growth and the transformations in its socioeconomic and political structures.

After 1959 Cuba's economic growth and development evolved through several different stages and periods. These evolutions were marked by various changes in strictly economic variables (endogenous and exogenous), in political approaches to economic development, and in the mechanisms of macroeconomic management. Table 2.1 summarizes these developments,[10] with the caveat that any attempt to define the boundaries of economic periods is necessarily approximate and subjective, and therefore yields only a general outline.

Beginning very soon after the Revolution, the government implemented major transformations in the economic and technical-productive bases of the Cuban economy. Following Rodríguez, these can be summarized as follows:[11]

- Creation of the infrastructure and provision of the necessary machinery to ensure the development of the agricultural sector and the humanization of agricultural labor
- Creation of the technical-material base required to produce capital goods, primarily to ensure growth in the agricultural-livestock sector
- Development of basic productive chains and human capital in the workforce to prepare for industrialization
- Pursuit of full employment
- Increase in the population's standard of living

The efforts to fulfill these objectives and their subsequent partial but ongoing achievement fueled a stable, positive growth trend that began in the early 1970s. This generated what could be called a prolonged wave of expansion continuing through the mid-1980s (see fig. 2.1). The short-term slowdown in 1979–82 was due mainly to losses from pest infestations in the country's main export products (sugarcane and tobacco) and from the drop in sugar prices between 1976 and 1980.

However, when the dynamics of growth are analyzed in more depth, a small reduction in the growth rate becomes apparent in the early 1980s compared

Table 2.1. Stages and periods of growth in the Cuban economy, 1959–1989

Stage		**Period**	
Main feature	**Dates**	**Main feature**	**Dates**
Attempts at accelerated industrialization and agricultural diversification	1961–65	Great changes	1959–63
		Economic recovery	1964–67
Preparation for and implementation of the ten-million-ton sugar harvest	1966–70	Ten-million-ton sugar harvest	1968–70
Transition	1970–75	Accelerated growth	1971–75
Gradual industrialization in the context of the international socialist division of labor	1975–89	Relative macroeconomic stability	1976–85
		Deceleration	1986–89

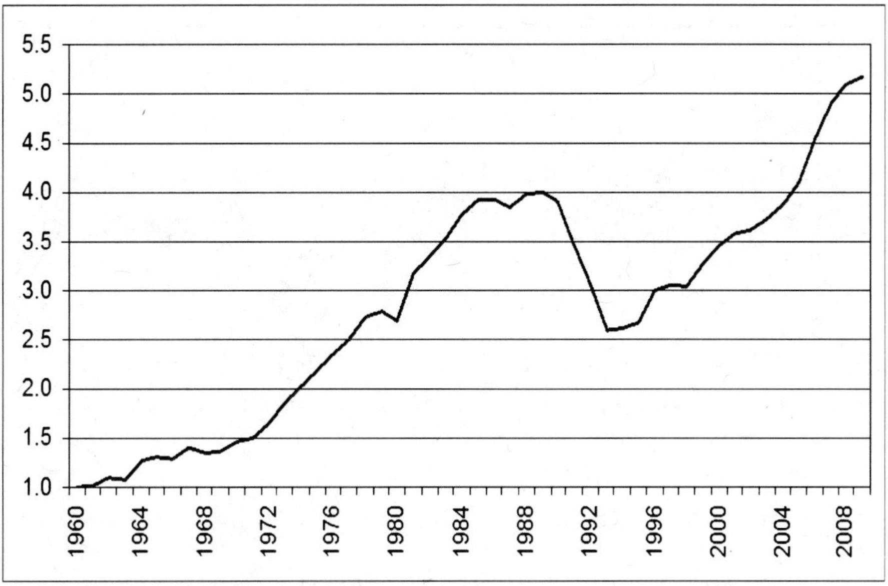

Figure 2.1. The Cuban GDP since the Revolution (1960 = 1). *Sources:* Estimates and approximations based on INIE, *Reconstrucción y análisis de las series estadísticas de la economía cubana, 1960–1975* (Havana: INIE, 1997); Juan Ferrán, "Producto interno de Cuba: 1903–1995 y proyección hasta el 2005" (investigation, January 1996); ONE, *Anuario Estadístico de Cuba* (Havana: ONE, 1997, 2001, 2003, 2005, 2007, 2010); and other specific information from the ONE.

to previous years, even though growth remained relatively strong (see fig. 2.2). Thus, the exhaustion of the economic model that had produced extensive economic growth in the 1970s was already foreseeable by 1980. This relative stagnation, which manifested much more clearly in the late 1980s and peaked in 1987, was closely connected to inefficient use of productive factors. Figure 2.2 also shows volatility in annual growth rates superimposed on an overall pattern of economic slowdown in the 1980s compared to the 1970s.[12]

With an understanding of the growth patterns in this period, it is next important to identify some of the general factors that contributed to these patterns.[13] Many different factors came together to launch the prolonged wave of expansion in the early 1970s. First, many aspects of Cuba's economic policies and mechanisms of economic management were radically changed in the late 1960s. A priority was improvement in economic and political institutions, including the imposition of a new political-administrative structure aimed at eliminating tremendous economic inefficiencies.

A second important factor was the reinstatement of the principle of remuneration based on work performed, which had broken down extensively in the late 1960s. The third important factor was Cuba's aforementioned integration into CMEA's international division of labor, which guaranteed supplies of produc-

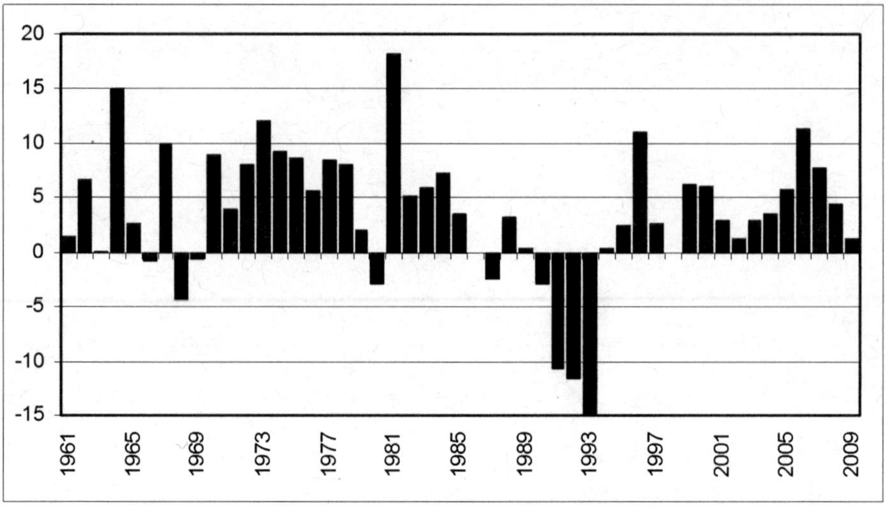

Figure 2.2. Annual growth of the Cuban GDP (%). *Sources:* Estimates and approximations based on INIE, *Reconstrucción y análisis de las series estadísticas de la economía cubana, 1960–1975* (Havana: INIE, 1997); Juan Ferrán, "Producto interno de Cuba: 1903–1995 y proyección hasta el 2005" (investigation, January 1996); ONE, *Anuario Estadístico de Cuba* (Havana: ONE, 1997, 2001, 2003, 2005, 2007, 2010); and other specific information from the ONE.

tive inputs, markets for products, and availability of financing. A fourth important factor was the reduction of domestic monetary circulation, which had increased substantially in the late 1960s. In 1965 accumulated liquidity amounted to barely 10 percent of GDP. By 1969–70 it had jumped to nearly 50 percent, but by 1975 it had been brought back down to 19 percent. All these changes had occurred by the First Congress of the Cuban Communist Party in 1975.

An additional important factor was the increase in government investment in the infrastructure of industrialization to support more balanced and prudent development across the different economic sectors (see table 2.2).[14] This increased investment was made possible, to a large extent, by the signing of commercial and credit agreements with the Soviet Union in 1972. Also important was the high price of sugar on the world market around 1974, although prices subsequently dropped precipitously. The economic slowdown, which became serious by the late 1980s, forced the government to suspend its massive capital investments in economic development.

The focus on industrialization[15] was another important factor contributing to the prolonged growth surge. Although growth had already started in previous periods, by 1976–85 the foreign trade and financial relations with the CMEA countries enabled more robust and accelerated improvement.[16]

As mentioned, Cuba's rate of economic growth dropped slightly in the early 1980s before falling sharply in the second half of the decade. Several of the economic problems that contributed to the economic downturn of the late 1980s

Table 2.2. Average growth rates of GDP and investment by period (%)

Period	Average growth rate		
	GDP	**Per capita GDP**	**Investment**
1961–67	5.0	2.8	14.0
1968–70	1.2	-0.4	-6.5
1971–85	6.8	5.7	11.9
1986–89	0.5	-0.5	1.2

Sources: Estimates based on INIE, *Reconstrucción y análisis de las series estadísticas de la economía cubana, 1960–1975* (Havana: INIE, 1997); J. Ferrán, "Producto interno de Cuba: 1903–1995 y proyección hasta el 2005" (January 1996); ONE, *Anuario Estadístico de Cuba* (Havana: ONE, 1997); and specific information from the ONE.

were in fact already apparent in the first half of the decade. These interrelated major problems were connected to the external links of the economy, which led to distortions in the domestic economy and to the failure to shift from a model of extensive growth to one of intensive (that is, based on improved efficiency) growth.

The only acute crisis in the first half of the decade was a hard-currency crisis in 1982, when credits were suspended and debt payments were rescheduled (debt payments were later suspended in 1986). Although at that time only 15 percent of Cuba's trade was in hard currency, that trade was a very specific and important economic input that could not be sufficiently offset by an increase in inputs from the CMEA countries.

The structural problem that began to appear in the early 1980s was, however, much greater than a continued vulnerability to hard-currency shortages. Despite the important advantages of Cuba's incorporation into CMEA, this integration left the domestic economy highly dependent on external inputs and with gaps in its domestic chains of production, particularly in manufacturing and industry. Cuba remained highly dependent on external inputs into the technological chains of production for some of its core resources, meaning that growth itself became a problem. A vicious cycle developed in which rapid growth rates increased the magnitude of the external inputs necessary to maintain that growth. Cuba was in a structural bind, where its need for productive imports and hence for sufficient exports to support these became the pivot of its economic growth model. In some (though not all) respects, Cuba's economic dynamics were little changed from what they had been before the Revolution. The country still relied extensively on its comparative advantage in natural resources such as sugar, which maintained its external vulnerability.

Thus, between 1975 and 1988 Cuba's import coefficient increased significantly, while its rigid internal economic structure prevented it from compensating for its increasing foreign debt via export expansion and diversification. Then after 1980 Cuba's terms of trade also deteriorated, as figure 2.3 shows.[17]

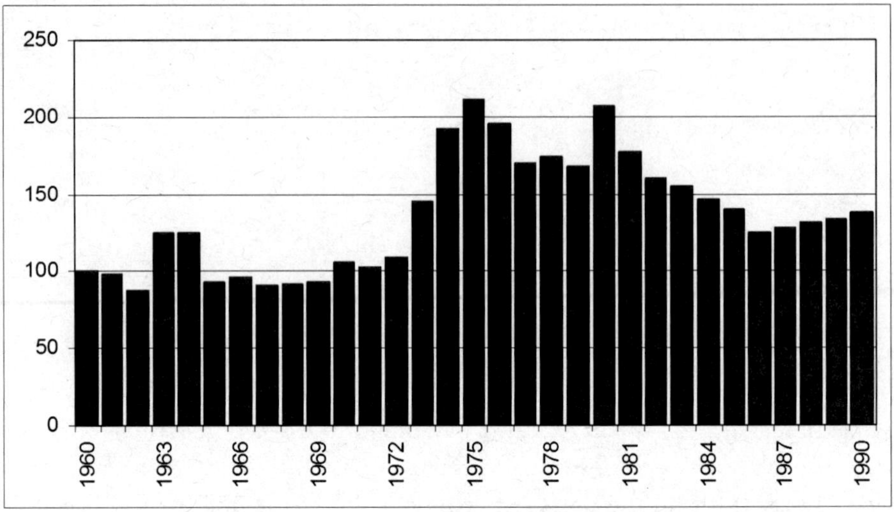

Figure 2.3. Evolution of Cuban terms of trade (1960 = 100). *Sources:* Estimates and approximations based on INIE, *Reconstrucción y análisis de las series estadísticas de la economía cubana, 1960–1975* (Havana: INIE, 1997); Juan Ferrán, "Producto interno de Cuba: 1903–1995 y proyección hasta el 2005" (investigation, January 1996); ONE, *Anuario Estadístico de Cuba* (Havana: ONE, 1997, 2001, 2003, 2005, 2007, 2010); and other specific information from the ONE.

This deterioration in terms of trade had a tremendous impact on the Cuban economy because the economy was undergoing a pattern of extensive growth.[18] By the time recession hit in the late 1980s and early 1990s, it became apparent that the crisis signaled that this model based on specialization[19] had reached its limits under the existing external conditions. In retrospect, clear signs of the impending problem were present by the end of the previous decade, though at the time they were masked by Cuba's integration into CMEA.

The slowdown and later near-stagnation of the economy brought with it some increase in the budget deficit, particularly in 1986–87. Until as late as 1990–91, this deficit was offset by international credits, which covered up to 70 percent of the domestic deficit and accounted for 8 to 10 percent of total national revenues in those years. As these credits ceased, the situation rapidly became more critical.[20]

On the expense side of the balance sheet, Cuba's continued high spending on social welfare contributed to the deficits. But more significant in the face of the worsening economic conditions were the increasing subsidies to enterprises, either directly through payments to cover losses, or indirectly through setting prices to prevent losses. The revenue side also suffered in the worsening economic climate, since a large part of government revenue came from the profits of economic enterprises, and there was as well an insufficient diversification of tax revenues. The tax on the circulation of goods alone contributed more than 40 percent to government revenue in those years.[21] Narrowly, this reflected the structural, functional, and organizational barriers that constrained the government's ability to raise income. But more broadly, it again indicated Cuba's inability to access the domestic resources necessary for economic reproduction and expansion.

By the second half of the 1980s, the underlying problem was a serious lack of economic surplus,[22] including that needed for economic expansion. As figure 2.4 shows, there were signs of loss of absorption and exhaustion in the extensive growth pattern.[23]

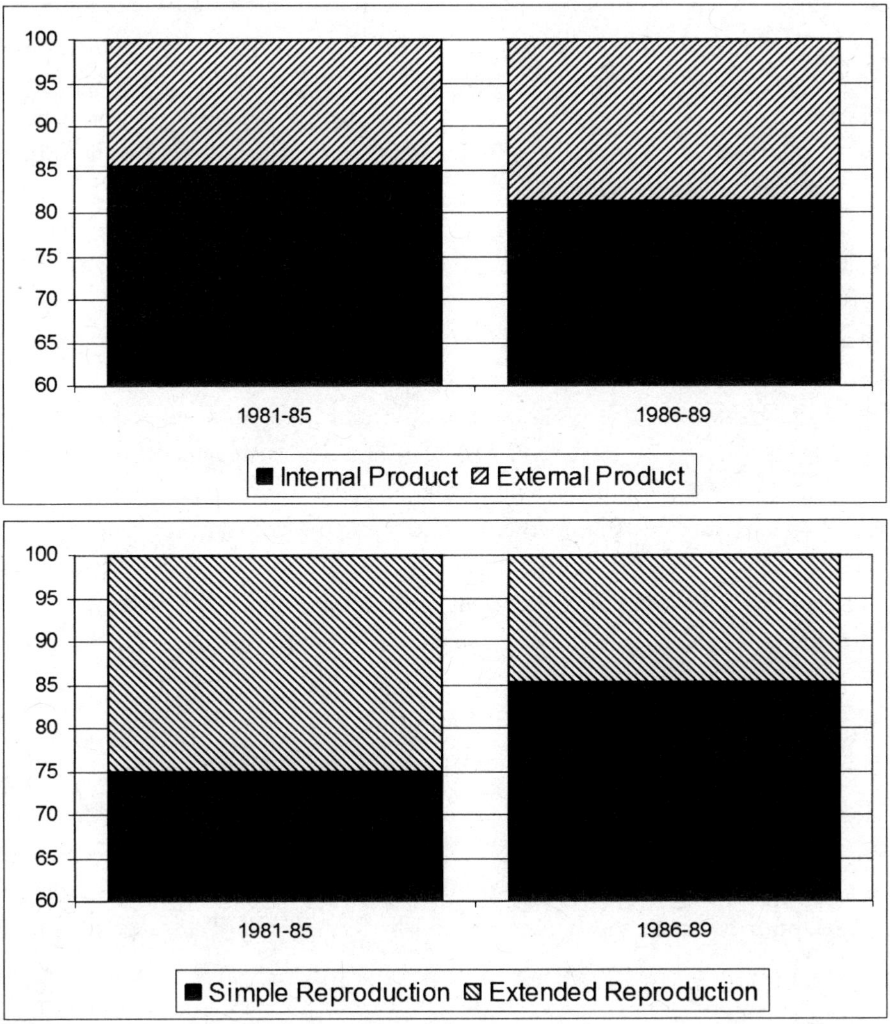

Figure 2.4. Product creation and reproduction (%). *Sources:* Estimates and approximations based on INIE, *Reconstrucción y análisis de las series estadísticas de la economía cubana, 1960–1975* (Havana: INIE, 1997); Ferrán, "Producto interno de Cuba: 1903–1995 y proyección hasta el 2005" (investigation, January 1996); ONE, *Anuario Estadístico de Cuba* (Havana: ONE, 1998); and CEE, *Anuario Estadístico de Cuba* (Havana: CEE, 1989).

Potentially this shortcoming could be offset by the economy's external sector. A consistent flow of external financing could in theory compensate for the lack of sufficient domestic savings (the savings gap) for the relevant productive processes. The question then would become to what extent this financing was actually present, as well as what its trends and basic proportions were.[24]

But even if such external support is present, as it was in Cuba in the first half of the 1980s, it really only creates a "silent crisis" by hiding the domestic shortcomings that eventually will manifest themselves one way or another. By late 1984, Cuban policymakers were already alert to the dangers of relying on foreign financing to support the economy. The central economic policies were consequently redrafted to initiate the process of "rectification of errors and negative tendencies," which addressed manufacturing efficiency and savings to resolve the most unsustainable aspects of the previous stage. It is important to stress that these changes were to be implemented without altering the framework of the existing economic model, as comprehensive and radical changes to the model were not deemed desirable at that time. These efforts had no sooner begun to be implemented and to yield some positive results when they had to be cut short. The economic catastrophe that resulted from the sudden dissolution of the socialist bloc left Cuba only two choices: radical economic restructuring for rapid economic recovery, or eventual collapse.

In macroeconomic terms these thirty years can be summarized extremely broadly as follows. By the late 1980s Cuba had largely managed to resolve the fundamental issues that had been outlined in the revolutionary platform—education, health care, and employment—and it had made considerable progress on industrialization. The economic model in place at the time, however, although still functional, was year by year showing greater signs of slowdown, and a process to rectify it was already under way when the crisis of the 1990s hit Cuba.

Crisis and Responses, 1990–2009

By 1989–91, for the second time in three decades, the Cuban economy suddenly faced highly adverse external conditions. Its central economic management and regulation were mainly structured on the physical allocation of inputs, supported by favorable external economic relations,[25] but the sources that supported those mechanisms abruptly disappeared. The scope of the required adjustments under highly unfavorable conditions in terms of Cuba's domestic equilibrium threatened the country's very survival. This time there were no mechanisms to offset the crisis as there had been in 1961–62. On the other hand, the country was better prepared to endure the resulting impact in terms of internal cohesion, social consensus, economic organization, and relevant experience.

Economic Recession

The magnitude of the macroeconomic crisis is summarized in table 2.3.

The sudden rupture of trade and financial relations with the socialist community was both the trigger and one of the fundamental causes for the economic crisis. At that time 85 percent of Cuba's foreign trade was with CMEA, with three groups of products accounting for some 75 percent of imports: fuels, food and agricultural materials, and machinery and equipment. But the concentration of trade and financial relations with CMEA was only the surface expression of much deeper and more extensive economic interconnections that penetrated all of Cuba's chains of production. This is why the disruption of economic relations with the socialist community had such widespread and extensive effects across the entire Cuban economy. The major internal structural problems in the economy that had been largely disguised under the "protective relations with CMEA" now became central to Cuba's economic performance, and the change occurred so suddenly that the country had essentially no time to adjust.

As noted previously, because of the economic contraction that began in the second half of the 1980s immediately prior to the onset of the crisis, by 1989 Cuba had increased its dependence on external capital to try to maintain its rate of gross investment. Following the onset of the crisis, foreign lending for capital formation nearly completely terminated. In addition, the economic cri-

Table 2.3. Macroeconomic performance indicators, 1989–1996

	1989	1990	1991	1992	1993	1994	1995	1996
Per capita GDP (1989 = 100)	100	96.0	84.9	74.6	63.1	63.4	64.8	69.6
Global supply (prices/81; 1989 = 100)	100	96.5	81.4	68.8	59.9	60.2	62.0	67.3
Household consumption (prices/81; 1989 = 100)	100	94.2	85.0	73.1	67.3	68.9	73.3	76.5
Unregulated price index	100	102.1	263.4	509.9	1,552.6	1,396.5	739.6	554.7
Accumulation rate (%)	24.3	25.0	14.9	6.9	5.8	5.0	6.3	7.5
Monetary liquidity[a] M_1 (millions of pesos)	4,163	4,986	6,663	8,361	11,043	9,944	9,251	9,534
Liquidity/GDP[b] (%)	21.3	23.9	38.0	51	86.0	77.3	70.2	67.1
Public deficit/GDP[b] (%)	6.7	9.4	21.4	29.7	30.4	6.9	3.2	2.2
Exchange rate[a] (Pesos/USD)	n/a	7	20	45	100	60[c]	25	19

[a] At year's end.
[b] In current terms.
[c] The rate peaked in the summer at 150 pesos/USD.
Source: Oscar U-Echevarría, "El modelo de ajuste macroeconómico: El caso de Cuba," *Cuba: Investigación Económica* 3, nos. 3–4 (1997).

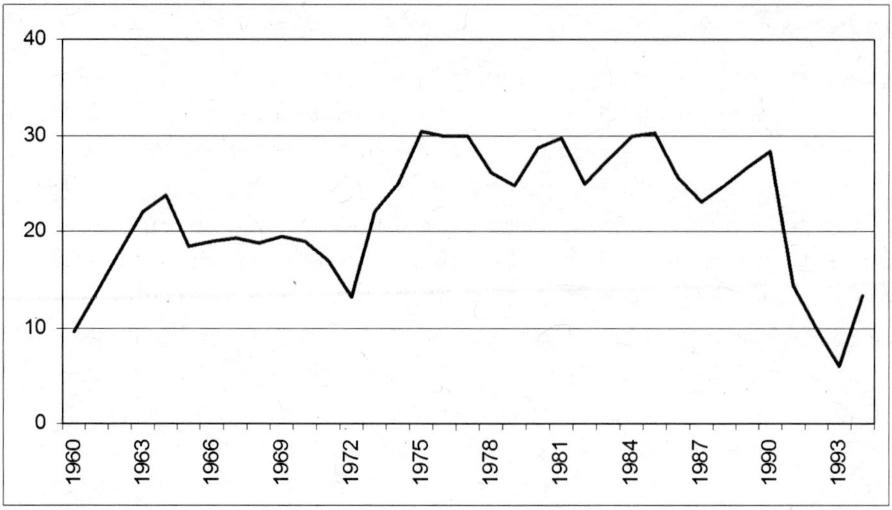

Figure 2.5. Gross accumulation rate, 1960–1993 (%). *Sources:* Estimates and approximations based on INIE, *Reconstrucción y análisis de las series estadísticas de la economía cubana, 1960–1975* (Havana: INIE, 1997); Juan Ferrán, "Producto interno de Cuba: 1903–1995 y proyección hasta el 2005" (investigation, January 1996); ONE, *Anuario Estadístico de Cuba* (Havana: ONE, 1997, 2001, 2003, 2005, 2007, 2010); and other specific information from the ONE.

sis brought a sharp reduction in internal saving. The gross accumulation rate therefore fell[26] and consequently so did gross capital formation, immediately creating a condition of undercapitalization (see fig. 2.5).

Traditional mechanisms for responding to this type of crisis, such as currency devaluation, were determined to be neither viable nor desirable. More importantly, they would have resulted in high and unpredictable social costs, in addition to other strictly technical costs.[27]

Instead, the crisis was approached with simultaneous sociopolitical and economic survival strategies. A central sociopolitical objective was to cushion the population as much as possible from the social costs of the crisis. Economically, the central focus was to carry out essential structural transformations and to realign the nation's economic policies with the new realities. The resulting emergency economic program, labeled the Special Period, was announced at the end of August 1990.

The early years of the Special Period had two distinct phases. In the first, from 1990 to 1993, economic survival was the main concern. The central focus was on ensuring that the inevitable immediate negative impact on public welfare would be as limited and, more importantly, as equitably distributed as possible. At the same time, the rupture of Cuba's foreign economic relations and the very open nature of its economy made creating the conditions for reinsertion into the world economy an immediate necessity (see chapter 3).[28] In the second phase, which began in 1993, the main concern shifted to economic recovery through macroeconomic stabilization[29] along with continued efforts to reinsert Cuba into international markets. The country's economic strategies and programs hinged on these objectives:

- To reduce the fiscal deficit, which had deteriorated significantly as a result of the steps taken to ameliorate the initial effects of the crisis on the population
- To sharply reduce the excess liquidity in circulation, a second effect of cushioning the social impact of the crisis
- To overcome the external gap that resulted from the initial shock by taking urgent steps to reestablish foreign trade[30]

Adaptation, Recovery, and Expansion

The overall strategy adopted in the Special Period actually retained many features of the approach that was being initiated in the late 1980s. The central concept was to create new sources of external revenue based on exploiting Cuba's comparative advantages in new ways. The two assets that became the most important to the recovery, and will continue to play important roles in the Cuban economy post-recovery, are Cuba's natural environment, which is conducive to international tourism (see chapters 9 and 10), and its half century of scientific-technical development in biotechnology and pharmaceuticals (see chapter 12).

Initially, tourism was the main driving force of incipient recovery. Between 1990 and 1998 gross revenues from tourism grew by 28.4 percent per annum,[31] making this the most dynamic sector of the Cuban economy. Tourism grew from 36.3 percent of total foreign earnings in 1993 to 53 percent in 1999,[32] as illustrated by a dramatic increase in the number of foreign visitors (see fig. 2.6).

Implementing the institutional, structural, and policy reforms called for in the Special Period required a number of profound economic and legal transformations, beginning with amending the constitution to legalize new economic activities.[33] Although these changes did carry certain economic, political, and social costs, they allowed Cuba to survive, to stop the decline in the GDP, and to establish the basis for a progressive recovery (see summary in table 2.4). Some of these changes entailed substantial modifications to long-standing structural policies, two of the more important of which occurred in agricultural property ownership and employment (table 2.5).

Another important structural change that began at this time and continues today is the diversification of exports. Of primary importance in this regard, both economically and for Cubans' very self-perception, is the decline in sugar

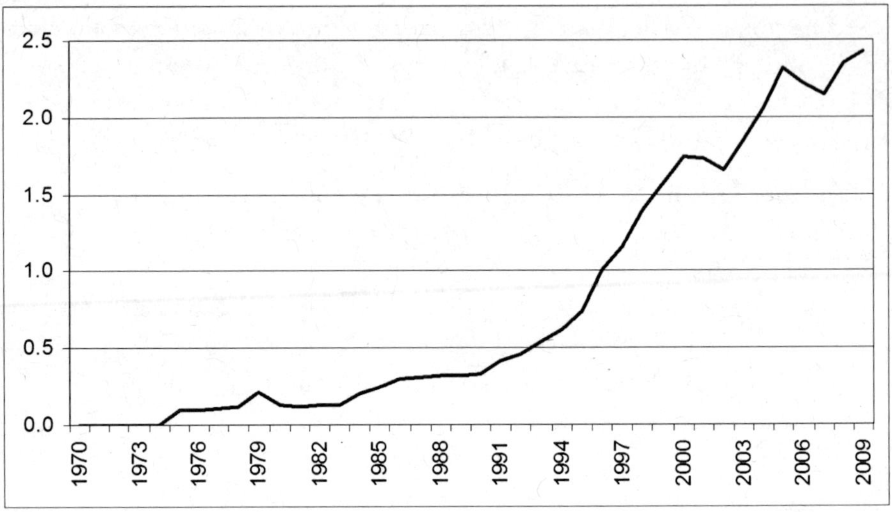

Figure 2.6. Number of foreign visitors to Cuba per year, 1970–2009 (millions). *Source:* Sección de Turismo del INIE, *Series estadísticas del turismo* (Havana: INIE, 2010).

Table 2.4. Summary of major Special Period reforms

Demonopolization	1992	Constitutional amendments eliminating the state and institutional monopoly on foreign trade
Deregulation	1992	Recognition of cooperative property and other forms of property ownership
	1993	Decriminalization of possessing hard currency
		Decree-law permitting self-employment
	1994	Decree-law creating free farmers' markets
		Decree-law creating small-scale industrial and handicraft markets
	1995	Foreign Investment Act
		Opening of CADECAs (currency exchange bureaus)
	1996	Decree-law establishing free-trade zones
		Modification to the law on tariffs
	1997	Restructuring and revitalization of the local markets for consumers
Decentralization	1993	Establishment of UBPCs
		Dissemination of hard-currency self-financing schemes in state enterprises
		Establishment of new forms of commerce
	1994	Restructuring of central administrative agencies
	1995	Changes in the enterprise and territorial planning processes
	1997	Decree-law reorganizing the banking system
Other measures	1994	Price increases for nonessential goods
		Elimination of unnecessary free social services

Source: Oscar U-Echevarría, "Estado, economía y planificación: Una primera aproximación," *Cuba: Investigación Económica* 5, no. 4 (1999).

Table 2.5. State versus private agricultural employment and landownership (%)

	1989		1994		1996	
	State	Non-state	State	Non-state	State	Non-state
Employment	95	5	83	17	76	24
Landownership	78	22	26	74	26	74

Source: Oscar U-Echevarría, "El modelo de ajuste macroeconómico: El caso de Cuba," *Cuba: Investigación Económica* 3, nos. 3–4 (1997).

exports, from 70 percent of total exports in 1992 to 40 percent in 1998 and to barely 8 percent in 2006. In turn, mining, tobacco, and fisheries products have increased their export shares.

The final structural change I will consider here concerns the shift in exports from goods to services. As mentioned, tourist services were the engine of the early recovery, and over the Special Period they came to replace sugar as the main source of foreign exchange (in recent years tourism earnings have occasionally been surpassed by nickel). As important as this change was, however, it left the Cuban economy dependent on the success of its international marketing of its natural endowments. It is important to recognize that such a situation, where the health of the economy rests in its insertion into the world market based on either primary goods or analogous services, leaves the country dependent and vulnerable to foreign events. Thus, growth tends to be compromised over the medium or long term, as Pedro Monreal, and before him CEPAL, have documented.[34] Fortunately, since 2000 a qualitatively different type of service based on knowledge has become important in Cuba's foreign trade, namely, the export of medical services and to a much lesser degree educational services. As I discuss later, these are not analogous to primary goods.

The increased diversification of export goods and the diversification from goods to services have not yet done much to resolve Cuba's persistent current account deficit. While in theory a current account deficit is problematic only if the offsetting capital inflows do not generate more time-discounted output than they cost, for Cuba it has been a fundamental constraint on growth. In this regard it is important to remember that the U.S. blockade has largely excluded Cuba from sources of low-cost long-term financing to cover its current account imbalances, forcing it instead to resort almost exclusively to expensive private and usually short-term financing, which has increased the costs of current account deficits. Very recent loans from Venezuela and China connected to (often joint) development projects have eased the situation somewhat, but lack of foreign financing for industrial projects and for a large number of ex-

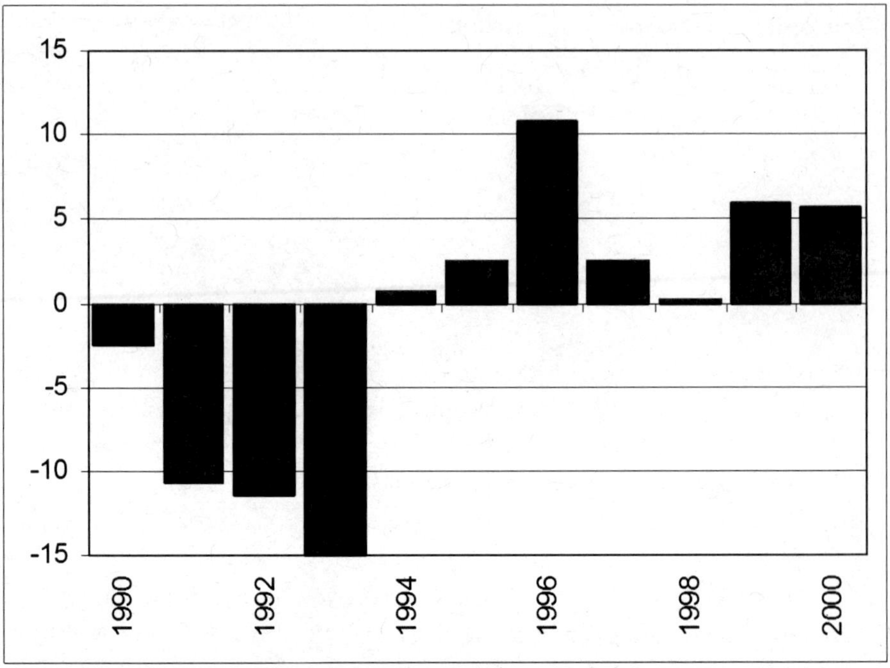

Figure 2.7. Annual growth of GDP during the first decade of the Special Period, 1990–2000 (%). *Source:* Estimates based on ONE, *Anuario Estadístico de Cuba* (Havana: ONE, 1997, 2001, 2003).

tremely necessary and long-overdue infrastructure repairs remains one of Cuba's central constraints on growth.

In the early years of the recovery, GDP growth was unstable, although annual growth averaged 3.5 percent to 2000 (see fig. 2.7). However, the pre-crisis per capita income levels were not yet restored in this period.

Despite the large fluctuations in growth, macroeconomic stability did improve somewhat in this period, as illustrated most dramatically in the reduction of the fiscal deficit as a percentage of GDP. The deficit was brought down from nearly 35 percent in 1992 and 1993 to around 2 percent as of 1996, with only minor increases after that. In addition, the excess liquidity, which had ballooned from 1991 to 1993, was brought down sharply and rapidly by reducing total liquidity as a share of GDP from 86.0 percent to 67.1 percent in annual adjustments between the end of 1993 and the end of 1996 (see table 2.3). Overall, then, the first decade of the Special Period saw the consolidation of the recovery process and several important structural changes in the economy.

The beginning of this century was marked by several problematic economic developments that largely emerged out of the various policies and practices implemented in the first decade of the Special Period specifically to promote short-term economic recovery. Three of these were particularly important and required careful attention and policy modifications:

- The external financial constraint intensified. In particular, the high vulnerability of tourism to exogenous factors was corroborated when the September 11, 2001, attacks in the United States led to significant reductions in visitors to Cuba in 2002.[35] It also became clear that although the tourism sector was highly profitable, it could not serve as the only engine for Cuba's economic growth.
- The gradual expansion of various schemes for enterprise self-financing in hard currency, implemented in a context of inadequate financial services and a lack of regulatory mechanisms, caused on the one hand serious distortions in the circulation of hard currency and, on the other, excessive devaluation of those activities not linked to the hard-currency sector.[36]
- Social stratification based on income was increasing, which was particularly problematic because in many cases wealth was either unrelated to labor or was derived from private employment not associated with the state sector, and the most negatively affected segments of the population were precisely those most connected with the essence of Cuban socialism.[37]

These concerns prompted the introduction of a number of new measures, starting with social programs in 2000–2001 and extending to finance and foreign economic activities in 2003 (see table 2.6). The latter measures represented a distinctly new stage in the economic management and oversight of monetary policy and foreign trade. Nationally centralized decision making was reinstituted for a very small number of "bottleneck" productive factors, such as hard currency and oil.

Table 2.6. Economic measures implemented after 2000

Nature of change	Specific reforms
Greater centralization in the management of hard currency	Ending of enterprise accounts in hard currency (2003)
	Establishment of the unified account at the Central Bank for all hard currency (2005)
	Currency-exchange controls (2005)
Changes in the style and methods of economic management	Improvement of planning procedures and their role in economic control and regulation
	Recentralization of foreign trade
Social policy	Enhancement of traditional welfare programs
	Individualization of social policy based on need
	Introduction of new "Programs of the Revolution"

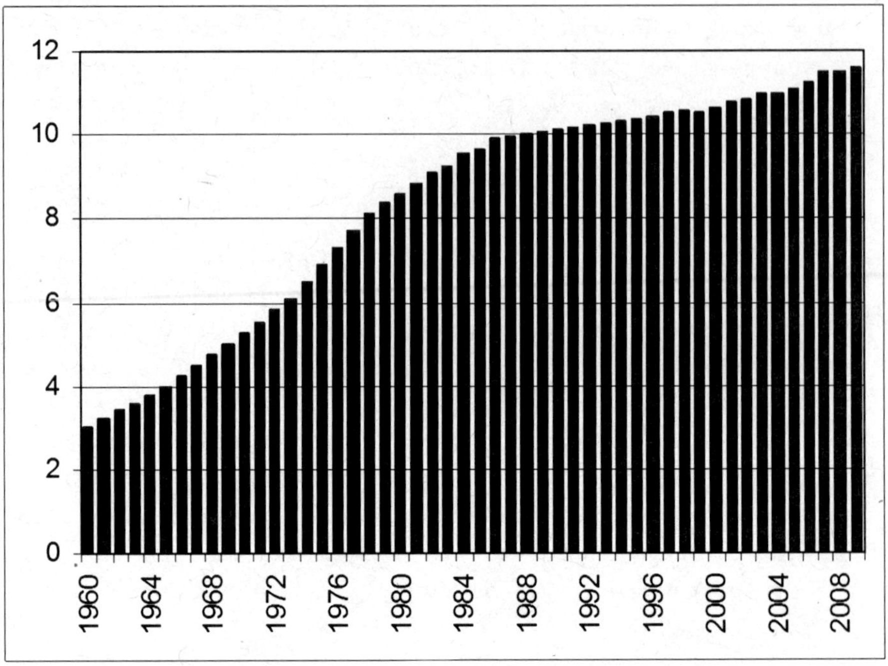

Figure 2.8. Development of human capital in the Revolution (average years of schooling of the workforce). *Sources:* Yenniel Mendoza, "¿Ha sido importante el capital humano en el crecimiento económico de Cuba?" (investigation, mimeo, INIE, 2004), and Carlos Fernández de Bulnes, "El capital humano en Cuba: realidades y alternativas" (investigation, mimeo, INIE, 2006).

In the middle of the decade, efforts to facilitate Cuba's medium- and long-term development turned to an issue of long-standing social pride. The educational and human development policies of the Revolution had accrued a large stock of human capital, as figure 2.8 shows. Yet with only a few exceptions, such as the biotechnology and pharmaceutical industries, this extremely valuable resource had not translated into new exports.

With favorable political circumstances both globally and specifically in Latin America, Cuba has begun exploiting its human capital potential to transform the national economy in important ways. In 2004 and even more so in 2005 Cuba began actively exporting high-value-added services, especially though not exclusively various medical services. Cuba's participation in ALBA (Bolivarian Alternative for the Americas) has been very important in promoting this growth, because ALBA members other than Cuba have medical needs that far exceed their domestic medical capacity. As a result, a trend has begun in which GDP growth depends increasingly on the provision of services rather than production of goods.

As a combined result of all the preceding factors, and in particular the

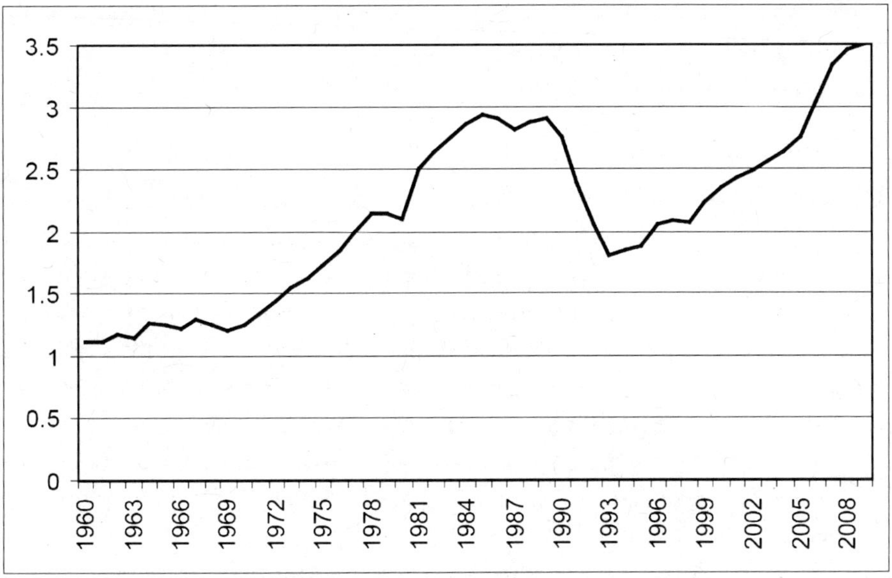

Figure 2.9. Per-capita GDP, 1960–2009 (thousand pesos/inhabitant). *Sources:* Estimates and approximations based on INIE, *Reconstrucción y análisis de las series estadísticas de la economía cubana, 1960–1975* (Havana: INIE, 1997); Juan Ferrán, "Producto interno de Cuba: 1903–1995 y proyección hasta el 2005" (investigation, January 1996); ONE, *Anuario Estadístico de Cuba* (Havana: ONE, 1997, 2001, 2003, 2005, 2007, 2010); and other specific information from the ONE.

solid economic base for economic recovery established in the 1990s, Cuba's economy began a period of consistent growth beginning in 1999. This lasted until 2009 when the effects of the world economic crisis hit Latin America hard and the year after Cuba also suffered the largest losses due to hurricanes in the history of the Revolution (see fig. 2.2). As figure 2.9 shows, per capita GDP reached 3,090 pesos in 2006,[38] surpassing the highest pre-crisis level of 2,950 pesos in 1985.

In sum, the first major macroeconomic outcome of the many policies of the Special Period was to cushion the effects of the crisis on social welfare through various stopgap measures. The second major macroeconomic outcome was a change in the nature of exports as a necessary step to avoid even greater shortages of critical inputs and as a first step toward building a new and expanded export capacity in the medium and long terms. Throughout the 1990s services (particularly tourism) were central to partially offsetting the current account deficit in goods. By the turn of this century, services (including medical services) began in some cases to show potential for generating a trade surplus. Together, tourism and medical services began to ease the long-term structural stranglehold on the economy produced by the chronically negative balance of trade. Finally, the economy began in 1999 to experience consistently higher rates of growth, which unfortunately were disrupted by the economic slowdown throughout most of Latin America due to the global Great Recession.

Structural Changes

Cuba's reinsertion into the international economy and leveraging of its human capital (knowledge) in order to restart economic growth entailed important structural changes in the economy. I next examine the changes in the composition of the national economy and in significant macroeconomic ratios.

The first fundamental structural change in the Cuban economy during the Special Period was a significant realignment of the sectoral contributions to the GDP.[39] Figure 2.10 shows an overall shift toward the tertiary sector driven by two main factors. The change between 1990 and 1996 primarily reflects expansion of tourism as the central engine of the early economic recovery. The change between 2000 and 2007 is the result of strong growth in social services, mainly health care and education, both for domestic consumption and as exports.

Table 2.7 makes clear that since 2001 this "tertiarization" has been driven

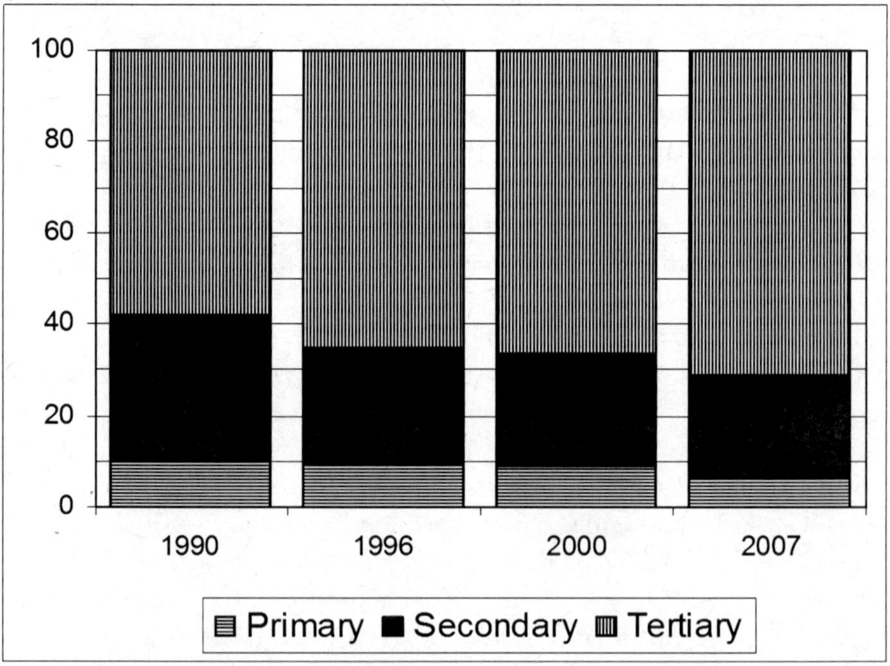

Figure 2.10. GDP composition by sector (%). Note: GDP has been calculated excluding tariffs in order to facilitate a comparison with the pre-crisis year 1990. *Sources:* Estimates and approximations based on ONE, *Anuario Estadístico de Cuba* (Havana: ONE, 1997, 2001, 2007, 2009) and specific information from the ONE.

Table 2.7. Changes in sectoral contributions to the economy, 1997–2009 (%)

	Annual change		
	Tertiary sector		Primary and secondary sectors
Year	Social services	Other tertiary	
1997	3.6	0.9	4.6
1998	0.2	7.1	-8.6
1999	4.7	5.8	8.0
2000	3.5	6.1	7.7
2001	5.6	5.0	-1.4
2002	3.4	1.5	-0.3
2003	7.7	3.9	0.3
2004	14.2	2.5	3.0
2005	29.6	5.0	2.0
2006	8.9	16.2	9.4
2007	11.4	3.3	8.8
2008	8.4	2.4	1.9
2009	1.5	2.0	0.5

Sources: Estimates and approximations based on ONE, *Anuario Estadístico de Cuba* (Havana: ONE, 2000, 2002, 2004, 2006, 2010), and specific information from the ONE.

by the dynamism of the social services sector, which has grown faster than not only the primary and secondary sectors but also the rest of the tertiary sector. Social services expanded most notably in mid-decade (2004, 2005, and 2007). The rest of the tertiary sector also outperformed the primary and secondary sectors in most years, reflecting healthy growth in such branches as transportation, telecommunications, and trade. However, the same table also reveals that the increasing weight of the tertiary sector is also a consequence of the relatively weak performance of the primary and secondary sectors in most years.

Beneath this structural change in the composition of output lies another structural change of fundamental importance to the Cuban economy. The primary driving forces for Cuba's structural changes, and the resulting healthy economic growth over the 2000s, have been the dynamism of the domestic economy, notably in social services, transportation, and communications. This stands in sharp contrast to the historic structural problem that the heart of Cuban economic dynamism was always located abroad.

A continued structural weakness, however, is that the economic expansion has largely consisted of extensive growth. This tends to limit the creation of a sufficient economic surplus to support expanded domestic demand and thereby generate truly endogenous growth. Stated differently, extensive growth for an open economy tends to be systematically reflected in a high dependence on imports to provide the additional resources needed for expanded reproduction. Notably, in the last few years efficiency in the use of factors of production has seen some improvement, which is the key to intensive growth.

Another important structural change involves the allocation of the GDP.

Table 2.8 shows that the growth of government spending has outpaced that of household consumption and of the GDP in most years since 1997. The steady but continual increase in government spending, from 30 percent in 2000 to 34 percent in 2007, could lead to two problems for the Cuban economy.

First, the continued growth of government spending as a proportion of GDP has the potential to generate deficit spending. As noted, the government deficit was brought down to around 2 percent of GDP in 1996 and has stayed relatively low since then. Recently, there has been a slight upward trend, hinting at a possible future deterioration, although to date the deficit has remained within acceptable limits and is fairly low by international standards.

The other side of the coin is government revenue. While the tax system introduced in 1994 represented a quantum leap in the government's taxation capacity, there remain indications of insufficient flexibility and diversity of revenue sources. An indication of this is the recent trend of indirect taxes (taxes on services and the circulation of goods) after 2005. In 1989 these taxes accounted for 80 percent of tax revenue. In 1996 they began declining significantly for a decade, bottoming out at 55 percent in 2005. But since then they have increased slightly, to more than 60 percent by 2007.

The second potential problem inherent in increased government spending is more subtle. As spending on social services goes up as a proportion of total spending, there is a corresponding decrease in the ratio of paid to unpaid consumption, where the latter consists mainly of subsidies on retail prices and free universal public services, such as health care and education. This in turn undermines an important microeconomic goal in Cuba today: to restore

Table 2.8. Government and private contributions to GDP growth (%)

	Annual rate of growth		
	Household consumption	**Government spending**	**GDP**
1997	2.3	2.7	2.8
1998	1.9	0.1	0.2
1999	5.1	5.1	6.2
2000	2.1	3.0	5.9
2001	3.8	3.3	3.2
2002	2.1	4.1	1.4
2003	6.2	7.3	3.8
2004	1.5	8.6	5.8
2005	0.4	10.4	11.2
2006	8.7	7.9	12.1
2007	1.5	10.5	7.3
2008	-1.8	2.6	4.3
2009	0.9	1.7	1.4

Sources: Estimates and approximations based on ONE, *Anuario Estadístico de Cuba* (Havana: ONE, 1996, 2000, 2006, 2008, 2010).

the contribution of wages and labor to an individual's standard of living, and thereby restore important labor incentives. All this has potentially negative consequences for macroeconomic efficiency.

The final major structural change in the macroeconomy has occurred in the external sector. I have already discussed the shift to service exports. This resulted in an overall macroeconomic structural transformation from services constituting 10 percent of exports in 1990 to 70 percent after 2005. A structural weakness that has improved only slightly is one common to most developing countries: the concentration of exports in a limited range of products or activities, which renders the national economy vulnerable in the current global environment. Cuba continues to have a notoriously low diversity of exports. Three groups of products account for 71 percent of exports of goods, and service exports are concentrated in two activities.

A final issue relevant to the external sector is the terms of trade. As figure 2.11 reveals, Cuba has had relatively constant terms of trade throughout the Special Period. Given its limited spectrum of exports, changes in world market prices for specific products (nickel, for example) can lead to short-term fluctuations in the purchasing power of exports, as evidenced in the increase from 2002 to 2005. In this case the rising value of exports was offset by both price

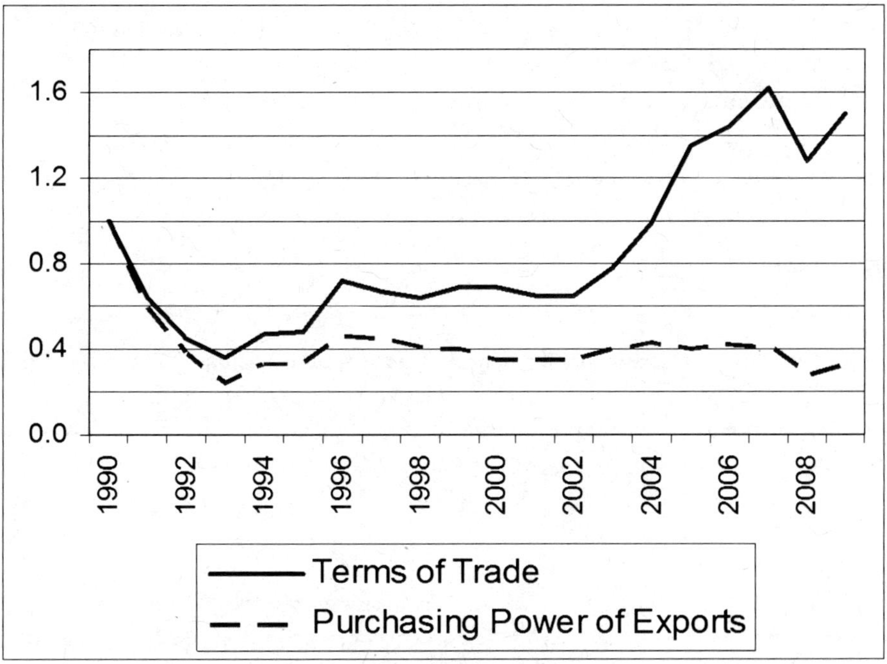

Figure 2.11. Evolution of terms of trade and purchasing power of exports, 1990–2009 (1990 = 1). *Source:* Estimates and approximations based on ONE, *Anuario Estadístico de Cuba* (Havana: ONE, 2000, 2006, 2010) and additional specific information from the external sector.

increases for imports (such as food) and an unfavorable structural shift in the national economy, an increase in the import coefficient and a reduction in the export coefficient. The key to long-term improvement in Cuba's terms of trade and the purchasing power of its exports is to continue expanding exports of high-value-added goods and services.

As for the future of the structural changes in Cuba's macroeconomy, all indications from both economists and political leaders are that the processes that have characterized the Special Period will continue in the short, medium, and long terms. The focus of Cuba's economic planning is specifically on addressing the remaining structural problems, while consistently protecting and extending existing social gains. At present the following nine issues are considered crucial to promoting the desired changes:

1. Increasing economic efficiency
2. Strengthening the connection between (socially useful) work and remuneration
3. Establishing efficient models of enterprise management and accumulation
4. Establishing a financial system appropriate to the needs of a socialist economy
5. Establishing appropriate domestic prices
6. Continuing the process of shifting the composition of output toward more high-value-added goods and appropriate end uses
7. Continuing the process of shifting the composition of exports toward high-value-added goods and services and toward greater diversification
8. Promoting internal savings
9. Resolving the issue of Cuba's dual currency

Notes

1. Carlos Rafael Rodríguez, "La defensa de la economía nacional" (conferencia en la Universidad Popular), in *Letra con Filo* II (Havana: Editorial Ciencias Sociales, 1983).

2. Specialization was sustained by the growth of the agricultural sector, rather than the industrial sector, which stagnated, resulting in very low yields. See Miguel Figueras, "Cambios estructurales en la economía cubana," *Cuadernos de Nuestra América* 7, no. 15 (1990).

3. The external sector has always been an essential link for the normal operation of the national Cuban economy, given the latter's small and highly open nature.

4. For further information, see the assessments by Alfredo González, "Cuba: los retos de la transición" (mimeo, Instituto Nacional de Investigaciones Económicas, 1994), and Miguel Figueras, "Realidades y cambios previsibles de la economía cubana" (Conferencia

magistral en el Forum "XXX Años de los Estudios de Economía en la Universidad de La Habana," 1992).

5. Important economic relations had previously existed with some CMEA countries, but they changed extensively both quantitatively and qualitatively in the early 1970s.

6. For further information, see INIE-JUCEPLAN, *Situación actual de la economía cubana: Perspectivas de colaboración con América Latina* (Havana: Editora JUCEPLAN, 1992).

7. Oscar U-Echevarría, "Apuntes para una discusión sobre sistema financiero cubano," *Boletín de Información Sobre Economía Cubana* 1, nos. 11–12 (1992).

8. See Elena Álvarez, "El ajuste importador de la economía cubana. Apuntes para una evaluación" (investigación, INIE, 1993), and Mario Fernández Font, "Cuba: 33 años después" (investigación, INIE, 1993). Both authors conduct a broad-based, meticulous, and detailed analysis of these aspects. The first is highly pertinent because it indicates that the external gap, the main obstacle and macroeconomic constraint on the country, is nothing more than an expression of the internal savings gap, which has been a permanent systemic constant in the national economy given the nature of its productive structure.

9. However, with the CMEA relations it was possible for a long time to cushion the effects resulting from the fluctuations in sugar prices and production, as the economy was isolated from the impact of external shocks.

10. An analysis of these stages and their manifestations up to 2000 can be found in INIE, *Reconstrucción y análisis de las series estadísticas de la economía cubana, 1960–1975* (Havana: INIE, 1997); Alfredo González, *Cuba: Escenarios del modelos económico en los años noventa* (Havana: INIE, 1993); and Oscar U-Echevarría et al., "Análisis del presupuesto y de los flujos financieros de la economía cubana" (investigación, INIE, 1992). Also illustrative are the references by Elena Álvarez, "Cuba: Un modelo de desarrollo con justicia social," *Cuba: Investigación Económica* 4, no. 2 (1998), and Oscar U-Echevarría, "El modelo de ajuste macroeconómico: El caso de Cuba," *Cuba: Investigación Económica* 3, nos. 3–4 (1997). The criteria and assessments in José Luis Rodríguez, *Estrategia del desarrollo económico en Cuba* (Havana: Editorial de Ciencias Sociales, 1990), are also important.

11. José Luis Rodríguez, *Dos ensayos sobre la economía cubana* (Havana: Editorial Ciencias Sociales, 1984).

12. Alina Hernández, "Volatilidad y crecimiento económico en Cuba" (ponencia, versión digital, Taller Científico 42 Años de los Estudios de Economía, Facultad de Economía, Universidad de La Habana, December 9–10, 2005).

13. This summary is based on information in González, *Cuba: Escenarios del modelos económico en los años noventa;* Gerardo Trueba, "Principales características de la economía cubana (panorama histórico y situación actual)" (investigación, INIE, May 1993); and INIE, *Reconstrucción y análisis de las series estadísticas de la economía cubana, 1960–1975.*

14. This aspect was incompletely achieved. One structural problem that was never overcome was the existence of incomplete technological chains of production for a number of core resources.

15. See an extensive analysis of industrialization in Gonzalo Rodríguez, *El proceso de*

industrialización en Cuba (Havana: Editorial Ciencias Sociales, 1980); also see a relevant periodization in Hiram Marquetti, "Industria manufacturera: Principales etapas de su desarrollo," in *Estructura económica de Cuba*, ed. Alfonso Casanovas, vol. 2 (Havana: Editorial Felix Varela, 2002).

16. This process of industrialization was, however, significantly limited by the poor technological development of the socialist community in some key fields, as illustrated in its high energy coefficient. See Miguel Figueras, *La industrialización en Cuba* (Havana: Editorial de Ciencias Sociales, 1991). We must realize, as Álvarez describes in "El ajuste importador de la economía cubana: Apuntes para una evaluación," that due to the harassment of the prolonged and ruthless U.S. economic blockade, Cuba could not always access the most advanced and efficient techniques on the international market even when it had the hard currency available to do so.

17. Figure 2.3 is calculated as the ratio of exports and imports at current prices and not, as the technical definition of terms of trade, based on a fixed set of products. Given relatively stable trade volumes, the two are very similar, and for the purposes of this chapter the ratio serves as a very good proxy.

18. Note that an extensive growth pattern does not necessarily have to be inefficient, but as explained it was economically problematic in Cuba's concrete conditions and a shift to intensive growth was necessary.

19. I refer particularly to the deteriorating terms of trade for sugar, the dominant export product at this time. Trueba, "Principales características de la economía cubana (panorama histórico y situación actual)," points out that this situation was already very apparent in 1981 and 1986.

20. See the analysis of these financial flows in U-Echevarría et al., "Análisis del presupuesto y de los flujos financieros de la economía cubana."

21. As a concept, a tax on the circulation of goods is a centralized way to equalize economic surplus by taxing one group of products in order to guarantee widespread access to another group of goods by using the collected revenues to subsidize them. As such a tax in practice begins financing other types of expenses, however, particularly when the government faces ongoing financial imbalances, it becomes a consumption tax, which always has a regressive distributional effect.

22. Based on studies of productive efficiency and cash flows. See U-Echevarría et al., "Análisis del presupuesto y de los flujos financieros de la economía cubana," and Alina Hernández and Oscar U-Echevarría, "Análisis de la economía cubana a partir de los complejos económicos productivos" (ponencia, Taller Científico sobre Eficiencia y Planificación, Facultad de Economía, Universidad de La Habana, November 1990).

23. For further information, see the analysis on the background of the 1990s crisis by Oscar U-Echevarría, "Cuba: La antesala de la crisis," *Cuba: Investigación Económica* 4, no. 2 (1998).

24. Interesting assessments of the issue can be found in Pedro Monreal and Julio Carranza, "Problemas del desarrollo en Cuba: realidades y conceptos," *Temas* no. 11 (July–September 1998); U-Echevarría et al., "Análisis del presupuesto y de los flujos financieros de la economía cubana"; and quantifications in Elena Álvarez, "La economía cubana en

los 80: Reflexiones en torno a una década compleja," *Cuba Económica* 1, no. 2 (1991), and "La apertura externa cubana," *Cuba: Investigación Económica* 1, no. 1 (1995).

25. For further information see González, *Cuba: Escenarios del modelos económico en los años noventa;* and Oscar U-Echevarría, "Regulación plan y mercado: El caso de Cuba," *Cuba: Investigación Económica* 2, no. 3 (1996); "El modelo de ajuste macroeconómico: El caso de Cuba"; and "Cuba: La antesala de la crisis."

26. Measured as the percentage of production set aside for gross accumulation.

27. See José Luis Rodríguez, "Perspectivas económicas de Cuba en 1996" (presented at the Word Economic Forum, Davos, Ministerio de Economía y Planificación, February 1–6, 1996), and "Panorama de la situación económica del país" (Segunda Conferencia: La Nación y la Emigración, Habana, Ministerio de Economía y Planificación, November 3–6, 1995). See U-Echevarría, "Regulación plan y mercado: El caso de Cuba" and "El modelo de ajuste macroeconómico: El caso de Cuba."

28. See José Luis Rodríguez, "Cuba 1990–1995: Reflexiones sobre una política económica acertada," *Cuba Socialista* 3, no. 1 (1996).

29. In particular to address a number of economic problems that evolved out of measures that had been taken in the first phase to immediately protect the welfare of the population.

30. Although Cuba had previously engaged in some foreign trade outside CMEA, largely because of the inadequate supply of certain goods in the socialist network, such trade was highly selective and conducted on a case-by-case basis. See Rodríguez, "Panorama de la situación económica del país"; "Perspectivas económicas de Cuba en 1996"; and "Cuba 1990–1995: Reflexiones sobre una política económica acertada."

31. Cited by Alfredo García, "Turismo," in *Estructura económica de Cuba*, ed. Alfonso Casanovas, vol. 2 (Havana: Editorial Félix Varela, 2002).

32. See paper by Gladys Alfonso, "Informe de la actividad turística, 1999" (mimeo, INIE, 2000).

33. For further information on the main measures of functional adjustment, see Alfredo González, "Economía y sociedad: Los retos del modelo económico," *Cuba: Investigación Económica* 3, nos. 3–4 (1997), and U-Echevarría, "Regulación plan y mercado: El caso de Cuba." See also Oscar U-Echevarría, "Estado, economía y planificación: Una primera aproximación," *Cuba: Investigación Económica* 5, no. 4 (1999).

34. Pedro Monreal, "La globalización y los dilemas de las trayectorias económicas de Cuba: matriz bolivariana, industrialización y desarrollo," in *Reflexiones sobre economía cubana*, ed. Omar Everleny (Havana: Editorial Ciencias Sociales, 2002); CEPAL, *América Latina y el Caribe: Políticas para mejorar la inserción en la economía mundial* (Santiago de Chile: CEPAL, 1995).

35. See U-Echevarría et al., "Aspectos Globales," in *Estructura económica de Cuba*, ed. Alfonso Casanovas (Havana: Editorial Félix Varela).

36. See Alfredo González, "El sistema de planificación y circulación monetaria dual en la etapa actual," *Economía y Desarrollo* vol. 134 (2003).

37. See Mayra Espina, "Efectos sociales del reajuste económico: igualdad, desigualdad y procesos de complejización en la sociedad cubana," and Juan Triana, "Prologo,"

both in Everleny, *Reflexiones sobre economía cubana*, and Ángela Ferriol, "Política social y desarrollo: Una aproximación global," in *Política social y reformas estructurales: Cuba a principios del siglo XXI*, ed. Elena Álvarez and Jorge Matar (Mexico: CEPAL, 2004).

38. At constant 1987 prices and without revaluations based on costs of social services, in order to maintain homogeneity in the series.

39. By convention, sectors have been structured by the type of economic activity as follows.

- Primary: agriculture; forestry; fisheries
- Secondary: manufacturing industries; construction
- Tertiary: electricity, gas and water; commerce; restaurants and hotels; transportation, storage and communications; real estate; financial establishments and services to companies; governmental; social and personal services; import rights

3

Cuba's Insertion in the International Economy since 1990

NANCY A. QUIÑONES CHANG

In the international context, Cuba is a small economy highly dependent on foreign trade. For 2000–2006 its participation in world exports of goods and services barely averaged 0.05 percent, while its ratio of foreign trade to GDP was 41.1 percent, an increase over previous years.[1]

In the early 1990s, several adverse factors converged to unleash one of the worst crises in the country's economic history. Some of the relevant factors included the dismantling of Cuba's markets in the CMEA countries, financial and commercial barriers to trade with non-CMEA countries, and the strengthening of the U.S. blockade.

With the demise of the socialist bloc, the Cuban economy lost

- its main markets for the purchase and sale of goods and services. In the late 1980s the socialist countries accounted for 80–85 percent of Cuba's total exchange;
- its favorable pricing terms. It has been estimated that in some years during the 1980s, the higher-than-world-market prices Cuba received for sugar, nickel, and citrus increased its income from exports by more than 60 percent;[2]
- its only external source of financing and credits. Cuba did not belong to any multilateral or regional financial bodies and had declared a moratorium on the service payments of its foreign debt in freely convertible currency since 1986;[3] and
- the type of relations and links prevailing in CMEA. The external sector operated on the basis of a state monopoly over foreign trade, government-level coordination mechanisms based on five-year plans, nonconvertible currencies, and physical trade quotas with prices fixed to guarantee a fair exchange.[4]

The country's external earnings took a severe hit. The terms of trade (at 1997 prices) declined from 1.48 to 0.70 between 1990 and 1992 (fig. 3.1), and the value of exports declined by 67 percent between 1989 and 1993. Sugar alone accounted for 50 percent of total export losses, as its price dropped from 51.4 cents per kilo in 1990 to 21.4 cents in 1992. The supply of credits was also interrupted, with the capital account in 1993 reaching barely a tenth of the 1989 figure.[5]

Due to these reductions in export earnings and credits, the current value of imports decreased by 72 percent from 1989 to 1993, returning to close to 1974 levels (fig. 3.1). The greatest contraction in the value of imports was concentrated in equipment, unfinished goods, and other consumer items. In 1993

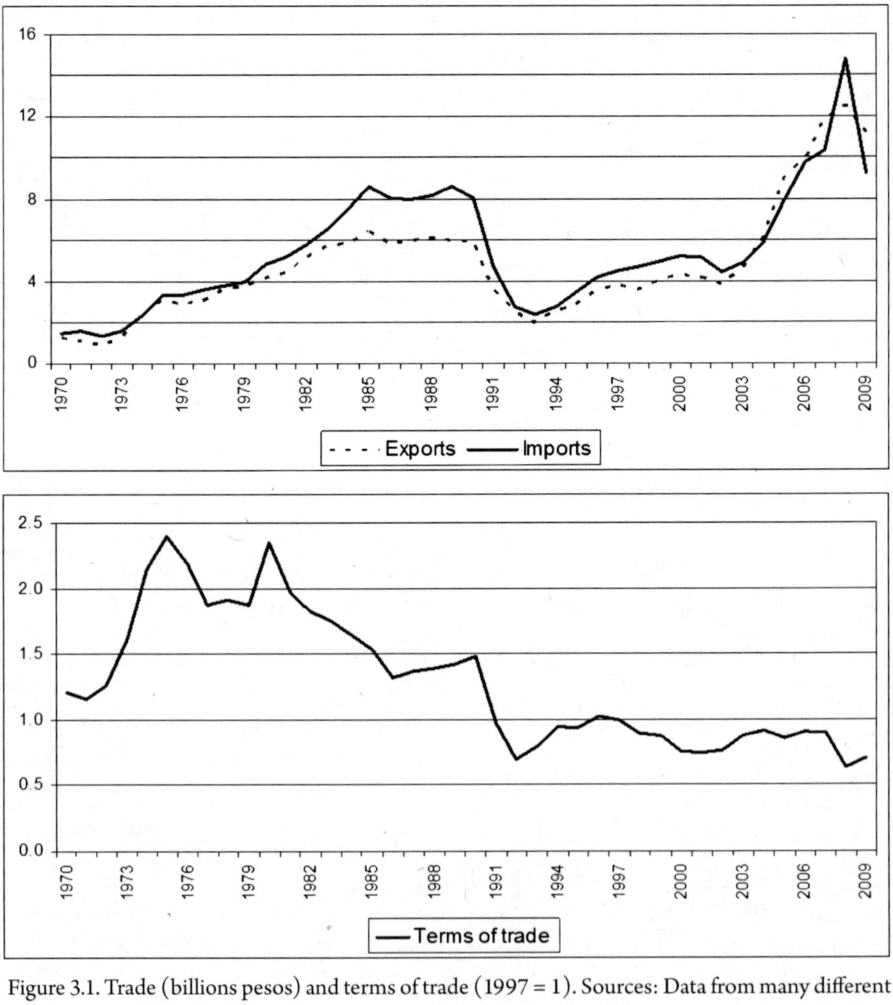

Figure 3.1. Trade (billions pesos) and terms of trade (1997 = 1). Sources: Data from many different publications of ONE, various years.

the combined value of these three groups equaled only 13 percent of the value imported in 1989. This caused a corresponding paralysis of installed manufacturing capacity, with estimated production at only 10 to 20 percent of capacity in 1993; moreover, the existing capital equipment was facing technological obsolescence for lack of upgrades.[6]

In order to guarantee minimum levels of economic activity and food supplies, priority for imports was assigned to fuels and foodstuffs. Their joint ratio in the import of goods was nearly 60 percent in 1993 and 1994, but their joint value still declined by 66.5 percent between 1989 and 1994. Import restrictions contributed significantly to a major deterioration in the population's quality of life through decreases in the supply of services—mainly transportation, electricity, health care, and education—and the availability of food. The per capita nutritional intake dropped from 2,845 kilocalories daily in 1989 to 1,863 in 1993.[7]

The situation in late 1993 was characterized by

- an overall drop in economic activity;
- an accumulation of internal financial imbalances that caused repeated devaluation of the Cuban peso. The fiscal deficit to GDP ratio was 33.5 percent, and the currency in circulation (liquidity) to GDP ratio was 73.2 percent;
- a deterioration in workers' real income; and
- a deterioration in labor productivity and social discipline.

This situation manifested in a high level of hidden underemployment, failure to seek formal employment, selective acceptance of employment, high labor turnover, high absenteeism, and a drop in the average retirement age.[8]

Thus, Cuba faced a situation similar to that in the early 1960s when the United States severed relations and, as occurred then, the authorities were forced to rethink Cuba's model of insertion into the international economy. This reevaluation brought about profound changes in the structure of markets, commercial specialization, financing sources, and the mechanisms to regulate external activities. Implementing the appropriate measures has been a particularly complex challenge for both internal and external reasons. For one, the Cuban domestic economy had been configured based on its comparative advantages within the socialist integration scheme. It was concentrated in the processing of natural resources, specifically sugar, minerals, and citrus. Both the structural dynamics of operating within this integration scheme and the majority of the products exported were not suited to developing new export markets with the rest of the world.

In addition, prior to the collapse of CMEA the United States, among other countries, had worked unceasingly to hinder Cuban trade outside of CMEA. Since 1960 Cuba had been barred from the U.S. market, the region's largest. Cuba did not belong to any international or regional financial bodies, nor did it receive the preferential access that developed countries granted to other Latin American nations (Lomé, Caribbean Basin Initiative, Sugar Quotas System). After the dissolution of CMEA, the United States attempted to completely isolate Cuba on the international scene and make trading even more difficult. The so-called Cuban Democracy Act of 1992, for example, prohibited ships from entering U.S. ports within 180 days of visiting Cuban ports, and it abruptly suspended Cuba's trade with the subsidiaries of U.S. firms based in third countries.[9] The Helms-Burton Act of 1996 codified into law all the provisions of the blockade and deepened its extraterritorial nature by attempting to halt the incipient foreign direct investment in Cuba. It completely barred officials and executives of any company that violated the U.S. blockade of Cuba from entry into the United States for business or personal reasons, regardless of their nationality. It even went so far as to restrict family visitation rights (the only part of this law so far relaxed by the Obama administration).

The Bush administration, following the recommendations of the so-called Commission for Assistance to a Free Cuba, in 2004 restricted Cubans residing in the United States to only one family visit to Cuba every three years, and limited visits to immediate blood relatives (parents, children, siblings). At the close of 2006, the economic losses to Cuba caused by the four-decade-long U.S. blockade were estimated at $89 billion. Some of the most important costs include much higher prices on international contracts, burdensome financing terms, higher transportation costs, the necessity of obtaining medications and medical equipment through third countries, the inability to procure high-efficiency technologies, nonpayment of copyrights, and the travel ban for U.S. citizens.[10]

In response to the crisis, Cuba launched the Special Period in August 1990. The policies for the first years focused on economic survival, but at the same time planning began on economic reforms that would substantially transform the structures and operation of the national economy. Introduction of these measures began in 1993. The Special Period became a two-decade-long process of economic reform that continues today. Two salient aspects of this reform process have been its gradual implementation and the leading role played by the state. Unlike elsewhere in Latin America, in Cuba the preservation of the major social gains achieved during the revolutionary period takes precedence over economic reforms.

Reinsertion into the international economy was one of the first major objectives of, and a trailblazing activity in, the economic reform process. Cuba's reincorporation into the international economy has been carried out via three key means: first, incorporation into the flows of international private financing, second, active participation in international and regional bodies and negotiations, and third, substantial changes in the regime and structure of trade.

Incorporation into the Flows of International Private Financing

Allowing the inflow of private financing into Cuba demanded substantial modifications to the legislative and regulatory systems, as well as the creation of institutions that would oversee the design and implementation of all the relevant policies. Remittances and foreign direct investment (FDI) have been the two main forms of private financial inflows into Cuba over the course of the Special Period.

In July 1993 the National Assembly of People's Power, Cuba's highest legislative and governing body, decriminalized the ownership of hard currency. At the same time it established a network of hard-currency exchange bureaus and retail outlets. These measures allowed the hard currency from remittances and from services in the incipient tourism sector to circulate through the banking system and the society.[11] According to estimates of the Economic Commission for Latin America and the Caribbean (ECLAC), the value of these flows ranged between $800 million and $1 billion in 2003–4 but dropped considerably following the sharply increased travel restrictions imposed by the U.S. government in May 2004.[12]

FDI had already begun in 1988, just before the crisis, but it greatly accelerated in the early part of the Special Period. This has been the only form of private capital inflows that Cuba has allowed. Other forms of investment used in a number of developing countries, such as bonds and stocks, would require fundamental changes in the operation of the Cuban system of production. In addition, they would leave the Cuban economy more vulnerable to international financial manipulation, and in particular to the endless U.S. economic aggression.

Cuba faced four disadvantages when it began seeking FDI. First, it began too late in the sense that its natural competitors in Latin America had accelerated their pursuit of FDI five or ten years earlier, as part of their conversion to neoliberal development policies. Second, those countries' neoliberal development policies imposed fewer restrictions on FDI, whereas Cuba sought to guarantee significant gains for its national economy at the possible cost of lower profits for the foreign investors.[13] Third, the U.S. blockade prevented Cuba from accessing the largest market in the hemisphere, one of the main advantages of FDI in other countries in the region. And finally, the United

States not only blocked access to its market but further attempted to prevent other countries from investing private capital in Cuba (or even trading with the Island, which is important for investment decisions) through the so-called Cuban Democracy Act of 1992 and the Helms-Burton Act of 1996.

For Cuba to receive private capital inflows required amending the constitution and passing laws to regulate such activity. In 1992 the Constitution of the Republic was amended to recognize property rights of joint ventures, to allow economic partnerships and associations, and to permit the transfer of economic entities to either partial or entirely foreign ownership. Act No. 77, the Foreign Investment Act, was adopted in 1995, regulating foreign investment within Cuban national territory.[14] It was designed around the following basic considerations: achieving national development objectives without compromising either national sovereignty or the principles of equity that have characterized the Revolution, and protecting the economy against the aggressive policies of the U.S. government.

In an attempt to ensure that FDI was consistent with the social objectives of the Revolution, particularly those relating to equity and the labor rights of Cuban workers (see chapter 8), foreign investment was excluded from the health and education sectors, and a Cuban employment agency was set up for Cubans working in foreign enterprises. To ensure adherence to the economic development and national sovereignty objectives, each business deal was approved on a case-by-case basis, the subsurface and marine property rights of the Cuban state were reserved,[15] and forms of economic association that would not compromise the sovereignty of national assets were extensively used (for example, joint production contracts and hotel management agreements). In order to protect Cuba against the ongoing U.S. aggression, the defense sector was also excluded. Transfers of registered shares of any joint ventures are strictly controlled, and authorization is required to change the members of an economic association.

The Cuban policy differs from the neoliberal policies of its neighbors in viewing these inflows as complementing national investment efforts, rather than as taking precedence over national economic development. Hence FDI in Cuba is required to contribute markets, technology, or productive capital that the Cuban economy lacks. In addition to this selective investment policy based on clear and consistent criteria for evaluating proposed foreign investments, Cuba employs centralized state decision making, including the establishment of a central negotiating body,[16] and active involvement of national agents in decision making, management, and follow-up on agreements reached. In this respect the main outlines of the Cuban policy are consistent with developmentalism, an approach to development that was most prominent in Latin America in the 1960s, with Raúl Prebish as one of its leading proponents.

Cuban law allows the free transfer of profits and repatriation of capital[17] and is relatively open with regard to the sectors where FDI is permitted, with exclusions only for defense, education, and health.[18] Other Cuban incentives for FDI include the Agreements for the Promotion and Reciprocal Protection of Investments and the Agreements on the Avoidance of Double Taxation.[19]

An overview of the main indicators relating to international joint ventures from 1994 to 2008 indicates that FDI has had positive effects on the national economy. Total sales increased at an average annual rate of 23.98 percent, and exports by 22.9 percent (fig. 3.2). These growth rates were much higher than

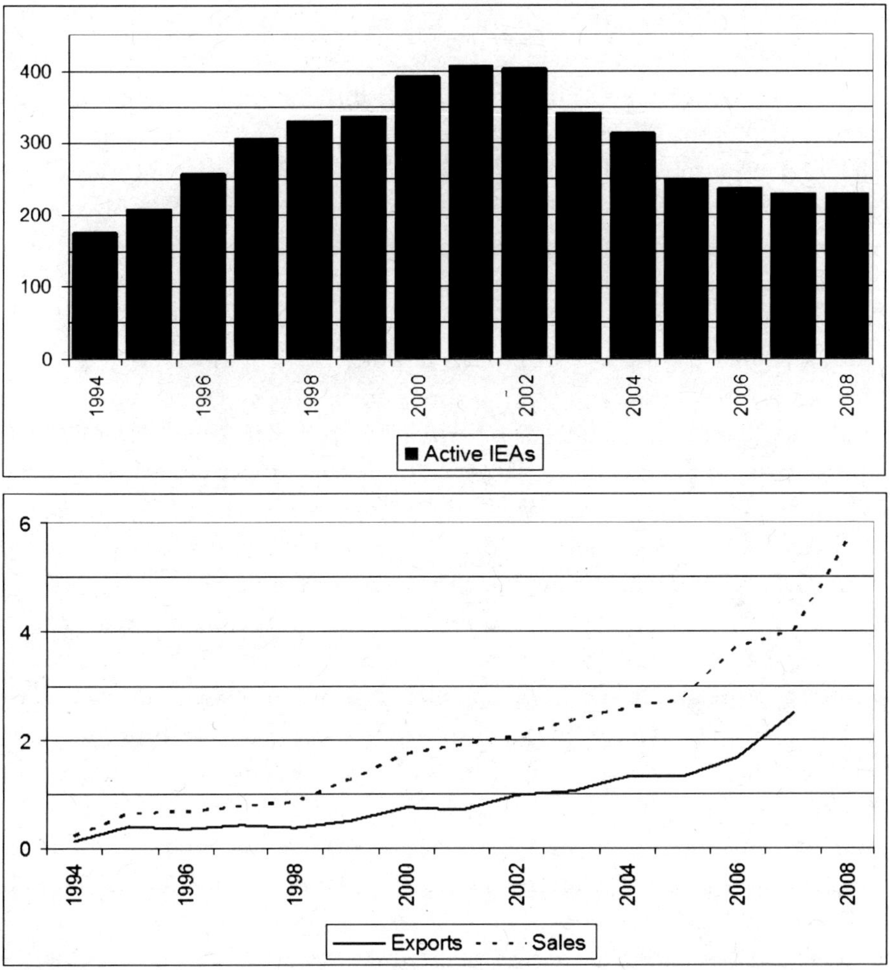

Figure 3.2. Economic performance of IEAs (number active and billions US$). *Source:* MINVEC, "La inversión extranjera: Situación actual y perspectiva" (presentation at the IX Reunión Nacional con Profesores de Economía Política, Havana, October 2007).

those for Cuba's GDP and total exports, and thus these ventures considerably increased their degree of penetration into the economy. For example, between 1994 and 2008 the contribution to GDP of revenue earned by international economic associations (IEAs) rose from 1.1 percent to 14.5 percent, while the share of exports expanded from 4.5 percent to 17.6 percent.[20]

In 2003 the Cuban government reviewed and amended its FDI attraction policies. One purpose was to bring the selection of proposals into compliance with the areas then being given top priority for development, because these had shifted somewhat since the previous decade. Another was that many foreign capital entities had failed to fulfill the economic and social plans they had outlined, necessitating stricter compliance mechanisms. These measures achieved greater efficiency, such that aggregate economic indicators continued to grow while the number of active joint ventures declined steadily (see fig. 3.2). This decline resulted from a reduction in new approvals (between 2003 and 2007 only twenty-nine were authorized) along with an increase in dissolutions (191 between 2003 and 2006). Some of the main reasons for the dissolutions were the foreign partner's failure to comply with its established obligations or to achieve the proposed social purpose and economic results, or simply the government's belief upon the expiration of the contract that this foreign activity no longer served Cuba's economic interests.

The pattern of FDI by sector and country of origin was relatively stable from 2000 to 2007. The sectors with the largest number of IEAs in 2007 were primary industry (mining and energy) and tourism (41 percent). Spain, Canada, Italy, and Venezuela were the main partners (64 percent). Venezuela in particular stood out in those years, as it went from eleven to twenty-six IEAs at a time when the overall number fell by more than 40 percent (table 3.1).

These joint business deals have been important to Cuba for two reasons. First, they have provided a more secure source of hard currency than if Cuba had attempted to penetrate international markets independently. Second, they have been a source of new or enhanced managerial skills and business knowledge. These are important for Cuba's efforts both to increase its domestic productive efficiency and to penetrate new foreign markets with its products and services. Thus, construction projects, which were among the pioneering joint projects, have been followed by, as two examples, franchises for the Floridita and Bodeguita del Medio restaurants and the production/marketing of a wide range of biotech and medical items, including vaccines, monoclonal antibodies, and SUMA diagnostic systems.[21]

Cuba's participation in the flow of international private finance has enabled the recovery and expansion of some industries that had been partially closed down after the breakup of CMEA, including nickel, tobacco, beverages, and

Table 3.1. Active IEAs by country and sector

	2000		2007	
Country	**No.**	**Pct.**	**No.**	**Pct.**
Spain	97	25	63	27
Canada	75	19	37	16
Italy	55	14	24	10
Venezuela	11	3	26	11
Total	238	61	150	64
Sector				
Basic industry	90	23	58	25
Tourism	70	18	38	17
Light industry	26	7	17	7
Construction	33	8	12	5
Food	19	5	12	5
Transportation	12	3	12	5
Agriculture	21	5	16	7
Iron and steel	20	5	9	4
Scientific clusters	5	1	9	4
Other	96	24	47	21
Total	392	100	230	100

Sources: Based on Omar Pérez, "La inversión extranjera directa en Cuba: Vientos a su favor?" (presented at the Seminario sobre Economía Cubana y Gerencia Empresarial by the Centro para el Estudio de la Economía de Cuba, July 2008), and Omar Pérez, "La inversión extranjera directa en Cuba," in Colectivo de autores, *Estructura económica de Cuba* (Havana: Félix Varela, 2002).

citrus. In other areas, such as tourism, telecommunications, and oil prospecting and extraction, the issue was not one of recovery but simply of the need for rapid expansion, sometimes almost de novo.

Participation in Regional and International Organizations

A vital element for the Cuban economy in this process of insertion has been the effective return to concessionary trading systems. Being excluded from these entails discriminatory treatment within international flows of trade and investment. Cuba became a full member of the World Trade Organization (WTO) in April 1995. Two of the most noteworthy outcomes of this membership are the preparation of a regulatory package governing external trading relations pursuant to WTO agreements and the international support in denouncing the U.S. blockade, which contravenes the principles of free trade. At the regional level the most important events have been Cuba's entrance into the Latin American Integration Association (LAIA) as its twelfth full member in August 1999, the signing of trade agreements with the Caribbean Community (CARICOM) countries in 2001 and with the South American Common Market in 2006, and the plethora of trade and investment agreements signed in the framework of ALBA since 2004. Since its entry into LAIA, Cuba has made intensive integration efforts, signing economic complementation agreements (ECAs) with the other eleven member countries.[22] At the same time, under the 1980 Montevideo Treaty, it has signed ECAs with Guatemala and CARICOM. These agreements are designed to reduce or eliminate tariffs in bilateral trade.

ALBA was proposed by Venezuelan president Hugo Chávez in 2001 as an alternative to the U.S. government–initiated North American Free Trade Agreement (NAFTA). Officially inaugurated at the end of 2004, ALBA is an inclusive alliance formalized through governmental agreements. Although it addresses trade, its main focus is energy integration, regional physical infrastructure, and resolution of the serious social problems that exist in the member countries. Other particularly important agreements address the development of transportation, communication, roads, agriculture, tourism, and certain industries.

Of all the aforementioned multilateral organizations, ALBA's objectives are the most closely aligned with Cuba's principles of socioeconomic development and international relations. Among the areas of accord are the balance between solidarity-based cooperation and economic benefits, the centrality of key social fields such as health care and education, the leading and proactive role of the state in the economy, the respect for national legal regulations, the development of physical infrastructure, the creation of joint ventures, the search for complementariness, and the preferential treatment for the most backward countries and regions.[23]

As of the end of 2009, ALBA members were Venezuela, Cuba, Bolivia, Nicaragua, the Dominican Republic, Antigua and Barbuda, Saint Vincent and the Grenadines, and Ecuador.[24] Cuba is a founding member, and since December 2004 its involvement has focused on

- development of education in the member countries, including both the eradication of illiteracy and university training in priority specialties;
- medical cooperation through extended primary health care, surgeries for ten million Latin Americans suffering from ocular diseases, construction of hospital facilities and diagnostic centers, and training of health professionals;

- development of regional energy integration through adhering to the Petrocaribe Agreement,[25] rehabilitating the Cienfuegos Refinery, developing ethanol production in Venezuela, prospecting for and exploiting hydrocarbons in Cuban national waters in the Gulf of Mexico, and conducting studies to identify and quantify oil reserves in the Orinoco oil belt;
- expansion of the economic interconnection among the countries in the region through construction and modernization of ports, development of railway infrastructure throughout Latin America, and participation in ALBATEL,[26] a large international telecommunications project;
- recovery and expansion of the capacities of certain Cuban industries, including pharmaceuticals, nickel, steel, and fertilizers, among others;
- pursuit of food security in the member countries through joint agricultural ventures, mainly involving rice, legumes, dairy products, poultry, and forestry resources;
- expansion of the tourism infrastructure, including the construction of three hotels in Cuba and one in Venezuela;
- defense and consolidation of Latin America's identity through cultural integration projects, such as the creation of the TELESUR TV channel, the Latin American and Caribbean Festival of Culture and the Arts, the Encyclopedia of Latin American and Caribbean Literature and Arts, and the ALBA printing press and record label, among other projects; and
- development of financial relations among member countries. The first branch of the ALBA Bank was opened in Havana on April 25, 2008. This institution was set up to help protect the region against economic crises and U.S. financial aggression and to promote the implementation of productive and social projects.

The massive agreements Cuba entered into under ALBA had an important impact on the economy in the 2005–9 period. In the external sector they led to modifications in the foreign trade regime and to structural changes in trade.

Changes in the Foreign Trade Regime

The institutions and the mechanisms regulating foreign trade were significantly transformed via the international commitments that Cuba entered into with new economic agents. This process can be divided into two stages based on the degree of centralization of Cuba's foreign trade.

The first stage, from 1990 until 2003, was marked by a process of decentralization. The number of entities involved in foreign trade increased dramatically, from only 50 in 1989 to 419,[27] along with the opening of 816 offices representing foreign companies by late 2003. This explosion of agents required that control mechanisms had to change from direct to indirect. The new measures included, among others, tariffs,[28] rules of origin, pest and disease controls, quality standards, and operational permits.[29] The major trade policy instruments, however, were programs that prioritized specific sectors whose activities offered a quick return on investment of the available hard currency, namely, tourism, medicines and pharmaceuticals, biotechnology, the agro-food industry, and national crude oil.

By mid-2003 several negative aspects of this regulatory framework were becoming substantially problematic, among them a reduction in Cuba's bargaining power, an increase in administrative costs, an excessive number of undertrained staff, the involvement of unnecessary intermediaries,[30] low efficiency in the management of trade, and foreign partners' noncompliance with contractual obligations. At the same time, in 2004 Cuba's external economic relations shifted positively through the signing of agreements with Venezuela within the framework of ALBA, treaties with the People's Republic of China, and the restructuring of short-term debts with some governments. These yielded a considerable expansion of the country's credit capacity such that between 2004 and 2007 the active debt increased by 3.102 billion pesos.[31]

These conditions ushered in a second round of modifications to the institutions and regulations governing foreign trade designed to increase centralization of foreign trade activities and control mechanisms. The three most significant aspects were institutional modifications, new monetary regulations (enacted in mid-2003), and the strengthening of planning instruments, primarily focused on centralizing and rationalizing overseas purchases. Their dual purposes were to increase compliance with all international commitments Cuba entered into and to channel resources toward Cuba's top socioeconomic development priorities.

The institutional modifications were intended to concentrate imports to improve Cuba's bargaining power. To that end, the number of enterprises authorized to engage in foreign trade operations was reduced from 192 in 2001 to 89 in 2005, and the activities of the purchasing committees were expanded. These committees operate as purchase cartels for widely used imports, such as metals, timber, tires, and plastic raw materials. Composed of national importers and producers, they operate under the Ministry of Foreign Trade (MINCEX), examining the initial offers of all competing suppliers, then negotiating the final price and total import volume with the party offering the most competitive terms.[32] In addition, the inclusion of domestic producers in the bid process served Cuba's goal of substituting for imports whenever possible.

The first of the new monetary regulations, in July 2003, was the obligatory exchange that eliminated domestic circulation of the U.S. dollar and replaced it with the CUC. At the same time, an exchange control was enacted at the Central Bank by means of the Hard Currency Approval Committee. Any enterprise seeking to pay for imports with hard currency must have the requisite funds in convertible pesos and have the transaction authorized. The committee also imposed a surcharge on the purchase of dollars as opposed to other hard currencies, because Cuba incurs increased costs with this currency exchange due to U.S. financial aggression.

In February 2005 all hard currency was placed in a single unified income account at the Central Bank. Enterprises deposit any hard-currency earnings into this account, and all hard-currency payments for any foreign transactions are made from it according to established priorities. At the same time, the purchase authorization mechanism was modified and the internal redistribution of resources in CUCs was reviewed.

In 2006 the Ministry of Economy and Planning drafted the Plan of Imports to complement the previous measures. This plan established frameworks and guidelines for all foreign trade activities, in particular for Hard Currency Approval Committee authorization of any hard-currency transactions.

Thus, as of the end of 2009, centralized planning mechanisms determine the structure and volumes of imports and even, to a large extent, the geographic distribution of purchases. Prices, although they are an important consideration in the analysis, do not by themselves determine the approval of imports. The determining factor is rather the availability of hard currency, which is allocated according to the priorities of the national economic plan. Individual enterprises can only make purchases that accord with this national plan.[33]

Structural Changes in Foreign Trade

The profound structural changes in the Cuban external sector involved trade patterns in both markets and products. The market structure of the trade in goods shifted from Europe, which in 1990 accounted for nearly 85 percent of trade, toward America and Asia, whose joint percentage rose to 73 percent in 2009. Within Europe, the share of trade with European Union markets rose while that with Eastern Europe declined (table 3.2).

Another distinct characteristic of this period was the diversification of trading partners. In 1990 nearly 68 percent of Cuba's trade in goods occurred with a single country, the former USSR. By 2009 a similar percentage was distributed among seven countries: Venezuela (26.6 percent), China (14.3 percent),

Table 3.2. Structure of Cuban foreign trade in goods, 1990 versus 2007 (%)

Region	Total trade		Exports		Imports	
	1990	2007	1990	2007	1990	2007
Europe	84.8	25.8	81.1	24.1	87.5	26.4
European Union	6.9	21.0	6.7	21.3	6.7	20.9
Americas	6.5	45.5	7.3	47.1	6.0	44.9
Latin America	5.3	31.0	5.4	20.7	5.2	34.8
Asia	6.8	25.9	8.1	27.0	5.8	25.5
Other	1.9	2.8	3.5	1.8	0.7	3.2

Sources: ONE, *Anuario Estadístico de Cuba* (Havana: ONE, 1998, 2010).

Spain (7.7 percent), Canada (6.2 percent), United States (5.7 percent), Brazil (4.9 percent), and the Netherlands (2.6 percent).

An unprecedented event in the history of the Revolution was trade with the United States conducted under special circumstances. This trade started in December 2001 with U.S. authorization of sales of food and pharmaceutical raw materials to Cuba in the wake of Hurricane Michelle, one of the strongest storms to hit the Island this century. U.S. authorities required that Cuba make all purchases in cash, pay for the goods before they were loaded for transit, and use only U.S. transportation. Notwithstanding these constraints the value of imports has increased steadily, from a mere 4.4 million pesos in 2001 to 675.4 million pesos in 2009, which made the United States Cuba's fifth-largest trading partner.[34] According to U.S. International Trade Commission (USITC) analyses, U.S. producers enjoy advantages in terms of geographic proximity and efficiency that as of 2008 made them the main suppliers of some staples, such as chicken (80 percent), corn (100 percent), wheat (42 percent), soybeans (100 percent), and animal feed (54 percent). These figures demonstrate the tremendous opportunities that the Cuban market could offer to U.S. growers and producers if the blockade were repealed.[35]

Exports

The geographic reorientation of trade was a compelling reason for Cuba to search for and maximize comparative advantages in new markets. Cuba's pattern of international insertion has transformed radically from an essentially sugar-based economy, with sugar accounting for 73 percent of total exports in 1990, to one specializing in services, which registered 72.8 percent in 2009 (fig. 3.3).

Beginning in the early 1990s, sugar production was severely hit by a drop in international market prices; a lack of external financing; adverse weather, including both an intense drought and hurricanes; lower sugarcane yields; and undercapitalization of the whole industry. These factors combined to cut production in half by the end of the decade, from 8.1 million tons (1989) to 3.9

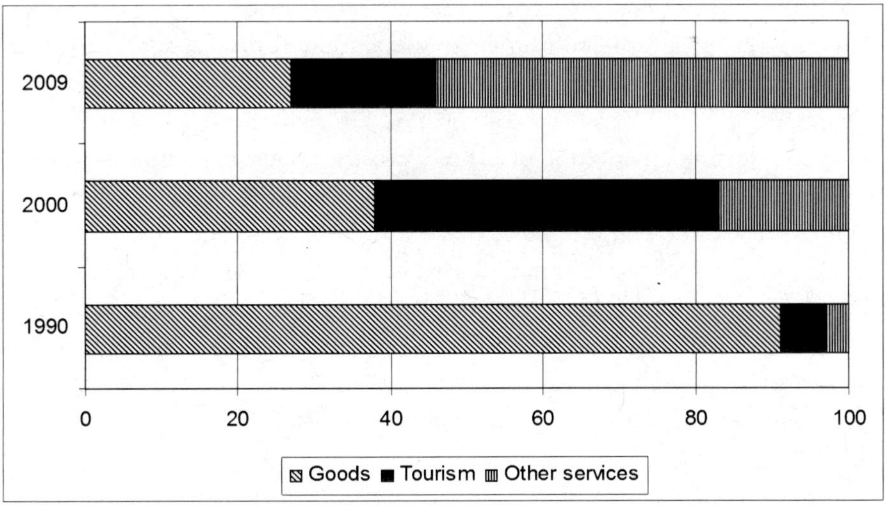

Figure 3.3. Percentages of Cuban exports of goods and services, 1990–2009. *Sources:* ONE, *Anuario Estadístico de Cuba* (Havana: ONE, 2005, 2010).

million tons (2000). Beginning in 2002 the government implemented various measures to increase the efficiency of the industry: closing 45 percent of sugar mills; converting 60 percent of sugarcane fields by area to other crops or livestock; diversifying the production of sugar by-products and derivatives; and streamlining the support industry, agricultural machinery, and other facilities.[36] Despite these efforts, production has continued to decline, dropping to barely 1.4 million tons in 2008.[37]

During the Special Period Cuba succeeded in inserting itself into the healthy growth of Caribbean tourism (see chapters 9 and 10). Fundamental to this success was the Island's bounty of beautiful locations, which were developed for tourism both rapidly and sensitively. Cuba also extended its tourist base by taking advantage of its skilled workforce to host scientific conferences and offer medical tourism. External earnings in this sector grew at an average annual rate of 9.5 percent between 1990 and 2009. This made Cuba the third-most-popular tourist destination among the Caribbean islands, surpassed only by Puerto Rico and the Dominican Republic. Tourism was Cuba's largest source of foreign revenue between 1998 and 2003. This growth required a significant domestic investment to increase Cuba's hotel capacity and associated infrastructure, such as transportation, communication, restaurants, and so on. Tourism was also one of the main sectors for IEAs, not only as a source of capital but equally to advertise Cuba as a destination in the tourism markets of the sending countries.

It must be emphasized that Cuba's tourism revenues were achieved without access to the U.S. market, the main source of Caribbean tourists. Only a very small percentage of the total U.S. population is permitted to travel to Cuba. In 2009, 65 percent of foreign tourists to Cuba came from Canada, the United Kingdom, Spain, Italy, Germany, France, and Mexico.[38]

Beginning in 2004 a second shift occurred in the structure of total exports, following the implementation of the ALBA agreements. Earnings from all services other than tourism recorded a more-than-sevenfold increase from 2003 to 2009, rising from 845.4 million to 6,028.2 million pesos. These other services include professional services linked to health care, telecommunications, sports, education, agriculture, industry, construction, culture, and informatics.[39]

During the Special Period, important structural changes also appeared in the export of goods. Mining, tobacco, and medicine products became the three main export categories, as their joint proportion increased from a mere 11.2 percent in 1990 to 55.8 percent in 2009 (table 3.3).

In mining Cuba exploited its natural advantage as possessor of one of the three largest nickel reserves in the world, making substantial investments to expand nickel production capacity. A joint venture with Canada's Sherritt International, in which Cuba owns 50 percent of shares, created a vertical chain of production, processing, and marketing of nickel. In 1996 the pre-crisis production level of 53,700 tons in 1989 was surpassed. Since 2000 production has remained above 70,000 tons,[40] despite wide fluctuations in the market price from less than $5 per pound to a peak of almost $25 per pound.

The expansion of health-related products, such as medicines and professional instruments, was enabled by Cuba's accomplishments in the biomedical field, including the creation of a research-production-marketing infrastructure. In 2008, forty Cuban products reached sixty-two countries. These included vaccines against tropical diseases such as hepatitis B, meningitis B, Leptospira, salmonella, H. influenza, typhoid fever, and cholera; medicines such as recombinant streptokinase, interferon, epidermal growth factor, Ateromixol, and monoclonal antibodies; diagnostic systems, kits, and equipment; gene therapy; and neuroscience equipment.[41] ALBA agreements were instrumental in boosting these exports in support of health campaigns initiated in many member countries. Thus, from 2000 to 2009 the annual average growth of medicine

Table 3.3. Percentages of exports of goods, 1990–2009

Group	1990	1993	2000	2009
Sugar	79.7	56.2	26.7	7.5
Tobacco and manufactured items	2.1	5.4	6.9	7.4
Minerals	7.5	15.5	36.9	30.3
Medicines and pharmaceuticals	1.6	5.7	2.0	18.1
Professional instruments and equipment	0.0	0.1	0.0	1.4

Sources: Based on ONE, *Anuario Estadístico de Cuba,* various years.

exports was 31.6 percent, while the increase in exports of professional instruments, mainly medical equipment, was 46.4 percent. As a result of this growth these groups came to rank second and fifth, respectively, in the Island's external sales of goods in 2009 (table 3.3).

In brief, Cuba's gradual adaptation to the demands of new markets has slowly restored the quantitative value of pre-crisis exports. Notable growth occurred in the middle of the first decade of the 2000s as the fruit of a decade of conscious efforts to transform the external sector, efforts that stalled recently only because of the world financial and economic crisis. By 2007 exports reached a value of 11.9 billion pesos, nearly doubling the all-time pre-crisis high of 6.5 billion pesos in 1985 (see fig. 3.1). Qualitatively, in less than twenty years the Cuban economy radically transformed itself. Its traditional export model specialized in basic products, mainly sugar. Its new export model is one where humanity, the most valuable and developed asset in the revolutionary process, plays an ever-increasing role, both in connection with natural resources via tourism and in other nurtured sectors such as health care, education, and sports. The overall dynamic is favorable growth in the value of exports.

Imports

The structure of imports was adjusted to support the process of restructuring the entire economy and the priorities set in the economic recovery plans initiated in 1990. As mentioned, during the severe economic contraction of 1990–93 foodstuffs and fuels were prioritized, and these two groups constituted 60 percent of foreign purchases. The machinery and equipment group suffered the most severe reduction in imports, dropping from 2,718 million pesos in 1990 to 244 million pesos in 1993, while imports of supplies and raw materials were also considerably reduced.[42] These cutbacks dramatically compromised the country's use, replacement, and expansion of its productive capacity (table 3.4).

Table 3.4. Imports by selected groups, 1990–2009 (%)

	Structure					Increase	
	1990	1993	2004	2008	2009	1990–93	2004–9
Foodstuffs and oils	12.1	24.5	19.7	16.6	17.7	-50.9	44.5
Fuels and lubricants	27.3	35.8	23.6	32.0	29.7	-64.5	102.1
Chemical and related items	5.7	8.2	9.6	8.3	9.2	-61.0	53.8
Manufactured products	11.6	8.6	12.2	10.9	11.8	-69.9	54.8
Machinery and transportation equipment	36.7	12.2	21.5	22.2	20.0	-91.0	49.2
Assorted manufactures	3.3	0.9	10.0	7.0	8.3	-92.4	32.8
Total						-72.9	60.2

Source: Based on ONE, *Anuario Estadístico de Cuba,* various years.

During the rapid recovery of import capacity from 2004 on, the foodstuffs and fuels groups continued to constitute more than 40 percent of total imports. For fuels, the increase in international prices was the central reason for that group's continued high contribution to total imports, despite successful strategic programs to develop national energy sources and conserve energy nationwide.[43] These efforts enabled a two-thirds reduction in the volume of crude oil imports, from 6.3 million tons in 1990 to around 2 million tons in 2005.[44] Otherwise, energy import expenditures would have been significantly higher. The agricultural sector, in contrast, was marked by erratic performance. Very few products managed to match their pre-crisis levels, which had an unfavorable impact on the balance-of-trade gap. The value of food imports increased 116 percent in the 1990–2009 period, and their proportion of total imports increased from 12.1 to 17.7 percent.

Imports of assorted manufactures also increased considerably in value, from 242.6 million pesos in 1990 to 736.0 million pesos in 2009, reflecting a basic problem common to much of the Cuban economy during the recovery. Most manufactured goods—such as garments, footwear, household and office supplies, furniture, and the like—were being produced in Cuba, but not in the quantities required to support the ongoing economic recovery. The result was that increased imports were necessary to maintain the recovery. This meant that, as was the case over the earlier course of the Revolution and even before that, Cuba's foreign-exchange balance during its recovery has continued to be a central factor in its domestic economic performance.

The annual value of machinery and equipment imports also increased considerably in the 2006–8 period, primarily because of the need to rehabilitate and expand the energy, transportation, communication, and water infrastructures. Adequate recapitalization of the industrial and agricultural sectors remains a major current challenge.

Impact on the Balance-of-Trade Gap

Cuba's efforts to diversify exports, capture flows of private financing, enter into regional agreements, and increase national efficiency successfully reduced the ratio of the current account deficit to GDP from 13 percent in 1990 to less than 1 percent in 2003–7 (fig. 3.4). There were even surpluses in 2004, 2005, and 2007, an unprecedented event in Cuba's economic history of chronic deficit over the last five decades.[45] As figure 3.4 shows, the primary factor in the improved current account balance from 2000 through 2007 has been the rapid increase in the export of services.

In 2008 the balance of payments took a turn for the worse as the result of a combination of two factors. First, the world economic crisis began to strongly

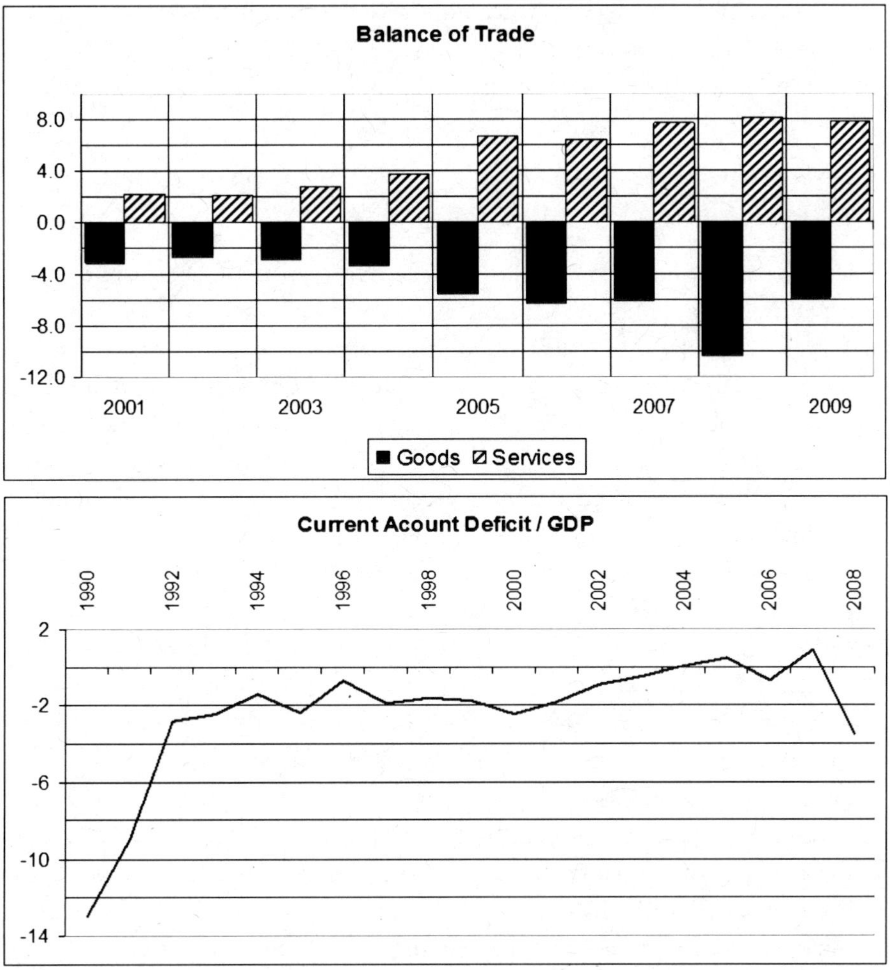

Figure 3.4. Balance of trade (billions of Pesos) and deficit-to-GDP ratio (%). *Sources:* Based on CEPAL, *La economía cubana: Reformas estructurales y desempeño en los noventa,* 1st ed. (Mexico City: Fondo de Cultura Económica, 1997); ONE, *Anuario Estadístico de Cuba* (Havana: ONE, 2006 and 2010); and Jesús García, "La economía cubana a inicios del siglo XXI, desafíos y oportunidades de la globalización," *Estudios y Perspectivas,* no. 32 (Mexico City: CEPAL, 2004).

affect Cuba through the fall in market prices for a number of its key exports, the rising costs of food imports, and the contraction of credit, among other effects. Second, Cuba was hit by three major hurricanes in barely two months, causing losses of $9.722 billion, or about 21 percent of Cuba's GDP. The effects were so immediate and severe that Cuba even had to temporarily suspend some of its debt repayments.

Cuba's response to this conjunction of problems was strongly proactive. Among other measures, it renegotiated its debts with its principal creditors, guaranteed financial resources for its export sectors in order to comply with its export contracts, deepened its import substitution process, and revised and prioritized its investment programs. These measures allowed the Island to maintain a positive balance of trade through the difficult year of 2009, and thus limit the downturn in the current account (shown in fig. 3.4).

Looking Forward

The Cuban external sector presently faces a dual challenge. On the one hand it must address the immediate effects of the world financial and economic crisis that was in full force by 2009 and almost certainly will continue for several more years. On the other, it must continue combating medium- and long-term structural problems, the topic of this chapter and an area where the country had made important progress by 2007. Both of these issues have been given high priority in Cuba's economic policymaking. Currency, planning, investment, finance, and trade measures have been implemented with a view to promoting the efficient management and use of external resources, from the signing of contracts to the payments. The top priority is to work to maintain the positive balance of trade, and then beyond that to return the current account to a surplus.

One of the most important structural problems still to be resolved in the country's current account is the high share of food and fuel imports, whose joint percentage increased to 47.4 percent in 2009 (see table 3.4). Only by reducing these percentages can the country afford increases in other lines of imports necessary to sustain and expand the economy. To that end, the Energy Revolution, started in 2005, has promoted conservation and rational use of traditional energy sources and the introduction of renewable sources.

In 2007 Cuba initiated a program to identify the import lines with immediate potential for domestic substitution, along with the investments necessary to carry out these substitutions. Particular attention was given to the agricultural sector due to its strategic importance for national security, the projected medium-term increases in agricultural prices on the international market, and its underutilized national reserves. A comprehensive change in agricultural management has been outlined, including adjusting the prices that the centers for collection and storage offer to producers; turning over land in usufruct to any individual, cooperative, or state enterprise that will guarantee production; attracting FDI; and redesigning institutional structures, among other measures. As this approach of import substitution continues, one could envision chains of production being built around the agricultural sector, such as developing the domestic capacity to produce inputs such as fertilizers, pesticides, agricultural implements, and machinery. Also, special attention should be paid to lines of use that extend from agriculture to industry, such as food packaging and processing for retail purchase.

One must bear in mind that the expansion of exports is an unavoidable necessity for financing imports and as a source of economic growth, given that the potential for import substitution is limited by the size of the national market. In this regard, extrapolating from the experience of the tourist sector, it is important that export promotion includes the creation of productive links that multiply its effect on economic growth without expanding the external trade gap. Three areas need to be considered for export development: traditional export goods and services, new export goods, and new export services.

There is room to expand the markets for a number of traditional export goods and services, such as tourism (see chapters 9 and 10), nickel, tobacco, citrus, and even sugar (especially its derivative products). Nickel continues to attract foreign capital, but citrus and sugar (despite large-scale changes to increase productivity in the early 2000s) have not reached their export potential during the Special Period.

The most promising new export lines of goods are biotechnological and pharmaceutical goods and medical equipment. All of these products are the fruits of Cuba's emphasis on education and human development. The development of further export lines of knowledge-based (and hence high-value-added) goods should also receive priority attention (see chapter 12). In addition, the agricultural sector has vast possibilities for potential new export goods (see chapter 11). The strong growth in international demand for fruits and vegetables in the early 2000s is one example of the potentials that exist in this largely underexploited field.

It has been the growth of services during the early 2000s (following tourism in the 1990s) that has made the greatest contribution to reducing the chronic structural problem of Cuba's current account deficit. After tourism, medical services followed by educational services have been the largest service exports. But the potential for knowledge-based service exports has barely been scratched (see chapter 12). International demand is particularly strong for a number of scientific-technical services in which Cuba has great expertise, among them information technology, environmental protection, nuclear energy, architecture, and agriculture. As with goods, development needs to be organized around the two principles of diversification of service exports to reduce the risks associated with export concentration and with promotion of high-value-added service exports.[46]

In summary, reducing the external finance gap requires the development of economic management and planning systems that, above all, are able to use existing productive potential efficiently, to promptly identify possibilities for both import substitution and export development and promotion, and to make global decisions on which of the various possibilities will yield the maximum returns on Cuba's limited investment resources.

Notes

1. Estimates based on Organización Mundial del Comercio, *Estadísticas del Comercio Internacional* (Geneva: OMC, 2007), digital version at http://www.wto.org, and ONE, *Anuario Estadístico de Cuba* (Havana: ONE, 2007).

2. Isis Mañalich, "Cuba, perfil exportador y competitividad" (Instituto Nacional de Investigaciones Económicas Working Paper, 1992).

3. As a result of U.S. pressure, Cuba was expelled from the Organization of American States in 1964, which vetoed the country's participation in the Inter-American Development Bank. That same year, Cuba withdrew from the International Monetary Fund and the World Bank, organizations where the United States has veto power.

4. Import prices were set according to the five-year average on the world market prior to the time of the transaction, and the prices of the main exports were set to compensate for any increases over time in input prices. CMEA deliberately adopted this policy to partially protect its least-developed members from the well-known historical relative deterioration of the terms of trade for exports from third-world countries. The result was that export prices were usually (though not always) higher than those prevailing on the international commodities markets.

5. Estimates contained in CEPAL, *La economía cubana: Reformas estructurales y desempeño en los noventa*, 1st ed. (Mexico City: Fondo de Cultura Económica, 1997).

6. Nancy Quiñones and Isis Mañalich, "Sustitución de importaciones un desafío impostergable," in *42 Aniversario de los Estudios Económicos.* Digital publication (Havana: Universidad de la Habana, 2004).

7. CEPAL, *La economía cubana: Reformas estructurales y desempeño en los noventa*, 2nd ed. (Mexico City: Fondo de Cultura Económica, 2000).

8. Ibid.

9. MINREX, *Cuba's Report to the UN Secretary General on General Assembly Resolution 57/11* (Havana: MINREX, 2003).

10. Alejandro Aguilar, "La política de hostilidad de los Estados Unidos contra Cuba: El bloqueo económico, comercial y financiero" (INIE Working Paper, 2008).

11. Alfredo González, "El sistema de planificación y circulación monetaria dual en la etapa actual" (mimeograph, 2004).

12. Jesús García, "La economía cubana a inicios del siglo XXI, desafíos y oportunidades de la globalización," *Estudios y Perspectivas* No. 32 (Mexico City: CEPAL, 2004).

13. In addition, neoliberalism allows incentives for FDI such as debt capitalization and privatizations that are inconsistent with the Cuban economy and its goals.

14. This act repealed the previous law regulating foreign investment, Decree-Law No. 50 of 1982.

15. For example, the Mines Act No. 76 of 1994 regulates any temporary concessions granting foreign investors rights to engage in mining activities (research, exploitation, and processing) on Cuban territory.

16. MINVEC was in charge of enforcing and overseeing government policy in this area until 2009, when its responsibilities were transferred to MINCEX.

17. As a comparison, Argentina and Brazil limit the free movement of capital via approval requirements, while Costa Rica withholds 15 percent of profits. This information is from a multimedia presentation at the Instituto Nacional de Investigaciones Económicas in 2003 by economic specialists from the *Wall Street Journal.* Their source was the Heritage Foundation's Index of Economic Freedom from that year. The current index is available at www.heritage.org/index.

18. As a comparison, Argentina prohibits shipbuilding, fisheries, nuclear energy, and real estate in certain areas. Brazil excludes the internal transportation of passengers, public services, and industries considered "strategic." Mexico limits oil, hydrocarbons, petrochemicals, electricity, nuclear energy, radioactive materials, telecommunications, and postal service. Chile sets restrictions on the purchase of land in certain areas, fishing in exclusive areas, maritime transportation among Chilean destinations, and gas and oil reserves. Ibid.

19. The Agreements for the Promotion and Reciprocal Protection of Investments are bilateral state-to-state treaties that set forth general terms to promote and guarantee the investors' economic and legal interests when investing in the territory of the other contracting party. From 1993 to 2002 a total of sixty-two such agreements were signed with seventy-one countries. The Agreements on the Avoidance of Double Taxation avoid the harmful effects of double taxation on the trade in goods and services and on the movements of capital, technology, and people. From 1999 to 2003 such agreements were signed with eleven countries. Cámara de Comercio de la República de Cuba, "Inversión extranjera: Por el desarrollo económico social," *Cuba Foreign Trade* No. 3 (2007).

20. MINVEC, "La Inversión Extranjera: Situación Actual y Perspectiva" (presentation at IX Reunión Nacional con Profesores de Economía Política, Habana, October 2007), and Omar Pérez, "La inversión extranjera directa en Cuba: Vientos a su favor?" (presented at the Seminario sobre Economía Cubana y Gerencia Empresarial by the Centro para el Estudio de la Economía de Cuba, July 2008).

21. CIGB, "Avances y Novedades de la Biotecnología en Cuba" (presented at the Center for Genetic Engineering and Biotechnology, 2007).

22. Argentina, Bolivia, Brazil, Colombia, Chile, Ecuador, Peru, Paraguay, Mexico, Venezuela, and Uruguay.

23. Lourdes Regueiro, "De la resistencia a las propuestas: ALBA" (presentation in the workshop La agenda hemisférica de la Segunda Administración Bush, un intercambio de visiones by the Centro de Estudios de América, Habana, April 2005).

24. Honduras used to be a member but withdrew in December 2009 under the ultraconservative government that came out of the elections conducted by the U.S.-backed government that took power in a coup in June 2009.

25. Petrocaribe is intended to coordinate the region's energy policy. Venezuela directly

supplies oil and oil by-products under favorable financial terms, with a guaranteed minimum price of $27.

26. ALBATEL encompasses the shared infrastructure of the international telecommunications system consisting of an underwater fiber-optic cable between Cuba and Venezuela and the Simón Bolívar Satellite System, the creation and development of the ALBA Internet supported by its own industrial and software production infrastructure conducive to technological sovereignty of the member countries, and the coordination of relevant national regulations.

27. These could be state-owned enterprises, private partnerships, or corporations.

28. These had been repealed as an early policy of the Revolution in 1961. They were reintroduced in 1996.

29. Susana Lee, "Balance de comercio exterior, crecieron 18% las exportaciones," *Granma*, February 28, 2004.

30. *Unnecessary intermediaries* refers to entities that do not have a necessary function in the production-trade chain and therefore contribute to excessively high commercialization margins. Some had even been created to operate only in the Cuban market. Elena Álvarez, Isis Mañalich, and Nancy Quiñones, "Impactos potenciales de la constitución de un espacio de libre comercio en los marcos de la ALADI" (Mimeograph, 2006).

31. This reflects active financial transactions, based on new financing obtained and the payments made. See ONE, *Anuario Estadístico de Cuba* (Havana: ONE, 2007, 2009).

32. Alfonso Casanova, information presented in the Taller de Sustitución de Importaciones which was held in Havana by the Asociación Nacional de Economistas de Cuba (October 2003); Luis Padrón, "Transformaciones en los mecanismos de comercio exterior" (MINCEX Working Paper, 2003).

33. Alvarez et al., "Impactos potenciales de la constitución de un espacio de libre comercio en los marcos de la ALADI."

34. ONE, *Anuario Estadístico de Cuba* (Havana: ONE, 2010). Imports peaked at 962.8 million pesos in 2008 due to Cuba's exceptional purchases of food following three major hurricanes that year.

35. Jonathan Coleman, *US Agricultural Sales to Cuba: Certain Economic Effects of US Restrictions: An Update* (Washington, D.C.: Office of Industries, USITC, 2009).

36. Juan Varela, "Cuba tiene posibilidades de ampliar, de ser necesario, su producción azucarera," *Granma*, January 12, 2004; Juan Varela, "Faltaron control y exigencia en la zafra," *Granma*, May 5, 2010.

37. ONE, *Anuario Estadístico de Cuba* (Havana: ONE, 2010).

38. Ibid.

39. Ibid.

40. Although production fell just below that figure in 2009. ONE, *Anuario Estadístico de Cuba* (Havana: ONE, 2008, 2010).

41. José Luis Rodríguez, "Una transformación singular, la biotecnología en la economía socialista cubana" (presentation at CEPAL, 2008).

42. These are subgroups of the chemicals and manufactured products groups in table 3.4.

43. Sizable investments were undertaken in energy exploration, enlargement of capacities, and adaptation of existing technologies for the use of national heavy crude. Between 1990 and 2004 crude oil extraction grew from just under 0.7 to 3.3 million tons, while natural gas production went from 33.7 to 704.2 million cubic meters. The sector's prospects improved considerably in late 2004, following the discovery of a new deposit of higher-quality oil north of Havana Province.

44. ONE, *Anuario Estadístico de Cuba* (Havana: ONE, 2006).

45. Some commentators have incorrectly asserted that Cuba's successful improvement of the current account balance in mid-decade hinged on the price of nickel. In 2007 nickel reached its highest ever average price, at more than $50,000 per ton, which was an important reason for the surplus that year. But the surpluses in 2004 and 2005 were different. While nickel prices were at times moderately good in those years, in October 2005 they dropped to a very low level of $10,000 per ton. Although nickel prices are one important factor, Cuba's current account no longer depends fundamentally on the price and production levels of a single good as it used to for sugar.

46. Isis Mañalich, "Inserción internacional de las exportaciones cubanas de bienes en el 2001–2005: Búsqueda de nuevas oportunidades" (INIE Working Paper, 2007); Nieves Pico, "Tendencias, actores, modos de suministro y sectores dinámicos del comercio internacional de servicios: En busca de oportunidades de inserción" (INIE Working Paper, 2007).

4

Medium- and Long-Range Planning in Cuba

Historical Evolution and Future Prospects

ELENA ÁLVAREZ GONZÁLEZ

As Commander Ernesto "Ché" Guevara underscored more than forty years ago, "centralized planning is the way of being of a socialist society, its defining category and the point where man's consciousness eventually manages to synthesize and channel the economy towards its goal: the full liberation of human beings in the frame of a communist society."[1] The objective of building a more developed society, and beyond that, one that is more just and oriented toward solidarity, necessarily entails a temporal horizon that transcends the short term. Many of these types of goals are attainable only in the medium term and after great effort. This fact lends special importance to medium- and long-range planning in socialism: a better future can be built only through systematic work beginning in the present.

A medium- and long-term perspective is necessary for achieving dynamic development through identifying socioeconomic objectives that will remove the structural deformations present in the economy and society. Such a perspective makes it possible to foresee the multiple interrelations between, and consequences of, various decisions and hence to determine the appropriate means to reach specific objectives. This is particularly true for issues that change slowly over time, such as technology, the development of scientific capabilities, the environment, and many social problems. A long-range perspective is likewise necessary in order to take into consideration the continually changing environments in which socioeconomic development plans are executed.

In examining the issue of medium- and long-range planning in revolutionary Cuba, it is important to stress that right from the beginning of the Revolution, strategic views for prospective development have always been present. This is true on both economic and social levels, whether or not these strategies were contained in formal medium- and long-range plans. For nearly fifty years strategic conceptualization has appeared in various long-range plans. Long-term strategic commitments to education and health care have been essential pillars of Cuba's socioeconomic development. The long-term prioritization and intense development of scientific-technical capabilities in general, and the fields of biotechnology and medical sciences in particular, have similarly been essential to Cuba's social and economic transformations. Since 2000 a number of qualitatively more advanced new social development programs have been launched. These programs seek to further develop the human potential of Cuban citizens, building on the country's prior achievements in this area. For these reasons medium- and long-range planning is critically important in the Cuban socioeconomic model.

Background

The initial attempts to take a prospective view of socioeconomic development in an independent Cuba are contained in such documents as "Algunos aspectos del desarrollo económico de Cuba" (Some Aspects of Cuba's Economic Development), written in 1957 by Regino Boti and Felipe Pazos at the request of the leadership of the 26th of July Movement and released in 1959, and "Programa del Partido Socialista Popular" (Program of the People's Socialist Party), published in early 1959.[2] Then in the early months of 1959 the new revolutionary government requested that ECLAC dispatch a mission to Cuba, which arrived in May of that year. Led by the Mexican economist Juan F. Noyola, its objective was to analyze the economic situation and make projections that would form the basis of a comprehensive overview of the country's economic development potential.[3] Through his findings, Noyola, who decided to stay in Cuba after the ECLAC mission departed, made an important contribution to the prospective view of the country's development potential at the beginning of the Revolution.

The early years of the revolutionary process drew the attention of foreign specialists, who also opined on Cuba's economic prospects. A well-known example is the Polish economist Michal Kalecki, who in 1960 drew up a global projection of Cuba's development for 1961–65. Kalecki provided, albeit at a highly aggregated level, a complete model of economic development. Another example from this period is the agricultural studies of the Chilean Jacques Chonchol.

In 1961 the Central Planning Board (JUCEPLAN) began drawing up the economic plan for 1962 and the projection for the four-year period from 1962 to 1965. This became the first attempt at prospective planning by the then-incipient national planning system. The JUCEPLAN economists and Professor Charles Bettelheim independently prepared similar economic projections, with greater disaggregation by economic sectors than Kalecki had provided. The 1962–65 projection outlined development goals for all the main economic sectors, along with plans for social development in education, health care, and the construction of housing and technical networks, among other areas. In September 1962 JUCEPLAN submitted the four-year plan to the government for approval, which included the main development guideline for the national economy up to 1965, especially for the investment plan.[4]

Several factors limited the opportunities to implement these initial studies. First and foremost was the urgent need to guide the economy through a period of huge difficulties, augmented by aggression from foreign governments, and in particular to organize and consolidate the incipient state-controlled economic sector. Furthermore, the projections were weakened by a lack of valid statistics, insufficient projects to operationalize the projections, and a low level of organization and inadequate training of economic officials.

In addition to this work, in 1963 JUCEPLAN created working groups or commissions to study various aspects of the economy. Many of these issues, by their nature, required taking a medium- or long-term view. Two notable efforts were a technical-economic study of the production, importation, and utilization of commercial containers and packaging, and a study of energy development up to 1970.

In 1964, JUCEPLAN was restructured. Along with its other responsibilities, it now spearheaded the preliminary work on the 1965–70 prospective plan. For this task, both an overall working group and sector-level working groups were established within JUCEPLAN. JUCEPLAN also assigned tasks to the other bodies of the central state administration.

The papers JUCEPLAN produced as part of this preliminary planning were based on a comprehensive diagnostic analysis of the economy from 1959 to 1964, with a view to identifying the primary problems to be solved. Based on this analysis, the main development guidelines were then specified to resolve these problems. These comprehensive analyses were supplemented with sector-level studies of the sugar, cattle-raising (including cattle feed), chemical (fertilizers and sugarcane by-products), electrical, mining and metallurgy (nickel, iron, and steel), mechanical, transportation, hydraulic, and construction (including building materials) industries, and the training of qualified personnel. Ultimately, the results of the studies, including the alternatives they recommended, were used to make projections for the main economic indicators of the national economy.[5]

Because of both the organizational structure adopted and the nature of the work undertaken, these papers became the most advanced experiment in midrange planning in Cuba to that time. They were, however, still limited in both scope and consistency, which is one reason why no medium-range plan encompassing all sectors and branches of the Cuban economy was officially announced at that time.[6]

In 1966 the country restructured its national agencies, JUCEPLAN among them. Its specific functions now included "drawing up prospective medium- and long-range plans that reflected the quantitative expression of the main priorities set forth by the revolutionary government, with a view to achieving sustainable development in the national economy."[7] In April 1966, JUCEPLAN led the development of the prospective plan through 1970. This involved the evaluation of the different branch-specific development guidelines then in existence, in order to build a national model that would provide the main directions for the economic development of the country.

At this time, an important element of prospective planning associated with economic research was the establishment of the Economic Research Teams of the Commander-in-Chief and the Research Teams of the University of Havana. Both of these groups played important roles in economic research, preparing a large number of applied research projects and projections in various branches of the economy, especially in the agricultural and livestock sector.

It is important to understand the degree of conceptual maturity in planning, particularly long-range planning, that had emerged in the country by this time. As stated in the paper Cuban representatives presented at the 1968 Seminar on Administrative Aspects of the Implementation of Development Plans held in Santiago de Chile,

> planning must be viewed as an integral part of the process of management that will transform the current society. Further, it must be taken into consideration that in order for the transformation process to be carried out with appropriate efficiency it must not constitute a simple series of tactical moves, but rather decisions on the immediate issues must fall within a general strategy that regulates the development of the process with a quite broad temporal horizon. . . .
>
> . . . If we agree that the main objective of long-range planning is to contribute to delineating the development strategy such that actions taken in the short term may effectively bring about the desired structural change in society, then it is impossible to conceptualize that planning activity unfolding in a neat and airtight fashion in an ivory tower, isolated from everyday events and decision-making centers. In that regard, long-range planning must be thought of as one of the mechanisms available to the Management System for its adequate operation and, therefore, as an integral part of a more complex whole that constitutes the Management System.[8]

In 1968, prospective planning efforts in Cuba were organized around very distinct features. The focus was

> to organize a work system based not on a disaggregated plan covering all the economy, but on the comprehensive study by the Central Planning Board of a rather large number of "programs" that constitute the most dynamic activities of the Cuban economy. Although the ultimate responsibility for these studies lies with JUCEPLAN, these involve . . . various entities and companies, as well as the Economic Research Teams of the University of Havana. The programs not only have a sector-wide content, but they also contain issues pertaining to macroeconomics, international economic relations, research, information automation, etc.[9]

This conception was intended to ensure that the midrange plans would not develop in isolation from the economic decision-making centers, and hence that they would have an operational content. For this reason no formal medium- or long-range plans for the entire economy were developed at that time. Nevertheless, there was a clearly defined development strategy, and a number of projections and projects in the main branches of the economy that could guide operational decisions related to that strategy.

The national goal of harvesting ten million tons of sugar in 1970 mobilized all of the country's efforts and resources toward that end, to the detriment of other activities. At the end of 1970, immediately following the country's failure to achieve this goal, a profound analysis of the national situation was completed, with important consequences for the field of planning. Following a review of JUCEPLAN's functions, it reassumed responsibility for preparing macroeconomic indicators and midrange plans and reactivated the Prospective Planning Unit created in 1969 to prepare the economic forecast through 1975. This comprehensive planning was instrumental in initiating talks with GOSPLAN (the State Planning Committee of the former USSR) at the end of 1970. These talks subsequently led to five-year agreements through 1975 between the two countries on trade (including establishing prices), investment credits, and debt settlement. Based on the same projections, similar trade agreements were also signed with the (former) German Democratic Republic and Czechoslovakia, and with Bulgaria. These agreements preceded what would eventually become the Coordination of Plans within CMEA.

The CMEA Era

In July 1972 Cuba entered CMEA, which was composed of the countries of the former socialist community. Its admission into CMEA entailed definite changes in the way medium- and long-range planning was undertaken, because these types of plans were the main tool member countries used to manage their economic coordination and integration. Since planned development took place somewhat differently within each country, coordination of national development plans was crucial for optimal development across the community as a whole.

CMEA countries had the latitude to coordinate aspects of common interest in their long-range economic plans or strategies either multilaterally with all or several countries in the community or bilaterally with a single country. Multilateral coordination in economic specialization and production was accomplished through the so-called Specific Long-Term Cooperation Programs in various fields. Notable areas of cooperation were energy, fuels and raw materials, manufacturing of machinery, consumer goods, the agriculture and food industries, transportation, and communication. Also established were integrated specialization programs, coordinated regulatory mechanisms for trade—such as principles for setting export prices, payment systems, and liquidation of accounts—and the Comprehensive Program on Scientific-Technical Progress. Multilateral long-term agreements were later formalized through bilateral arrangements. In the bilateral arena, prospective planning was undertaken to prepare Long-Term Cooperative Programs and Coordination of Five-Year Plans. In Cuba, the five-year and long-range plans became hallmarks of its ties with CMEA member countries. The agreements that were concluded contained specific procedures and time frames, all in the framework of the community.

Five-Year Plans and the Coordination of Plans

Given that the Cuban economy is very open, and that development was now conceived of within the framework of the International Socialist Division of Labor and with external collaboration, the Coordination of Plans became an essential pillar of internal five-year planning activities. The overall process of preparing five-year plans then became an "iterative" procedure of establishing national plans and aligning them with the coordinated plans through bilateral negotiations with each country.

This medium-term international coordination, in turn, was based on strategic lines and agreements on long-range plans or programs among the CMEA countries. Cuba, however, did not have an operational long-range strategy when it joined CMEA, merely the previously mentioned generic long-term goals. The work to develop operational long-range strategic plans was not undertaken until the late 1970s, as will be discussed below. Once that system was operational, JUCEPLAN would receive guidelines from the Cuban Communist Party for the development of a five-year plan that would align with Cuba's long-term goals. Then, once JUCEPLAN elaborated the main objectives of the national plan, they were submitted to and discussed at the Communist Party Congress.

In this context, the work of midrange domestic planning resumed in the country. In late 1972, the Politburo of Cuba's Communist Party adopted a resolution to draw up, by 1973, an economic development plan for 1976–80. This ushered in a new stage in which planning both formally and in practice assumed a much greater role.

JUCEPLAN had to start work on the first five-year plan without any guidelines or regulations from higher bodies, since, as noted, Cuba did not then have long-range strategic plans to provide such guidance. Therefore, JUCEPLAN drew up a global model that served as a starting point and, to some extent, as training for the work ahead.

Dr. Osvaldo Dorticós Torrado, then president of the Republic and of the Central Planning Board, said of this beginning:

> Obviously, under normal conditions and in the future, the preparation of a plan of this nature should always be preceded by general development guidelines issued by the leadership of the Party. But as things are now, the Politburo does not have what it needs to issue concrete guidelines. For the task we are facing of constructing a plan, the Planning Board itself will have to, based on some very general concepts that have been outlined and some development paths that are pretty clear, develop appropriate ideas. We will consult with the Politburo to define the development concepts, as we will have to simultaneously create and implement the general development concepts, the general development guidelines, and the concrete and specific tasks involved in preparing the plan.
>
> . . . Our international relations in CMEA also require that we do this. But even aside from our membership in CMEA, it would have been necessary to have done this. It was not possible to continue working only on annual plans. I think it was impossible to have done otherwise.[10]

The process of preparing the five-year plans improved over time. Beginning with the 1976–80 plan, they contained extensive details on targeted production levels, investment projects and the amount to be invested by component, export and import figures, material balance accounts, projections for employment and qualified labor, global indicators, and estimates of the balance of payments. By the 1981–85 and 1986–90 plans JUCEPLAN was able to draw up a general framework, later approved by the government, for preliminary discussions on the Coordination of Plans with other CMEA countries. For

1986–90 this framework was grounded in a long-range plan, which had been under development since 1978.

The goal of these five-year plans was to procure as many resources as possible for economic development. This involved negotiating with the CMEA countries to secure fair prices for exports, on that basis obtaining the largest possible volumes of imports and investment resources, and seeking financial solutions for any resulting imbalances. The agreements in the Coordination of Plans guaranteed nearly 85 percent of imports and more than 80 percent of investments and provided market and price guarantees for around 80 percent of exports. Resources purchased in freely convertible currencies had a secondary, although very important, role, particularly in closing certain productive processes and chains. All these factors lent a high degree of certainty to the preparation of the midrange plan and security for the national economic development plans.

As mentioned, the five-year plans were prepared in several stages in an iterative process in which the closure elements, or pivotal elements on which completion of the plan depended, were external. This was expressed in what was obtained in the Coordination of Plans with CMEA countries, as well as in the hard-currency financial projection. The general procedure was as follows:

1. Production projections for major export products and preparation of material balance accounts
2. Analysis and projection of external factors, such as prices, markets, agreements with other countries, and external financial commitments, such as debt service payments
3. Estimation of external revenues and consequently of import capability
4. Projection of activity levels of the most important branches of the economy and preparation of material balance accounts
5. Specification of import demands, including investments
6. Analysis of the external financial balance, given the current demand for imports and investments
7. Adjustment of the projection accordingly

In essence the planning process just outlined involved adapting the national economy's needs and possible performance parameters to the needs and capabilities of the external sector. For example, requirements were set for the various productive branches in order to meet the quality standards as well as the desired volume and variety demanded by foreign markets. Conversely, economic development, the introduction of new products, and improvement in the standard of living demanded that the external sector deliver to Cuba certain quantities of raw materials, fuels, equipment, and other items, with specified deadlines and standards of quality.

The existence of five-year plans with high degrees of guaranteed supplies and demands was determinative for annual planning. Thus, in essence, the annual plan was a yearly correction of the goals contained in the five-year plan, based on evaluating the possibilities of honoring both Cuba's and its trading partners' external commitments. Again the biggest constraint, on which adjustments usually pivoted, was the availability of hard currency.

It should be noted that one of the major limitations throughout the entire five-year planning process was the minor involvement of the enterprise structures. This issue will be returned to below, as it is an important topic in the developing of the new planning models in Cuba today.

As described, the Coordination of Plans among CMEA member countries were developed multilaterally for issues of common interest. Bilateral planning was done for issues of mutual interest to two specific countries and, most importantly, to detail and finalize multilateral agreements. The Coordination of Bilateral Plans involved examining and discussing the following issues:

- Production specialization and cooperation
- Investment objectives in the various branches where cooperation would occur
- Nomenclature, volumes, and delivery deadlines for supplies of goods and services
- Terms of trade for those supplies (price-setting formulas, forms of financing, and other economic issues)
- Handling of payment imbalances
- Aspects of scientific-technical cooperation

These issues were formalized in protocols signed by the leaders of the central planning bodies of both countries. Afterward, these would take the form of intergovernmental agreements signed by the relevant agencies (trade agreements, price agreements, government credit agreements, and so on).

Overall, the coordinated plans sought to establish efficient and stable economic structures based on the advantages that integration offered. These plans were designed to be instrumental in enhancing the effectiveness of social production and maximizing the use of material, financial, and labor resources available in the member countries. In the particular case of Cuba, the Coordination of Plans took into consideration the Island's degree of economic development relative to the other member countries and emphasized those aspects that would contribute to Cuba's catching up to their levels of development.

The central planning body in each country was in charge of organizing, managing, implementing, and overseeing the whole process of producing the Coordination of Plans. In each country, the planning bodies either made or endorsed all decisions. The general procedure followed in Cuba was as follows. The Coordination of Plans process regularly started two and a half years prior to the period set for coordination. The deadlines, terms of the process, and general instructions for all member countries were established through a program approved by the Session (the highest body of CMEA).

The CMEA planning process was preceded in Cuba by a period of intense domestic diagnoses, forecasts, and preparations for negotiations. To carry out the tasks necessary for the coordination of plans, working groups were established, generally composed of representatives of branches or groups of the economy, presided over by officials from the central planning bodies. Entities concerned with specific industries, foreign trade, supplies, and whatever else might be relevant participated as appropriate. In successive group meetings participants would define and specify the issues of common interest and eliminate irrelevant ones. As the processes in the Coordination of Plans became operational, responsibilities were established that continued from one period to the next. These working, or branch, groups were overseen by central groups (also called global groups) led by vice-presidents of the central planning bodies and made up of representatives of national bodies (foreign trade, economic cooperation, technical-material supply, domestic trade, and the Central Bank). The central group summarized and assessed the recommendations of the branch groups, determining the final proposals for submission to the presidents of the central planning bodies. Finally, the presidents endorsed the proposals and signed the final protocols.

In brief, this process can be characterized as a series of very intense negotiations whose main features were a high degree of centralization of decision making and a detailed inventorying of the products to be exchanged and the investments to be undertaken. This detail facilitated the subsequent completion of trade agreements, five-year credits, and annual allotments of guaranteed imports. In Cuba's case the number of detailed current import items rapidly expanded in subsequent five-year periods, from more than 400 items in 1976–80, to more than 900 items in 1981–85, and to more than 1,100 items in 1986–90.[11]

Major criticisms of this process included that it was rigid, slow, and bureaucratic. A major limitation was that the entire five-year planning process was almost entirely carried out by planning agencies, with very limited involvement of the actual primary productive links (production or consumption enterprises).

Cuba's participation in the Coordination of Plans deepened in each successive five-year period from 1976–80 to 1981–85 and 1986–90. The preliminary work for the 1991–95 period was complicated by an extensive restructuring of

CMEA that began in late 1986. These changes were intended to improve the mechanisms of cooperation and integration. An "intensive model of cooperation" was proposed, in which the center of gravity was to shift from the macro (national government) level to the micro level of productive enterprises, trusts, cooperatives, and the like. Direct contact among producers was now viewed as key to the development of specialization and cooperation among CMEA member countries. This development necessitated a corresponding change in many economic mechanisms, including planning, because the centralized methods of the preceding model could not connect thousands of producers.[12] But that restructuring became irrelevant, and Cuba's work on the 1991–95 plan was terminated early on when CMEA disintegrated and socialism rapidly dissolved, first in Eastern Europe and shortly thereafter in the former USSR.

Long-Range Planning

Long-range planning—for ten-, fifteen-, or twenty-year spans—was mainly programmatic in nature and constituted one of the basic ways that the international socialist division of labor was organized. The long-range plans and associated guidelines were intended to provide the framework for both the five-year planning tasks and the international Coordination of Plans. Thus, long-term planning must be understood as one element in a system of long-, medium-, and short-range time horizons.

Preparing a long-range plan requires engaging in intense prior analysis and diagnosis and preparing forecasts, all for use in international negotiations over the Coordination of Plans. Within each country, long-range planning was generally the basis for the Programs of the Communist Parties, whose temporal horizon was generally between ten and fifteen years.

In Cuba, long-range planning—that extending more than five years in the future—was initiated in 1976 with the establishment of the National Institute for Economic Research (INIE), which was charged with creating a socioeconomic development strategy through the year 2000. INIE's first task in preparing this report was to analyze the Cuban economy, particularly its evolution from the victory of the Revolution to 1975. The main purpose of this analysis was to identify the central problems of the economy post-1959 that remained to be resolved and to determine the trends and specifics of economic development since then that could influence any planned future development.[13] This analytical and diagnostic work took nearly two years to complete, and by 1978 the foundation was in place to complete the first macroeconomic forecast through 2000.

In the first half of 1978 INIE drew up this national forecast and, based on its findings, published preliminary recommendations about objectives of and premises for prospective economic development. Simultaneously, INIE formulated organizational and methodological principles intended to govern subsequent strategic (that is, long-range) planning. Both the preliminary recommendations and methodological principles were examined and approved at a joint meeting of the Politburo and the Executive Committee of the Council of Ministers on July 20, 1978, thus marking the nationwide commencement of strategic planning.[14]

The Joint Resolution of the Politburo and the Executive Committee opened by acknowledging that despite Cuba's efforts, the country had not completely overcome the economic problems stemming from underdevelopment. It further stated that continued advancement of the socialist revolution required accelerated economic development and profound social and economic transformations, which were only "possible to achieve fully in the framework of long-range prospective planning." Furthermore, "outlining the socioeconomic development objectives, and specifying and fleshing out the program of action and the possible solutions to development problems is the essence of a prospective socioeconomic development strategy, as the first phase in creating a long-range prospective plan."[15]

The resolution recognized that deepening Cuba's integration into CMEA was a decisive factor in its prospective economic development and that a task of such magnitude required coordinated efforts from all state bodies. JUCEPLAN was assigned to manage, organize, and oversee the work, as well as to synthesize the findings.[16]

Importantly, the work that started in 1978 relied on solid conceptual and methodological guidelines, published by the advisory services and presented to the working commissions that conducted the different studies. Particularly interesting were those aspects relating to the initial description of the problems, the scope of the forecasts, the premises of the forecasts, and the projection of variants, which used the most advanced techniques known at that time.[17]

The long-range planning went through several stages:

- 1978–80: Large-scale specific forecasts were prepared by forty-four inter-ministerial commissions. This made it possible to gather and organize numerous ideas on prospective development and served as the basis for the programmatic guidelines on development through the year 2000 adopted at the Second Congress of the Cuban Communist Party in December 1980. However, it was not possible to achieve internal conformity and compatibility of all these studies.
- 1980–mid-1982: The different specific forecasts were integrated and

aligned into an integral forecast, with appropriate internal compatibility, realism, and feasibility, to serve as the basis for subsequent prospective planning tasks.[18]

- Mid-1982–mid-1984: With regard to the external economy, an overall development scheme was drawn up between Cuba and the former USSR and, subsequently, long-term cooperation programs with the USSR and the rest of CMEA were developed. Those programs were intended to serve as the basis for the Coordination of Plans for 1986–90 and subsequent years. Relevant to the internal economy, existing data were updated and an institutional strategy was formulated for preparing a prospective plan to the year 2000. The first draft of that plan was submitted for consideration to the country's senior management in mid-1984.
- Mid-1984–late 1986: Different bodies received instructions to build on their previous prospective planning efforts. In fact, however, the greatest efforts focused on the coordination of Five-Year Plans and on finalizing negotiations on long-term programs with CMEA countries. At the same time, internal events in late 1984 directed increased emphasis to planning for the 1986–90 period and led to the strategic decisions being postponed, because the strategic concepts themselves were largely dependent on current events and on short-term changes in the upcoming 1986–90 period.[19]
- Late 1986–1989: The so-called restructuring of CMEA started in late 1986, affecting Cuba's ongoing planning concepts and methods. At the multinational level this triggered a review of the concepts of integration and the methods of achieving it, including planning. Within Cuba, the rectification process was under way and hard-currency shortages heightened financial tensions. All these events led to a substantial transformation in long-range planning, carried out in a centralized fashion with no involvement of the productive entities. This planning focused on assessing the possible impacts of a change in Cuba's external conditions, based on the events unfolding in the former socialist countries, rather than on updating the existing prospective plan. The work done at INIE in this period provided a comprehensive view of the challenges ahead for the Cuban economy in the 1990s. This turned out to be very important, because when complex decisions suddenly had to be made in the early 1990s, the prerequisite analysis already existed for use in decision making.

First and foremost, conceptually, Cuba's socioeconomic development strategy consisted of determining the country's social, economic, and scientific-technical development objectives and prospective policies that would support each of these. Second, it was focused on specifying the program of action that would resolve the problems of development. Because the strategy constituted a system of ideas, objectives, and measures for the conscious transformation of society, it was regarded as a category of planning and, in particular, of prospective planning. Conceptually, it was recognized that the strategy and prospective plan were inextricably linked and that the relationship between the two was similar to the dialectical link between form and content. The strategy was the essence of the prospective plan and the basis upon which it was designed. The prospective plan was the rationally structured expression of the objectives and concrete benchmarks.[20]

In fact, in the mid-1980s Cuba came close to achieving a structured planning system following the steps outlined in figure 4.1. The intent was to conduct a five-year review of the long-term plan and advance its horizon by five years. The demise of socialism in Europe and the dissolution of CMEA prevented the consolidation of this system.

In terms of the external economy, long-range planning was materialized with the former CMEA countries through bilaterally agreed-on long-term development programs for economic and scientific-technical cooperation up to the year 2000. This planning was programmatic in nature and constituted the framework, or point of reference, for the Coordination of Plans. This coordination was preceded by active discussions and negotiations with these countries to obtain feedback for the preparation of the strategy and the pro-

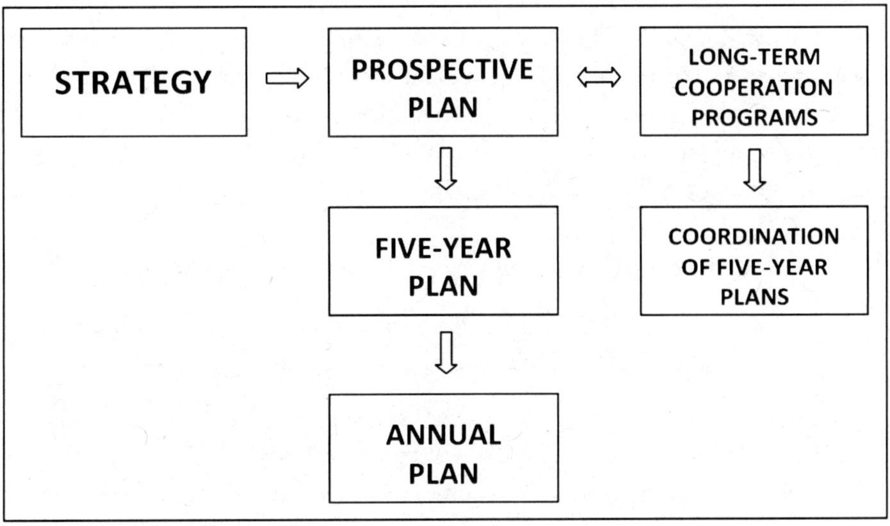

Figure 4.1. Cuba's intended planning process.

spective plan. Cuba and the USSR discussed an overall concept of prospective development in the early 1980s, as a decisive element for the realization of the domestic strategy and a preparatory step for formulating the bilateral long-term program. The program, signed in October 1984, was updated in light of the CMEA restructuring, and a new programmatic document was drawn up: "Conception of the Development of the Foreign Economic Relations between the Republic of Cuba and the USSR for 15–20 Years."

At the international level, negotiations were under way from the time of Cuba's admission into CMEA to define the country's economic specializations. These were to take advantage of existing comparative advantages and favor development by guaranteeing markets, prices, financing, and supplies. Agreements were eventually hammered out on nickel, citrus, and sugar within the framework of the "Specific Programs of Long-Term Cooperation" documents; these agreements were subsequently finalized on bilateral bases.

As part of the restructuring of CMEA in 1986, the cooperation policy toward its least-developed countries (Vietnam, Cuba, and Mongolia) was reviewed. The findings indicated that their integration into CMEA was slow and, hence, that their progress in attaining the same level of development as the rest of the CMEA countries was being hindered. Accordingly, the new document titled "Collective Concept of the International Socialist Division of Labor" presented procedures to expedite the development of these countries. Specifically, "Special Integral Programs of Multilateral Collaboration of the European Member Countries of CMEA with Vietnam, Cuba, and Mongolia" was drawn up to effect these procedures. Cuba's program was signed in 1988, but that was too late to have any effect.

One last aspect of long-range planning worth noting is the Overall Comprehensive Transportation Development Scheme. This was drawn up with the assistance of the Institute for Integral Transportation Problems, which was attached to GOSPLAN in the USSR. Established by 1972 and operating for more than fifteen years, it provided a valuable methodological and analytical basis for Cuba's work in this field, as well as important training for specialists.

Medium- and Long-Range Planning in the 1990s and 2000s

The demise of CMEA triggered a series of events that directly affected the conditions for planning in Cuba. The primary ones were as follows:

- Loss of the external conditions that supported the plans (export markets, negotiated prices, imported supplies, credits)
- Severe economic crisis. The plunge in the levels of economic activity until 1993 prevented the stable assurance of the annual plans. Opera-

tional mechanisms had to be established to respond rapidly to new problems that unexpectedly emerged almost daily.

- Changes in the domestic economic policy and in the economy's operational mechanisms that had to be established to manage the crisis

Under these circumstances where many pressing problems had to be addressed immediately, long-range planning had to be postponed for some time. Some believed it was almost impossible to forecast the future in such a difficult and hostile environment and in the face of such great uncertainty. But as the economic transformations put in place in the early 1990s, and more intensively after 1993, evolved, planning became not only once again possible, but necessary. However, the new situation called for a new method of overall planning that accounted for a number of changed factors:

- Increases in the margins of uncertainty
- Changes in property relations and the emergence of new forms of property with associated new economic agents (joint ventures, UBPCs, self-employed workers)
- Modifications in the forms of state property (new types of state-run enterprises, such as corporations)
- Modifications in the way the state monopoly on foreign trade was exercised and decentralization of the management of external economic relations
- Restructuring of the Bodies of the Central State Administration (OACE) with new structures and functions and greater enterprise autonomy
- Emergence of hard-currency self-financing schemes (which were gradually enlarged and evolved into hard-currency income and expenditure budgets) in light of the financial unsustainability of the system of material balances
- Changes in the allocation of resources whereby instead of resources being allocated to producers, producers accessed resources according to consumer demand, making resource utilization more efficient and obliging producers to increase their competitiveness
- Different plan-to-market correlation with expansion of private market relations including farmers' markets, cottage industries, and self-employed workers
- Legalization of the possession and circulation of hard currency, the existence of non-labor channels to obtain income (remittances), the creation of hard-currency markets, and the emergence of the dual-currency economic system

- Domestic financial cleanup process, which involved changes in the methods of management, distribution, and consumption

It made sense that these changes were first addressed in new annual plans. But a temporal horizon of one year was inadequate to address them, and the need for a midrange framework quickly became obvious. A longer-term view was required to "maintain the ability to make decisions in terms of strategy, economic policy, and the system of management."[21] Previously it had been said that five-year plans were feasible because of external guarantees. Now, precisely because those conditions had vanished, a view of the future was important for decision making.[22]

In the new conditions, a changed focus was very important for medium- and long-range planning. Such planning had to take into account numerous new factors in Cuba's internal and external economic environment:

- Loss of guaranteed supplies that had been present in the old five-year plans
- Greater uncertainty in the medium and long term
- Changes in the organizational and institutional framework
- Variety of economic agents tied to the existence of different forms of property
- Recognition that production outside economic plans is possible
- Recognition of active external restrictions, given the complexity of the world's political and economic environment and Cuba's subjugation to the U.S. blockade

The working methods that had prevailed until the late 1980s were mainly based on projections or forecasts with a "genetic" or a "normative" approach.[23] The multiplicity of changed conditions necessitated a shift to new methods appropriate to the new circumstances. Important concrete changes have occurred in various planning processes. The working principles have been modified. Frameworks are no longer used as starting points, but rather each field's potential, restrictions, and alternatives are examined to build compatible variants. The financial feasibility of branch-specific projections is subjected to analysis based on the new means of resource allocation. Sensitivity analyses are used. Organizational and institutional changes are now part of each projection. Variants are outlined in terms of possible achievements, decisions, and external factors. Strategies are formulated taking into account external factors and economic agents.[24]

At a broader conceptual level, the new principles are integrated around a methodology of scenarios, based on the concept of strategic prospects. For more than a decade now, the methodology of scenarios has been applied effectively to analyze the existing conditions in the Cuban economy. It is a proactive approach, with some degree of balance between extremes. It recognizes that there are elements of uncertainty and unpredictability, but at the same time recognizes that it is possible to use various methods to act on and design the future.[25] The methodology of scenarios is implemented internationally, with applications to the study of economic, political, and social issues and international relations. Operationally it consists of analyzing cause-effect relations for complex systems, taking into account the factors of uncertainty and alternative decisions. To that end, the strategic elements (key variables) defining a situation are determined and then combined to form different scenarios.

Strategic prospects view the future as "a product of randomness and chance, of the system's own limitations but, above all, as a result of will, desire, and ambition. In other words, the future cannot be explained only through the past. It is also conditioned by the will to change, and to control the new rules of the game that allow us to direct our future."[26]

It is useful to define some of the main concepts in the methodology of scenarios:[27]

Projection: an extrapolation into the future of a past activity or indicator

Prediction or forecast: a projection evaluated according to the probability of its occurrence

Prospect: a set of predictions constituting an overview of possible futures

Scenario: the description of a future situation together with the course of events that will enable a shift from the initial condition to that future situation

Plan: a set of compatible projections together with a description of the ways and means that are highly likely to achieve those projections (note the difference between a plan and a scenario)

The overall methodology of scenarios can be outlined as follows:

Starting point: Identify the system, namely, the phenomenon to be projected and its environment. Because the two interact, both have to be examined.

Phase 1, Diagnosis: Analyze the phenomenon in terms of trends, potentials, limits, and restrictions; economic-financial aspects; identification of agents and their behaviors; international comparisons (it is insufficient to study the phenomenon's evolution in isolation; it must be compared to others); and specification of what constitutes the seeds of change.

Phase 2, Structural Analysis: Delimit the system, identify strategic variables, and determine the links among them with a view to establishing the structure of the phenomenon in order to build a model.

Phase 3, Projection: Consider the behavior of the variables (internal and external) according to inertial trends, introduction of changes, and consideration of new trends. Calculate the financial feasibility of projections and estimate projections of the variables.

Phase 4, Strategies: Consider the environment of the phenomenon, its interactions within that environment, and the related agents to specify the most appropriate strategies.

Phase 5, Comprehensive Scenarios: Define objectives and policies, and actions to achieve them.

An important point to emphasize is that the new planning approaches involve the productive enterprises in preparing the scenarios for their industry, based in many cases on the business plans they have introduced into their operation. The current principles are perfectly suited to the new operating environment of enterprises, which are increasingly required to operate strategically, with a view to enhancing and sustaining their competitiveness. Likewise, these principles also call for the participation of experts from different fields to enrich the strategic approaches.

Medium-range planning resumed in Cuba in 1993, for the reasons just indicated; although the methodology of scenarios had not yet been introduced, many of its underlying planning requirements and techniques were put into place then. In 1994 INIE conducted an initial study in a very centralized manner. This study recommended a number of solutions to the serious problems Cuba faced at the time and served as a vehicle to inform the top political leaders of the economic impacts and modifications that were both foreseeable and necessary.

In mid-1996, work began on a medium-range projection titled "Socioeconomic Scenarios up to the Year 2000." Its objectives were

- to define the general framework in which the Cuban economy would operate through 2000 and, in some cases, through 2005;
- to propose objectives, policies, and organizational changes that would maximize the revitalization and development of the economy; and
- to determine strategies for various different possible situations in the context of the economic and related political environment in which Cuba was operating.

For this study multiple scenarios were created to represent many different possible trajectories of the economy. Then, for practical reasons, this large diversity of possibilities was narrowed down to two scenarios: (1) *trend-based*: what would need to occur to maintain the existing trends; and (2) *active:* everything necessary to achieve the desired economic growth and development, taking into account the coherence of various solutions to specific issues and any required complementary measures.

To carry out this work the Ministry of Economy and Planning set up the following eighteen working groups, each addressing a particular strategic problem: Macroeconomic Model; Population; External Revenues; Agriculture, Food, and Sugar; Industrial Policy; Energy and Fuels; Infrastructure and Equipment; Domestic Finances; Employment Restructuring; Income Distribution and Social Policy; Education and Qualified Labor; Transformation of Institutions and Business Systems; Social Agents; Effects of the Economic Blockade and Helms-Burton Act; Trends in the International Economy and Trade; Foreign Financing; Scientific Research and Technological Policy; and Use of Natural Resources, and Protection of the Environment.

These groups—composed of more than three hundred experts from organizations, entities, and research and academic centers—met through the second half of 1996 and part of 1997. The synthesis and national-level analysis, completed by mid-1997, provided important input for drafting the Economic Resolution that was passed at the Fifth Party Congress, held in October. At the same time, this study provided a framework for the drafting of annual plans. It was updated in early 1998 in order to guide the 1999 annual plan and subsequently updated again for the 2000 plan. Since the second half of 1999 a number of midrange scenarios have been produced, shifting the temporal horizon first to 2005, then to 2010, to 2013, and in some cases to later years.

An important feature of the present planning system is that although the scenario-based approach predominates, not all the groups always use it in their research. Instead, participants use this and other techniques flexibly, adapting them to the specifics of each task.

Higher political agencies in the government have important influence on the final formulation of plans by continually interacting with the technical economists in the ministries and the research centers who are responsible for planning. In each stage of the process, the economists' findings are reviewed at higher levels of the government, which issue important feedback on additional issues to consider or reconsider. This feedback affects the final outcome of each stage, and hence the basis for the subsequent stage.

So far, this discussion has been confined largely to the national economy. It is worth briefly noting that the new prospective and scenario-based approaches have also been applied in many economic plans for specific areas. These have included regional development, urban planning, sectoral development, and the blockade and Cuba-U.S. relations (which was completed in 1993), among others.

At the broadest conceptual level, the central principle that emerges from the previous discussion of the new planning approach is that the radically different conditions in which the Cuban economy operates today have generated new methods of planning. But the goal of planning remains the same as before: the generation of comprehensive medium- and long-range views of the economy as essential instruments for steering the country on the path to development.

Future Challenges

Although medium- and long-range planning has restarted and moved forward with more flexible and much more participatory methods better suited to current economic conditions, important challenges still remain. For the purpose of provoking thought on the issues involved, here is a list of what the author considers the most significant challenges:

- Achieve greater comprehensiveness and continuity among the short-, medium-, and long-range visions. Although much progress has been made in establishing midrange sectoral or branch-specific projections, these projections must be better linked with the creation of annual plans, while more elements from the annual plans must be incorporated into the longer-range projections.
- Carry out specific sectoral and social programs as integral parts of the prospective vision, while simultaneously ensuring overall balance in the economy. Even when all the individual programs are justified, the medium- and long-range plans must consist of more than just the sum of these individual programs.
- Establish conditions that combine decentralization and greater enterprise autonomy with the degree of centralization necessary to guarantee Cuba's social interests. Even though this problem relates to planning in general, it is particularly relevant for the medium- and long-range horizon, because this is the time frame relevant to the development process itself, which must not be compromised.
- Integrate territorial aspects into the economy's strategic prospective vision.
- Transform the planners' understanding of planning, in the sense that

prospective and strategic views must always be taken into account and that making projections is a continuous process, not something to be done at specific intervals on the calendar.

- Create efficient organizational and institutional structures and mechanisms for completing prospective planning studies. This raises again the old question of who should be in charge of ensuring that prospective planning is compatible with the contents of the annual plans, in terms of both timing and necessary human resources.

In conclusion, I hope that my observations here will promote and contribute to the debate on this centrally important issue for the Cuban economy.

Notes

1. Ernesto Guevara, "Sobre el sistema presupuestario de financiamiento," *Nuestra Industria. Revista Económica* 2, no. 5 (1964): 16; also compiled in *Ernesto Che Guevara: Temas Económicos* (Habana: Editorial de Ciencias Sociales, 1988), 315–16.

2. José Luis Rodríguez, "40 años de Planificación en Cuba," an interview in *El Economista de Cuba*, January–February 2000.

3. JUCEPLAN, *Apuntes históricos de la Junta Central de Planificación*, vol. 1 (Havana: JUCEPLAN, 1985).

4. Ibid.

5. Ibid.

6. JUCEPLAN, *La Planificación Económica en Cuba* (Havana: JUCEPLAN, 1968).

7. JUCEPLAN, *Apuntes históricos de la Junta Central de Planificación*, vol. 1.

8. JUCEPLAN, *La Planificación Económica en Cuba.*

9. Ibid.

10. JUCEPLAN, *Apuntes históricos de la Junta Central de Planificación*, vol. 1.

11. Elena Álvarez, "Problemas actuales que presenta la Coordinación de Planes en los marcos del CAME" (INIE, mimeo, 1989).

12. Elena Álvarez, "Hacia un nuevo modelo de colaboración en los marcos del CAME" (INIE, mimeo, 1989).

13. JUCEPLAN, *Apuntes históricos de la Junta Central de Planificación*, vol. 1.

14. Ibid.

15. JUCEPLAN, *Programa de Estudios para la elaboración de la estrategia de desarrollo perspectivo económico y social hasta el año 2000* (Havana: JUCEPLAN, 1978), 10–16.

16. JUCEPLAN, *Programa de Estudios.*

17. For a detailed presentation of these issues see ibid., especially 63–66.

18. JUCEPLAN, *Apuntes históricos de la Junta Central de Planificación*, vol. 1.

19. These events related to an in-depth review of economic concepts and policies triggered by the remarks of Commander-in-Chief Fidel Castro at the closing session of the National Energy Forum and at the National Assembly of People's Power in late 1984, as

well as to the rectification of errors and negative tendencies that was launched in 1986. Also in those years, hard-currency constraints became particularly problematic, forcing additional review and adjustment of economic goals. Furthermore, the CMEA countries showed preliminary indications that the existing model of relations would soon change, as evidenced in the Coordination of Plans.

20. Francisco Martínez Soler, "Hacia una estrategia de desarrollo económico y social de Cuba hasta el año 2000," *Cuestiones de la Economía Planificada* No. 8 (1981): 13–14.

21. José Luis Rodríguez, "Escenarios económicos y sociales hasta el año 2000," *Temas de Economía y Planificación* No. 2 (1996): 1.

22. Alfredo González, "Notas de conferencia impartida en el Seminario sobre los Escenarios Económicos y Sociales hasta el 2000" (June 14, 1996).

23. The "genetic" approach consists of attempting to directly infer the future performance of phenomena based on past knowledge, taking into account the trends, regularities, and inertia of the different processes. The "normative" approach is essentially based on setting forth the development objectives and then determining what measures must be adopted to achieve them. JUCEPLAN, *Indicaciones metodológicas para la elaboración de los estudios de la estrategia de desarrollo perspectivo económico y social hasta el año 2000.*

24. González, "Notas de conferencia impartida en el Seminario sobre los Escenarios Económicos y Sociales hasta el 2000."

25. Ibid.

26. Juanjo Gabiña, "El futuro revisitado," *Prospektiker* (1995): 2–3.

27. González, "Notas de conferencia impartida en el Seminario sobre los Escenarios Económicos y Sociales hasta el 2000."

Part II

Socioeconomic Issues

5

Creating a Better Life

The Human Dimension of the Cuban Economy

RITA CASTIÑEIRAS GARCÍA

Hunger, destitution, disease, ignorance, unemployment, lack of opportunity, lack of security, inequality, hopelessness, those are the words that could summarize the living conditions of a large portion of the current population of the planet.

Fidel Castro

As we enter a new millennium, humankind has to address two unresolved challenges: stopping the decimation of the environment and ending poverty. The search for a better life or, in other words, for an improved quality of life or human well-being, has existed since time immemorial. The emergence of the concept as such, and the concern with its systematic and scientific evaluation, is, however, relatively new.

During the 1950s and early 1960s, there was growing interest in understanding human well-being, and it became necessary to measure this condition with objective data. Social science fields began to develop social indicators that allowed quantitative measurement of conditions and events connected with a population's social well-being. Over the course of the 1960s, the issue became much more popular. In the mid-1970s and early 1980s, social well-being started to take shape as an integrated and multidimensional concept, involving all walks of life and both objective and subjective components. Quality of life has now become a widely used concept in many different fields, such as health care, mental health, education, economics, politics, and the world of services in general. There is, of course, still a lack of consensus on both its definition and proper evaluation.

Quality of life is linked to humans' satisfaction of their material, social, psychological, and spiritual needs, and hence encompasses a large number of elements. It is based on the security and availability of health care and education, sufficient food and decent housing, a healthy natural environment, justice, equality between the sexes and races, dignity, and security. Humans are entitled to safety and security not only in terms of protection against avoidable damage, but also in terms of freedom from the fear of such damage. Personal safety is closely linked to social and economic security, as well as to national and international peace and security. Because of its intrinsically multidimensional nature, quality of life cannot be summarized with some single social indicator, nor can an average quality of life be calculated.

It is becoming daily more obvious that a healthy natural environment is an important component of quality of life. Sustainability is a recognition that natural resources are limited and that appropriate stewardship is the basis for the survival of the environment, society, economies, and individuals. If the means of human existence and prosperity cannot be sustainably protected, they cannot be guaranteed. Sustainability is therefore a necessary component of security.

Sustainability also has another, less discussed aspect: the sustainability of society. Sustaining human society requires maintaining diversity in human beings by allowing them to develop their individuality. This central goal of socialism is also directly relevant to quality of life. Achieving the development of every human persona in turn rests on the development of health care, education, and other social services.

Equity is a fundamental principle that should govern every society. True equity is based on real equality of opportunity, which in turn is possible only through greater equality in the distribution of income, wealth, and access to services. When a country's existing policies are indeed governed by equity, all its members have greater security, longer life expectancy, a more sustainable environment, and in general a better quality of life.

Measurement of Human Well-Being

Several institutions have created indexes for quality of life as a whole. Such an index results from the combination of various indicators and attempts to represent the true, overall well-being of individuals. One of the first indexes synthesized was the physical quality of life index,[1] based on three indicators: infant mortality rate, life expectancy at birth, and adult literacy rate. In 1990 this indicator was replaced by the Human Development Index (HDI), published by the United Nations Development Programme (PNUD). HDI is conceptually very similar to the earlier index, but education level is measured by combining the adult literacy rate (weighted two-thirds) and the median number of years of schooling (weighted one-third).

All indexes have problems and dangers, however. The numerous disparate elements of quality of life cannot be synthesized into a completely satisfactory index, because the choice of elements making up the index and the weight attached to each element largely depend on value judgments. The resulting indexes are always expressed numerically, which too many users accept as signifying objectivity. The inherent subjectivity of the concept, however, means that the numbers generated, and hence the rankings of groups and countries, vary greatly according to the value judgments made in the choice of the component indicators and their weighting. Quality-of-life indexes are thus much less objective than their numerical form suggests.

A look at the different aspects of the concept of human well-being necessarily leads to an analysis of social policies and how they influence quality of life. This is demonstrated by an analysis of the situation in Cuba.

Cuba's Social Problems Prior to 1959

Very briefly, Cuba's social problems prior to 1959 can be summarized as follows:

- Widespread and ever-increasing poverty
- Highly polarized income distribution: the wealthiest 20 percent of the population received 58 percent of the income, while the poorest 20 percent received only 2 percent.
- Widespread unemployment: 24 percent of the working-age population was unemployed.
- Inadequately remunerative employment: around 60 percent of wage-earning and self-employed workers earned less than the low minimum wage then in effect.
- Absence of a social safety net: social security, besides being insufficient, covered only 50 percent of workers, and welfare was nonexistent.
- Absence of universal health care accessible by the entire population: communicable diseases, such as enteritis, diarrheic diseases, and tuberculosis were among the top ten causes of death.
- Evidence of social decay: drug use, prostitution, and corruption, among other vices, were widespread.
- Lack of guaranteed access to education: more than one million Cubans were illiterate.
- Critical and ever-increasing housing shortages and high rents
- Lack of social protections for children, senior citizens, and people with disabilities
- Rampant discrimination based on skin color and gender
- Disengagement of the most marginalized sectors from the social and political life of the country

The Orientation of Cuba's Social Policies

In Cuba, the term *social* encompasses everything that relates to society. It is multifaceted in nature and includes the fields of education, health care, food, housing, water and sanitation, employment, social security, and welfare. Social policies, therefore, have been correspondingly diverse in their goals. Since they are comprehensive, they take into account the important element of complementarity among objectives. Social policy goals address improvement in the standard of living and material well-being; increase in equity; and transformation of values, behaviors, and social relations. The 1976 Constitution of the Republic of Cuba defined the Cuban state as a socialist state of workers whose goal was to promote the enjoyment of individual and collective well-being, based on social justice and human solidarity.

From the time of the attack on the Moncada garrison and Fidel Castro's "History Will Absolve Me" speech at his trial, the ultimate objective of the Cuban Revolution has remained constant: progressively and systematically to improve the population's conditions of life. Central to the objective is the premise that economic growth is not an end in itself and that social and economic development must progress hand in hand.

Hence focusing on and addressing social problems was a high priority in the initial changes undertaken after the victory of the Revolution. The state was centrally responsible for formulating and implementing a social development policy that, in conjunction with the activity of the economic sector, radically modified the living conditions of the majority of the population. The initial large-scale, people-oriented social programs, such as the literacy campaign, land reform, and the elimination of evictions, approached social issues with a breadth that was unusual prior to that time.

Of all the previously listed facets of society, education, health care, and employment have been the three main pillars of Cuba's social policies since 1959. Education is particularly interesting because it has many spillover effects to other social policies and aspects of the economy and society. For example, an educated population can become active agents in implementing all social projects, which is why education has always been seen as pivotal for the success of all of Cuba's social policies. In addition, greater levels of schooling and qualifications tend to decrease fertility and, correspondingly, affect the age composition of the population. Increased education also tends to increase the involvement of women in the out-of-household workforce, improve the economic situation of households, and change lifestyles.

Cuba's social policy has been broadly characterized by its universal, free, and planned nature. Planning, in particular, has made it possible to reconcile the various elements in the complex framework of social policies in terms of objectives, time (providing the appropriate resources for each stage of a project), and space (balancing different territorial needs). In addition, consistent political commitment has been important for the continuity of state financing, implementation, and monitoring of social programs.

An important aspect of Cuba's social policies that should be stressed is the strategic role of equity. Merely granting the entire population equal opportunities to satisfy their needs is insufficient to achieve equity; it also requires providing greater opportunities to social groups that are disadvantaged due to historical conditions and as a result will likely fail to maximize their available opportunities. One example is the facilitation of women joining the out-of-household working population and beyond that their promotion to leadership posts throughout society. Another example is the attempt to raise rural living standards to urban levels. Humanizing the toughest jobs and bridging existing salary gaps were two other attempts, through specific regulations and actions, to increase equity throughout society.[2] In addition, equity promotion extends beyond Cuba's national borders through social policy projects designed to assist other developing countries in health care and education, among other areas. Such solidarity is not just left to the population's spontaneous charity, which would inevitably lead to low levels of international aid. Cuba has put in place institutional mechanisms that channel these actions through intergovernmental cooperation agreements or through UN bodies.

General Achievements of Social Policies Implemented in Cuba

Throughout the entire revolutionary process, Cuba has endeavored to enhance its social, political, and economic development under the principle of the right to social justice and equity for all, which includes guaranteeing the basic needs of the people. The social policies implemented in Cuba have aimed at progressively meeting each of the human rights that contributes to a dignified quality of life, as recognized in the legal instruments of the United Nations. The rights of all types of citizens—children, women, senior citizens, people with disabilities, men, and the family—are explicitly embedded in the country's legal, administrative, and political culture.

In this context, the first achievement of the Revolution was eliminating citizens' fear for their physical security through the removal of the repressive practices characteristic of previous governments. These had violated arguably the most basic human right: the right to life.

The difficult economic period known as the Special Period, which officially began in 1990, revealed four achievements of the social policies Cuba had put in place over the previous thirty years. First and most obviously, the crisis revealed once again the commitment of the revolutionary process to do everything possible in the face of any problem or crisis to minimize social harm to its citizenry. Cubans often comment that throughout the worst of the depression not a single school or hospital closed, nor was a single citizen abandoned by society to fend for him- or herself. People whose workplace could no longer offer them productive work because of the economic crisis often were entitled to continue receiving their salary. This was designed to protect Cuba's social policy of full employment and to avoid shifting the cost of the crisis onto workers. This response should be compared to the way the majority of third-world and even first-world countries have responded to large (or even small) economic downturns in order to fully appreciate what it reveals about Cuba's commitment to defend the gains of the previous thirty years of social policies.

Second, it showed the depth of the commitment to equality underpinning so many of Cuba's social policies. Many other countries facing similar (or even less dramatic) economic implosions carried out IMF and Washington Consensus policies that threw the major costs of adjustment onto the poorest and most vulnerable in society. Visitors to Cuba frequently commented on the degree of "shared sacrifice" across all levels of Cuban society.

Third, it showed the degree of democracy that had developed in Cuba over the previous three decades. Several discussions concerning fairly severe and fundamental government-proposed economic belt-tightening measures were organized in neighborhoods and workplaces throughout the country. These heavily attended meetings led to large numbers of revisions to the original proposals. But beyond that, they represented a step toward making men and women into the subjects, rather than just the objects, of the process of social development. Finally, the absence in the social discussions of a significant degree of support for the dominant world alternative, neoliberal adjustment, revealed the fourth achievement of Cuba's social policies: its degree of development of social solidarity. This certainly came in part from both the shared sacrifices and the popular participation in decision making.

In brief, the general achievements of Cuba's social policies have resulted in a gradual growth of well-being for the Cuban population. These will be discussed in detail in the rest of this chapter.

Characteristics of the Cuban Population

As of December 30, 2006, there were an estimated 11,239,000 inhabitants living on the Island. The average annual population growth in the 1990s was very low, at about 5 per 1,000 inhabitants, and between 2000 and 2007 the population experienced almost zero growth. The population rates for all the provinces remained fairly close to the national average, except in Havana, whose population has declined from 2001 to 2007.[3]

Whereas in the 1950s women had an average of 4 children, that number has dropped to 1.6 at present, which is comparable to the average childbirth rate of 1.71 in developed countries. For thirty years the birthrate has been below the level of population replacement, indicating that not every woman is leaving at least one daughter to replace her reproductive function at the end of her childbearing years. With this low fertility rate, the population between infancy and fourteen years of age has been decreasing as a proportion of the whole. At the same time, mortality levels have declined while life expectancy at birth has increased, increasing the proportion of the population who are age sixty or older. From a quantitative point of view, these facts are highly significant for Cuba's age profile over the last several decades.

Conceptually this process is associated with the so-called demographic transition from high to low birth and mortality rates. With its very low levels of fertility and mortality, Cuba is currently in the last of these stages as defined by the Latin American and Caribbean Demography Center, although some analysts and researchers believe that the Island is already in a post-transitional stage. The country has gone from 11.3 percent of the population being older than fifty-nine in 1985 to 16.6 percent falling in this age bracket in 2007. According to estimates by the Population Division of the United Nations, Barbados and Cuba will be the most rapidly aging countries in Latin America and the Caribbean in the immediate future (see chapter 7 for more information on Cuba's demographics).[4]

Human Development

The 2007–8 UN Human Development Report ranks Cuba fifty-first of a total of 177 countries. Since 2001, it has been classified as a country of high human development.[5] As can be seen from table 5.1, which breaks down the components of the HDI, Cuba's development is higher than that of Latin America and the Caribbean except in per capita income. The combination of high HDI ranking with low per capita GDP indicates the high priority Cuba attaches to social policies. Cuba also outranks the HDI average for central and eastern Europe and the CIS due mainly to its high life expectancy at birth, a result largely of its healthcare policy. Note that the difference in HDI between Cuba and the high-income countries results almost entirely from Cuba's low level of per capita income relative to those countries. In terms of quality of life this difference manifests mainly in a greater degree of comfort and quality of services in those societies.

Table 5.1. Human Development Index for Cuba and various world regions, 2005

	Human Development Index	Life expectancy at birth	Adult literacy rate	Combined gross enrollment rate	Per capita GDP (in US$)[a]
World total	0.743	68.1	78.6	67.8	9,543
Developing countries	0.691	66.1	76.7	64.1	5,282
Latin America and the Caribbean	0.803	72.8	90.3	81.2	8,417
OECD countries	0.916	78.3	—	88.6	29,197
Central and Eastern Europe, CIS	0.808	68.6	99.0	83.5	9,527
High-income countries	0.936	79.2	—	92.3	33,082
Upper-middle-income countries	0.776	70.9	89.9	73.3	7,416
Low-income countries	0.570	60.0	60.2	56.3	2,531
Cuba	0.838	77.7	99.8	87.6	6,000

[a]Purchasing Power Parity.
Source: United Nations Development Programme, *Informe sobre desarrollo humano* (Madrid: Mundi-Prensa Libros, 2007).

Inequality

As noted earlier, in 1959 the poorest 20 percent of the Cuban population received 2 percent of the total income while the wealthiest 20 percent received 58 percent. By 1989 this situation had changed radically, with the 20 percent of the population with the lowest income receiving 8.9 percent while the highest-income 20 percent received 34 percent. Subsidized food and the many free social services in Cuba made the reduction in inequality much greater than even this large change in income inequality indicates. One of the major successes of Cuba's social policies has been the elimination of extreme inequality.

The dire economic situation in the early 1990s and the measures adopted to address the crisis resulted in a significant increase in income disparity. Even so, Cuba continues to have the lowest income inequality in Latin America and the Caribbean. Available estimates of the inequality of income distribution in urban areas, measured by the Gini coefficient, placed Cuba at 0.38 for the 1996–98 period (see table 5.2).

The main factor associated with the largest inequalities in the current income distribution in Cuba is presence versus absence of a stable source of hard-currency income. Some basic commodities and consumer goods, such as toiletries and cleaning items, among others, are available in insufficient quantities on the rationed market, so must be purchased in hard-currency shops. Hence, those families without hard-currency income must spend a large amount of their Cuban peso income to purchase the necessary hard currency to supplement their rationed allotment of these basic items. Government-subsidized investments in food, education, health care, social security, and welfare, among

Table 5.2. Gini coefficient for urban income distribution in selected Latin American countries

Country	Gini coefficient
Colombia	0.56
Panama	0.54
Ecuador	0.52
Bolivia	0.51
Uruguay	0.44
Cuba	0.38

Sources: CEPAL, *Panorama social de América Latina, 2002–2003* (Santiago de Chile: CEPAL, 2003), except Cuba; Ángela Ferriol, "El modelo social cubano: Una aproximación a tres temáticas en debate," *Cuba: Investigaciones Económicas* 7, no. 1 (2001).

other services, reduce the effects of the heightened inequality of the primary income distribution. Likewise, the solidarity in Cuban society plays an important role in mitigating its effects, as friends and relatives offer significant assistance in food and other items. The growth in income inequality, however, remains a major social issue in Cuba today.

Employment

Fidel Castro clearly reiterated Cuba's fifty-year position on unemployment at the closing session of the Fourth International Meeting on Globalization in 2002:

> The category of unemployment has to disappear. A man cannot be redundant, and a society where man is redundant is useless. It does not withstand an ethical analysis; it does not withstand a human analysis and therefore it is condemned from a moral and a human standpoint. . . . In Cuba there will be no unemployment. We will continue to train our people. We have promised every young person guaranteed employment, on one condition: that they are trained.

The Revolution's employment policy has been aimed at creating the conditions in which people can find useful jobs, freely chosen within the options and limits set by Cuba's socioeconomic development. Again, this social policy is based on Cuba's solid principles of equity and social justice. Some important elements of this policy include banning wage differentials by gender or territory, placing special emphasis on increasing female employment outside the household to incorporate women into collective work experiences, and fulfilling the commitment to employ graduates of higher and intermediate education. Above all, the goal of eliminating unemployment, essentially ac-

Table 5.3. Unemployment rates in several developed countries, 2006 (% of working population)

Country	Rate	Country	Rate
Cuba*	1.8	Canada	6.3
OECD	6.0	Italy	6.8
Norway	3.5	Sweden	7.0
Japan	4.1	Germany	8.4
United States	4.6	Spain	8.5
Australia	4.9	France	9.4
United Kingdom	5.3		

*2007.

Source: United Nations Development Programme, *Informe sobre desarrollo humano* (Madrid: Mundi-Prensa Libros, 2007).

complished prior to 1989, has remained a high priority in Cuba's labor policy even during the economic difficulties of the Special Period. In 2007 the unemployment rate was only 1.8 percent, very low by international standards (see table 5.3 for unemployment rates of some OECD member countries).

In the face of the economic slowdown of the Special Period and the associated restructuring of productive enterprises, the low unemployment figures for 2007 required deliberate employment programs, particularly over the last decade. Particularly important was the large program of skill upgrading or further schooling for the unemployed or underemployed population. In the short run this "employment in studying" made a measurable contribution to reducing unemployment. But its purpose was long term: an investment in knowledge that will eventually become the country's most valuable asset (see chapter 12) and that is a necessary component of the effort to restructure enterprises to operate more efficiently and create high-value-added goods. The Comprehensive Training Course was a part of this program aimed specifically at youths aged seventeen to twenty-nine who were neither working nor studying. Significant unemployment in this age group is particularly problematic, not only for individuals but for their families and communities. Many of these young people were trained in scientific-technical areas such as information technology and computer science. But a larger number were trained to expand Cuba's social policies in health care, education, culture, and in particular, new social welfare services. (I will describe this major welfare program in the next section.)

Cuba today faces two important problems related to employment. The first is underemployment, which trended upward during the economic crisis when the decision was made to keep many workers at their workplaces in the state sector even though there was no work for them to do. This situation was at its worst in the early and mid-1990s, and it has improved somewhat as the economy has been recovering and producing more productive employment. Another part of the improvement has come from reductions in excessive state enterprise workforces, especially over the last decade as part of the enterprise reform program of *perfecionamiento empresarial* (enterprise improvement). As of the middle of 2010, however, this continues to be a major problem and there is an ongoing discussion in the government regarding a large-scale reduction in the state enterprise workforce in the near future. As always, a central part of the discussion is how to undertake this reform without placing the costs associated with this socially beneficial action onto the particular workers laid off.

The second major employment-related problem today is that adhering to the full employment policy during the Special Period and the recent economic slowdown that began in 2008 has delayed efforts to increase the real wages of various labor groups. This in turn has hurt productivity, generating a negative feedback loop that makes resolution of the country's economic problems still more difficult.

Social Security and Welfare

Upon coming to power in January 1959, the new revolutionary government took immediate action to secure social security and welfare. It seemed likely that some companies would renege on their commitments to their workers and appropriate the pension and workers' funds for their own benefit. A program was immediately put in place to guarantee the fulfillment of all such obligations. At the same time, the first long-range steps were taken to expand the existing social security and welfare systems to protect all workers against liabilities such as common accidents and occupational hazards, work-related and common illnesses, maternity complications, partial disability, old age, death, mendicancy, and social neglect.

Afterwards a social security system was established based on intergenerational solidarity, referred to as "sharing." This system encompasses two complementary programs: social security and welfare. In 2006 the social security and welfare system delivered benefits to 2.1 million people, 18.8 percent of the population. Given generous retirement rights and benefits, the aging of the population, discussed earlier, has caused a fairly rapid increase in the number of people receiving benefits from this system.

The welfare system protects in particular those elderly people without resources or protection and any other people who are unfit to work and lack relatives in a position to provide assistance. Overall, it covers everyone whose material needs are not secure and those requiring state protection due to their living conditions or health status. There are social programs that provide community-based services to the elderly, offer employment to single mothers, look after socially disadvantaged children, provide comprehensive care for people with disabilities, and cater to other vulnerable groups.

A major new welfare program was initiated in the twenty-first century. This involves a ten-month social work course that offers intensive training to young people who have non-university-level postsecondary education. After graduating, these social workers provide highly individualized welfare services to the community. Each is responsible for a specific territory. The social worker's job is to become acquainted with all the citizens in that area and to identify any problems they have. The worker then goes on to identify the needs and problems at the community level and propose solutions to help resolve them.

Schools have been set up in most provinces, from which more than thirty-one thousand such social workers have graduated. These are then grouped into work brigades that operate in nearly all of the country's People's Councils.[6] These graduates are also guaranteed access to university courses connected with their employment.[7]

These social workers have already carried out or begun work on several important projects:

- Individualized care of every student in the Behavioral Schools, every young person in the Comprehensive Training Courses, and every senior or disabled citizen, among others
- Gradual transformation of prisons into schools
- Comprehensive study of infants and youths up to age fifteen, focused on evaluating the nutritional status, education, family environment, and living standards of every child. This study involved 2.2 million children and identified approximately 283,000 cases in need of food or educational, medical, psychosocial, or other assistance.

Women's Involvement

An area of social policy that has achieved noteworthy results relates to the incorporation of women into the workforce. In addition to the lower fertility rates discussed previously, the social policy of creating networks of child-care centers and services has been key for this result. The 2007–8 UN Human Development Report ranked Cuba among the countries in the world with the best index of women's social involvement. In 2007 women accounted for[8]

- 67 percent of Cuba's teaching staff
- 65 percent of university graduates

- more than 60 percent of the workforce in the sectors of education, public health, economics, and banking
- 56.7 percent of doctors
- more than 55 percent of attorneys
- 49 percent of professional judges and around a third of those working in industry[9]
- 43 percent of the 614 members elected to the Eleventh Legislature of the National Assembly of People's Power (2007–12)
- 38 percent of senior managers
- 38 percent of the workforce in the economy
- 48 out of 199 directors of scientific research centers
- tens of thousands of the Cubans who have enrolled in internationalist missions to many countries of the world, as for example, in the cooperative medical efforts carried out in Africa, Central America, and the Caribbean

In the area of sports Cuban women have also achieved equality of rights and opportunities. On one hand, they participate extensively in competitive and elite-level sports, with both qualitatively and quantitatively significant results. But at least as socially important, and unlike women in many other countries and in prerevolutionary Cuba, they have also increased their participation in recreational athletics and exercise, especially in the schools, which are very important for developing and maintaining healthy bodies and minds.

Food

Cuba's policies concerning food have been and continue to be a high social priority. The Revolution's history since 1959 clearly demonstrates two achievements. First, the government has succeeded in guaranteeing every Cuban at least a minimum amount of basic food, even under the most difficult economic conditions, such as some years in the 1960s and at the beginning of the Special Period. This is no small achievement, and it contrasts with almost all other third-world countries and many first-world countries. It is, for example, notable that Cuba spent very scarce foreign exchange that it desperately needed for many other economic tasks to import food during the early Special Period in order to guarantee food security. The other achievement that so many visitors commented on during these economic calamities was the degree to which the reduction in food intake was shared across all levels of the population.

Cuba's economic crisis of the early 1990s had a very negative and acute impact on the availability of food for two reasons. First, in the CMEA integration scheme that prevailed prior to the crisis, Cuba had imported much of its food; therefore, with the crisis-induced, abrupt drop in the country's import capacity, food imports plummeted. Second, much of its domestic food production was integrated into international chains of production that necessitated certain imports like fertilizers, pesticides, and petroleum for farm machinery; therefore, domestic food production plummeted as well. The most tangible expression of the crisis was the emergence of an epidemic neuropathology, which peaked in the first quarter of 1993 and mainly affected the adult population aged twenty-five to sixty-four.

The recovery of food consumption in Cuba from its nadir in 1993 took a decade. By 2000 food intake was approaching the pre-crisis level, and it continued to improve in subsequent years (see table 5.4). By 2006 caloric intake surpassed the recommended minimum daily allowance by nearly 37 percent and protein intake by 16.8 percent.[10] Fat intake, however, remained at only 66 percent of the recommended value. It should be noted that Cuba is currently updating its recommendations in light of the recent marked increase, also occurring in much of the rest of the world, in problems of overweight and obesity in the population, particularly among young people.

An important part of Cuba's half century of success in food security has been that a sizable portion of the total available food has been subsidized and distributed based on social criteria. In 2006, food accessed through state-subsidized channels accounted for 64.1 percent of total caloric intake and 62.7 percent of protein. As of 2008 the Cuban state has been giving clear indications that it intends to sharply reduce, and perhaps eventually even totally eliminate, such subsidized distribution because of the inefficiencies involved. The slow progress to date on this goal is connected to the difficulty of designing a system that will eliminate the subsidies but at the same time continue to fulfill Cuba's promise of guaranteeing food to all its citizens.

Table 5.4. Average nutritional intake in Cuba, 2000–2006

Nutrient	Unit	Recommended nutritional value	2000	2003	2006
Calories	Kcal	2,400	3,007	3,241	3,290
Protein	g	72	70.2	81.8	84.1
Fat	g	75	55.9	44.8	49.8

Sources: S. Jiménez, *Recomendaciones nutricionales* (Havana: INHA, 1996); ONE, *Hojas de Balance FAO* (Havana: ONE, 2000, 2003, 2006); and Ministro de Economía y Planificación, *Informe de Cuba sobre seguimiento acuerdos de la Cumbre Mundial sobre la alimentación* (Havana: MEP, 2008).

Public Health

An internationally recognized component of the development and consolidation of Cuba's health-care social policy has been the community doctor plan. Under this system a medical doctor and a nurse become the personal primary health-care providers for approximately five hundred people who live in a particular community. The doctor and nurse also live and have their office in that community. The system also extends to day-care centers, schools, workplaces, and other public facilities. The primary care level is supported by a polyclinic that is equipped to treat more complicated medical problems and that periodically carries out medical reviews of its area of responsibility. Two further objectives are to expand specialized medical services to all the polyclinics in the country and to develop centers for specialized training and for medical research, all with a view to providing the entire population with the highest possible level of medical services.

Based on this objective, the following measures have been adopted to further improve the quality of Cuban medicine:

- Opening physical therapy centers in all polyclinics
- Introducing new hemodialysis, ophthalmology, and intensive care services in the municipalities
- Upgrading technology in all primary and secondary services. This has the added advantage of bringing the most important high-quality medical services closer to the household.
- Establishing new schools for training and requalifying professionals in the new services being provided
- Establishing the National Center for Medical Genetics, opened in 2003, intended to coordinate the country's genetic network. This institution both trains human resources and conducts research on genetic health problems, integrating population, clinical, and laboratory studies.

The Cuban population's health indicators compare favorably to those of the region, and some even match the levels of developed countries. Even throughout the economic crisis of the 1990s Cuba preserved the social policy of assigning high priority to health care. The result was that there was minimal decline, and in some cases even continued improvement, in the global indicators. The indicators from the UN Human Development Report reflect Cuba's social policy of a high level of commitment to health care (see table 5.5). Another reflection of the high priority Cuba assigns to health care is the ratio of doctors to inhabitants, which stood at 1 to 158 in 2006, the lowest registered value for this indicator even among countries with a high HDI.[11]

Table 5.5. Selected health indicators for Cuba, 2005

	Population with access to clean drinking water (%)	Infant mortality rate (per 1,000 live births)	Mortality rate of children under 5 years of age (per 1,000 live births)	Mothers receiving medical care in childbirth (%)
World total	83	52	76	63
Developing countries	79	57	83	60
Latin America and Caribbean	91	26	31	87
OECD	99	9	11	95
Central and Eastern Europe, CIS	94	22	27	97
High-income countries	100	6	7	99
Upper-middle-income countries	84	28	35	88
Low-income countries	76	75	113	41
Cuba	98	6	7	100

Source: United Nations Development Programme, *Informe sobre desarrollo humano* (Madrid: Mundi-Prensa Libros, 2007).

Cuba's epidemiological situation is similar to that of developed countries. The main causes of death are mostly noncommunicable chronic diseases. The top five causes of death in 2006 were heart disease, malignant tumors, cerebrovascular disease, influenza and pneumonia, and accidents, which accounted for 73.6 percent of total deaths in that year. The country has managed to eliminate through vaccination programs six preventable diseases that were major health problems prior to 1959, including poliomyelitis, measles, whooping cough, and rubella.

Acquired immunodeficiency syndrome (AIDS) is considered a latent epidemic in Cuba due to its low prevalence in high-risk groups. Cuba's HIV prevalence of about 0.1 percent of adults between fifteen and forty-nine is one of the lowest incidence rates in the world and is ten to thirty times lower than the rates of its neighbors in the Caribbean. An early short-lived quarantine program to stop the spread of the virus in the population ended in 1993. People declared HIV-positive are cared for under the HIV/AIDS Control and Prevention Program and the Epidemiological Surveillance System of hospital units. AIDS incidence increased by only 25.1 cases per million inhabitants in 2005.[12]

Cuba offers cooperative medical assistance to third-world countries, thus helping to alleviate the shortage of medical personnel and resolving the serious health issues in Latin America, the Caribbean, and Africa. This medical cooperation is currently conducted in twenty-one countries, including Guatemala, Haiti, Venezuela, Paraguay, Nicaragua, Gambia, Honduras, Ghana, Equatorial Guinea, Namibia, Zimbabwe, Cambodia, Guinea Bissau, and Burundi. In addition, the cooperative project with Latin America, Asia, and Africa under the Comprehensive Health-Care Program gave rise to the Latin American School of Medical Sciences. This center's mission is to train future doctors from third-world countries who will return to their home countries to replace the members of the Cuban medical brigades currently providing services there.

Finally, the Alma-Ata Declaration of 1978 and the Global Strategy for Health for All by the Year 2000, a proposal the World Health Organization adopted unanimously in 1981, enshrine a principle of equality that gave momentum to the medical activities that member countries were carrying out to benefit their senior citizens. In 1985 Cuba began providing specialized hospital care for its senior citizens by establishing the country's first geriatric service and by developing an internship in this medical specialty. Subsequently, geriatric services were set up in the capital's main teaching hospitals and in other provinces. In 1992 the Ibero-American Center for the Elderly, a tertiary-level facility, was established. This center established guidelines for the development of the geriatric specialty, not only in Cuba but throughout Ibero-America. These resulted in Cuba's current Comprehensive Health-Care Program for Senior Citizens.

Education

Transformations in the educational system began immediately after the triumph of the Revolution with the literacy campaign, the boost in primary education, the training of teachers, and the process of raising the education level of workers and farmers in general. The Teaching Nationalization Act of 1961 defined teaching as a duty of the state, declared that all education would be free, and prohibited private education. A central pillar of the entire national education system has been the combination of study and labor, whose essential objective is both individually formative and socially pedagogical.

Cuba's ever more educated human capital is seen as key to both the Island's new economy and, in keeping with the Revolution's central goal from the beginning, to its ongoing social development and improvements in quality of life. A wide range of complementary educational programs have been implemented with the following objectives:

- Creating various alternatives to guarantee continuing education for the entire population
- Achieving greater comprehensive training for children and youths
- Developing a complete and stable national teaching staff
- Creating the necessary material conditions in the schools to enable better educational services

In order to achieve these objectives, the following efforts have been or are being carried out:

- Broadcasting two educational television channels in all the provincial capitals, reaching 62.7 percent of the population
- Renovating school libraries and the resource centers attached to the National Education System, with the goal of developing the habit of reading
- Equipping all educational centers (particularly small rural ones) with electricity
- Expanding audiovisual aids
- Expanding the widespread use of information technology and computer science from an early age and turning informatics into an essential tool of economic efficiency, quality, and development
- Reducing primary classrooms to twenty students and expanding the primary curriculum to cover three times more knowledge
- Implementing a program to improve and streamline secondary education. Under the new plan, each teacher should have no more than fifteen students. To that end, thirty thousand youths are currently being trained to work as comprehensive secondary education teachers who cover all academic subjects and move with their students from grade to grade.
- Expanding the universal nature of higher education by setting up more than seven hundred municipal university centers. These centers are a new type of university facilitating postsecondary study in students' home municipalities, thus guaranteeing the entire population a continuum of studies at the territorial level.
- Establishing the University of Computer Science for training new information technology professionals and upgrading the skills of existing ones, and for the production of software and related services with the goal that intellectual property will eventually become an important sector for the national industry and for exports. This school will also support the IT-readiness program for Cuban society.

Culture and the Arts

The goal of Cuba's social policy for culture and the arts is to facilitate public assimilation of the values of national and universal culture and thereby enrich quality of life. This mission informs the operational goal of the cultural sector to provide an atmosphere that nurtures artistic and literary creation; facilitates popular participation in the country's cultural life; and increases the production, promotion, and circulation of cultural products and services in order to preserve and enrich Cuban cultural heritage.

These objectives have been pursued through the following efforts:

- Training art instructors, with a target figure of thirty thousand by 2012
- Expanding the teaching of art, including the fine arts, to all the provinces by opening seventeen new art schools and adding new capacity at the National Ballet School
- Extending the International Book Fair—which has had an extraordinary cultural, social, and political impact—to the entire country
- Creating a Family Library containing the best of Cuban and global literature and making it available very inexpensively to the population
- Creating the Open University, a nationwide program that complements the existing educational system and provides useful practical knowledge
- Consolidating the Rural Television Halls, located in the country's remotest areas, which are instrumental in disseminating culture, knowledge, and information through television. These halls simultaneously offer recreation and education to the inhabitants of these areas through television broadcasts.
- Consolidating the municipal Youth Video Clubs, which can be thought of as neighborhood-based movie theaters, as a cultural service for the communities where they are located. These centers are intended to enhance the general and comprehensive culture and quality of life of the population, particularly for children and youths.
- Disseminating the Round Tables that are broadcast on television in order to promote and consolidate the population's political culture as an essential element of creating a comprehensive general culture. These Round Tables are considered a political university.
- Increasing the production of cartoons that transmit and instill revolutionary and patriotic values and sentiments
- Consolidating the Tribunas Abiertas (Open Rallies), which are an exceptional instrument of struggle aimed at showing the people's sup-

port for the Revolution and their massive, overwhelming rejection of the aggressions of the Empire

Sports

In Cuba sports are considered to be an essential element of both recreational and spiritual enrichment of the society. They serve as an important link in Cuba's entire spectrum of people-oriented social policies. Sports are considered both a constitutional and a human right.

Professional sports were eliminated in 1959. Since then programs have been put in place to promote the extensive practice of sports and physical education throughout the country. Many programs operate on a community level and promote various physical activities designed to involve as much of the community as possible. Sports and physical activity are also considered part of Cuba's system of health throughout its municipalities, as part of its general approach to disease prevention as well as for physical rehabilitation in therapeutic wards. Physical education is also an established subject in the national education system. Every province has a university-level school of physical education, there is a national institute of physical education, and there are many lower-level educational institutions for preparing physical education instructors.

Sports is another field where Cuba has extensively shared its human capital internationally in support of a better quality of life for all humanity. For many decades Cuban trainers and sports specialists have worked in countries around the world, developing both elite national teams and broader national social programs. Cuba established the International School of Physical Education and Sports in 2001 as a world-class university to train physical education and sports professionals from around the world; in this institution human solidarity has been the value on which all the technical aspects rest. Its goal is to graduate students capable of subsequently integrating this education back into their own countries. The student body is primarily African, although students also come from Asia, Latin America, and the Caribbean.

Starting in 2002, the National Olympiad of Cuban Sports has been held every two years. At the first Olympiad an unprecedented event was held in Revolution Square: a massive simultaneous chess match with 11,320 boards, a world record. On the elite level, the results of Cuba's policies in the field of sports are reflected in the medals the country has won in the Central American, Pan-American, and Olympic Games.

Another goal being addressed is establishment of the Scientific Sports Cluster, with a certified anti-doping laboratory and a sports clinic, designed to guarantee excellence in specialized scientific-technical services, research, and postgraduate medical teaching. The anti-doping laboratory, the twenty-ninth of its kind in the world (there are still only thirty-four today), opened in 2001 and has been accredited by the International Olympic Committee.

Housing

The basic principle of the right to housing is enshrined in the Constitution of the Republic of Cuba, which establishes that the state should endeavor to provide comfortable housing to every family. In addition to being a reaction to the terrible housing conditions that existed among the poor majority of the population before 1959, this is another pillar of the country's overall development strategy. As an initial step to address the severe housing shortage extant at that time, the state enacted two primary measures in 1959–60: the Rent Reduction Act, enacted in 1959, brought rents down by 30 to 50 percent; while the Urban Reform Act, enacted in October 1960, enabled every rent-paying family eventually to own their house, as rents were to be considered as amortization. The rent for new houses was capped at 10 percent of a family's income. The other principal regulation governing housing in Cuba today was passed in the middle of the economic difficulties of the Special Period. The General Housing Act of 1998 set forth rules and regulations to ensure access to housing, regardless of income.

An overall assessment of the housing situation indicates that the policy implemented in 1959 has had a positive social impact. For example, as the population increased by 60 percent between 1959 and 2002, the housing stock increased by more than 80 percent. More than a million new houses, including replacement homes, were added to the housing stock at a rate of construction that increased gradually up to thirty to fifty thousand houses per annum (although this number fell precipitously in some years of the Special Period). The growth of the housing stock was due not only to the building of new houses but also to the creation of new housing capacity as homeowners have expanded and subdivided their homes. In 2002 there were 3.5 million houses in Cuba.[13]

In relation to overcrowding, a study using the Unsatisfied Basic Needs Measure and other studies indicate that for most of Latin America and the Caribbean the critical threshold is more than three people to a room.[14] It is left open, however, "as deemed most appropriate in each case," whether this refers only to bedrooms or to all available spaces other than the kitchen, bathrooms, corridors, and garage. For Cuba, the 2002 Population and Housing Census found that the average number of people sleeping in the same room was 1.34. This aggregate national average does not support the common foreign perception of Cuba as suffering from severe overcrowding by Latin American standards.

The significant housing concern for many Cubans lies elsewhere, with the condition of the existing housing stock. On one hand, important progress has been made over the course of the Revolution. Between 1959 and 2002 deteriorated housing declined from 47 percent to 13 percent in urban areas and from 75 percent to 30 percent in rural areas.[15] But at the same time, decades of insufficient maintenance and rehabilitation of the housing stock have allowed its progressive decay. By early 2004 this problem had progressed to the point where, while 61 percent of homes (1.93 million homes) were classified as in good structural condition, the combined inadequate categories of fair and bad constituted 39 percent of homes. Measures enacted during the economic upturn in the first years of the twenty-first century have significantly increased the availability of materials for maintenance to homeowners, resulting in a marked increase in housing repairs. The downturn due to the worldwide Great Recession of 2008 and especially 2009 has reduced that rate. However, the requisite laws and practices are in place to resume the high rate of housing repairs once the present economic slowdown ends.

The Environment

Socioeconomic development cannot be viewed separately from environmental protection and natural resource conservation, because the two interact. On one hand, exploitation of natural resources is an indispensable requirement for economic growth and rising standard of living. On the other hand, productive processes generally degrade the environment. The ever-increasing and ever-accelerating deterioration of the global environment is currently the most serious danger affecting humanity and is one of the factors aggravating the deteriorated standard of living in many countries.

While a few aspects of environmentalism were present from the beginning of the Revolution, such as the project to reforest Cuba, concerns with industrial and agricultural production largely overrode environmental concerns for its first three decades. This began to change in the mid-1980s and especially over the course of the 1990s. At the end of 2001 Cuba took another big step forward in its commitment to environmentally sustainable development by launching the LA21 Bayamo Project. This was part of a UN effort to promote local application of the environmental development principles codified in Agenda 21 adopted at the UN Conference on the Environment and Development in 1992. In 2003 the state then launched the Cuba National Local Agenda 21 Programme to reproduce the successful Bayamo experience in other locations across the Island, starting with building a training center in Santa Clara to develop the necessary national expertise. Today, world-class environmental principles are applied to development throughout Cuba and allow it, in a rational and coherent manner, to promote steady and environmentally sustainable socioeconomic development.

The Battle of Ideas: Special Social Development Programs

The fight for the return of Elián González in 2000 directly posed the following question to all Cubans: Should Cuban society pursue material consumerism as epitomized by the United States and the people holding Elián in Florida in particular, or should it continue to pursue the long-standing humanist vision of a better life that Cuba had pursued for four decades despite its limited resources (social inclusion, culture, and human development)? Out of that debate Cuba launched the Battle of Ideas, a multidimensional social, ideological, and cultural counterattack against consumerism. Over the following years it came to consist of more than two hundred special programs, many already mentioned earlier. Some were enhancements of longtime programs, others were new. The three main pillars were, across the entire population, (1) to enhance the quality and quantity of education, (2) to elevate the comprehensive level of culture, and (3) to reinforce and extend the Revolution's social achievements and, accordingly, enhance the population's quality of life.

At the closing session of the Fourth International Meeting on Globalization in 2002, Fidel Castro stated in reference to the special programs, "There are two types of capital: financial capital, which is of utmost importance; but there is a capital with far more value, which is human capital. With it, Cuba is not only progressing in the economic field but also moving swiftly down the path to social development." And he went on to add that "a social revolution is an educational revolution."[16] It is internationally recognized that increasing a population's educational level is a prerequisite for a higher and ever-improving quality of life.

It is a goal of the Revolution that Cuban society should enjoy comprehensive, general culture as a vehicle to achieve one of Martí's maxims: "Being educated is being free." To that end, one priority of Cuba's overall social development policy is its cultural dimension. I have already mentioned a number of specific cultural programs that comprise the Battle of Ideas. Beyond those specific programs, culture is one of the central concepts of the Battle of Ideas. In 2004, Minister of Culture Abel Prieto noted that Cuba could not and should not compete with capitalist consumer societies by trying to provide every Cuban family with two cars, a swimming pool, and a vacation house. Rather, "we can guarantee conditions of a decent life and at the same time a rich life in spiritual and cultural terms. This is a conception of culture as a form of growth and personal realization that is related to the quality of life. In this sense, we are convinced that culture can be an antidote against consumerism and against the oft-repeated idea that only buying can create happiness in this world."[17]

Funding Social Policies

This chapter has argued that Cuba's social policies have been directed at creating a better life for all Cubans, and it has presented as evidence a large number of policies addressing many different aspects of society. The question that arises immediately is how committed Cuba is to such policies, in the sense of how much of its limited wealth it invests in them. Table 5.6 shows that in this regard Cuba ranks first in Latin America by a substantial margin. In addition, notwithstanding the economic difficulties of the new millennium, the Cuban state continues to increase the fraction of its wealth dedicated to social policies at a faster rate than its wealth is growing. The real amount of social expenditure (at 1997 prices) grew at 8.6 percent per annum on average between 2001 and 2006, while Cuba's GDP grew at only 7.0 percent.[18]

Table 5.6. Social expenditures as a percentage of GDP for Latin American countries, 2005–2006

Country	Pct. of GDP[a]	Country	Pct. of GDP
Cuba	29.2	Venezuela	11.7
Uruguay	20.9	Mexico	10.5
Argentina	19.4	Paraguay	9.0
Brazil	19.1	Peru	8.0
Costa Rica	18.6	Dominican Rep.	7.4
Panama	17.3	El Salvador	7.1
Chile	14.8	Guatemala	6.5
Bolivia	13.6	Ecuador	5.7
Colombia	13.5	Latin America and the Caribbean[b]	13.1
Honduras	13.1	Latin America and the Caribbean[c]	15.1

[a]Based on information from the ECLAC database. Figures are based on spending through the second quarter of 2005.

[b]Simple average, excepting El Salvador.

[c]Adjusted average, excepting El Salvador.

Source: CEPAL, *Panorama social de América Latina, 2005–2006* (Santiago de Chile: CEPAL, 2006).

Brief Concluding Remarks

Over the fifty years of its Revolution, Cuba has given high priority to social policies directed at creating a better life for its citizens. These policies have been backed by a relatively large portion of Cuba's limited wealth. Even in very difficult economic times they have been protected and consolidated, and in some cases even enhanced and extended. A combination of Cuba's remaining aspects of underdevelopment (notwithstanding its important gains in human capital) and the open-ended nature of human well-being make it clear that all of Cuba's important achievements to date are no more than a preamble to what still needs to be done. The road ahead is clearly much longer than the road already traveled. Keeping this in mind, the fundamental principle of Cuba's social policies remains, today as much as ever, that the road is being consciously built in the direction of human well-being and not, as in so many other countries, toward promoting capital accumulation under the pretext of "trickle-down well-being."

Notes

1. David Morris, *Measuring the Condition of the World's Poor* (New York: Pergamon Press, 1975).

2. In Cuba, "humanizing" work entails transforming jobs that require only the exertion of force, with no use of the unique human ability to think, into work that utilizes the ability to be creative and problem solve.

3. ONE, "El envejecimiento de la población Cubana 2007" in the CD by the Centro de Estudio de Población y Desarrollo, *Información para estudios en población y desarrollo 2007* (Havana: ONE, 2008).

4. Ibid.

5. PNUD, *Informe sobre desarrollo humano* (Madrid: Mundi-Prensa Libros, 2008).

6. The People's Council is a local, representative body of the People's Power system of government in Cuba. It encompasses a given territorial area, supports duties of the Municipal Assembly of People's Power, and facilitates greater knowledge of, and attention to, the needs and interests of the inhabitants of its area of responsibility (Act No. 91 of People's Councils).

7. ONE, *Inicio del curso escolar 2007/08 y resumen del curso escolar 2006/07* (Havana: ONE, 2008).

8. ONE, *Panorama económico y social: Cuba 2007* (Havana: ONE, 2008).

9. Cuba has a system of professional judges trained in all aspects of the law, who have full-time legal employment. In addition, there is an extensive network of workers trained in workplace law who adjudicate legal challenges by workers (or enterprise mangers) concerning the work process. Typically, these industry judges do not earn their livelihood

through their legal work, but rather through employment in one of the workplaces under their authority.

10. The average recommended daily allowance is the amount of macronutrients and micronutrients that an individual must consume according to medical criteria to meet physiological requirements, carry out regular activities, and preserve the health of an entire population. It includes a margin of security for the diversity of food habits.

11. ONE, *Anuario Estadístico de Cuba 2006* (Havana: ONE, 2007).

12. Ministerio de Salud Pública Dirección de Estadísticas, *Anuario estadístico de salud* (Havana: MINSAP, 2006).

13. ONE, *Censo de población y viviendas* (Havana: ONE, 2002).

14. J. C. Feres and X. Mancero, *El método de las necesidades básicas insatisfechas (NBI) y sus aplicaciones en América Latina* (Santiago de Chile: CEPAL, 2001).

15. S. Gomila, *Política y estrategia habitacional: La experiencia cubana* (Havana: INV, 2003).

16. A speech by Fidel Castro in the closing session of the IV Encuentro Internacional de Economistas in Havana on February 15, 2002. Available at http://www.cuba.cu/gobierno/discursos/2002/esp/f150202e.html (accessed February 10, 2011).

17. Prieto's comments are available at www.walterlippmann.com/abelprieto-11-7-2004.html (accessed February 10, 2011).

18. Specifically because this figure is compared to many other Latin American countries, I use the standard method of considering the contribution of social expenditures to GDP, evaluating them at their market prices, rather than the more meaningful way of correcting to include free and subsidized social services, which are dominant in the case of Cuba.

6

Fighting Poverty

Cuba's Experience

ÁNGELA FERRIOL

The main goal of the Cuban economic model since 1959 has been to build a society marked by equity and social justice in which every person has the right to satisfy his or her basic needs, not as a consumer but as a citizen. The objective was to build a society based on the principle of equality of opportunity and the practice of solidarity as the essential criterion for distribution. With regard to policies, this model sought to strengthen social, economic, and political connections in order to create a virtuous cycle conducive to accelerated development, where the state would be the principal agent that would guarantee this objective.

In 1953 Fidel Castro outlined the major problems facing Cuba in his historic legal defense speech, "History Will Absolve Me": "The problem of land, the problem of industrialization, the problem of housing, the problem of unemployment, the problem of education, and the problem of health for the people: those are the six points that our efforts would have resolutely determined to address, along with the achievement of public freedoms and political democracy."[1]

Cuba's strategies of political, economic, and social development in the 1960s focused on eliminating the mechanisms that caused extreme economic inequality and, along with it, acute social stratification. This was the key prerequisite for the new model that was to distinguish the subsequent Cuban social and economic performance from the rest of Latin America. Transformations in the system of ownership and the active role of social policies were the main axes of the revolutionary strategy. The combined effects of economic and social policies sought to ensure the population's well-being by guaranteeing full employment, equity in income distribution, a gradual increase in individual consumption, and the satisfaction of basic needs through the state provision of free health care, education, and social security services, among others. Poverty, in particular, was to be eradicated from Cuban society.

The 1959–1989 Period

The transformations in Cuban society in the 1960s after the victory of the Revolution included changes in economic structure, operation of the labor market, and distribution of property and wealth, among other aspects. These structural changes had a profound social impact. *The Eradication of Poverty in Cuba* (1983), by J. L. Rodríguez and G. Carriazo, was the first study of poverty published in the country after 1959.[2] Their analysis demonstrated the elimination of that scourge by providing carefully documented information on both the poverty-eradication policies that had been implemented and their positive effects. It also highlighted popular participation in health-care and educational campaigns and other specific programs as a distinct feature of the Cuban model that contributed to its efficacy.

The key to Cuba's achievements from 1959 to 1989 was its implementation of social policies. At the most basic and immediate level, policies were enacted to quickly eradicate blatant evils such as organized crime, corruption, prostitution, child abuse, and drug addiction. But the goals of Cuba's overall social policy were much more profound than these immediate issues. At their heart was the human condition. On one level they addressed the essential issue of improving the people's material standard of living and well-being, first and foremost by eliminating poverty. But beyond that, they included the goals of increased social equity and the transformation of values, behaviors, and social relations. In particular they aimed at building new human relations based on the value of solidarity, where improved individual well-being for every citizen was to be created as part of building social well-being for all citizens. All these nonmaterial goals themselves had implications for material well-being and the end of poverty.

Guaranteeing education, health care, and employment have always been three top priorities among Cuba's social goals. It is an important reflection of the Island's overall social policy and the very nature of its revolutionary society that Cuba in its constitution guarantees the right to free health care and to free education at all levels and, in turn, defines work as both a duty and a right, which subsumes rights to rest and to work-related safety, security, and health care. The concern with solidarity is reflected in the right to not be socially abandoned. All these rights are guaranteed to everyone, without discrimination based on gender, skin color, national origin, or religious beliefs.[3]

Other important subjects of Cuba's social policies include food, water and sanitation, housing, and social security and welfare. In assessing the efficacy of Cuba's social policies, the important effect of the complementarity of its sector-wide policies must be taken into consideration. Because of interactions among policies, particular policies have synergistic effects in relation to both economic growth and social transformations.

Education has many social effects. It is a necessary prerequisite for instilling revolutionary values and the related elevation of popular culture. Because it enables people to be the active agents in social transformation, Cuba made education the foundation for advancing the remaining social projects. Over the last two decades, in a narrow economic sense knowledge-based goods and services have become one of the most dynamic sectors of the emerging new Cuban economy (see chapter 12), both for domestic industries and for exports. Education is considered one element in ending poverty in all societies in the world. Higher levels of schooling and professional training increase women's involvement in employment and improve household economic status. They also tend to decrease fertility levels and accordingly affect the dynamics of the population and its age composition. Finally, at a very broad level, increased education affects the lives people choose and how they choose to conduct them.

Providing full employment has been a top-priority social policy since the 1960s. It is viewed as one means to the Revolution's goals of ending poverty, increasing the population's material well-being, and creating the conditions for a dignified life. The state is responsible for generating the necessary jobs. The employment policy includes reconciling the supply of and demand for labor, by both economic activity and geographic location. Economic planning is used to guarantee both an adequate supply of labor and its efficient use. Along these lines, and as a particular response to its history of underdevelopment, Cuba has directed special attention to the training and employment of qualified personnel. The amount of qualified labor that Cuba will need is projected for each level of training and specialty, based on the requirements of the various economic development programs. This determines the allotted enrollments in various specialized training and educational courses.

The employment policy also contains measures to protect workers against arbitrary layoffs, guarantee adequate rest breaks, protect against occupational hazards, provide a healthy work environment, and establish social security regulations. In addition, it is intended to create equity. In order to keep salary differences within a set range and to avoid gender discrimination, mechanisms were put in place to guarantee equal salaries not only for the same type of work but also for "equivalent work." All jobs in the economy were examined to determine their complexity and required skill level. A centralized and uniform salary system was established with a single wage scale, and then salaries were paid according to the job's established complexity and skill level.

For several decades, the measures in place throughout the economy were very effective at diminishing inequality. In the late 1980s Cuba had a narrow spread between its salary extremes, a factor of only 2.5, and about 80 percent of family income came from salaries.[4] Ownership income was very limited. Equitable access to well-being was further reinforced by sizable transfers from the state via free services and subsidies.[5] By 1986 income distribution was very equitable, with a Gini coefficient of just 0.25.[6] Whereas in 1953 the poorest 20 percent of the population received only 2.1 percent of the total income and the wealthiest 20 percent received 58.9 percent, by the 1980s the ratios were 9.0 percent and 34 percent, respectively.[7]

One pillar of the equity achieved in that period was the so-called income-consumption model then in effect.[8] The population's main income source was salaries and, therefore, labor results effectively determined access to goods and services that needed to be bought. Overall, the state provided these goods and services at low and stable prices, and it also subsidized the high prices of international goods that were available. These measures gave meaningful purchasing power to salaries. The other pillar of equity in that period was, as previously noted, that a large proportion of total consumption came from free and universally accessible services. The proportion of these services was significantly higher than in most other countries, especially because although the purpose was to cover essential basic needs, in Cuba these included relatively complex and costly services in health care, education, and other areas not usually classified as basic in other countries.

Thus, a rationed market of products provided the recommended nutritional values for the Cuban population, in addition to, for example, minimum needs for footwear and clothing, all at subsidized prices. There was a complementary market of goods and services at unrestricted prices. Plus, there were important nonmarket ways to access durable household appliances, automobiles, houses, and tourism. In 1980 it was estimated that 56 percent of the total consumption of goods and services was covered by income from labor, that is, from salaries and from revenues of cooperatives and private owners. The remaining 44 percent of consumption was obtained through economic redistribution, that is, by transfers from the state to the population in subsidies, social security, or free services.[9]

Two other social policies were particularly important for homogenizing the population's standard of living and thereby reducing poverty. The first was facilitating women's incorporation into the out-of-household workforce and their promotion to leadership positions in society. The second was the then historically unprecedented attempt to bring the rural living standard up to that in cities.

This model established procedures for upward social mobility connected with labor and educational training. These criteria, unlike ownership of capital or land, tended to homogenize the standard of living of the population. Improvements in the social development indicators (some of which were even comparable to the developed world) and the process of equalizing the living standards of families across the Island are signs of the progress in the Cuban population's standard of living and, more broadly, its quality of life.[10] By the 1980s the concept of poverty was no longer part of the social consciousness.

In the late 1980s the economic model started to show signs of weakness through decreases in the rate of growth and economic efficiency. This was followed only a few years later by the demise of first the socialist community then the former USSR. The massive economic crisis these events unleashed in Cuba and the resulting urgent need to introduce some market economy reforms in order to reinsert the country into the global economy led to a number of transformations that significantly altered the model then in place. These events and the resulting economic changes also reintroduced poverty as an issue.

The 1990–1999 Period

Between 1989 and 1993 economic activity declined abruptly, with an accumulated decrease of 35 percent in the GDP and of 75 percent in imports. In just two years, from 1991 to 1993, the country lost nearly 50 percent of its purchasing power and was cut off from sources of international credits.[11] This, of course, had a severe impact on the population's well-being.[12]

The principal effects of the crisis in these years were declines in standard of living and the quality of basic services, including even health care and education. The most critical problems were limited food; widespread deterioration of housing; and shortages of electricity, transportation, communications, and cooking fuel.[13] Concerns over the possible reemergence of poverty in Cuba appeared in this constellation of circumstances.

A unique adjustment and transformation process was launched to address the economic difficulties. The economy continued to be defined as socialist, albeit with a new balance between planned and market economies. A dollar economy was legalized parallel to but distinct from the peso economy. The economy's external sector was opened up but, again, in a way very different from the standard trade liberalization applied in the region. The use of monetary-based exchange processes was greatly expanded, both internationally and domestically. The search for market niches in internationally segmented markets became essential for obtaining the foreign income that Cuba's small and extremely open economy needed. The state enterprise management system was fundamentally altered in a number of ways, including being progressively decentralized. Although state property continued to predominate, a variety of new types of property were created and coexisted with it.[14]

The most important economic changes began in 1993 and were directed at achieving necessary increases in the efficiency and competitiveness of the economy. These were consolidated in 1995 once the recovery process took off. These changes were notable for their gradual and cautious nature in the midst of Cuba's highly unfavorable economic conditions. The reform measures focused on four areas:[15] macroeconomic adjustments, introduction of structural and institutional changes, microeconomic modifications, and social measures.

Five significant social policy measures were adopted in 1990 to mitigate the effect of the crisis on the population. First, even in the period of abrupt economic contraction, workers were not dismissed from their jobs and continued to receive at least their nominal income. Second, a very gradual employment adjustment process began as part of the process of reforming economic enterprises. Third, the nominal income of all pensioners under the social security and welfare system was maintained. Fourth, the majority of available consumer goods was shifted to the rationing system so that their distribution would be as equitable as possible. And fifth, the government attempted to preserve the social programs in health care and education in their entirety. A distinct feature of the Cuban response was, in fact, rejection of "increased labor flexibility" mechanisms and, consequently, avoidance of unemployment as a major problem.[16] As a result of these measures, unemployment never rose above 7.0 percent.

As can be deduced, these policies were aimed at preventing the social costs of the external shock and of the required economic adjustments from falling disproportionately on particular groups and aimed instead to spread them out across the entire population. Thus, for example, the impact of the shock fell not only on the group of workers that would have been laid off but on the entire population due to the foreseeable fall in real wages that followed from printing money to pay salaries without the corresponding production of goods and services to spend them on. Between 1989 and 1993 the real wages of workers dropped by 50 percent, although subsequent gains over the rest of the period being considered then recuperated part of these losses.[17] At the same time, some adjustment of the workforce did occur. Some of this was problematic, as was the large movement of labor trained for other work into the emerging tourism sector and the closure of workplaces in other key sectors of the economy, such as agriculture and construction.[18]

The size and structure of the population's income and spending were modified through the implementation of these economic reform measures, the legalization of the circulation of the U.S. dollar alongside the Cuban peso, and the establishment of new economic spaces. Particular groups of citizens registered increases in monetary income, mainly from self-employment, tourism, offshore remittances, and the new labor incentive systems enacted, particularly in the hard-currency sectors. All these changes gradually increased income differences and hence certain dimensions of social differentiation.

The available information on the population's average income in local currency for 1996–99 indicates that the largest incomes belonged to self-employed workers and salaried workers in foreign companies, joint ventures, and Cuban foreign trade enterprises. State workers earned the lowest incomes, causing a labor shift from this sector to those offering better wages. This group of state workers includes technicians and professionals who had historically been at the upper end of Cuba's wage spectrum. In addition, the nature of their work meant that most of them did not have access to alternate sources of income. For these workers the crisis years brought a sharp reduction in the value of their qualifications, causing dissatisfaction and instability in this highly qualified segment of Cuba's labor force. However, regardless of income differentiation through salaries and other sources in local currency, the main source of income inequality that developed during the crisis resulted from some citizens developing direct accesses to sources of hard currency, as there was a very favorable rate of exchange between hard currency and Cuban pesos.[19]

Based only on the population's monetary income, the Gini coefficient in 1999 had risen to 0.38. Of course, the continuing large state nonmonetary transfers in health care and education significantly contributed to limiting social inequality. Estimates that account for these effects and housing ownership put the Gini coefficient at 0.30.[20]

Beyond increasing income inequality, the structural transformations contributed to the internal fragmentation of existing classes and social levels and the emergence of new social groups. Along with other processes, this increased the heterogeneity and complexity of the social structure.[21] Certain groups faced a gradual decrease in their prospects for general social progress and opportunities to realize well-being. Other groups that emerged and consolidated were marked by their high levels of income and consumption relative to the average population. A widening gap opened between vulnerable and advantaged groups.

On an individual level, the reforms also altered the traditional channels of socioeconomic mobility and undermined the education-occupation-income triad that had been a central factor in the previously achieved social homogenization. Access to certain resources and other factors—particularly access to remittances and income from underground activities—became keys to socioeconomic mobility.

The crisis also reaggravated the territorial inequalities that the previous economic and social policies had largely eliminated. By the late 1990s access to goods and services had developed a strong spatial component. The greatest opportunities appeared in physical and social spaces with advantages for supplying and marketing products,[22] spaces that were distributed unevenly across the provinces. Research by the Physical Planning Institute identified the territories with the highest vulnerability to insufficient food production and unemployment.[23] In this analysis, thirty-four of forty-two municipalities that were classified as having high and very high vulnerability were located in the eastern region of the country.

In brief, the Special Period crisis and the reforms have had differentiated impacts on various social groups, despite the social policies that sought to protect the entire population on equal terms. Overall, households employed various strategies to offset the decline in their standard of living and achieve social reinsertion, with varying degrees of success. During the crisis and subsequent recovery, the greatest opportunities have been available to those families that managed to find their way into activities generating hard currency, including activities connected with the flourishing underground economy.

The acute nature and profound impact of these economic and social processes refocused the attention of academicians and politicians on questions regarding poverty: Has the phenomenon of poverty reemerged in Cuba? Is poverty in Cuba the same as poverty in the rest of the underdeveloped world? Is poverty compatible with a socialist society? And finally, how can social policies be adapted to the new conditions in order to address the needs of disadvantaged groups?

Does Poverty Exist in Cuba?

In order to study poverty it is necessary to recognize the complex and multifaceted nature of the phenomenon. The 1995 World Summit on Social Development in Copenhagen was an important event in regard to establishing an appropriately complex definition of poverty. There was consensus at the meeting that poverty manifests in many forms, among them a lack of income and sufficient productive resources to guarantee a sustainable livelihood; famine and malnutrition; ill health; lack of or limited access to education and other basic services; increase in morbidity and mortality due to disease; lack of housing or inadequate housing; lack of resources to ensure security; and social discrimination and exclusion. It is also marked by lack of participation in making decisions in society's civil, social, and cultural life.[24] Such conditions of poverty frequently persist across generations.

It is obvious that a person does not have to demonstrate all these manifestations of poverty to be considered poor. The close relationship among the various fields of social development suggests, however, that a vicious cycle is frequently created in which the poor population develops most of these manifestations simultaneously.[25]

It is important to stress that in this approach the measure of basic needs used to determine who is poor is distinct from the desires and expectations of the individuals themselves. In other words, "conditions of deprivation" must be distinguished from "sentiments of deprivation."[26] The latter are unquestionably important, but they are more closely linked to the concept of relative poverty, in which a person compares his or her situation to that of others, taken as the point of reference. A whole approach to the study of poverty, the so-called subjective approach, can be built around these sentiments of deprivation. This approach solicits the participation of the poor in the investigation, for example through giving their views on what constitutes poverty, how their living conditions compare to others in their society, and what they view as the processes of impoverishment and survival strategies.

Studies of poverty in Cuba are relatively scarce.[27] Estimates in the 1990s suggested that a portion of the population had insufficient monetary income. Yet, this population still enjoyed guaranteed access to education, health care, and social security. Thus, to answer one of the questions posed earlier: poverty in Cuba is qualitatively different from poverty in the rest of the Latin American region. Among the factors that differentiate poverty in Cuba are the following rights and services that are guaranteed to the entire population, especially to those with low or insufficient incomes:

- Food that supplies a minimum of 50 percent of nutritional requirements is available at subsidized prices affordable to everyone. Additional subsidized food may be made available, depending on necessity, vulnerability, or job placement.
- A community doctor is continuously present and practices both preventive and curative medicine in the neighborhood, providing both primary and intermediate services for free. Whenever more intensive treatment is needed, everyone has the right of referral to receive free, high-technology, specialized medical services available across the country.
- Pregnant women and infants up to one year old receive monthly care, including all required services. Diagnostic tests for the early detection of congenital malformations and specialized services for high-risk pregnancies are free.

- Basic education through ninth grade and the guarantee of full training for employment are free of charge. This is an important right and service, not only for the young person who directly receives it but for the family he or she comes from who benefits both monetarily and psychologically from knowing their child will find employment, a major concern of most poor families worldwide.
- People with specific or special needs—such as women and people with physical or mental disabilities—are offered special jobs that accord with their capabilities.
- Higher-education studies are totally free of charge. Young people who did not pursue university studies can take courses to upgrade their skills.
- A social security system offers complete coverage for all workers, including protection against losses from disease, partial or total disability, maternity, and old age.
- A welfare system offers monetary transfers, allocations in kind, and employment to people needing assistance because of disability, lack of household income (particularly for single mothers), and losses due to natural disasters.
- An advantageous payment system facilitates homeownership.

These benefits are provided at levels above the critical thresholds for Latin America to classify a household as being in poverty and having unsatisfied basic needs.[28] Some items—such as advanced studies, complex medical treatment, or homeownership—are not even considered basic needs by any other country in the region. Because poor Cubans are able to receive general social protection and a number of essential goods and services not accessible to the poor throughout the rest of Latin America, the term "population at risk" has been proposed to refer to that portion of the Cuban population with insufficient income to purchase all the basic food and nonfood items it needs.[29]

Figure 6.1 shows the sharp increase in the population at risk during the early part of the Special Period.[30] Between 1988 and 1996 the percentage of the urban population at risk more than doubled (P0). The risk gap (P1) shows that the difference between the poverty line and the average income of people in poverty was not great but grew in that time. This indicates that, independent of the number of people at risk, their poverty intensified. Intensity of poverty (P2), a more nuanced measure, yields the same qualitative result: that the intensity of poverty increased.

As mentioned, the effects of economic contraction were more pronounced in Cuba's eastern region, where 30 percent of the urban population lives.

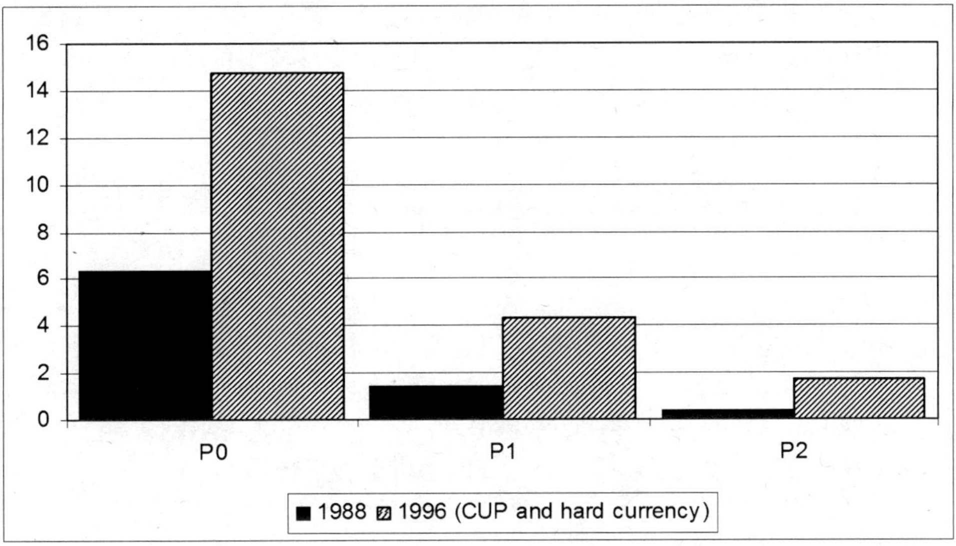

Figure 6.1. Urban population at risk in Cuba, 1988 and 1996 (%). *Source:* A. Ferriol, G. Carriazo, O. Echevarría, and D. Quintana, *Efectos de políticas económicas y sociales sobre los niveles de pobreza: El caso de Cuba en los noventa* (Havana: INIE, 1997).

Nearly 22 percent of these people were at risk, compared to the national average of 14.7 percent for the urban population. But because the eastern region already had a greater population at risk than either the western region or the city of Havana pre-crisis, the latter two regions suffered a greater deterioration in their risk incidence than the east did.[31]

National GDP did not stop falling sharply until 1994, when it stabilized at 0.7 percent growth. In 1995 growth was consolidated at a rate of 2.5 percent as Cuba tried to restart large parts of its economy that had been closed down or severely curtailed. Not until 1996 did Cuba see its first year of strong growth after the crisis, with growth at 7.8 percent.

The estimates for the city of Havana in table 6.1 are an important indicator of the government's concern with poverty during the beginning of the recovery. The table shows the immediate attention Cuba gave to its growing population at risk as soon as it had funds to do so. The percentage of the population at risk in Havana dropped in one year from 20.1 percent to 11.5 percent, and the P1 and P2 indicators both show that the intensity of poverty was sharply reduced as well. Moreover, despite the significant deterioration in its indicators of poverty during the crisis, figure 6.2 shows that by the new millennium Cuba compared favorably with its Latin American neighbors.[32]

Recently, an international poverty line of $1 per day adjusted for purchasing power parity has come into common usage. This measure was created to

Table 6.1. Population at risk in Havana, 1988, 1995, 1996 (%)

Year	P0	P1	P2
1988	4.3	1.2	0.4
1995	20.1	5.2	1.8
1996	11.5	3.0	1.1

Source: A. Ferriol et al., *Efectos de políticas económicas y sociales sobre los niveles de pobreza: El caso de Cuba en los noventa* (Havana: INIE, 1997).

facilitate distinguishing between classes of poor (for example, from those who have between $1 and $2 per day) and also for evaluating compliance with the UN Millennium Development Goals. This much lower poverty line of course yields much lower poverty numbers. In 2005 only 1.9 percent of the Cuban population were in poverty according to that criterion.[33]

A comparison of the socioeconomic and socio-demographic characteristics of at-risk versus high-income households indicates a number of factors associated with the former's disadvantaged situation.[34] First of all, these households were more likely to have preadolescent children: 39 percent of families in the lowest decile of per capita family income, and 29 percent of those in the next lowest decile, had preadolescent children.[35] In comparison, only about 14 percent of households in the top two deciles had preadolescent children. A similar pattern held for households with adolescents.

A second socio-demographic factor concerns households consisting of only senior citizens. These comprised roughly 10 percent of households at every income level. However, for low-income seniors, age and limited resources interacted to increase their vulnerability, and they were more likely than younger families to experience multiple characteristics of poverty (for example, health problems and housing problems).

A third factor was the sector of the economy the household wage earners were employed in. This was related to a fourth factor: the level of education in the family. The average schooling level of low-income families, albeit relatively high at nearly tenth grade, was lower than that of high-income families.[36]

In most countries, housing conditions correlate fairly directly with household income, due to the existence of a housing market. In Cuba, where the housing market was largely eliminated, precarious housing conditions were a causal factor for many of the negative conditions that constitute poverty. The final factor was the number of people in a family who were "economically active" (that is, people who earn income). In 40 percent of the households in the lowest income decile, no one was economically active. This was also the group with the highest percentage of homemakers. In the next lowest decile, the family employment situation was better but still far worse than in the high-income

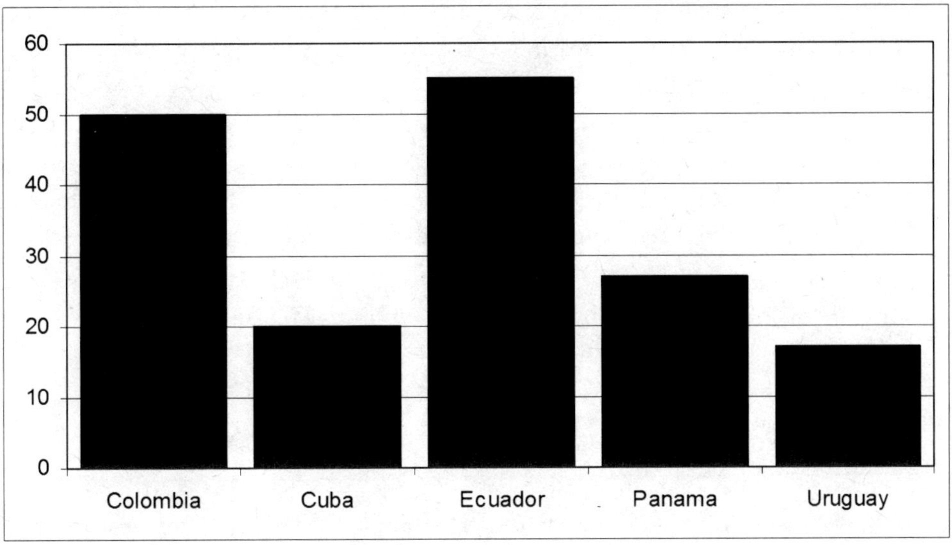

Figure 6.2. Urban poverty in select Latin American countries, 2001–2002 (%). *Sources:* CEPAL, *Panorama social de América Latina, 2002–2003* (Santiago de Chile: CEPAL, 2003); and A. Ferriol, "El modelo social cubano: Una aproximación a tres temáticas en debate," *Cuba: Investigación Económica* 7, no. 1 (2001).

groups, where only around 13 percent of households had no economically active members.

Vulnerability to many of the problems of poverty was not confined to the two lowest family income deciles. A 2001 study of households at risk in the city of Havana found that a significant number of families in the third to fifth deciles from the bottom had similar poverty-related problems in terms of containing only senior citizens, having chronically ill members, or having members who could work but did not.[37]

Qualitative studies revealed the interrelation of families' values and behaviors with demographic and socioeconomic factors such as those just discussed. Negative values and behaviors aggravated household vulnerability to poverty. Two common negative compounding factors were the presence of significant domestic conflicts and of gender inequality in family roles.[38]

Finally, it is important to know what a population thinks about its own socioeconomic situation. The previously mentioned Havana study also addressed this issue.[39] A representative sample of families was asked to indicate the three main problems affecting their daily lives. The top two problems were insufficient income and insufficient food. The two next highest concerns, mentioned by significantly fewer respondents, were deteriorating housing and shortage of transportation. Unemployment, insufficient education, and lack of social protection against emergencies were indicated only extremely infrequently. This finding once again shows both the similarities and the important differences between the population at risk in Cuba and people in poverty in other underdeveloped countries.

The presence of economic vulnerability and the risk of poverty are, however, not compatible with the objectives of socialism to build a just society that provides all people with extensive opportunities to develop their human capacities. Therefore, reducing the number of vulnerable and disadvantaged people in Cuba and eliminating the processes that give rise to these phenomena continue to be important challenges for the state. The accelerating aging of the Cuban population adds an extra dimension to these problems.

Coping with Economic Vulnerability and the Risk of Poverty, 2000–2010

In response to the reemergence of economic vulnerability, the government implemented a number of special social programs beginning in 2000 to supplement its traditional social policies. Given that these were responses to the deterioration of the population's living situation during the Special Period, they are often referred to as "emergency programs," although many are clearly general improvements on the previous social policies that will continue after full economic recovery. Eventually constituting more than two hundred social programs, they collectively are revolutionizing Cuba's provision of social services. Like all the traditional policies, the new measures were informed by Cuba's commitment to effective equality in its social policies, which meant that many targeted specific disadvantaged groups facing heightened vulnerability and risk of poverty.

A major innovative concept for addressing the problems of the most disadvantaged and economically vulnerable has emerged during this period. The concept of wherever possible providing personalized welfare services is slowly spreading throughout Cuba's welfare system. As a rule, this approach should place social policies on a more equitable, effective, and efficient footing. The training of a large body of social workers with new mandates has been key to implementing this concept.

A large body of young people have been formally trained in new schools of social work. Upon graduation, they are assigned specific tasks in the communities, but their overarching function is to prevent social exclusion. In pursuit of this goal they maintain stable links with a group of families, evaluate their needs on-site, select those families requiring the most support, and try to provide the type of care or solution needed. This approach was piloted in a program where social workers went door to door to every family in Cuba, identifying all the underweight children up to fifteen years of age and arranging for them to regularly receive additional high-quality food. An area of social policy where personalized care is extremely important is geriatric care. The new social workers are presently transforming policies for the elderly as part of the National Plan of Action for Senior Citizens.

Cuba's combination of universal social policies with personalized attention to the needy contrasts with the neoliberal "focusing" approach to fighting poverty that is used in the rest of the region. In fact, focusing is simultaneously a standard of inclusion and of exclusion.[40] According to ECLAC, in light of the characteristics of social vulnerability present in most countries of the region and the disadvantaged groups' lack of local participation, focusing seems to yield disappointing results.[41]

These are the most frequent activities of Cuban social workers:

- Providing personalized benefits in kind to socioeconomically challenged families in unhealthy neighborhoods
- Providing young people up to fifteen years of age whose growth and weight are inadequate with a supplementary monthly quota of free food
- Improving the living conditions, physical activity, employment, social protection, and integration of people with disabilities
- Giving needy senior citizens personalized assistance with nutrition, in-home care, income, and living conditions. The assistance could be monetary, in kind, or in services.
- Promoting physical, cultural, and community-integration activities among senior citizens
- Providing people who are ill with special diets, allocating the appropriate baskets of food for each case
- Assisting families who have sustained losses from natural disasters by providing food, personal belongings, household appliances, and construction materials for housing repairs
- Providing assistance aimed at socially reintegrating youths ages seventeen to thirty who are neither studying nor working. In particular they receive employment offers, priority access to higher education, and access to a specially tailored program of intermediate-level education courses plus a stipend.
- Assisting a wide variety of other vulnerable groups to access numerous extant social programs, such as those for pregnant women; orphans; former inmates; and families in mountainous areas, the least-developed provinces, and high-unemployment municipalities

There has been wide discussion in Cuba of problems with the traditional social policies enacted over the years from 1959 to 1989 and into the Special Period. On one hand, they had yielded outstanding results in transforming the population's social situation, eradicating poverty, and even diminishing the significant inequality and problems of vulnerability that reemerged during the crisis of the 1990s. But on the other hand, and incompatible with the Revolution's goal of building social equality, the disadvantaged groups still retained some characteristics of being intergenerationally disadvantaged. As an important example of this, the level of schooling in at-risk households was lower than average. To address this concern, a group of new programs was designed beginning in 2000, with the primary objective of supplementing the effective equity of traditional social policies in the current times of growing inequality. Primary among these were a large number of new policies directed at education:

- The individual teaching needs of primary students are examined, with greater attention given to those children facing educational difficulties. Work is under way to ensure special education for all children with any degree of limitation, no matter how severe. This is another example of the concept of personalization of services spreading throughout Cuba's social policies.
- Schools were reorganized to have one teacher to a maximum of twenty students in all primary schools, enabling the teacher to become better acquainted with the students, their learning limitations, and their socioeconomic situation. This allows differentiated education to be provided to each student.
- The conditions and furnishings of rural schools were equalized with those of urban schools. Recent investments in personal computers and audiovisual aids have provided comparable equipment to all schools. This makes it possible to consolidate the classes of excellence that are prepared and taught throughout the country and to universalize the teaching of computer science and informatics.
- Active community involvement is promoted in cases of school absence, to prevent school dropouts.
- School lunches and snacks have been fortified in order to increase the nutrition of students living in families at risk. This is also important for promoting their learning.
- A similar initiative has been implemented in secondary education. Specialized assistance is provided to examine teaching needs at the intermediate level, with a structured plan of one teacher to every fifteen students, two sessions, and a school brunch. New options for special-

ized study, such as computer science, art, and social work, have been added to the traditional offerings for career preparation coursework.

- Tertiary education has been considerably expanded. The goal of universal higher education is being promoted with the establishment of university campuses in all municipalities. University students in day courses receive stipends, and 50 percent of these enjoy free room and board.

Other new public health programs have been implemented:

- Intermediate and emergency medical services have been brought closer to the community to facilitate access, particularly by senior citizens. In this model secondary health care blends into primary care. Primary health-care settings are now equipped with ECGs, medications for thrombolysis in the early treatment of cardiac arrest, high-resolution ultrasound equipment to examine vital organs and conduct prenatal sonograms, traumatology and rehabilitation, and endoscopic services for the early detection of diseases in the digestive tract, among others.
- The community doctor program has been strengthened for providing personalized care and reducing health risk factors in the community. Universal vaccination programs have been expanded to include thirteen vaccines. Priority care plans are being put in place to address high-prevalence diseases in vulnerable groups, importantly tuberculosis and genetic conditions.

The other key factor for the success of the new policies being initiated has been the conditions of their implementation, including issues of management, personnel, consistent funding, collection of information, monitoring, participation, dissemination of information, and integration with previously existing social services. The following are some of the factors in the execution of these programs that have been essential to their efficacy:

- The type and quality of program management has been important for both their short-term success and long-term sustainability. Political leaders at the highest levels initially oversaw the new programs. Although the programs were implemented through existing institutions, a parallel, independent organization was set up to supervise their use of resources and ensure their smooth operation and progress.
- Because the quality and commitment of its personnel is a limiting factor for any program, human resources in these new programs have received special attention right from the beginning. The focus has been on the quality of training and the establishment of a vocational com-

mitment among the staff. This continues to be a fundamental factor in the performance of these programs and is continuing to be addressed.

- Starting up a new program requires particular management activities and skills that differ from managing an established program. The initial managers must establish the appropriate teams of experts to design the programs and draft the training syllabi for staff. They must then launch initial pilot experiments, closely monitor them, and make continual corrections and improvements, more in the capacity of an experimental scientist than a typical program manager, before the program goes into widespread practice.
- Intermittent programs can never develop sufficiently to achieve significant social results, and consistent funding is one requirement for the necessary continuity. Therefore, the state fully funded all new programs out of an initial independent and centralized fund. Once the new facilities and programs were up and running, they joined the traditional service network and were funded in the same way as traditional programs.
- A preliminary component of information collection concerns determining the appropriate beneficiaries for the new programs. Social workers played a key role in this regard. They were assigned to complete systematic studies in their communities, conducting semistructured or in-depth interviews with every family to determine which ones needed assistance and to follow up with those that did.
- A second aspect of collecting information was to determine the specific needs of the beneficiaries. Censuses were carried out with specific objectives, such as evaluating the nutritional status of young people up to fifteen years of age and the situations of people with disabilities, senior citizens living alone, and youths who were neither studying nor working. These projects are continuing at present. The social workers again played a major role in conducting these censuses, along with community doctors, school personnel, and community-based social organizations, depending on the specific census.
- A particular type of essential information collection concerns program monitoring and evaluation. Here again, social workers are on the front lines, constantly monitoring all aspects of the life situation of the families assigned to them. Additionally, particular evaluative censuses are conducted with target groups in order to gauge the results of specific programs. With regard to ensuring that efforts are successful, the program and project officers, along with specialists from sector-wide bodies and scientific institutions, conduct ongoing, systematic control of

the inputs and supplies used and activities carried out. They also assess the need for further adjustments to the programs to improve their performance.

- In addition, the various channels of civic control continue with their traditional mechanisms for monitoring and evaluating social policies. These include the People's Councils, the meetings where delegates report back to their constituencies, the local government departments responsible for receiving and addressing citizen complaints, and the reports to the National Assembly by state agencies in charge of these programs.
- Local governmental and social organizations of the people (such as Committees for the Defense of the Revolution, trade unions, and the Federation of Cuban Women) play roles in some aspects of information gathering, as well as in monitoring the programs, through both social and local governmental channels.
- The dissemination of extensive information is essential for monitoring and other forms of participation. Cuba adapted its traditional information dissemination systems to include the new programs. Key information channels are the national statistical system; the complementary, sector-wide information systems (health and education are the most advanced); the surveys on the economic situation of households, workplaces, and other venues; the Food and Nutrition Surveillance System; the monthly review of the economic plan; the monitoring of the execution of the state budget; and the systems for soliciting the comments and views of the people.
- An integrated public information dissemination strategy is essential to mobilize the population in support of the social programs and of the Cuban government's decision to devote a relatively large portion of its scarce resources to those programs. The system involves both written and televised dissemination on the national and provincial levels. Added to this are public presentations that government and social agencies use for explaining the programs on the provincial and municipal levels. These presentations are carried out at a meaningful level of sophistication. For example, they commonly present the degree of social access to a program through such indicators as the coverage achieved; the amount of qualified staff, equipment, and general infrastructure the program needs; and the benefits provided in kind, in monetary terms, and in the quantity and quality of services. Also the strategic objectives and main goals of the program are systematically presented along with these results achieved.

- A different important aspect of the dissemination of information is the widespread transmission of the new approaches and practices ("best practices") in service delivery from one institution and program to another. This has been a key to the overall "revolution and transformation" of Cuba's social policies by the new programs.
- The continuation of the traditional social policies (such as assistance to senior citizens, to single mothers, to disadvantaged minors, to people with disabilities, and to needy families, among many others) and of the traditional mechanisms citizens use to apply for assistance serves to unify the new programs with the old.[42] This functional linkage facilitates social integration for the beneficiaries of the emergency programs to prevent their situation from deteriorating when certain emergency programs fulfill their objectives and are terminated.
- The universal, comprehensive, and free nature of Cuba's social policies enables the beneficiaries of the new emergency programs to join traditional programs they had failed to utilize before, and even to receive simultaneous assistance from both sources, again contributing to the integration of the programs and the sustainability of the emergency measures.

In 2004, after several of the programs had been in force for a year, various censuses and studies were conducted in the communities, indicating progress in the situation of the vulnerable population in a number of dimensions. Among these dimensions were greater access to medical services, including emergency services; greater equity in children's real opportunities for physical and mental development; better standards of living for disadvantaged families; and an increase in the survival rate of senior citizens.[43]

Building on the improvement registered in 2004, another group of structural measures was put in place in 2005. These were intended to introduce changes in the prevailing income-consumption model, in view of Cuba's improved economic situation at that time and its likely continuance in the medium term. Some of those decisions were significant for people in the lowest income deciles. For example, the country's minimum wage was increased by 125 percent, a measure that benefited around 38 percent of working people. The base salaries of workers in health, education, justice, and law enforcement have subsequently been increased gradually. Social security pensions below three hundred Cuban pesos were also raised, benefiting 98 percent of pensioners and increasing the average pension by 47 percent. Gradual pension increases will continue as long as economic conditions indicate that they will not produce inflationary effects. A challenge for the authorities in managing the current income-consumption model is to appropriately adjust the universal tax and subsidy system to the current characteristics of household monetary income.

Lessons from Cuba's Experiences

A set of lessons that might be applicable in other cases can be drawn from the Cuban experience:

- It is possible to increase the quality and efficiency of educational and health services while keeping them in the public domain.
- Equity must be a central, strategic objective of social policy.
- Based on the goal of ensuring a certain base level of social development for all citizens, the universal and free character of social policies must be supplemented with one or more other characteristics to guarantee effective equity. Personalizing services is one possible supplementary characteristic.
- An appropriate balance is required between centralization and decentralization to implement effective controls and regular evaluations.
- The best results are obtained when the program combines the efforts of different agents with common purposes (government, political and social organizations, families).
- It is essential to have qualified and dedicated staff capable of assimilating scientific advances to practice.
- Political will is necessary for poverty-eradication programs to have sufficient budgetary priority and continuity.
- It is essential that programs be designed with the required comprehensiveness, which is the only way that social policies can effectively protect and involve disadvantaged groups.

To fight poverty it is necessary but not sufficient to focus on optimizing the performance of antipoverty institutions. In addition, it is necessary both to address other, more general socioeconomic problems and to create appropriate social values and a public sentiment of solidarity with the neediest in society. Without these values it will be practically impossible to reach out to the very poor. The Cuban experience indicates that through humanistic values it is possible to provide quality basic services to the entire population and to ensure a decent living for the people with the lowest incomes, even with a low level of national economic development.

Notes

1. F. Castro, *La historia me absolverá* (Havana: Editora Política, 1973).

2. J. L. Rodríguez and G. Carriazo, *La erradicación de la pobreza en Cuba* (Havana: Editorial de Ciencias Sociales, 1983).

3. For further information on citizens' rights, see the *Constitución de la República de Cuba* (Havana: Editora Política, 1997).

4. D. Quintana, "¿Es el trabajo la principal vía de acceso al consumo?" (INIE Research Report, 1991).

5. A. Ferriol, "El empleo en Cuba 1980–1995," *Cuba: Investigación Económica* 2, no. 1 (1996).

6. A. Zimbalist and C. Brundenius, "Crecimiento con equidad: El desarrollo cubano en una perspectiva comparada," *Cuadernos de Nuestra América* 6, no. 13 (1986).

7. A. Ferriol, R. Castiñeiras, and G. Therborn, *Política social: El mundo contemporáneo y las experiencias de Cuba y Suecia* (Montevideo: Editorial TRADINCO, 2005).

8. A. Ferriol, "El modelo social cubano: Una aproximación a tres temáticas en debate," *Cuba: Investigación Económica* 7, no. 1 (2001).

9. Quintana, "¿Es el trabajo la principal vía de acceso al consumo?"

10. Centro para Investigaciones de la Economía Mundial, *Investigación sobre desarrollo humano y equidad en Cuba en 1999* (Havana: CIEM, 2000).

11. A. Casanova, ed., *Estructura económica de Cuba* (Havana: Editorial Félix Varela, 2002).

12. A. González, "Economía y sociedad: Los retos del modelo económico," *Temas* No. 11 (1997); A. Ferriol, G. Carriazo, O. Echevarría, and D. Quintana, *Efectos de políticas económicas y sociales sobre los niveles de pobreza: El caso de Cuba en los noventa* (Havana: INIE, 1997).

13. For further information on the social effects of the crisis, see Colectivo de autores, *Cuba: Crisis, ajuste y situación social (1990–1996)* (Havana: Editorial Ciencias Sociales, 1998).

14. J. L. Rodríguez, "Cuba: El camino de la reforma económica," *Cuba Socialista* No. 16 (1999).

15. For further information see A. González, "Economía y sociedad: Retos del modelo económico," *Temas* No. 11 (1997).

16. Ferriol, "El empleo en Cuba 1980–1995."

17. After the reforms that began in 1993, the economy slowly but steadily recovered. See Ferriol et al., *Efectos de políticas económicas y sociales sobre los niveles de pobreza: El caso de Cuba en los noventa.*

18. For further information, see the remarks by C. Lage and J. L. Rodríguez at the V Congreso de la ANEC and the X Congreso de Profesionales de las Ciencias Económicas en Centroamérica y el Caribe. Reproduced in *El Economista*, Havana (1997).

19. Ferriol, "El modelo social cubano: Una aproximación a tres temáticas en debate."

20. These studies have significant methodological value because in calculating the Gini coefficient they considered transfers via state spending on food, health, education,

and housing ownership. These estimates were made using a rate of exchange of ten pesos to one dollar. For further information on the factors determining the greatest inequality in income distribution, see A. Ferriol, "Apertura externa, mercado laboral y desigualdad de ingresos" (INIE Research Report, 2000).

21. For further information on the socio-structural impact of the economic readjustment and the social re-stratification process, see M. Espina et al., *Impactos socio estructurales del reajuste económico* (Havana: Centro de Investigaciones Sicológicas y Sociológicas, 1996).

22. L. Iñiguez and M. Ravenet, "Precedencias y efectos de los procesos de la década de los noventa en las desigualdades espaciales y sociales en Cuba" (Centro de Estudios sobre Salud y Medio Ambiente, Universidad de La Habana Research Report, 1999).

23. For more information see Instituto de Planificación Física, *Vulnerabilidad de los territorios a los procesos de cambios* (Havana: IPF, 1997).

24. Naciones Unidas, *Informe de la Cumbre Mundial sobre Desarrollo Social* (Ginebra: NU, 1995).

25. For further information on the pillars of social development and their close interrelation in the economic development process, see the findings in A. Ferriol and A. González, "Política social: Un enfoque para el análisis," *Cuba: Investigación Económica* 1, no. 4 (1995).

26. A. Sen, "Sobre conceptos y medidas de pobreza," *Comercio Exterior* No. 4 (1992).

27. R. Muñoz, *Concepto y medición de la pobreza* (Havana: Comité Estatal de Estadísticas, 1992); O. Hernández, "Algunas consideraciones acerca del concepto de pobreza y su medición de acuerdo a las condiciones de Cuba" (Comité Estatal de Estadísticas Working Paper, 1994); J. Torres, "Pobreza. Un enfoque para Cuba" (a presentation at the INIE, 1992); Ferriol et al., *Efectos de políticas económicas y sociales sobre los niveles de pobreza: El caso de Cuba en los noventa;* M. Ramos, "Contribución al estudio de la pobreza. Reseña analítica" (INIE Research Report, 2003); Colectivo de autores, "Reforma econoómica y población en riesgo en Ciudad de La Habana," *Cuba: Investigación Económica* 12, nos. 1–2 (2006).

28. For a complete study on the usefulness and applications of the method of unsatisfied basic needs in Latin America for poverty-related studies see J. C. Feres and X. Mancero, *El método de las necesidades básicas insatisfechas (NBI) y sus aplicaciones en América Latina* (Santiago de Chile: CEPAL, 2001).

29. Ferriol et al., *Efectos de políticas económicas y sociales sobre los niveles de pobreza: El caso de Cuba en los noventa.*

30. These three indexes refer to a class of measures of poverty developed by James Foster, Joel Greer, and Erik Thorbecke in "A Class of Decomposable Poverty Measures," *Econométrica* 52, no. 3 (1984). P0 is the percent of the population with income below the poverty line. P1 measures the gap between the middle income of the poor and the poverty line. P2 is a more nuanced measure of the intensity of poverty than P1 is, as it is sensitive to income distribution among the poor.

31. For further information on conceptual and methodological issues connected with the Cuban social model, see Programa de las Naciones Unidas para el Desarrollo, *Efecto*

de políticas macroeconómicas y sociales sobre los niveles de pobreza: El caso de Cuba en los años noventa (Mexico City: Ediciones Mundi-Prensa, 1998).

32. Starting at the end of the 1990s the way the at-risk population was calculated in Cuba changed, so the data in this graph, for example, is not directly comparable with the data in the previous table and graph.

33. A. Ferriol, A. Hernánez, A. González, and X. Hoang, "Cuba: Export Promotion, Poverty, Inequality and Growth in the 1990s," in *Who Gains from Free Trade? Export-led Growth, Inequality and Poverty in Latin America*, ed. R. Vos, E. Ganuza, S. Morley, and S. Robinson (London: Routledge, 2006).

34. Programa de las Naciones Unidas para el Desarrollo, *Efecto de Políticas macroeconómicas y sociales sobre los niveles de pobreza: El caso de Cuba en los años noventa.*

35. Households were ranked in ascending order according to their per capita income level, and then this whole ordered population was divided into 10 deciles, groups of equal size.

36. The household's average school level was calculated as the average number of years of studies completed by people aged fifteen and older.

37. Colectivo de autores, "Reforma económica y población en riesgo en Ciudad de La Habana."

38. M. Zabala, "Aproximación al estudio de la relación familia y pobreza (Doctoral thesis, Havana, 1999); B. Díaz, I. Guasch, I. and B. Vigaud, "Caracterización del niño en riesgo por condiciones socioeconómicas adversas" (Informe del Ministerio de Educación, 1990).

39. Colectivo de autores, "Reforma económica y población en riesgo en Ciudad de La Habana."

40. CEPAL, *La brecha de la equidad: Una segunda evaluación* (Santiago de Chile: CEPAL, 2000).

41. Ibid.

42. Traditionally, the two main mechanisms have involved individuals either delivering petitions to public government offices at all levels that are responsible for dealing with popular complaints, or submitting requests to their People's Power delegate.

43. This in turn increased life expectancy in Cuba, which in 2005–2007 was 77.97 years, 76.00 for men and 80.02 for women. ONE, *Indicadores demográficos de la población cubana: Cuba y sus territorios 2007* (Havana: ONE, 2008).

7

The Cuban Population

Major Characteristics with a Special Focus on the Aging Population

JUAN CARLOS ALFONSO FRAGA

By the end of 2007 the median age in Cuba had risen to 37.0 years. There were 1.9 million senior citizens (people sixty years old and older, or "over fifty-nine"), constituting one in six Cubans, or 16.6 percent of the population of slightly more than 11.2 million.[1] The age profile in these figures is characteristic of the world's developed countries. And as in those countries, Cuba's aging population is the result of secular decreases in both fertility and mortality.[2]

The problems an aging population causes for a society are well known. The largest of these is the increased demand for health care and social services correlated with the growth of a population that has greater functional limitations. A second major problem is the changing balance across the generations. In terms of the number of people, this means that more people require care while relatively fewer are able to provide it, regardless of whether that care is provided through public channels or individual channels (mostly within families). Economically, this means that there is an ever larger number of nonworking people requiring formal or informal intergenerational transfers from a relatively smaller number of working people.

Many problems of aging are more acute for senior citizens who live alone. Due to changing family residence patterns and simply to people living longer, the percentage of senior citizens who live alone in Cuba is constantly increasing. Because women live longer than men on average, there are more elderly women in this situation. And because women have had a lower workforce participation rate, their status as senior citizens living alone can be even more vulnerable than that of men, despite all social efforts to pay special attention to this group.

Fertility and mortality have declined in nearly all Latin American countries. However, Cuba's demographic history differs from those countries in at least three respects, all of which have an impact on the nature of its aging profile. First, Cuba has the lowest birthrate in the region. Although there was a small baby boom in the 1960s after the victory of the Cuban Revolution in 1959, the total fertility rate (TFR) has been below 2.0 children per woman since 1978.[3] In 2007, Cuba's TFR stood at 1.43 children per woman.

This is a result, to some extent, of changes in fertility patterns connected with the increase of women working outside the home, their high educational and health levels, and, in general, with the increase of women's social empowerment. Among Cuban women, 59.1 percent are now part of the workforce, with 65.6 percent of these being professional workers or technicians.[4] But a second factor is transformation in the patterns of family formation. Although marriage is even less a prerequisite for childbearing than before, and people have been marrying at earlier ages, these changes are more than offset by opposing factors. One factor is that many young couples reside with other family members in living situations with limited space for additional children. Another important factor is the decreased stability of couples, whether formally married or not.

The second aspect relates to the structure of households and families. Three related family mechanisms are typically used to address the pressure from the significant growth in the Cuban senior population. The first involves their increased cohabitation with younger family members. The second involves the adaptation of existing family networks specifically for regular transfer of both material and emotional resources to senior citizens. The third involves the exchange or swapping of living quarters among family members.

The children of the 1960s baby boom are now between forty and fifty years old. So although the rapidly increasing number of senior citizens is already putting pressure on these family support mechanisms, there is still a sizable base in the working population to make these mechanisms possible. With the very low fertility rates that set in by the 1970s, however, when the baby boomers reach retirement age in a decade, these mechanisms will be much more severely stressed. There will be fewer chances for intergenerational transfers of any kind, including shared living quarters. Cuba's significant emigration over the last five decades is a second factor that has to be considered due its impact on family structure.

The third distinct aspect of the demographic changes in Cuba is the role played by its health-care system and, of particular concern to this article, its senior health care. Cuba's enormous commitment of resources to and its centralized management of its health-care system have been instrumental in providing care for acute and chronic conditions and in offering intellectual and emotional support. Cuba's system supplies resources that help minimize the isolation of senior citizens in ways that are simply impossible in societies where such resources are privately owned. Even with the constraints imposed by Cuba's adverse economic situation in the past two decades, the centralized national system has been able to maintain universal support and to minimize the deprivation and neglect that are so prevalent in societies where senior citizens are only partially assisted by public services.

A key demographic result of Cuba's social policy has been a continuous reduction in the mortality rate among Cuba's senior citizens. This has been particularly true for the cohort who entered the senior population bracket since 1990. At the root of their decreased mortality rate is a decreased morbidity rate: prior to the extensive use of modern medical techniques such as immunization, illnesses were frequently lethal for senior citizens, but that is no longer the case.

Current Situation

At the end of 2007, Cuba had a population of 11,236,790.[5] Twelve years earlier, in January 1996, Cuba had reached 11 million. The level of 10 million was reached in 1984. According to current population projections, Cuba will not reach 12 million in the near future. In 2006 and 2007 the Cuban population actually decreased very slightly. It increased in 2009, but again only very slightly.

This trend, virtually unique in the context of today's developing countries, is characteristic of a very late stage in the standard demographic transition. Fertility, as the main demographic variable influencing population growth, has declined significantly. Many specialists consider Cuba's situation to be one of the most intense declines worldwide.

Cuba had actually developed a relatively low rate of population growth by the world standards of the time even before the Revolution. The main decline, however, has been over the last forty years. In addition, this decline has been surprisingly homogeneous across different social levels and regions of the country. "Within the developing world, Cuba stands out both for the early initiation of its process of demographic transition in the beginning of the twentieth century and for its accelerated, homogenous culmination of that process in the last few decades."[6]

Cuba's social policies, in addition to all the other effects they have had on the population, have been central to the accelerated demographic transition of the last forty years through the known population-development correlation.

These policies have occurred in a country that, even despite obvious economic difficulties—many imposed from the outside—has attached priority to the basic aspects of socialist development. A number of the policies in basic social areas such as health care, education, social security, welfare, and public safety have yielded demographic changes that mimic the first world, such as these:

- In 2007 there was a doctor for every 158 inhabitants and a stomatologist (specialist on oral problems) for every 1,049.
- In 2007 the mortality rates for infants and children under five were 5.3 and 6.7 per 1,000, respectively, and the maternal mortality rate was 31.1 per 100,000 live births, the lowest in Latin America.
- For 2005–7 the life expectancy at birth was 77.97 years and was 22.08 years at age 60 (23.37 for women).
- In 2006 the net enrollment rate in primary education was 99.31 percent, while the percentage of students starting first grade who reached fifth grade was 98.5 percent.
- At the time of the 2002 population and housing census, the over-fourteen population had an average educational level of 9.5 years, while the working population had more than 11 years of education.
- In 2006, 74.0 percent of women in the workforce had an intermediate-higher (non-university postsecondary training) or higher (university) education. In the same year 51.2 percent of workers in the science and technology sectors were women.
- In 2007, the unemployment rate was barely 1.8 percent.
- Out of the population of 11.2 million in 2006, 1.5 million received social security benefits.

In addition, abortion was decriminalized in 1965 both as part of a policy of sexual and reproductive rights and as a health-care policy, and 77 percent of women of childbearing age use contraceptives with their partners. The overall result has been that the demographic transition in Cuba, like the epidemiological transition, can be said to have reached the highest stage. The main demographic variables, fertility and mortality, have maintained low levels. The former has been below the generation replacement level since 1978. As of 2007, the fertility level in Cuba is so low that some writers refer to the country as being in a post-transitional stage. Cuba's first-world levels of fertility, life expectancy at birth, infant mortality, and other socio-demographic indicators put it a quarter century ahead of the rest of the continent in this process of transition.

In slightly more than a quarter century, from 1980 to 2009, Cuba's population has shifted from a low to an essentially zero rate of growth. In 1980–85 the annual average rate of growth was 8.1 per 1,000 inhabitants, dropping to

5.5 in 1990–99. Throughout these two decades the population increased by slightly more than 1.5 million, yielding an annual average growth of 75,000. However, back in the 1980s the average annual increase was roughly 97,000, whereas by the 1990s it had dropped to around 48,000. The trend of declining growth rate has continued into the twenty-first century, with the average annual rate of growth in 2000–2007 registering around 13,000. The above-mentioned small absolute declines in 2006 and 2007 reduced the population by a total of 7,045 over those two years.

To assess Cuba's population growth in the context of Latin America and the Caribbean, we can begin by noting that in 1950 Cuba was the region's seventh-most-populous country. At the end of 2009 it ranked tenth, behind, in order, Brazil, Mexico, Columbia, Argentina, Venezuela, Peru, Chile, Guatemala, and Ecuador. By 2015 it is projected to rank thirteenth, being surpassed also by the Dominican Republic, Haiti, and Bolivia.

Demographic analysis techniques, essential in population studies, identify three factors in population dynamics: fertility, mortality, and migration. Quite a few scholars also identify gender and age structure as a fourth factor. The latter two can have significant impacts on a population's growth potential through their effects on the other three factors in terms of the numbers of individuals in school, of reproductive age, and of older age. These factors also have an important although less immediately obvious effect through the number of individuals of working age and hence the availability of labor and the ability to earn sufficient income for raising children. This highlights the importance of including the population's age and gender structure in population growth considerations and in the design of social and economic policies based on those studies. The population's gender structure is of interest because of its impact on the number of births, deaths, and emigrants, as well as on other aspects of society determined by the relation between the sexes (see table 7.1).

The falling predominance of men shown in table 7.1 can be explained by the population history of the Cuban archipelago, the increase in overall life expectancy, and the higher male mortality. During the first quarter of the twentieth century Cuba was a country of many immigrants, particularly from mainland Spain and the rest of the Antilles. Mostly men, they arrived on Cuban shores by the hundreds of thousands amid the frenzied boom of the sugar monoculture. This explains the pattern in the early years of table 7.1. This massive immigration subsequently ceased for several reasons, and there was a positive, though more gender-balanced, emigration. This explains the sharp drop recorded by 1953. As is the case everywhere in the world, more boys than girls are born in Cuba, and its birth masculinity ratio of roughly 1,060 is very close to the world average.[7] Higher male mortality then lowers the masculinity ratio

Table 7.1. Masculinity ratio (MR) for Cuba, selected years, 1899–2007 (males per 1,000 females)

Year	MR	Year	MR
1899	1,076	1970	1,052
1907	1,103	1981	1,022
1919	1,127	2002	1,003
1931	1,131	2006	1,003
1953	1,050	2007	1,003
1960	1,050		

Sources: From 1899 to 2002, data come from the population censuses. Figures for 2006 and 2007 are from the *Anuario Demográfico de Cuba, 2006* and *2008,* prepared and edited by ONE-CEPDE.

through progressively older age brackets. The primary cause for the gradual but continuous decline in the masculinity ratio after the Revolution was increased life expectancy. A larger and larger percentage of the population consisted of senior citizens, and for that age group the masculinity ratio is always less than 1 because of higher male mortality. The result, as shown in table 7.1, is that over the course of the Revolution the masculinity ratio for the entire population consistently trended toward a more normal and expected value reflecting a more balanced gender structure.

The continued existence today of a higher rate of male mortality can be seen in table 7.2, which displays the general trend that the higher the age bracket, the lower the masculinity ratio. Today it is only after childhood that the higher male mortality sets in.

With regard to age structure, for many years now the country has been undergoing a change in its age profile due to the continuous decrease in fertility and, to some extent, the increase in life expectancy. There has been a continuous decrease in the percentage of the under-fifteen population and increase in the percentage of the over-fifty-nine population. Conceptually speaking, this process is referred to as "population aging," and it is considered the main population-related challenge that Cuba must address in its prospective socioeconomic development. Figure 7.1, displaying age profiles by five-year intervals for 1907, 1953, and 2007 and the projection for 2025, presents this issue visually.

In 2007, senior citizens accounted for 16.6 percent of the total population, an increase of more than 50 percent in their population share since 1981 (see table 7.3). This increase in senior citizens brought the median age in Cuba up to 37.4, placing the country among the fastest-aging nations in Latin America and the Caribbean, surpassed only by Uruguay and Argentina. Estimates are that by 2025 Cuba will have the largest percentage of elderly people in its

Table 7.2. Masculinity ratio for Cuba by general age ranges, selected years, 1985–2007 (males per 1,000 females)

Year	Total	0–14 years	15–59 years	60+ years
1985	1,015	1,045	1,015	1,017
1995	1,008	1,054	1,023	952
2006	1,003	1,058	1,012	908
2007	1,003	1,059	1,002	902

Source: ONE-CEPDE, *Estudios y datos de la población de Cuba, 2007* (Havana: ONE, 2008).

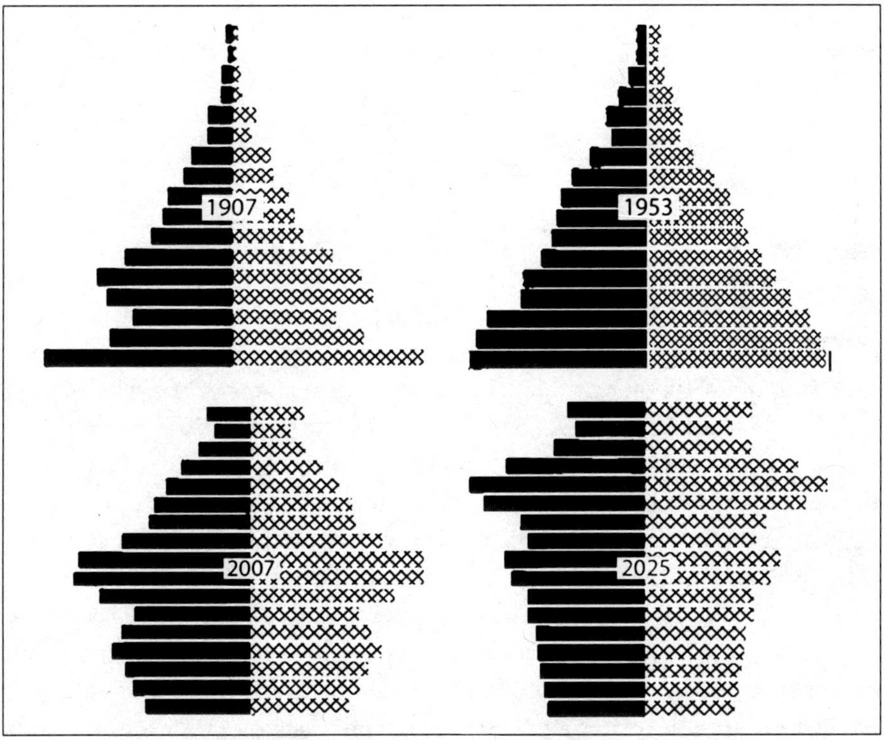

Figure 7.1. Cuban population pyramids by sex and age group, 1907, 1953, 2007, and the 2025 projection. *Sources:* Selected years of the census and ONE-CEPDE, *Anuario Demográfico de Cuba* (Havana: ONE, 2008); and ONE-CEPDE, *Cuba proyección de la población cubana: Nivel nacional: Período 2007–2025* (Havana: ONE, 2006). Starting with the bottom bars and moving upward, the bars give the relative percent for the given year in the age groups 0–4, 5–9, and so on. The top bar is "80 and over." The female population distribution is the right half of each pyramid and the male the left half.

population of all Latin American countries, with more than 26 percent of its population in the over-fifty-nine age bracket (see table 7.4).

From the socioeconomic standpoint, it is very important to examine the relationship between the youngest (under age fifteen) and oldest (over fifty-nine) population segments, on the one hand, and the working-age population

Table 7.3. Evolution of Cuban population structure by general age ranges, selected years, 1907–2007 (%)

Year	0–14 years	15–59 years	60+ years	Median age
1907[a]	36.6	58.8	4.6	24.1
1919[a]	42.3	52.9	4.8	23.7
1931[a]	37.4	57.5	5.1	24.7
1943[a]	35.5	58.9	5.6	25.7
1953[a]	36.2	56.9	6.9	26.6
1970[a]	36.9	54.0	9.1	27.0
1981[a]	30.3	58.8	10.9	29.5
1995	22.2	65.1	12.7	34.2
2002[a]	20.5	64.8	14.7	35.1
2006	18.4	65.7	15.9	36.9
2007	18.0	65.4	16.6	37.4

[a]From Population and Housing Census.

Sources: ONE-CEPDE, *Estudios y datos de la población de Cuba, 2006* and *2007* (Havana: ONE, 2007, 2008); *Anuario Demográfico de Cuba, 1995* (Havana: ONE, 1996).

(fifteen to fifty-nine years), on the other. The age dependency ratio (or more simply, the dependency ratio), which specifies the number of nonworking people in relation to those of working age, is commonly used for this purpose. The following figures show the fluctuation in the dependency ratio over the past two decades: 1985: 592; 1990: 533; 2000: 547; 2006: 523; 2007: 528.[8]

These figures show that over the last twenty years, despite some fluctuation, the dependency ratio has been relatively stable. This turns out to hide an important aspect of the Cuban reality that was mentioned earlier. The over-fifty-nine population is increasing while the under-fifteen population is decreasing, and over the last twenty years these changes have largely canceled each other out, as the dependency ratio reflects. Clearly, this balance cannot continue, because the percentage of the under-fifteen population cannot keep falling far enough to continue offsetting the constantly increasing over-fifty-nine population as Cuba's aging process continues.

The changes in the absolute size of the three groups—pre-working age, working age, and post-working age—offer more information on this issue. Because of the dataset used for this calculation, the first group consists of the under-seventeen cohort, the second group is seventeen to fifty-nine for men and seventeen to fifty-four for women, and the last group is sixty and over for men and fifty-five and over for women. Table 7.5 shows that from 1985 to 2007 the pre-working-age population declined by a little more than 741,000, while the working-age population increased by nearly a million and the post-working-age by about 832,000. First, this clearly shows again the aging of the population. Second, this shows why the dependency ratio remained relatively

Table 7.4. Aging index according to demographic transition stage, Latin America and the Caribbean, 1980, 2005, 2025

Demographic transition stage	Country	Aging index[a]			Percentage increase		
		1980	2005	2025	1980–2005	2005–25	Transition year[b]
Highly advanced	Cuba	33.8	80.9	184.6	139.3	128.2	2010
Advanced	Uruguay	54.5	74.2	106.3	36.1	43.3	2020–25
	Chile	24.7	46.1	103.1	86.6	123.6	2025
	Argentina	39	52.2	77	33.8	47.5	2035
	Brazil	17.1	31.3	68.6	83	119.1	2035
	Colombia	14.2	24.6	65.4	73.2	165.9	2035
	Costa Rica	18.8	28.8	75.5	53.2	162.2	2035
	Mexico	12.1	27.1	69.4	124	156.1	2035
Full	Peru	13.3	25.2	51	89.5	102.4	2045
	Panama	16.5	28.5	58.7	72.7	106	2040
	Ecuador	13.8	25.1	53.8	81.9	114.3	2045
	Venezuela	12.4	23.7	53.6	91.1	126.2	2045
	Dominican Rep.	11.2	23.7	45.6	111.6	92.4	2050
	El Salvador	11.4	22.1	39.9	93.9	80.5	2050
	Paraguay	13.6	19.2	39.4	41.2	105.2	2055
	Nicaragua	9.1	14.8	34.9	62.6	135.8	2050
	Honduras	10.1	14.5	29.1	43.6	10.7	2055
Moderate	Haiti	15.3	16.6	27.3	8.5	64.5	2065
	Guatemala	10.2	14	20.8	37.3	48.5	2055
	Bolivia	12.9	17.2	31	33.3	80.2	2065

[a]The aging index is the ratio of the population aged 60 and over to the population aged 0–14.
[b]Approximate year in which the 0–14 and 60+ groups become the same size.
Source: Centro Latinoamericano y Caribeño de Demografía (CELADE, the population division of CEPAL), *Estimaciones y proyecciones de las poblaciones de América Latina y el Caribe* (Santiago de Chile: CEPAL, 2007).

Table 7.5. Cuban population distribution in relation to the working age, selected years, 1985–2007

Years	Pre-working age[a]	Working age[b]	Post-working age[c]	Median age of workers (years)	
				Men	Women
1985	3,082,862	5,727,154	1,342,623	33.6	32.4
1990	2,802,917	6,398,984	1,492,564	34.2	33.7
2006	2,418,149	6,721,100	2,099,794	36.4	36.2
2007	2,340,988	6,721,344	2,174,458	37.8	37.3

[a]Ages 0–16.
[b]Ages 17–59 for men and ages 17–54 for women.
[c]Ages 60+ for men and ages 55+ for women.
Source: ONE-CEPDE, *Estudios y Datos de la Población cubana 2007* (Havana: ONE, 2008).

stable despite the aging over this period. And third, the disaggregation of the population shows the relative increase in nonworking dependents that will become a problem in the near future despite the stability of the dependency ratio over the last two decades. The number of dependents increased only slightly over the last two decades because the rapid increase of 58 percent in the post-working-age population could be balanced by a fall of 24 percent in the pre-working-age population, given that the absolute number of the latter group was more than twice as large as the former at the beginning of the period. Today the absolute numbers in the two groups are about the same, and the rate of growth of the post-working-age group should remain about the same in the near future. This means that the rate of decline in the pre-working-age group would have to double to maintain balance. In fact, however, given its small size today the rate of decline in the youngest age group can actually be expected to level out. So the absolute number of dependents should start to grow in the near future, slowly at first and then at an accelerating rate. The number of people of working age grew by 17 percent over the two decades but had almost completely stopped growing by 2006. This rate should stay low in the near future as the number of people entering the group from the ever-smaller pre-working-age population becomes less and less able to offset those leaving the group as they reach fifty-five or sixty. Cuba's labor base for its entire population will grow more slowly than the number of nonworking dependents.

Another aspect of the aging process of the population relates to the working-age population itself. As table 7.5 shows, the median age of working-age men and women has been rising steadily. This trend too is projected to continue in the near future.

Detailed Profile of the Senior Population

The Research Project on Health, Welfare, and Aging (SABE) was carried out in 2000 under the auspices of the Pan-American Health Organization (PAHO) in seven capitals or major cities in Latin America and the Caribbean. Surveys were conducted to determine a series of important indicators on senior citizens. In the case of Havana, where more than 20 percent of Cuba's elderly population was then living, these surveys revealed a large amount of detailed information. These were matched and confirmed by the subsequent findings of the 2002 Population and Housing Census.

There was at least one senior citizen in 42 percent of houses visited. Women accounted for 59.1 percent, and men for 40.9 percent, of the senior population. The estimated median age was 70.0. As expected, the ratio of women to men increased with age due to the higher mortality rate of males. The overall femininity ratio (women per thousand men) among senior citizens was 1,443.

Regarding marital status, the largest percentage of the senior population was married or cohabiting (40 percent), followed by widows (approximately 33 percent). Of the seniors interviewed, 97 percent reported that they had cohabited with a partner at some time in their lives.

At the time of the research, 89 percent reported that they had living children. By age, this represented 94 percent of the population in the sixty-to-sixty-four age bracket and 84 percent of the over-seventy-four population. Among respondents 9 percent still had a mother living, and 3 percent a father. As life expectancy continues to increase, there will be larger numbers of senior citizens with one or both parents still living.

Regarding education, 44 percent reported having an intermediate or university-level education. Only 4.5 percent reported having no schooling. The education level of men was higher than that of women. The predominant educational category for women was the primary level (56 percent), while for men it was the intermediate level (46 percent). Also, a larger percentage of men (7 percent) had university degrees.

Of the senior population, 56 percent practiced some type of religion, while the remaining 44 percent had no religious affiliation. For both men and women the percentage practicing a religion increased with age. Thus, the over-seventy-five group had the highest percentage of people practicing some form of religion.

At the time of the survey, 20.1 percent of the senior citizens were working. (Cuba has no mandatory retirement age.) Of this percentage, 0.7 percent worked in the informal economy and a similar percentage worked in households. The remainder, almost the entire senior working population, worked in the formal labor market. By age, 47 percent of working senior citizens were sixty to sixty-four. Almost three-quarters (74 percent) of working senior citizens were men.

The survey found several types of family arrangements with sufficient frequency to be considered a household family-structure category. The most frequent was "living with children without a husband/wife," which accounted for 34 percent of the senior citizens. This was followed by 21.3 percent "living with children and a husband/wife." Together these groups constituted more than half the senior population. This high incidence indicates the importance that Cuban senior citizens attach to living with their children, for a combination of material, cultural, and emotional reasons. After these two groups, the next largest group, 11.2 percent, reported living with only a spouse or partner, and 10.7 percent were living alone. These two categories combined, accounting for a little more than one-fifth of the senior population, are considered an important group at risk. A revealing result was that after all the family arrangements just listed, the next most frequent one was living with unrelated others. While some among this group had lived with unrelated people all their lives, others had begun living with others after being left alone for any of several reasons, apparently adopting this lifestyle to avoid the economic or emotional challenges of living alone. Family arrangements and their significance remained similar across all age subgroups of the senior population.

If we look at the population at greatest risk, those living alone, we see an important gender issue. The percentage of women living alone was 30 percent higher than that for men: 11.8 percent of senior females lived alone, compared to only 9.1 percent of males. When this finding is combined with the fact that there are more senior women than men, the result is that this most vulnerable of all groups contains many more women than men.

Concerning the critical issue of income, 93.3 percent of the seniors were receiving some income at the time of the study: 76.3 percent received retirement benefits or pensions, 26.3 percent received family assistance from inside the country, 20.1 percent earned wages, and 15.2 percent received family remittances from another country. The remaining categories had such low percentages as to be irrelevant.

In relation to housing, an index was drafted with stringent parameters for housing quality. According to this criterion, 11.5 percent of housing was in good condition, 79.3 percent was in fair condition, and the remainder was in bad condition.

Projected Evolution of the Cuban Population

A 2006 study by ONE and CEPDE projected the Cuban population evolution out to the year 2025 on the basis of current trends (see table 7.6). Having reached essentially zero growth by 2006, the Cuban population was projected to decline at a slowly increasing rate, reaching -0.8 per 1,000 by 2025. The rate of decline is so small, however, that the population can be characterized as essentially stable over the eighteen years, dropping only 74,000 to 11,165,475 by 2025.

The existence of a relatively stable population for two decades is in itself a condition that requires further careful consideration on many dimensions related to the basis for Cuba's social and economic development. In this chapter, however, the focus is kept on the evolving process of population aging.

The effects of Cuba's low fertility rate and low mortality rate (or in roughly equivalent terms, its high life expectancy) are projected to intensify in the near

Table 7.6. Projected population and average annual growth rate (AAGR) by five-year periods, 2007–25

Year[a]	Population	AAGR (per 1,000)
2007	11,239,128	0.0
2010	11,236,362	-0.1
2015	11,226,738	-0.2
2020	11,211,208	-0.3
2025	11,165,475	-0.8

[a]Yearly population estimates are dated from midyear, and therefore these projections are calculated the same way.
Source: ONE-CEPDE, *Cuba proyección de la población cubana. Nivel nacional: Período 2007–2025* (Havana: ONE, 2006).

Table 7.7. Projected Cuban population structure by age group, 2007–25 (%)

Year[a]	Ages 0–14	Ages 15–59	Ages 60+
2007	18.4	65.4	16.2
2010	17.2	65.4	17.4
2015	15.7	64.8	19.5
2020	14.6	63.7	21.6
2025	14.2	59.7	26.1

[a]Yearly population estimates are dated from midyear, and therefore these projections are calculated the same way.
Source: ONE-CEPDE, *Cuba proyección de la población cubana. Nivel nacional: Período 2007–2025* (Havana: ONE, 2006).

future. The result will be further acceleration of Cuba's process of population aging, with many social and economic effects. Just to name three major ones, there will be a relative reduction in the supply of labor; the demand for health care will become both quantitatively greater and qualitatively more complex; and there will be a relative reduction in the age groups actively engaged in the largest educational services: preschool, primary, intermediate, and both university and non-university postsecondary education. But beyond these major effects, all sectors of the economy and all social programs will be affected.

As of mid-2010 more than one-sixth of Cuba's population of approximately 11.2 million is more than fifty-nine years of age. This yields an absolute number of almost 2 million people. By 2025 this group is projected to rise to 26.1 percent of the population (see table 7.7). Given the relatively stable population indicated in table 7.6, the total number of senior citizens is projected to surpass 2.9 million by then.

The sixty-plus population will be the only age group experiencing continuous growth. Both the total population and the populations in all other age groups will experience absolute declines. There will be a decline in the number of childbearing women and, within that group, a more acute drop among those in the most fertile ages, fifteen to thirty-four. In the social and family environments this will mean not only more elderly people needing more, and more complex, support, but also fewer young and working-age people to provide it. Cuba's population pyramid is projected to evolve by 2025 as shown above in figure 7.1.

An important element in Cuba's aging process is the evolution of the oldest portion of the senior age group, those over seventy-nine, which is sometimes referred to as the "fourth age." This is the top bar in the population pyramids in figure 7.1. Although not growing quite as fast as the overall senior citizen population (projected to grow 55 percent between 2007 and 2025), their 38 percent growth, from 325,000 to 450,000, makes them, like their younger peers, a rapidly growing segment of the population.

Along with the decline in the size of the working-age population, the current trend of its increasing median age, which is one important component of Cuba's population aging process, will continue. The mean and median ages of the working-age cohort of the population will increase from 39.1 and 38.7 in 2010 to 41.7 and 41.2 in 2025 (see table 7.8).

It is essential when considering the current and prospective demographic developments to keep in mind that these are the direct results of the social advancement that Cuba has achieved. It would therefore be inappropriate to view them negatively. To the contrary, the increased life expectancy that is changing Cuba's age structure is clearly a positive effect, in line with Cuba's central goal of human development. Likewise, reduced fertility is both an effect of and one contributing cause of the advances of women in society and in the family, and hence again is a sign of heightened human development. Yet, these demographic changes in general, and Cuba's accelerated aging process in particular, nevertheless pose major challenges to Cuba's overall social and eco-

Table 7.8. Projected mean and median ages of the working population, 2007–25

Year[a]	Mean age	Median age
2007	37.8	37.4
2010	39.1	38.7
2015	40.8	39.6
2020	41.5	40.7
2025	41.7	41.2

[a]Yearly population estimates are dated from midyear, and therefore these projections are calculated the same way.

Source: Author's estimates based on information from ONE-CEPDE, *Cuba proyección de la población cubana. Nivel nacional: Período 2007–2025* (Havana: ONE, 2006).

nomic development. Careful study of their consequences is required, leading to the implementation of policies to address any new effects.

Some Consequences of the Aging Process

Regardless of whether the forecasts just discussed turn out to be exactly accurate, it is a fact that today the age structure of the Cuban population is already undergoing profound changes. This situation is often referred to as Cuba's main demographic "challenge," again with the caveat that longer, healthy lives are a desired result of successful social policies over the next fifteen years, and even beyond 2025 in some cases. The consequences of aging are directly connected with changes in the social context. These include, among many other factors basic to a country's socioeconomic development, consequences in the following areas that will be specifically discussed in this section: health care, social security, labor resources, and household dynamics. Because the aging process affects all ages—infants, school-age children, childbearing women, working people, and senior citizens—it has consequences for all these socioeconomic factors.

Most immediately obvious, an aging population raises costs for a national health-care system because of these people's higher rates of morbidity, mortality, and chronic and degenerative diseases. Higher health-care costs of course mean a corresponding decrease in funds available for the country's other social and economic development efforts. In this respect medical costs for the elderly directly influence the entire social structure, the rate of improvement of the quality of life of the entire population. It is important to recall the aforementioned rapid growth of the fourth age group, those more than seventy-nine years old. Per capita medical expenses are far higher for this age group than for the average senior citizen.

Because all retirees are entitled to social security, the increased percentage of retired senior citizens in the population immediately increases the cost of the social security system. This is a major problem under discussion in all first-world countries as a result of their advanced-stage demographics, and because Cuba shares those first-world demographics it shares this problem. The issue is the dependency ratio: how many working people contribute to the support of a no-longer-working elderly person. The dependency ratio worsens as a country advances demographically, meaning that the contribution needed from every working person continually increases. And whereas first-world countries have such relatively high per capita GDPs that (if the political will is present) citizens can pay a great deal to support the nonworkers and still be left with high incomes, this is not the case for a third-world country.

The first impact of the aging process on labor resources is the prospective diminution of not only the percentage but the absolute numbers of the working-age population. A second effect discussed earlier partially negates this quantitative decline: the increase in the average age of the working population. Given Cuba's extensive recent and ongoing efforts to further educate and upgrade the skills of its workforce, a marginally older workforce can also be marginally better qualified. The quantitative decline in labor resources can be partially offset by their qualitative increase, which is marginally favored by a slightly older workforce.

The relationship between population aging and family dynamics is one of the most complex and relatively least studied issues connected with Cuba's demographic transition. This relation depends not only on material resources but also on educational aspects and on the continually changing roles of the members of Cuban families. The family's responsibility to care for senior members is a major issue in family dynamics in Cuba. As noted, based on census data and Project SABE, more than 40 percent of Cuban households currently contain an over-fifty-nine family member. Whether or not seniors live in the same household as younger family members, their financial, physical, and psychological well-being are strongly influenced by, and a strong influence on, the family's dynamics and even functionality. The amount of care seniors require from family members, in addition to the extensive social support for their health care and other needs, can become a major demand on a family's financial, temporal, and psychological resources. And again, all these issues are much more acute for those families with members in the fourth age. Two key factors that help to prevent these tasks from becoming harmful to family dynamics are family education and additional community assistance when needed.

Social Policies and Programs for the Aging Population

In a broad sense, all of Cuba's social policies and programs concern aging. Cuba's high life expectancy is rooted precisely in its social policies on health care, education, food security, and so on. In that context, the first consideration for Cuba's current policies and programs on aging is that its traditional general social policies have remained in place while new ones have continuously been added. This has occurred despite the two-decade-long economic crisis whose severity would have caused serious reductions in such programs for most third- and even first-world countries. Yet there has been no change in Cuba's principles or strategic goals of human development, or in their general implementation. In the ten years from 1994 to 2004, when Cuba was just beginning to come out of the severe economic downturn, its per capita spending on health care and education increased by 97 percent and 169 percent, respectively.

Another important aspect to take note of concerning Cuba's current ongoing efforts to develop and introduce new and ever-more-effective implementation mechanisms is that no activity relating to basic public social services has been privatized. The state continues to contribute to social equality through the universal and cost-free nature of basic social services, such as health care and education from primary right through university levels. And the government-provided social services go beyond those that are internationally regarded as basic. As an example, the state guarantees a basic level of food and commodities, with special treatment for children, pregnant women, senior citizens, and medical patients.

A few of the many new social programs and extensions of traditional ones introduced since the late 1990s include the following. Higher education has been made even more accessible to all citizens through a large-scale program of extending delivery to people locally in their municipalities. Wage scales for the country's working population have been raised, especially since the middle of the first decade of the 2000s and continuing today. A direct and immediate improvement in the population's standard of living has been achieved by providing or replacing some basic household items and appliances and by increased housing repairs. Welfare for vulnerable people, those in the lowest income brackets or experiencing other difficulties, has expanded in degree and coverage and is currently streamlining its identification of needy people and its protective policies, which have been particularly important for senior citizens.

With a view of aging as a current and prospective social success but also a problem, many additional policies and programs have been designed, drafted, and implemented, specifically to give priority care to senior citizens. The largest numbers of these have been in health care, social security, and welfare. Together these represent a society-wide effort to address this all-encompassing issue.

The Senior Citizen Comprehensive Health-Care Program, in force since the 1990s, is modeled on a concept dating from the 1970s contained in official state documents and records from the Cuban Parliament.[9] The driving force behind this early concept was the priority attached to projected health care and social security problems on the basis of Cuba's aging population, which was already obvious then. For implementation, the current program is divided into several fundamental aspects, as follows:

Community assistance programs: These offer social security and services for senior citizens on their own, including a subprogram promoting lifestyle changes, the prevention of diseases and disabilities, and both ongoing and timely health care, in which community doctors play an important role. The basic principle for compliance was to have communities generate their own solutions, and then to provide each community with the appropriate instruments, methods, and structures to implement those solutions. In this framework, evaluations of community-level efforts were treated as mechanisms not only of supervision but also of feedback.

Hospital assistance: These interventions are directed at solving health problems that cannot be resolved in the community, but with the prospect of returning the patient to the community if possible, with plans coordinated at the various levels of care.

Institutional assistance: Nursing homes or assisted living homes are viewed as a necessary link within the social health-care program for senior citizens who do not have the resources or ability to live in normal housing or are otherwise vulnerable (as determined by an evaluation). For several reasons this is not a preferred option whenever it can be avoided, and therefore a number of alternatives have been created for dealing with this level of need. One is the so-called grandparents' houses, founded more than two decades ago, where the elderly receive services as outpatients. Another is grandparents' clubs, connected with the primary health-care level, which focus on, among other things, physical education, sharing experiences, and carrying out common activities.

Training of specialized human resources: Personnel trained in geriatrics, gerontology, psychology, and social work are able to assimilate the newest information and international recommendations.

Multidisciplinary research: A final basic component relates to multidisciplinary research, combining the medical perspective with psychological, sociological, economic, demographic, and other information.

Several initiatives have been implemented to follow up on the Senior Citizen Comprehensive Health-Care Program and as part of the efforts to make the country's response to the needs of the elderly more dynamic. These initiatives also derive from Cuba's efforts to address the principles and recommendations of the World Congresses on Aging, held in Vienna in 1982 and in Madrid in 2002, and the Regional Plan adopted in Santiago de Chile in 2003 and updated in Brasilia in 2007. Among other specifics, these initiatives include the following:

- Establishment of specialized health-care centers for senior citizens
- Creation of lecture halls for the elderly in the country's major universities, designed to teach senior citizens how to cope more proactively with this stage of their lives, in order to improve their quality of life
- The undertaking of studies and proposals on policies and programs at several academic and research centers

- The participation of the Social Workers Program in research on, and direct and individualized fulfillment of, the needs and aspirations of this segment of the population

The existing programs for senior citizens provide economic assistance, aid in kind, household support, and institution-based services, such as the following:

Pension and social security payments: The 1.5 million current social security beneficiaries represent an increase of approximately 200,000 in the last decade despite the minimal population growth. Spending on social security and welfare increased by 65 percent between 1994 and 2004, and the government has been working to increase the level of these payments since the early twenty-first century as the financial state of the country has allowed.

Day centers or grandparents' clubs: Such centers operate during the day, providing seniors with adequate food, medical care, and occupational therapy. A goal of these centers is to keep the elderly with their families as much as possible. They are more economical for society than full-time institutions. The facilities are large houses adapted to accommodate groups of forty to sixty senior citizens per day.

Housekeeping services: Those elderly people who live alone or have needs beyond what their relatives can meet receive services to help them stay in the community, such as assistance with house cleaning, food preparation, and laundry.

Food services: Elderly people who live alone can receive food deliveries with the goal of contributing to their adequate nourishment.

Assisted living homes: Homes are available for those senior citizens who are capable of looking after themselves to some extent but have some physical or social problem that limits their independence. The goal is to maintain, and to whatever degree possible restore, the patient's capabilities.

Proposals to Improve Senior Care

Notwithstanding these efforts, Cuba requires and will require more comprehensive and integrated efforts given the magnitude of the aging population and its impact on society as a whole. To that end, the government set up a committee to outline actions and measures to be carried out at present and in coming years. The guidelines are characterized by functional sustainability and integrated viability based on Cuba's political and socioeconomic realities, on its family and cultural traditions, and, above all, on its population trends. These actions can be summarized and grouped as follows:

Informative actions: These are designed to diagnose and evaluate, with appropriate frequency and detail, the issue of population aging, taking into consideration regional and social differences and projected evolution.

Integrating actions: A first aspect of integration concerns the need to integrate the ever-increasing requirements of this population group, both general and specific, into both the global plan of the economy and its sector-wide and social development programs, particularly health care. A second aspect concerns promoting cooperation across government agencies in order to meet the population's existing demands, plus any others that may arise during the implementation process, including those that may arise from the interaction between different social plans and programs. A third aspect of integration concerns the need to maximize and integrate the participation of all the local organizations in Cuban society within communities, workplaces, and schools. Beyond social organizations such as the Committees for Defense of the Revolution (CDRs), unions, the Federation of Cuban Women, high school and university student groups, and so on, this includes social workers, as well as organizing the senior citizens themselves in formal or informal groups. A final type of integration concerns the need for social actions aimed at integrating and fulfilling both material and spiritual needs, as an investment in both a longer and richer life.

Educational and dissemination actions: These efforts are designed to educate the population of all ages to prepare them for the aging process. They must include very practical matters, such as self-care, as well as cultural and ideological issues, for example, cultivating the respect for the dignity of senior citizens that they deserve. Another important aspect of education and dissemination to be addressed is to project a social image that emphasizes the positive elements of different life stages by means of oral and written traditions and through the mass media. This will contribute to creating an important culture "about" and "for" senior adulthood in Cuban society. School syllabi from primary education onward must also incorporate these messages.

Environmental and cultural activities: These are designed to adapt and improve established policies and practices in aspects of Cuban society in which senior citizens play a role, including the physical environment and Cuban culture. This is more than an issue of recognizing and addressing existing constraints on the participation of those senior citizens who already consider such activities an important part of their life. It also must promote the participation and personal enrichment of those who do not, as part of improving the quality of life of all senior citizens. These actions will take place in different settings, such as the community, the family, senior citizens' organizations, and others. With regard to aging, these actions will contribute not only to extending good health into old age but also to healthy aging throughout the whole life cycle.

In broad terms, the purpose of these actions is both to add years to a person's life and, through enrichment, to add life to a person's years.

Actions to enhance protection: These actions are designed to strengthen the legal and civic protection of the aging population, including with regard to their residence in households and in the family. Another aspect concerns improving the existing mechanisms for providing material, and often emotional and psychological, protection against the difficulties faced by the vulnerable senior citizens who are disabled, alone, or facing other difficulties.

Monitoring and evaluation: The implementation and results of policies and practices need to be monitored through the established channels for public participation, for example, oversight through political, governmental, and state organizations. These serve as a source of constant feedback on required modifications, and in particular help with the often problematic issue of finishing projects in the scheduled time frame.

Research actions: One type of research provides the statistical data to support the previously described diagnosis and evaluation. A second type of important research concerns the development of necessary methods and procedures to achieve the goals that have been set. But beyond these functions, research is vital in maintaining Cuba's role as an important contributor to the worldwide efforts to address the international issue of population aging. Interchanges at professional conferences and sharing of research results enable Cuba both to greatly strengthen its own response to this problematic result of its successful social policies and to highlight the extensive measures it has taken in providing integral care to its ever larger elderly population. Thereby, the rest of the world has opportunities to learn from both the problems and successes of Cuba's policies and practices concerning its senior citizens.

Notes

1. Oficina Nacional de Estadística—Centro de Estudios de Población y Desarrollo (ONE-CEPDE), *Anuario Demográfico de Cuba 2007* (Havana: ONE, 2008).

2. ONE-CEPDE, "Condiciones de vida, participación en la fuerza de trabajo y estado de salud de los adultos mayores cubanos" (Proyecto de Investigación entre la OPS, Universidad de New York y el CEPDE, unpublished, 2000).

3. J. C. Alfonso Fraga, "Cuba: De la primera a la segunda transición demográfica: El descenso de la fecundidad," in CEPAL-CELADE, *La fecundidad en América Latina ¿Transición o revolución?* (Santiago de Chile: CEPAL, 2003).

4. ONE, *Panorama económico y social de Cuba 2007* (Havana: ONE, 2008).

5. J. C. Alfonso Fraga, "Description of Population and its Interrelation to Socio-Economic Development," in the Ministry of Economy and Planning, *Cuba's Economic Structure* (Havana: MEP, 2009).

6. UNICEF, UNFPA, ONE, CEDEM, and MINSAP, *Cuba: Cambio social y conducta reproductiva: La transición de la fecundidad* (Havana: ONE, 1996).

7. The ratio is the number of males per thousand females (alternatively it can be calculated on the basis of one hundred).

8. Data from author's estimates and ONE-CEPDE, *Esperanza de vida en Cuba y provincias 2005–2007*: *Cálculos por sexo y edades* (Havana: ONE, 2008).

9. Ministerio de Salud Pública and Centro Iberoamericano de la Tercera Edad, *Atención del anciano en Cuba: Desarrollo y perspectiva* (Havana: MINSAP, 1996).

8

Labor Relations, Labor Rights, and Trade Unions

Their History in Cuba

ALFREDO MORALES CARTAYA

The basis for Cuban workers' specific rights and labor relations is the country's socialist character. The 1976 Constitution legally established the socialist nature of Cuba as fundamental to all of its policies and legislation, including all of its labor legislation. The constitution opens with this statement in Article I:

> Cuba is a socialist state of workers, independent and sovereign, organized by all and for the good of all, as a unitary and democratic Republic, for the enjoyment of political freedom, social justice, individual and collective well-being, and human solidarity.[1]

The constitution establishes labor as a right, a duty, and the basis of honor for every citizen. In accordance with Cuba's socialist nature, it establishes that the state, as the collective power of the people and at the service of the people, guarantees that no man or woman who is able to work will lack the opportunity to obtain employment, in order to contribute to both the objectives of society and the satisfaction of his or her personal needs.

Not only was the socialist constitution of Cuba created for the well-being of working people, but workers actively participated in its formulation and adoption. More than six million Cubans discussed the preliminary drafts, resulting in modification of 60 of its 141 articles. It was then submitted to a popular referendum and adopted by 97.7 percent of the voting-eligible population.

The rights and labor relations of Cuban workers are not, however, a result of the Cuban Constitution. To the contrary, the Cuban Constitution is the result of a history of struggle by the entire Cuban nation for its rights and sovereignty and for the socioeconomic well-being of its citizens. And, of course, working people constitute the majority of any population. From the beginning workers were central to the overall national struggle in Cuba, while at the same time they fought for their own rights and well-being as rural and urban working people.

Historical Background

Cuba was the last Latin American colony to obtain independence from Spain. The U.S. intervention in Cuba's war for independence turned it into a neocolony. The United States imposed the Commercial Reciprocity Treaty and the Platt Amendment on Cuba, giving Americans the right to intervene militarily, exploit Cuba's natural resources, secure privileges for U.S. capital investments, and thwart any attempt by the Cuban people to establish a system of law and order of their own choosing.[2] In the early years of the neocolony, U.S. interests promoted sugar monoculture, the structural deformation of the economy, and government corruption. The unrestricted inflow of U.S. capital to purchase land, sugar mills, tobacco factories, railway lines, and other sources of wealth reinforced exploitation, hunger, unemployment, low wages, lack of health care, racial discrimination, and other social ills among Cuban workers.

The trade union movement began to emerge and to struggle for improved labor conditions and a higher standard of living right from the creation of the neocolony. In 1925 the National Workers' Confederation of Cuba was established with the goal of creating a united front for all workers to fight for their rights. Its main leader, Alfredo López, was assassinated a year later by the country's repressive forces.

Right from its birth the Cuban workers' and trade union movement had to fight simultaneously for improved working conditions and for workers' democratic rights. Workers suffered brutal exploitation, precarious labor conditions, unemployment, seasonal unemployment in sugar production, meager salaries, and more broadly, social neglect. They suffered not only from the absence of basic labor laws to protect them but also from much outright discriminatory legislation: Decree-Law No. 3 prohibited strikes, Decree-Law No. 52 allowed the government to deport any immigrant workers at its discretion, Decree-Law No. 63 banned many workers' organizations and nullified labor contracts, Decree-Law No. 65 prohibited the collective assembly and action of civil servants, and finally Decree-Law No. 92 suspended labor leaders for two years if they did not accede to all the authorities' demands. Hence, protests, demonstrations, strikes, and clashes, often bloody, characterized the country's political situation in the first half of the twentieth century. These actions were directed not only against the discriminatory legislation and for labor rights and improved labor conditions, but also more broadly against the oligarchic regimes, coups d'état, and threats of U.S. intervention.

In 1939, through these struggles, the Confederation of Cuban Workers (CTC) was founded as a vehicle to coordinate the unity and solidarity of workers. From its inception it led the struggle for improved working conditions and the strengthening and enforcement of the little labor legislation that existed. It opposed labor discrimination against blacks, women, and youths, but more broadly, it fought against fascism and war. It worked for consensus among workers on measures of popular and national interest at the Constituent Assembly convened for the country's alleged democratization. Due to the influence of popular and democratic currents within the assembly, the 1940 Constitution was advanced and progressive for its time, including with regard to labor issues.[3] The 1940 Constitution established these rights:

- Labor as an inalienable right of every citizen
- A maximum eight-hour workday and forty-four-hour workweek
- The right to unionize
- Paid vacations
- Protection for pregnant women
- The Cuban state's obligation to find work for the unemployed

However, although the constitution recognized these rights on paper, their application turned out to be nonexistent.

The CTC, spearheaded by its historic leader Lázaro Peña, was steadfast in its efforts to defend and promote the organization and rights of Cuban workers. The government, in contrast, never ceased its efforts to divide the trade union movement. In June 1947, following the April 12 U.S. official announcement of its anticommunist policy (the Truman Doctrine), the Cuban government moved to eliminate the unified leadership of the CTC, despite the fact that most workers supported it. In a blatant violation of the law, the Ministry of Labor nullified the Fifth CTC Congress and convened a new, government-sponsored meeting. Out of that false splinter meeting within the trade union movement came an artificial organization bearing the same name as the authentic CTC. It usurped the latter's official position and declared itself the promoter of anticommunist, democratic unionism. Its actual goal, however, was to subordinate the workers' interests to the government's positions and the interests of Cuba's oligarchy. From that time until the triumph of the Revolution two different trade union organizations coexisted in Cuba: the authentic CTC, which represented the genuine interests of the workers, and the government-imposed, imposter CTC, intended to splinter the movement. Popular idioms branded the latter organization the CTK, in reference to its illegal appropriation of funds earmarked to pay the wages of teachers and professors under Section K of Law 7 of 1943.

The creation of the CTK, which fragmented the trade union movement, was accompanied by increased attacks against workers and their true leaders. These included threats, layoffs, persecution, assaults on trade unions, and the assassination of militants and legitimate trade union leaders who had influence among the workers. The list of assassinations includes Jesús Menéndez, a leader of the National Federation of Sugar Workers (killed by army captain Casillas Lumpuy); Aracelio Iglesias, a national port leader (killed by trade union gunmen); Miguel Fernández Roig, a tobacco grower; and José María Pérez, from the transportation sector. Today, Cuban workers consider these men and others martyrs in the fight for workers' rights and dignity.

Under the fallout of the drop in world sugar prices, Cuba's economic and social situation continued to deteriorate in the 1950s. Enormous sugar and livestock estates predominated, with 8 percent of the population controlling 75 percent of the land. One-third of the working population was unemployed or underemployed; 27.3 percent was illiterate; the average level of schooling was third grade; and only 55 percent of children between six and fourteen attended school. There was only one rural hospital in the country, and medical doctors were concentrated in the large cities, where they received incomes far exceeding those of the masses. Yet the infant mortality rate was sixty per thousand live births. The wealthiest 20 percent of the population earned 58 percent of the income, while the poorest 20 percent received only 2 percent.[4] At that time the United States controlled more than 56 percent of Cuba's sugar production and more than 60 percent of its foreign trade.

The condition of the rural peasantry was catastrophic. Their rate of illiteracy was 43 percent. Although they grew and produced food, only 11 percent drank milk, 4 percent ate meat, 3 percent ate bread, 2 percent ate eggs, and 1 percent ate fish. Seventy-four percent of rural housing was in deplorable condition, and only 10 percent had electricity.[5]

These objective conditions strained the country's political system, leading Fulgencio Batista to stage a coup d'état on March 10, 1952. Batista installed a dictatorship characterized by corruption, the handing over of Cuba's economic resources to foreign capital, business dealings with the U.S. Mafia (Lucky Luciano and Meyer Lansky, among other mob bosses), and violent repression of workers and the population.[6] Batista crushed popular protests and trampled on the 1940 Constitution. He was supported by Cuba's repressive forces, the corrupt trade union leaders in his service, and the U.S. government, which considered him their strongman. Throughout Batista's 1952–58 dictatorship, the trade union movement remained divided. There was the official trade union, which was controlled by corrupt leaders who negotiated with the regime, and the underground trade union movement, constantly subjected to brutal repression.

The attack on the Moncada and Bayamo garrisons on July 26, 1953, ushered in a struggle that ended in the final defeat of the tyranny on January 1, 1959. The final sustained armed struggle in the Sierra Maestra began after the landing of the yacht *Granma* on Cuban shores in December 1956. Beginning with a handful of combatants, the rebel army slowly but steadily grew in size and began to score important victories, expand its theater of operations, and liberate territories. During these two years the workers, the trade union movements, and the farmers' associations started to take shape as the main bases of support for the Revolution.

The call for the Congress of Workers in Arms, held in one of the liberated areas of the Frank País II Eastern Front, led by Commander Raúl Castro Ruz, had significant repercussions for the trade union struggles. Some of the resolutions adopted by the delegates to this congress included the following: to initiate a struggle for payment of the sugar premium; to ensure repairs to the sugar mills and hence employment by the beginning of the sugar harvest; to revoke the authorization of pro-government trade union leaders to negotiate with landowners and tenant farmers on behalf of the sugar workers; to convene assemblies in workplaces to dismiss the false trade union leaders from office; to support the peasants in real land reform; and to back the actions of the rebel army.

The spirited struggles for worker unity and rights, and the very victory of the Revolution itself, were not mere historical accidents. They were instead rooted in the humiliating standard of living of the Cuban people, which Fidel Castro Ruz denounced in his famous "History Will Absolve Me" speech. Some of the conditions he cited were these:

> 600,000 Cubans out of work; 500,000 rural laborers who work for four months a year and starve during the rest; 400,000 industrial workers and seasonal farm laborers whose retirement pensions have been embezzled; 10,000 young professionals—doctors, engineers, lawyers, veterinarians, teachers, dentists, pharmacists, journalists, painters, sculptors, etc.—who leave the classroom with their degrees, longing to fight and full of hope, only to find themselves in a blind alley, with all doors closed; the 85 percent of Cuban small farmers who pay rent and live under constant threat of eviction from their land; 200,000 rural families who do not even have a vara[7] of land to plant food for their hungry children . . . 2.8 million people in our rural and suburban population lacking electricity.[8]

Basis for the Current Situation: Transformations in the 1960s

Following the revolutionary victory of January 1959, these social ills were eliminated. The new government initiated a period of transformation and radical changes that undermined the foundations of the neocolonial and dependent capitalist state. For the first time in the history of the republic, power passed into the hands of the humble, the workers in close alliance with the peasants.

The government immediately began implementing important measures in support of the people. The old army and the repressive instruments of the national oligarchy and foreign capital were dismantled. The judiciary that was complicit with them was purged. The public administration was rid of corrupt officials, and those who had amassed their wealth at the expense of the people had their ill-gotten gains confiscated. The first Land Reform Act was enacted. Electricity costs and housing rents were lowered. A widespread construction program of public works, housing, and hospitals in rural areas was launched. Gambling, drug trafficking, and prostitution were eliminated. A campaign of nationalization took over those companies that had monopolized the country's sources of wealth. Thousands of workers laid off during the tyranny were reinstated. The splinter trade union bureaucracy that had thrived at the expense of workers' interests was eliminated. The main leaders of the corrupt trade union fled the country. The gangster Eusebio Mujal, who for several years had usurped the leadership of the trade union movement, escaped with the other agents of the deposed regime. Five of his estates, on which hundreds of employees and seasonal laborers worked, were confiscated, totaling sixteen hundred hectares of land, thousands of head of cattle, and other property.

The Tenth Congress of the CTC—also known as the First Congress of the Revolutionary CTC—was held in November 1959, less than a year after the revolutionary victory. Its central goal was to restructure the fragmented trade union movement. Many foreign workers' organizations sent representatives, including the Confederation of Latin American Workers, the Inter-American Regional Labor Organization, the Latin American Confederation of Christian Trade Unions, and the World Trade Union Federation. Other union representatives came from Chile, Uruguay, Venezuela, Guatemala, France, Italy, Spain, the Soviet Union, India, and the People's Republic of China, among other countries. Several important agreements came out of this congress:

- Strong support for the recently victorious Revolution
- The purge of divisive and corrupt leaders from the union movement

- The suppression of strikes and other trade union actions that could negatively affect the revolutionary transformations
- A 4 percent contribution from the workers' salaries to foster Cuba's industrialization
- The termination of affiliations with reformist organizations and those submissive to big capital, such as the International Confederation of Free Trade Unions
- The establishment of relations with all democratic trade union confederations in the world

At this time, the government enacted many profound revisions in the laws governing labor relations, with the following outcomes:

- It increased salaries.
- It created new and productive jobs.
- New legislation standardized workers' rights and duties, creating a new system of labor relations.
- The fifty-five embezzled insurance funds received monetary resources to cover workers' retirement pensions. (Many workers had not received their pensions for a year or more.)
- Welfare programs were initiated to eliminate poverty and care for people with disabilities and those in nursing homes.
- Social Security Act 1100 furnished the country with its first comprehensive and universal system of protection for workers and their families.
- The CTC and the trade unions were recognized as autonomous organizations and legitimate representatives of the workers, an unprecedented event in the history of Cuba.

Overall, the laws adopted by the revolutionary government declared workers to be the collective owners of the national economy and the country's wealth.

Labor in Cuba Today

The labor relations of wage-earning workers are legislated in the Labor Code.[9] Complementing this code are a number of laws specifically regulating certain activities for all the legal entities in the country that have their own assets, including state-owned enterprises, joint ventures, foreign branches, cooperatives, and employment agencies. There are also regulations addressing the labor relations of wage earners in small private enterprises as well as self-employed workers.

General Working Conditions, Including Safety and Health

The work regulations specify an eight-hour workday and an average forty-four-hour workweek. The Ministry of Labor and Social Security has approved exceptions for special types of jobs, such as longer shifts in cyclical, seasonal, and other activities with special characteristics, and shorter shifts on jobs that may pose health risks or have other specific circumstances. Workers receive at least one day off per week, generally Sunday. When dire necessity or social interest dictates extra labor needs, workers may work overtime, do double shifts, or work on days off, as determined by an agreement between the enterprise administrators and the trade union, with a limit of 160 additional hours per year in total. Workers receive thirty calendar days of annual vacation for every eleven months of work, plus eight days off per year for national holidays, which are paid in full.

Child labor is prohibited, and violations are severely punished by law. Fifteen- or sixteen-year-old youths can enter into a work contract upon completion of their basic education if they have parental consent, authorization from the Ministry of Labor and Social Security, and a medical report documenting their ineligibility to pursue further studies due to underachievement or other justifiable reasons.

Safety and health on the job, in addition to being enshrined as a labor right under Article 49 of the Constitution of the Republic, are regulated by the Labor Protection and Hygiene Act of 1977 and the General Labor Safety and Health Guidelines of 2007. These laws and regulations simultaneously serve to preserve the physical well-being of the workers, the facilities, and the environment. Their implementation in individual enterprises rests fundamentally on the active participation of the workers and trade union organizations. They give workers the rights to demand safe and hygienic labor conditions from their employers, as well as the safety equipment needed for personal and collective protection. Those who sustain work-related accidents or diseases receive a subsidy until their medical discharge or recovery. Legal punishments are prescribed for accidents caused by employer violations of safety and protection standards. Even with an increase in the level of economic activity over the last fifteen years, workplace accidents continue to trend downward, in conjunction with increased attention to risks and adoption of additional preventive measures in most enterprises. However, employers and some workers still have a long way to go in terms of compliance with the existing standards and rules.

Women Workers

A particularly important part of Cuba's overall commitment to universal social equality is its labor policies for women. Cuba was the first country to sign and the second to ratify the UN Convention on the Elimination of All Forms of Discrimination against Women.

In 1959 only about 194,000 women worked outside their homes, accounting for 12.1 percent of the working population. Of these women, 70 percent were engaged in household or informal activities, and only 58,200 had maternity benefits. Today, having been granted equal rights and social and professional development, women make up 46 percent of workers in the dominant state sector of the economy and more than 66 percent of the country's technical workforce. Furthermore, women account for 70 percent of teachers and professors, 63 percent of university graduates, 55 percent of attorneys, 53 percent of executives, 52 percent of medical doctors, 52 percent of grassroots trade union leaders, and 49 percent of judges.

Current legislation stipulates that with medical certification, pregnant workers who are unable to carry out their normal job duties should be transferred to another job that they can perform and be relieved of night shifts if that is an issue. Maternity benefits comprise the following:

- Leave of six days or twelve half days for prenatal and dental care
- Compulsory leave from work as of the thirty-fourth week of pregnancy
- Paid maternity leave of eighteen weeks, of which twelve are for postnatal care
- Pay equal to the woman's average weekly salary while on leave
- Economic assistance after the postnatal leave until the child is one year old
- Unpaid leaves as needed to look after children until they are sixteen years old

Labor Contracts and Collective Labor Agreements

Labor contracts are an important feature of the formalization of labor relations. These are signed between each enterprise and all workers at least seventeen years old. They specify the working conditions and the length of employment, whether for a specific period, an indefinite period, or the implementation or execution of a project or task. More than 80 percent of the contracts signed are open-ended contracts for permanent employment, whether continuous, intermittent, or cyclical; these have no specified termination date. Workers under this type of contract are part of the permanent workforce of an enterprise.

The specifics of the labor contract can be modified as agreed by the parties. Modifications may reflect negotiations on a worker's job description, clauses in the collective labor agreement, or legal requirements. In the event of a dispute over the labor contract, the employee is entitled to lodge a complaint with the relevant body to seek a resolution.

Legislation sets forth justified reasons for temporary suspension of labor relations without breaking the labor contract. This assures the worker of the continuity of his or her employment in the event certain reasons for absence arise, such as participating in trade union and other congresses; testifying under subpoena; acting as a lay judge in the people's courts; undergoing medical tests and checkups; donating blood; being mobilized into the army; taking leave on the death of a parent, spouse, or child; taking maternity leave; and other special situations. Termination of the labor relation is subject to preestablished causes. Employees may contest their termination and are entitled to job reinstatement and to moral and material compensation if the complaint is settled in their favor.

Another and more collective aspect of the formalization of labor relations is the use of collective labor agreements. These constitute an agreement between the enterprise management and the trade union on the terms of labor and the best ways to enforce each party's reciprocal rights and obligations. Such agreements cover increases in the enterprise's production of goods and services, administrative and managerial relations with the workers, and promotion of workers' proactive participation in various aspects of the operation of the enterprise. In theory, before it is formalized in writing and becomes legally binding, the collective labor agreement must be discussed and approved at a workers' assembly. However, such meetings are often not held because of "operational routinism" or a lack of knowledge about this regulation.

Resolving Labor Conflicts

The system for resolving labor conflicts has three pillars. The first and primary one is a grassroots board set up in each enterprise to investigate and settle the claims of workers who believe that their labor rights have been abridged or that they have been unjustly sanctioned. These bodies are composed of one member elected in the workplace assembly, one member appointed by the trade union, and one management representative, with backups for these three positions. These members are re-ratified or replaced every three years. These bodies thoroughly investigate, publicly and promptly make rulings, and thereby resolve nearly 70 percent of claims filed annually by workers. The work of these bodies has been instrumental in reducing the number of disputes each year, lowering procedural costs and compensations and, most importantly, improving the atmosphere in workplaces, particularly because coworkers resolve the claims.

The second pillar for conflict resolution is the municipal people's courts. These are composed of both professional and lay judges. Here either party can present its case for overturning the ruling of the grassroots labor board, after which the court makes a decision. The Labor Division of the People's Supreme Court can overrule the decision of a municipal court.

The third pillar for conflict resolution is the National Office for Labor Inspection, attached to the Ministry of Labor and Social Security. This body oversees compliance with labor legislation, systematically verifying the enforcement of labor, salary, occupational safety and health, and social security provisions. Upon discovering an offense or violation, the labor inspection team may levy fines against the offenders, idle the plant machinery, close down the enterprise, or invoke other disciplinary measures, as the case calls for. Any cases of alleged criminal behavior are submitted to penal authorities.

Salaries

Salary policies have been created with a central concern for equity. A unique salary system guarantees that payment corresponds uniformly with the worker's qualifications and the work performed, without discrimination based on gender, age, or place of employment. This system operationalizes the constitutional precept of equal pay for equal work.

Salaries constitute the main source of income for workers and their families, and hence their main means of obtaining consumable goods. They are not, however, the only source, nor are they sufficient, for that matter, to satisfy all a family's needs. The state provides several basic services, either for free or at heavily subsidized rates. Among these are health care, education, day care, a basic food ration, housing, medications, transportation, drinking water, and community sanitation. These greatly supplement the goods that workers and their families consume, and hence the effective purchasing power of their income. Because it is widely known that the Cuban state provides extensive goods and services, the assertion in some international media that the average Cuban worker only earns the equivalent of $17 a month is nothing more than an indecent lie. To be sure, if one converts the average monthly salary of 436 Cuban pesos (CUP) to dollars at the CADECA exchange rate, it comes out close to $17. But obviously no person in any capitalist county in the world could obtain the goods and services that a Cuban worker receives free for $17 per month, nor even for twenty times that amount (considering that this includes health care, education, and housing with running water and electricity).

Salaries are paid in legal tender at least once a month. A portion of the salary can be withheld only by a legal decision (up to a third of the salary) or by garnishment by appropriate authorities to pay alimony or debts (up to half of the salary). In particular, and in stark contrast to the standard capitalist practice, salaries cannot be withheld because of a temporary suspension of work that is not the fault of the worker. In this case the workers are ensured their salaries until conditions allow them to begin to work again.

On a periodic basis the state readjusts the minimum wage and the salary levels for different jobs. Salaries depend on the complexity of the labor and its conditions and are set in consultation with the relevant trade union organization. Supplementary salaries for work under abnormal conditions, nighttime work, and work that requires advanced professional training are set similarly. Wages and salaries have progressively increased, starting with the lowest salaries. In 2005 the minimum wage was doubled to 225 pesos to make up for the loss of purchasing power during the Special Period. Since then, the focus of Cuba's wage policy has been to improve the correspondence between wages and workers' productivity in terms of goods and services. The intent, as discussed further in the next section, is to motivate increased production and thereby create the basis for a continued increase in the wage scale. Over the last two decades wages have more than doubled in nominal terms: whereas in 1989 the average monthly salary was 188 CUP, today it stands at 436 CUP. At the same time, the amount of free and heavily subsidized goods and services distributed to the whole population through the ration card and other channels has decreased, so these increased wages also play a more central role in a worker's consumption than they did in 1989. There is universal recognition in the Cuban government that the present wage scale is insufficient for a dignified standard of living.

Increasing Enterprise Efficiency and Labor Productivity

Despite all the advances Cuba has made in the process of its recovery from the economic shock at the beginning of the 1990s, wage earnings are still insufficient to satisfy the population's needs. Cuba believes that the key to resolving this problem lies with increasing enterprise efficiency and labor productivity. On the one hand, if workers' incomes are tied more closely to their individual work contributions, so that everyone earns a salary based on the results of their work, then the desire to earn a higher salary will cause workers to put greater thought and effort into their work. This will yield the desired increased efficiency and productivity, and is the rationale for Cuba's current drive to increase the connection between salary and results achieved throughout the economy. This issue is complicated however by the fact that although Cuba is promoting a closer connection between pay and work performance, the Revolution does not and will not use neoliberal shock measures nor even let the full impact of economic difficulties or crises fall on workers' shoulders.

On the other hand the causal link between higher salaries and increased efficiency and labor productivity simultaneously runs the other direction. Only a sustained increase in the production of goods and services and in labor productivity can create the basis to make any nominal increase in salaries a real increase. With that in mind, short- and medium-term direct efforts to increase the efficiency and productivity of the workforce are being carried out with the goal of allowing for an ongoing increase in workers' salaries. Major conceptual and structural changes are being implemented, bottlenecks in the productive processes are being opened, labor legislation is being streamlined, workers' participation in searching for solutions to these issues is being enhanced, and the role of trade unions is being reinforced. For example, as part of the multifaceted search for efficiency, hundreds of enterprises are implementing a new management system (*perfeccionamiento empresarial*) that increases the powers of managers and trade union leaders (instead of government ministries) to make decisions regarding the enterprises' internal processes and to resolve labor problems. They have the prerogative to determine the structure of the enterprise, the number of workers required, the payment systems, and the criteria for performance evaluations. That includes the rational use of labor and the elimination of internal underemployment by reallocating redundant workers to other useful and necessary tasks.

It must be stressed, however, that management cannot resort to layoffs as a strategy to increase productivity and profits. In addition to the rational use of labor through its reorganization and reallocation, a vital means of increasing productivity is via increased technology and improved human capital. Labor skills must be continuously enhanced by ongoing training. For example, workers are entitled to a number of days of leave every year to attend daytime university courses and, further, to receive a loan equaling the salary they would have received for those days of work. The continually increasing importance of educated and highly skilled labor in the Cuban economy has already manifested in the steady increase of the tertiary sector, and in particular its knowledge-based components, for both Cuba's internal economy and its foreign trade (see chapter 12). Building on five decades of progress in education under the Revolution, in 2007 services accounted for 67.7 percent of GDP with important contributions coming from medical services, genetic engineering, biotechnology, informatics, and tourism.

Social Security and Pensions

An important complement to salaries in providing for the well-being of the population of any country is a comprehensive and universal system of social security and pensions. Cuba has a social security system in place that establishes fundamental rights, duties, and guarantees for all workers incapable of working due to age, disability, accidents, or disease, and for their families in case of their death. It provides support to senior citizens with insufficient resources, as well as (together with the welfare system) to any needy person who cannot work and lacks sufficient family support. Social security is provided without discrimination based on age, gender, skin color, religious belief, or political ideology. In Cuba, as in all countries, comprehensive health care is an important issue for senior citizens and people with disabilities, though in Cuba social security blends into the universal and comprehensive health-care system for the entire population.

The Cuban state guarantees that pensioners will receive the income, services, health care, and other systematic care they require, particularly those who are disabled or belong to other socially vulnerable groups in the population. Policies are shaped to address pensioners' specific and individual needs. For example, senior citizens living alone or those with a disability receive subsidized in-home services to assist with food preparation, personal care, social orientation, and delivery of their pensions, among other services. There are now more than 2 million pensioners out of a total population of 11.2 million, so this guarantee entails an outlay of extensive resources. In 1959, 114 million pesos were spent on social security. Forty-five times that amount is earmarked today for pensions alone; that is, more than 5 billion pesos, or 7 percent of GDP.[10]

Unemployment

The General Regulations on Labor Relations, dated March 1, 2005, set forth under Article 1 that

> the policy on employment is part of the state's socioeconomic policy, structured to incorporate eligible and willing people into socially useful employment, without any discrimination; it guarantees the employee's income, security, and stability of work against structural or cyclical changes; permanent training and development of the labor force; and broad-based forms of participation of workers and workers' organizations at all levels of the decision-making process on such policy.[11]

As mentioned, in the event of any contingency affecting a worker's job security, the employer is obliged to exhaust all possibilities to offer the worker other productive employment. This may require the employer to send the worker to courses to refresh or augment the worker's skills. Any new job assignment cannot prejudice the worker's income. These provisions have made a major contribution to minimizing frictional unemployment over the years, and particularly during the last two decades of the Special Period.

In the event that a significant number of jobs are eliminated in a given enterprise or industry,[12] and no alternative jobs can be found for some workers in that enterprise, Cuban employment policies at the supra-enterprise level take force. No worker willing to work is left without employment. Redundant workers receive offers of employment in other enterprises, or when necessary, training in new skills for their subsequent reinsertion into the labor force, again with their income protected. This procedure was applied on a large scale in the early 2000s when the jobs of 100,000 workers were eliminated due to the downsizing of the sugar industry. None was abandoned to his or her individual fate.

By 2007, before the effects of the world's Great Recession reached Cuba, the unemployment rate had been brought down to 1.8 percent according to the National Office of Statistics, which follows International Labor Organization (ILO) methodology. Despite what was by international standards a very impressive level of unemployment, Cuba was and still is pursuing an intensive plan to increase employment, in accord with its commitment to offer jobs to all workers who are able and willing to work. A first target was to ensure the availability of jobs for graduates of universities, polytechnics, and trade schools, in keeping with the drive to continually upgrade the educational level and skills of the Cuban labor force. The second target was to ameliorate Cuba's frictional unemployment by prioritizing jobs for young people and soldiers discharged from military service. The third target was to address Cuba's small structural unemployment by finding jobs for, and often providing further education and training to, former inmates, people who have a criminal record but did not spend time in jail, and those disabled people who are able to do certain kinds of work.

Self-employment

Contrary to the belief of many foreigners, the Cuban Revolution has always had self-employment, and it is regulated by law. Prior to 1990 the large majority of the self-employed were small private farmers, but there were also always several tens of thousands of self-employed people in the cities as well. In current discussions on Cuba, the term *self-employed* usually refers to the latter, urban group and so I will use it that way in this section, even though there are now more self-employed small farmers than ever.

In the 1990s self-employment peaked at more than 200,000, and there are now 166,000 self-employed, accounting for 3.4 percent of the total workforce. These workers supply their own (usually simple) means of production and are employed in activities that complement social production. Based on supply and demand, they manufacture and sell products and services; rent houses; transport cargo and people; and create music, literature, and plastic arts. They pay taxes on their income to the Tax Administration Office. This small-scale self-employment in Cuba entirely lacks the informality, precariousness, and lack of social protection that characterizes such employment in other countries.

The government has been indicating for several years that it intends to reduce the excess workforce in the state sector. Presently in 2010 it is working on the details of how to do so, as always without leaving unemployed those whose jobs are eliminated. A significant expansion of the self-employed sector is one way to absorb workers laid off in this necessary improvement in state enterprise labor efficiency. At the same time, self-employment will increase the availability of a number of personal services that have been in inadequate supply in the past.

International Labor Agreements

Cuba is a founding member of the ILO and actively cooperates and participates in its activities. Cuba has ratified eighty-eight conventions on a wide range of labor rights, making it one of the top ten countries in the number of ratifications. These conventions entail organizational responsibilities for Cuba both to comply with the accords and to disseminate information about its compliance. Cuban labor legislation provides the legal framework for enforcing the provisions of all the conventions. In many cases the laws exceed international norms, as Cuban workers have more rights, broader benefits, and stronger social protections.

Cuba has also ratified seven of the eight major international conventions. It has ratified and—despite claims to the contrary from enemies of Cuba's Revolution—has complied with Conventions Nos. 87 and 98 on the freedom of association and the right of workers to organize and bargain collectively. Convention No. 182, prohibiting the worst forms of child labor, is under study for ratification, even though there is no child labor of any type on the Island.

In the current global environment, powerful countries intent on dividing the international labor movement, and on undermining the political systems of those nations that refuse to accept the unjust international order, have engaged in campaigns of false propaganda regarding the labor practices of their enemies, while themselves engaging in selective practices and judging their actions by a double standard. Table 8.1 shows eight major labor conventions and which of several developed countries have ratified them, from which readers can draw their own conclusions.

Cuba responsibly complies with the international commitments it enters into. When it ratifies an international labor standard, it does so because it has existing legislation and national programs that provide the framework for an instrument that can be used to fulfill the commitment. An example of this

Table 8.1. Fundamental labor rights conventions and countries ratifying them

Country	Freedom of association and collective bargaining Conventions		Elimination of forced or obligatory labor Conventions		Elimination of discrimination in employment and occupation Conventions		Abolition of child labor Conventions	
	87	**98**	**29**	**105**	**100**	**111**	**138**	**182**
Spain	x	x	x	x	x	x	x	x
United Kingdom	x	x	x	x	x	x	x	x
Germany	x	x	x	x	x	x	x	x
France	x	x	x	x	x	x	x	x
Italy	x	x	x	x	x	x	x	x
Canada	x			x	x	x		x
United States				x				x
Japan	x	x	x		x		x	x
Cuba	x	x	x	x	x	x	x	

honoring of international conventions is indicated in the UN Development Programme second report on Cuba's compliance with the Millennium Development Goals. The report states that, based on ongoing actions and those scheduled to be implemented, three of the eight goals have already been achieved, and three more are likely to be fulfilled within the established time frame.

Trade Unions

The CTC and its twenty trade union members play an important role in representing the interests of workers. They are independent of the Cuban state apparatus. Because they are workers' organizations, their members elect and determine their leadership. Each union approves its own bylaws, structure, funds, operating procedures, and relations with other organizations and the outside world. All entities and workplaces have active trade unions, the secretary-general of which is entitled to participate in senior management meetings whenever an issue is raised that pertains to labor relations or workers' problems. In terms of both legal provisions and daily activities trade union representation and decision making occur on different levels: local, national, and the CTC. The twenty national unions comprise the CTC, and through the decisions of the workers themselves in its congresses, the CTC expresses the desire for unity in the Cuban trade union movement.

More than 3.4 million workers are affiliated with the CTC's branch unions, accounting for 97 percent of all workers in the country. This high rate of affiliation is based on voluntary membership decisions: union dues are not withheld from workers' paychecks, so workers must make an active decision to pay them. This is evidence of the unity and cohesion achieved by the Cuban trade union movement. The significance of this achievement by and for Cuban workers is underlined by the low levels of union affiliation found in most other countries, particularly the world's most developed economies. Furthermore, in those countries several of the formally existing basic labor rights are undermined by the government and politically powerful conservative institutions (for example, the press), including the most basic rights to organize and to bargain collectively. A glance at the level of union affiliation in the G8 countries sets off an alarm bell concerning the ongoing deterioration of the previous important achievements of labor there. According to the June 2008 Global Report of the International Labor Conference, the union affiliation rate in the United States is 12.2 percent, and the rate in the private capitalist sector is less than two-thirds of that. In Canada the Labor Congress, held in May 2008, estimated that 31.5 percent of Canadian workers are union members. European Union data list union affiliations in member countries as follows: Italy, 38.1 percent; United Kingdom, 30.4 percent; Germany, 29.2 percent; Spain, 16.3 percent; and France, 9.8 percent. Japan's rate is less than 5 percent.

In their domains of activity, Cuban trade unions have, among others, the following recognized rights:

- To participate in the drafting, implementation, and control of enterprise production or service plans
- To represent the individual and collective rights of workers in the workplace, and to advocate for the improvement of working and living conditions
- To demand and oversee compliance with labor legislation and the regulations governing salaries, safety, health, and social security
- To continuously improve the overall environment where the worker carries out his or her duties
- To promote technical, professional, and cultural training activities
- To promote recreational and entertainment opportunities for workers during their nonworking or break times
- To promote the proactive participation of workers in every aspect of the labor environment
- To contribute to workers' discipline, productivity, efficiency, and concern with quality

- To organize and promote tasks pertaining to trade union work, as provided for in union bylaws
- To negotiate the collective labor agreement with management

In order to protect trade union leaders in the discharge of their duties, enterprise management by law cannot transfer them or terminate their employment due to their union activity. It must also provide the trade union, free of charge, with areas in the enterprise for use in its activities.

By law, trade unions must consult in and evaluate government and management decisions. Hence, every new legal standard or economic measure that may affect the rights or well-being of workers is subjected to a rigorous discussion process at all levels of the trade union movement, in consultation with enterprise management and the state central administration, prior to being adopted. The Constitution of the Republic even authorizes trade unions to present opinions on, or amendments to, drafts of national legislation. In many cases the trade unions decide to submit the draft legislation for discussion among the workers in their workplaces. The opinions and suggestions that are presented in that forum amend and enrich the final legislation that is subsequently adopted.

An eloquent example of the level of respect for trade unions and for participatory democracy in Cuba was the establishment of workers' parliaments, convened by the CTC and its branch trade unions in 1994. These were convened to assess the set of government measures submitted to the National Assembly to address the severe economic crisis that had resulted from the demise of the socialist community and the simultaneous intensification of the U.S. blockade. Some three million workers discussed the proposed measures in workplace assemblies, which members of the National Assembly attended. The result was that workers themselves contributed to finding more efficient solutions to the problems of the budget deficit, price increases, the domestic financial imbalance, and other economic difficulties. Workers in the assemblies objected to the imposition of taxes on salaries as long as salaries remained low and stagnant due to the economic recession, although there was consensus that wages should be taxed when the salary situation improved. The National Assembly took those opinions and criteria into account and postponed taxation of wages until after the economic situation improved.

A final comment should be made concerning trade union activity in Cuba. One variant of the not-so-covert war that the Empire to the North has waged against Cuba has been the fabrication of false trade union organizations composed of people who neither work nor represent any collective of workers or workplaces in Cuba, and who are financially supported by money from overseas. Then when these organizers are punished, not for union activity but rather for breaking Cuban laws, this is presented to the world as an instance of Cuban noncompliance with the labor agreements on the freedom of association and the right to organize. This situation has reached the point where the "ghost" trade union organizations have even lodged complaints with the Committee on Trade Union Freedom over alleged violations of the rights of their workers in Cuba. These groups in fact have nothing to do with the issues of labor rights and relations in Cuba because they do not involve Cuban workers. On the contrary, the majority of Cubans consider them to concern the very different issue of Cuba's right to sovereignty.

Challenges Ahead

The material in this chapter on the status of labor and labor relations in Cuba today makes it clear that many challenges lie ahead—as has been the case over the constantly evolving fifty-year history of the revolutionary process. The most immediate challenge is to raise the standard of living of Cuban working people. This requires ongoing increases in their salaries, which in turn requires continual increases in their labor productivity. Fundamental changes in the Cuban economy were necessitated by the demise of the socialist community, but those changes, which have been unfolding for the last twenty years and continue to develop today, now must have increased efficiency and labor productivity as one of their central goals. But while labor conditions and relations throughout the capitalist world and, in particular, the developed world have been deteriorating over the last twenty years in the service of increased profits, Cuba's chosen goal of building socialism precludes that path as an option to achieve the required improvement in the productivity of its enterprises. In contrast, Cuba must improve its efficiency and labor productivity while maintaining its many labor rights and positive labor relations, extending them, and maintaining and extending the many other achievements of the Revolution for its working people. Its new labor relations must, just like the old ones, be created and understood as a central part of its project of building socialism, now under changed world conditions.

Notes

1. *Gaceta Oficial de la República de Cuba*, http://www.gacetaoficial.cu/html/constitucion_de_la_republica.html.

2. Emilio Roig de Leuchsenring, *Análisis y consecuencias de la intervención norteamericana en los asuntos interiores de Cuba* (Havana: Imprenta Siglo XX, 1923).

3. Group of Authors, *La neocolonia: Organización y crisis: Desde 1899 a 1940* (Havana: Editora Política, 1998).

4. See José Luis Rodríguez, "La economía neocolonial cubana," *Cuba Socialista* No. 37 (1989).

5. Asociación Católica Universitaria, *Encuesta ¿Por qué reforma agraria?* (Havana: ACU, 1957).

6. Enrique Cirules, *El imperio de La Habana* (Havana: Editora Letras Cubanas, 1999). This is a study about the business and operations of the Mafia in Havana.

7. A unit of length approximately equivalent to one yard.

8. Fidel Castro, *La historia me absolverá* (Havana: Oficina de Publicaciones del Consejo de Estado, 1993). Annotated edition.

9. *Gaceta Oficial de la República de Cuba,* http://www.gacetaoficial.cu/html/codigodetrabajo.html.

10. ONE, *Panorama económico social, Cuba, 2007* (Havana: ONE, 2008).

11. *Gaceta Oficial de la República de Cuba.* http://www.gacetaoficial.cu/.

12. A central goal of the current program of enterprise restructuring is to eliminate internal underemployment by reducing enterprise workforces while maintaining output, in order to raise labor productivity and thereby salaries.

Part III

Specific Branches of Production

9

The Evolution of International Tourism in Cuba

MIGUEL ALEJANDRO FIGUERAS

Until the beginning of World War II, international tourism catered largely to the elite. The large and luxurious passenger liners such as the *Titanic*, or the safaris of the style Ernest Hemingway wrote about in the "Snows of the Kilimanjaro," could be considered typical of international tourism in those years. After World War II the nature of tourism changed. Advances in medicine, low-cost air-conditioning, large-fuselage jet aircraft, progress in satellite communications, personal computers, and credit cards enabled international tourism to mushroom from twenty-five million people in 1950 to nearly a billion international tourists in 2010.

Key factors for the early development of tourism in Cuba were its proximity to the East Coast of the United States, the World War I travel ban that prevented wealthy Americans from visiting Europe, the elimination of lotteries and gambling in the United States, and the subsequent implementation of the Volstead Act, which was intended to enable the Eighteenth Amendment establishing Prohibition. Cuba's leaders then, with the support of powerful external forces, came to view Havana's future as the Great Destination of Gambling Tourism for Americans. Havana, not Cuba as a whole, received one out of every two Americans traveling to the Caribbean between 1920 and 1930. In the 1920s new, large, and lavish hotels were built in Havana almost every year to host the ever-increasing flows of American visitors yearning for alcohol, gambling, wild parties, and other activities frowned on in their own country.

Then came the Great Depression of the 1930s, followed by World War II. In those two decades from 1930 to 1950, tourism-related activities declined in Havana, and many hotels and other enterprises connected with the tourism sector struggled to avoid closure and bankruptcy. In the 1950s tourism flows sharply increased again, and along with them new investments in hotels and a major boom in casinos and related irregular activities.

The latter were largely promoted and run by the National Crime Syndicate in the United States. In 1950–51 leaders of that syndicate were brought before the Senate Committee to Investigate Organized Crime in Interstate Commerce, presided over by Senator Estes Kefauver. Facing this heightened pressure, they began to fear that the government might move against their investments and enormous profits throughout the United States, particularly in Las Vegas.[1] Consequently, they chose Havana as a base outside the United States where they could relocate their Las Vegas–style gambling and associated businesses if that were to become necessary, and they began to build the industry there accordingly. These criminal elements affiliated themselves with Fulgencio Batista, the dictator who controlled Cuba's destiny for seventeen of the years between 1934 and 1958.

> The parallels to Las Vegas were everywhere. As more than 300,000 American tourists streamed into Havana in the fifties, casino after casino went up, some built by venerable corporations like Hilton and Pan American. . . . Cuban politicians eager for tourism and part of the take welcomed the "professionalism" of gangsters.
>
> So great was the migration of casino operators and floor men to Havana at one point in the decade that Nevada officials worried about the depletion of Las Vegas's own "professionals." There was talk in Carson City of prohibiting Nevada owners from operating in Cuba. . . . In 1959 . . . [the] Foreign Gaming Rule [prohibited] Nevada casino licensees from being involved in casinos anywhere else—legal or illegal.[2]

In 1958 two-thirds of the tourist rooms in Cuba were in Havana. The other third were scattered throughout the rest of the country, almost all in low-class hotels. Places in the country with special tourism potential, sites of breathtaking natural beauty, went undeveloped. Tourists in Havana could enjoy extremely lavish hotels, with their great neon signs, as symbols of a city of attractions. These majestic tourist facilities gave the appearance that Havana was a modern developed city. But there was a huge contradiction between the surface of ostentatious luxury these tourists experienced on the one hand, and the misery and abject poverty of the majority of the population on the other.

In the late 1950s, earnings from tourism became the third-largest source of foreign exchange for Cuba. At this time, 90 percent of tourists came from the American market, while national tourism in Cuba was very limited. Upper-class Cubans preferred to spend their holidays overseas. Every year, eighty thousand Cubans residing on the Island would travel abroad, most of them as tourists. Although the inflow of foreign visitors to the Island was higher than this, the length of stays and level of spending of Cuban tourists abroad caused Cuba's income from tourism to be less than its expenditures in most years, resulting in an overall negative balance.

A Different Course for Tourist Development, 1959–1989

With the victory of the Cuban Revolution in 1959, difficulties started to arise between Cuba and the U.S. government. In January 1961 the Eisenhower administration unilaterally severed relations and imposed measures to isolate the Island from the rest of the world. Within three weeks of the break in diplomatic relations, a travel ban was imposed to prevent U.S. citizens and residents from traveling to Cuba without a special license from the U.S. government. From that time on, Cuba's tourism situation changed radically. International tourism suddenly vanished, domestic tourism was promoted, and the number of Cuban tourists traveling abroad steadily declined.

It was not possible for Cuba to replace U.S. tourism with other markets. Europe, after reconstructing the damage caused by World War II, was waking up to tourism, and northern Europeans were discovering the sun and beaches of Greece, Italy, and Spain. Just before the imposition of the U.S. travel ban to Cuba, the first Boeing 707 and Douglas DC-8 aircraft took to the air, substantially diminishing the transportation costs for tourists. But as Mediterranean beaches opened up to tourism, few Europeans were interested in spending their vacations in Cuba. In the first place, the flight there was much longer and more expensive. But beyond that, Cuba was made less desirable through being the target of U.S.-backed attempted invasions, ongoing acts of sabotage, and threats of total destruction, all hallmarks of the U.S. policy toward Cuba in the 1960s.

The new Cuban policy of domestic tourism promotion aimed to initiate a nationwide movement for all Cubans to enjoy the scarce recreational tourism centers then in existence.[3] Primary among these were Cuba's spectacular beaches, which until the Revolution had been the private property of foreigners and Cuba's oligarchy. Act 270, enacted in April 1959, declared all Cuba's coasts and beaches to be public property that every person was free to walk on.[4] The general measures and actions to promote domestic tourism included organizing excursions, tours, and even travel programs. The state did not rule out promotion of legitimate foreign tourism, and soon there were relatively limited measures to draw tourists from the socialist countries, but this was a very different type of foreign tourism from what Cuba had endured before.

In cooperation with the Confederation of Cuban Workers and other social and government organizations, the government informed the population of domestic and foreign tourism options available to them.[5] The banking sector started to grant low-income Cubans credits to pay for vacations. In addition to the relatively small number of hotels at beaches and recreational sites, the Cuban public was offered rooms in villas, houses, and cabanas, most of which had formerly belonged to members of Cuba's oligarchy who had left the Island.

The revolutionary government founded the National Institute of the Tourism Industry (INIT) as the first agency specializing in tourism. The law creating INIT specified that tourism, aside from its economic significance, should be conceived of as the organized dissemination of information about the attractions of Cuban natural settings and national culture. It should serve the twofold purpose of educating Cubans about the assets of their homeland and of presenting the Island and its people to other people around the world, in order to deepen links of solidarity. Another objective that was emphasized even back then was conservation of the natural attractions and protection of the historical and cultural heritage that were the basis for tourism. In line with this mandate, INIT organized a number of different types of tourist activities for the enjoyment of Cuban tourists (workers, farmers, soldiers, students, and retirees).[6]

As national tourism became consolidated from 1960 to 1969, INIT gradually increased its offerings of excursions and package tours for tourists from the socialist countries. But a significant amount of international tourism could not really be said to have reemerged until the 1970s. Cuba's tourist policy then envisioned the following order of priorities:

1. To facilitate national tourism
2. To cater to tourism from the socialist countries
3. To foster tourism from the rest of the world

The main report to the First Congress of Cuba's Communist Party, in December 1975, clearly indicated these priorities:

> The nationalization of hotels and the main recreational facilities gave people access to them.
>
> Tourist facilities have received an investment of 50 million pesos. Of that figure, 15 million was used in the early years for public beaches.
>
> . . . .
>
> International tourism, after almost entirely disappearing, has experienced a slight increase over the last few years, with quite a different composition and quality than in the past. That [quality] will have to characterize the tourists who visit us in the future, making up a healthy trend of visitors seeking our natural attractions or interested in becoming acquainted with the social changes that have taken place in our homeland. It is estimated that more than half a million tourists will visit us in the next five-year period, mainly during the winter season.

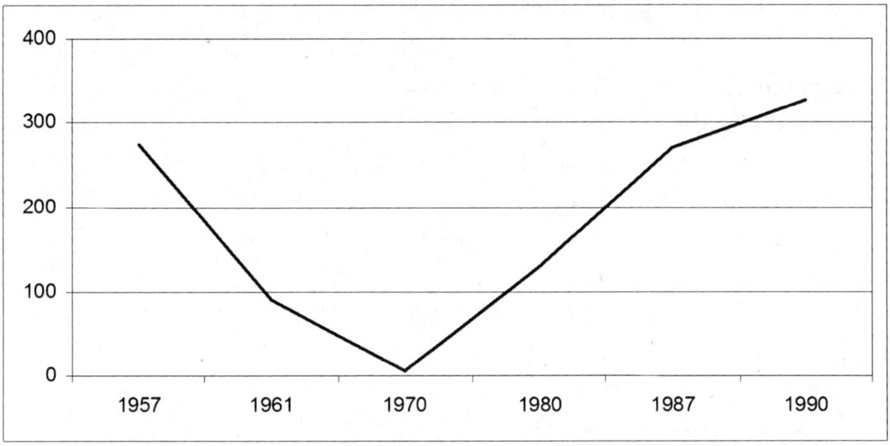

Figure 9.1. Tourist arrivals in Cuba, 1957–1990 (thousands). *Source:* Rogelio Quintana, Manuel Figuerola, Mariano Chirivelia, Damarys Lima, Miguel Alejandro Figueras, and Alfredo García, *Efectos y futuro del turismo en la economía cubana* (Havana: INIE, 2004).

With a more active policy on tourism, Cuba started to make investments and implement a plan of action to foster international tourist flows between 1975 and 1989. In 1983 the Reagan administration reimposed the ban on travel to Cuba from the United States, which had been allowed to lapse during the Carter administration. But even though the U.S. market was cut off again, remaining markets continued to grow (see fig. 9.1). The level of arrivals rose to 270,000 tourists in 1987, matching the number of tourists who had come thirty years before. Unlike in 1957, however, almost no one came from the United States, and the visitors were coming for very different reasons.

Intensive Development of International Tourism, 1990–2009

By the late 1980s the demise of the Soviet Union and the other socialist countries of Eastern Europe was foreseeable, even though most of the world did not recognize the possibility until it happened. In light of the potential loss of Cuba's main trading partners, the need arose to develop new sectors of the Cuban economy in order to enable it to survive, and eventually transcend, the extremely difficult situation that might arise. Most importantly, these sectors would need to be able to rapidly generate hard-currency earnings, given what such a disruption would do to Cuba's foreign exchange constraint. Tourism was a clear option, but building that sector to the required scale would require creating new capacities, as well as setting aside a portion of the existing national tourism capacity, to cater to ongoing increases in international tourists. President Fidel Castro clearly defined and expounded on that policy in mid-1988:

> There are people who still don't understand, and they don't understand that we have to exploit the sun, that sun and that moon which are shining their light on us. We don't live at the North Pole or at the South Pole. We don't live in a cold country. We live in a country that is, by the way, very hot. . . . Exports are difficult. We must also compete hard in the field of tourism. Now, the field of tourism can be a source of employment for tens of thousands of fellow citizens, who have to be well-trained workers capable of looking after tourists the right way.
>
> With a lot of realism and common sense, we are developing the plans for tourism, because we must turn tourism into one of the sources of hard currency for the country.
>
> Of course, there are many good things for the foreign tourist that the population also receives. If we build an aquarium, the population will enjoy it and so will the tourists; if we build a zoo, the population will enjoy it and so will the tourists; if we build recreational centers for children and young people, like the ones in Baconao, children will enjoy them. Such tourist development is also going to help the population in many respects, as well as providing the country with important revenue.[7]

The collapse of socialism in Eastern Europe, the possibility that Fidel Castro had foreseen, started in mid-1989 and terminated in December 1991 with the disintegration of the Soviet Union. In the following years, Cuba plunged into the so-called Special Period: GDP dropped by 35 percent, imports declined by 50 percent, export values were reduced to one-fourth of their 1989 level, and less than half the usual amount of oil was available. The caloric intake per inhabitant was reduced by a third, protein consumption by a half, and fats by even more. Due to this sudden deterioration in diet, hundreds of thousands of people were affected by optical neurosis and peripheral neuropathology, unknown in Cuba until then. Hundreds of thousands of hectares could not be farmed for lack of fuels, fertilizers, supplies, and agricultural equipment, and harvests plummeted. Half the non-sugar industrial production came to a halt. All transportation, public and private, rapidly declined. Power generation fell by 27 percent, causing electrical service to become insecure, with frequent blackouts. Hundreds of thousands of workers, though subsidized rather than being left to their individual fate, no longer had productive work.

Internationally, the discussion was not about *whether* the Cuban Revolution could survive, but rather about how many more months it had to live. In order to expedite the destruction of the Revolution, its main enemy designed a number of additional aggressive policies and carried out a series of provocations and attacks. All these actions in this period had as at least one of their goals to hinder Cuba's development of tourism:

- The Torricelli Act (1992) blacklisted vessels that called at Cuban ports, removing the possibility of developing cruise tourism to its potential.
- The Track II policy[8] attempted to undermine the Revolution from within.
- The rafters' crisis (1994) generated an image of large-scale, illegal migration and social chaos.
- The provocation of U.S. airplanes flying over Havana and the rapid adoption of the Helms-Burton Act (1996) increased fears among potential investors, scaring off many.
- The terrorist campaign involving bombs planted in hotels and other tourist facilities (1997) sought to cause panic.
- The Bush Plan derived from the Commission for Assistance to a Free Cuba report (2004) contained new and harsher restrictions on travel to Cuba.

Many people thought it would be impossible for international tourism to develop in Cuba in the face of such aggression from the United States. That it did was a result of the strategic conception of tourism development that Cuba defined and then put into practice with the personal involvement of Fidel Castro. As the crisis unfolded, Cuba concentrated a large part of its few available resources on building this industry. Thereby, the Island achieved the most dynamic tourism development of any country in the Caribbean in the last part of the twentieth century.

In 1990, Cuba received a little more than 300,000 tourists (see fig. 9.2). It

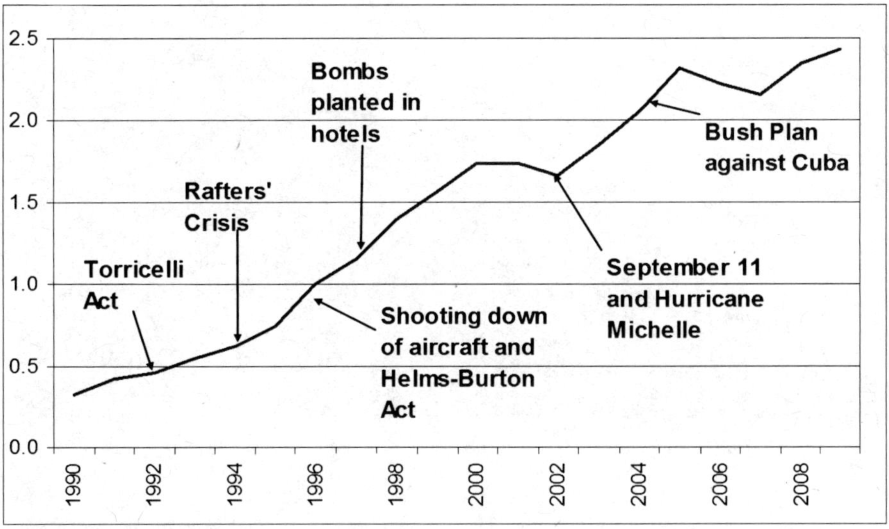

Figure 9.2. Tourist arrivals in Cuba, 1990–2009 (millions). *Source:* ONE, *Anuario Estadístico de Cuba* (Havana: ONE, 2001, 2010).

was ranked twenty-third among the tourist destinations in the Americas. By 1997 tourist arrivals exceeded the one million mark, moving the country up to eighth in the Americas and above Jamaica and the Bahamas in the Caribbean. In 2004 the Island passed the two-million-tourist-per-year mark, ranking it third in the Caribbean.

Over the years of the Special Period, roughly one in every three dollars of income from the export of goods and services has been generated by tourist activities. In absolute numbers, over the period from 1991 to 2010, tourism export earnings contributed on the order of $34 billion, not only to the Cuban economy generally but more specifically and crucially to the Cuban current account. In 1990, earnings associated with tourism were $243 million, only 4 percent of the total income from the export of goods and services (see fig. 9.3). In 2005 they hit a record of $2.4 billion and have remained at or over $2 billion since 2003.

Over the Special Period from 1990 to 2007, total economic investments in Cuba were $45 billion. The tourism development program received roughly one-seventh of that, $6.8 billion, leaving $38 billion for other purposes. In the most difficult years of the Special Period, which were also when the tourism industry was just being initiated, up to one-fourth of Cuba's total investment was set aside to build the industry.

A third of the amount spent on tourism development was allocated to the creation of airports and other necessary infrastructure and to the expansion

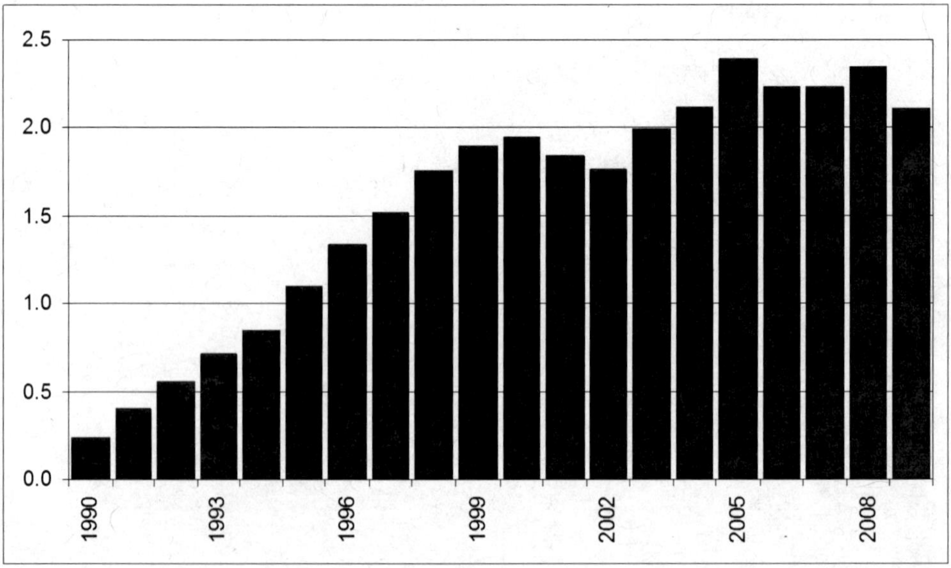

Figure 9.3. Tourism-related earnings, 1990–2009 (billions of US$ and CUCs). *Source*: *Anuario Estadístico de Cuba* (Havana: ONE, 1997, 2001, 2010).

of capacity and development of new technologies in branches of the economy that supply items for tourism and communications. In retrospect, this ratio between direct tourism investments and infrastructure appears to have been appropriate in light of what Cuba needed to do to develop the industry. Other countries that have neglected these associated investments have in the end had to pay a high price for that neglect.

Development of the tourist sector was diversified throughout the country. Whereas in the 1950s, Havana had two-thirds of hotel capacity, now it has only one-fifth. The largest concentrations of development occurred in the eight main tourist regions: Havana, Varadero, Jardines del Rey, northern Camagüey, northern Holguín, Santiago de Cuba, the south-central coast, and Cayo Largo del Sur.

The construction of modern tourist facilities (hotels, airports, roads, communication networks, and so on) has decentralized the industry, benefiting a variety of regions and communities. While they benefit directly from increased employment and income, beyond that they receive upgraded roads, electricity, water, and communications infrastructure, among other services.

The Impact of Tourism on the Economy and Society

The main impact of tourism on the Cuban economy was, of course, the generation of foreign exchange. But it played a second, more subtle role as a test case and model for a central task in all Cuban production: increasing efficiency and quality. Because of the particularly sharp competition in the Caribbean tourism industry, the considerations that are important for all Cuban production are particularly acute for the tourism industry. With regard to efficiency, earnings or sales per worker have increased fivefold. This success was achieved both by maximizing the large existing reserves and, more important as a model for other Cuban production, by enhancing productivity. Increased productivity does not often go hand in hand with dynamic growth, in that successful growth can mask the need for continually improved productivity. At present, hotels average 0.90 workers per room, half the ratio in early 1990s.

One reason for the improved quality in the industry is the large inflow of extremely competent labor. The tourism sector has 20,205 university graduates, a figure that is eight times higher now than in 1990. At the depth of the Special Period when the economy as a whole was severely depressed, thousands of high-level specialists in many economic branches were either subsidized or underutilized. Fifteen thousand university graduates eventually left their previous careers and moved into the rapidly expanding tourism sector. This flow was the main source for the sector's continual qualitative improvement.

Another economic influence of tourism also involves important lessons the industry offers for the Cuban economy as a whole. One characteristic of an underdeveloped economy that is central in hindering its development is its disarticulation: the absence of strong domestic forward and backward linkages or strong domestic chains of production. When tourism started to explode in 1990, an extremely high percentage of the earned foreign exchange immediately leaked out of the country to pay for required imports of goods for the operation, and investment goods for the expansion, of the industry. Specifically, in the early 1990s only 12 percent of the purchases by tourist entities were met by local producers. A critical issue for the tourist industry's success in becoming the major short-term supplier of foreign exchange for Cuba.was to develop backward linkages, namely, the capacities of Cuban producers to meet the input needs of the tourist industry. Success in this regard was significant and rapid, with national suppliers meeting up to 68 percent of the needs of the industry by the early 2000s and remaining at roughly that level today. Similar success should be reproducible in some other sectors in the Cuban economy, generating import substitution and a more balanced and diversified economy.

Achieving this success has required fundamental changes. In the first instance, Cuban producers simply did not have the capacity to produce the needed input goods for the tourist industry. Investments were required to either restore existing or create new capacity. But the most important element was the need to improve the quality of Cuban products, often through technological transformations. Five fundamental changes were necessary for Cuban producers to create these backward linkages in the tourism industry:

- Intrinsic durable quality
- Presence and image
- Flexibility to diversify
- Timely deliveries
- Division of massive standardized production into personalized, custom-order production

These types of technological and procedural changes took place in a wide range of economic activities. Because they were essential to the success of the Cuban tourism industry, it is worth listing a number of them in detail.

- More advanced packaging systems were adopted to produce beers and soft drinks in cans, fruit juices and yogurt in plastic containers, aseptic milk in Tetra Pak, mineral water in PET bottles, and coffee in vacuum packs.

- New, higher-quality slaughterhouses and factories were built to provide cooked meats and sausages.
- Modern techniques were adopted for the milling of rice and wheat to achieve the standards that tourists expect.
- Beginning in 1992, 1,270 greenhouses were introduced for protected cultivation of produce for tourist consumption. A portion of those structures were later replaced under a new program that introduced 636 more technologically advanced greenhouses.
- State-of-the-art technologies were adopted for the production of better-quality towels more efficiently. The new equipment is capable of changing sizes, colors, and stamping dies in a matter of minutes (the previous process took twenty-one days).
- The quality of production, in particular the durability, of suits and hotel uniforms was improved in order to meet the requirements of a wide range of tourist enterprises. The system of maintaining a single design and color for each enterprise for many years allowed important cost savings because these clients could replace only a portion of their stock of uniforms annually.
- Design centers for uniforms and furniture were established with the capability of determining and transferring into production the wide range of demands from the tourist chains.
- The technologies used to produce yarn, fabric, and garments for assorted hotel apparel, linens, and draperies were modernized.
- Small factories were created to produce hotel footwear, using high-quality leathers and other raw materials to turn out modern and durable shoes, with a differentiated output to accommodate the demands of different buyers.
- The capacity was developed to produce the amenities for hotel bathrooms, meeting the standards required by the different hotel brands.
- Elevators and air-conditioning systems were manufactured and assembled domestically.
- The advanced, high-speed communications technologies necessary for processing credit card payments, making long-distance reservations, and maintaining phone and Internet connections with tourists' home countries were introduced. The pressure to meet these demands expedited the introduction of digital and mobile communications and expanded the use of the Internet and e-mail.
- The capacity of the construction industry and the stocks of building materials were expanded to permit the undertaking of many hotel

projects simultaneously, particularly in the tourist regions of Varadero, Jardines del Rey, and northern Holguín.

- New products were produced domestically, including modern plumbing, quality ceramic tiles for bathroom floors and walls, and many others.
- New organizational and technical measures were adopted in the construction sector in order to execute the substantial investments in accommodations, such as implementing the Integrated Project Management system and strengthening the authority of and expectations for the senior project manager, contractor, and schedulers of the building projects.
- New hotels initially had to be largely designed abroad and adapted to Cuba's specific conditions. To significantly develop the domestic design capacity required in turn the expansion or development of many other components; for example, a large increase in the computers and specialized software required for many different engineering processes.
- Assimilating the expertise and organizational methods of foreign construction companies that participated in the design and construction of some tourist infrastructure made it possible to reduce construction schedules considerably (for example, through turnkey projects, the design-construction concept, and other methods).

A final important effect of tourism on the Cuban economy and society was its rapid provision of jobs at a time when unemployment suddenly soared.[9] Between 1990 and 2006, direct employment in tourism doubled, while hotel capacities nearly tripled and income increased tenfold. And while direct employment in tourism has doubled, indirect employment has quadrupled, mainly in support branches and those supplying goods and services (see fig. 9.4). Adding the employment generated in the private sector, it can be estimated that tourist activities generate employment for around 335,000 workers. That accounts for 7 percent of the 4.7 million people employed in the total national economy.

Jobs created in the tourism industry disproportionately serve three groups to whom the Revolution has made special commitments for ensuring jobs: youth, women, and recent graduates.

- Half the workers in tourism are younger than thirty-five.
- Women make up 41 percent of the labor force.
- Seventy-two percent of the workforce in tourism completed the twelfth grade or higher.

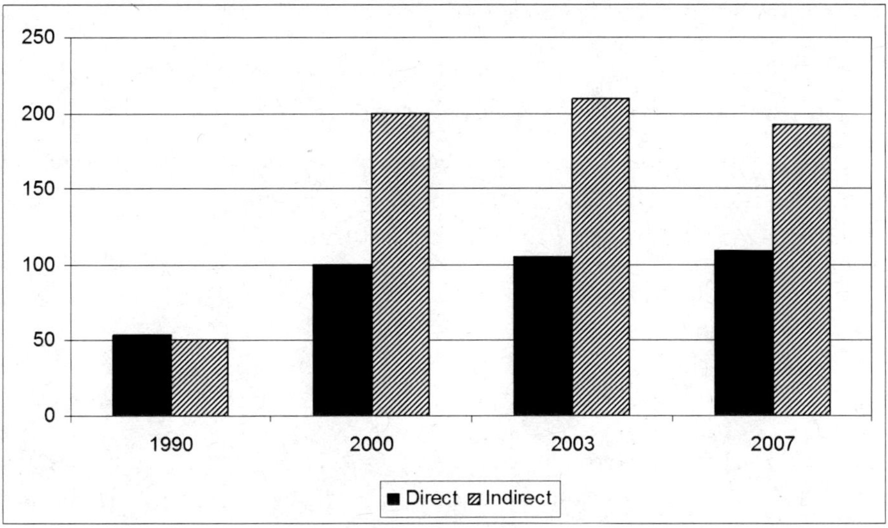

Figure 9.4. Direct and indirect employment connected with tourism (thousands). *Source:* Unpublished data from INIE and MINTUR, 2000 and 2004.

Environmental Impact

In 1992, at the UN Conference on Environment and Development in Rio de Janeiro, Fidel Castro indicated that the then-incipient tourist industry in Cuba would be built on the principle of achieving sustainable development: "Based on the strategic priority attached to tourism as a vehicle for development in the material conditions of the country, all works being undertaken on beaches, keys, and other areas with tourist potential are carried out after a careful evaluation of their possible environmental impact."[10] Environmental protection is an ever-present dimension of the regional development plans that are prerequisite to any tourist resort development. Regulations and measures are put in place to protect and preserve the beaches and dunes, the existing flora and fauna, and other aspects of the affected environment. The regulations address limits on the amount of construction, minimum construction distances from the coastline, maximum allowed building heights, types of construction systems to be used, and other features.

Environmental studies conducted when the period of high growth of international tourism started indicated that Cuban beach and resort areas could potentially support up to 210,000 hotel rooms without environmental damage. Only one-fourth of that potential has been used so far. Before the first hotel opened in the new region of Jardines del Rey in 1991, the Center for Research on Coastal Ecosystems was founded there. Its mandate is to provide recommendations for protecting beaches and coasts, particularly those with tourist developments.

The Impact on Cuba's International Image

In assessing the impact of tourism development on international relations, the central consideration is that 34 million people from more than one hundred countries visited Cuba between 1990 and 2010, including

- fifteen million from European countries;
- ten million Canadians;
- five million from Latin America and the Caribbean; and
- nearly one million from the United States.

Most tourists reported that their visit gave them a favorable impression of Cuba, its people, and its political system. In particular, a visit to Cuba usually exposes the disingenuousness of the many disinformation campaigns carried out against Cuba, primarily by the United States and people in its employ. Tourists in general return home with an image of Cuba that is very different from their preconceptions derived from hostile propaganda. With regard to the important issue of Cuba's relation with its diaspora, it is important to note that between 1990 and 2010, almost three million expatriate Cubans have visited their country of birth.

Challenges, Unresolved Problems, and the Search for Solutions

It is essential always to bear in mind that the accomplishments of Cuba's tourist industry have been achieved despite the obstacles and prohibitions erected by the U.S. government. Half the tourists visiting the Caribbean every year are American. Hence, if Cuba ranks highly among tourist destinations in the Americas as a whole, it does so despite operating without access to half the region's market. In some of the most competitive Caribbean destinations, American tourists account for up to 70 percent of total visitors. Equally important, they are the biggest spenders. But that tourist segment is forbidden to Cuba because the U.S. government does not allow them to freely visit the Island.

Beyond the enormous loss of revenue, the absence of American tourists contributes centrally to another adverse result: greater seasonality. Canada, Germany, and France send high concentrations of tourists to Cuba during the so-called high season, from December through March. In contrast, half of American tourists travel to the Caribbean between May and August. In other islands of the region Americans balance out to some extent the concentration of European and Canadian visitors during the cold months. Hence the curve of tourist arrivals reflects a greater seasonality in Cuba compared to the rest of the Caribbean: the high season is higher and the low season is lower (see figure 9.5). That translates into lower average annual occupancy of tourist accommodations, which affects the profitability of hotels. As long as the American tourist market remains closed to Cuba, its next best option to address this issue is to promote other markets with relatively low variability of arrivals throughout the year. The United Kingdom, for example, is currently Cuba's second-largest market, and its seasonality is low compared to that of Canada, Germany, or France.

It is expected that someday sanity will prevail among the leaders of the U.S. government, the travel ban will be lifted, and American tourists will be able to visit the Island. Many analysts and specialists on Cuba in the United States and around the world have asked how large a flow of tourists would result immediately and how that flow would evolve in the early years. Countless research reports have made forecasts addressing these questions. The following are three of the best recent studies. The University of Colorado and the Washington-based Battle Group consultancy were hired, respectively, by the think tanks of the Democratic and Republican Parties. During the summer of 2003 they both released studies whose forecasts had similar figures. More recently, the vice-president for legal affairs of the American Society of Travel Agencies testified at a U.S. congressional hearing on the expected effects of the eventual elimina-

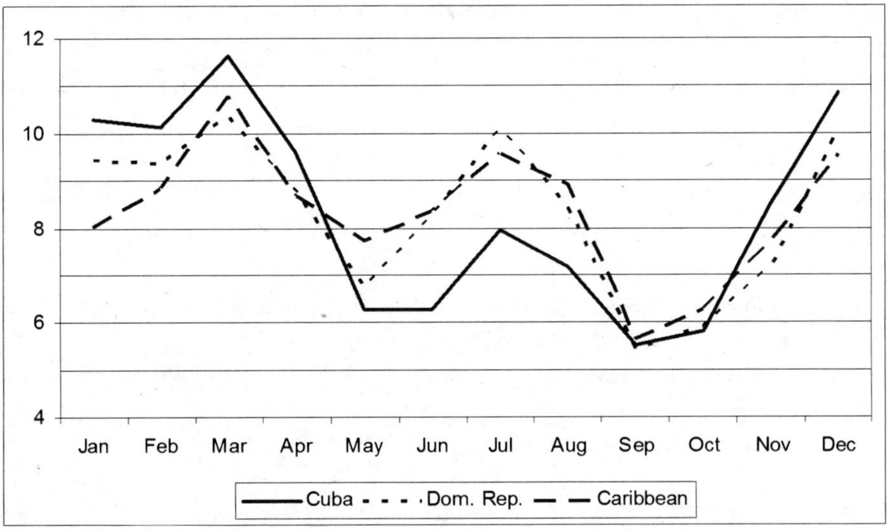

Figure 9.5. Seasonality of tourism in Cuba (2007) versus the Dominican Republic (2007) and the Caribbean (2002) (% of area's yearly total). *Sources:* Caribbean Tourism Organization, *Caribbean Tourism Statistical Report, 2001–2002* (St. Michael, Barbados: CTO, 2002); ONE, *Anuario Estadístico de Cuba* (Havana: ONE, 1997, 2001, 2010).

tion of the travel ban on Cuba. Combining these forecasts yields the following as a likely scenario:

- A year after the lifting of the travel ban on Cuba, between 750,000 and 1,000,000 Americans would visit the Island.
- Within two years, the figure would have increased to 1.8 million a year, including half a million tourists on cruises.
- Within five years, arrivals could be on the order of 2.6 to 3 million American tourists traveling to Cuba annually.

In addition to looking forward to the end of the U.S. travel ban, the other important prospective near-term issue is to resume the growth of other international tourism. Key to this will be to diversify (1) Cuba's international sources of tourists, (2) the segments of the international tourist market that it attracts, and (3), related especially to the latter, the types of tourist products it offers and supplies.

In summary, even though the main enemy of the Cuban Revolution has harassed, hampered, and attempted to destroy it, the international tourism sector in Cuba has continued to grow and diversify. First and foremost, this has provided an indispensable inflow of foreign exchange that has been essential, especially in the 1990s, to Cuba's survival and eventual recovery from the Special Period. Beyond that, a number of successes in the tourism industry can provide important lessons for the broader economic restructuring that Cuba is now going through. Equally important and too often overlooked in studies of the effects of international tourism on Cuba is that the tens of millions of international visitors over the last two decades are presenting the world with a more truthful picture of Cuba to counterbalance the widely disseminated hostile propaganda of the enemies of the Cuban Revolution.

Notes

1. Gambling was legalized in Nevada in 1931. In the 1940s casino-hotels mushroomed, largely funded and often even managed by organized crime.

2. Sally Denton and Roger Morris, *The Money and the Power: The Making of Las Vegas and Its Hold on America, 1947–2000* (New York: Knopf, 2001), 203–4. Like state regulations in general, this statue was easily circumvented and had almost no effect in practice. Different overseers and floor men from Las Vegas ran the Syndicate operations at the Riviera, Nacional, Capri, Havana Hilton, and Sans Souci at various times.

3. Recall that most of the extensive tourist facilities that existed then were oriented toward gambling, sex, and parties in Havana, not nature tourism or even beaches.

4. This act was passed within months of the triumph of the Revolution and was in-

tended not as an early measure to promote domestic tourism but rather as a symbol to the population of the Revolution's commitment to social equality. It was, nevertheless, an important basis for the national tourism program that soon developed.

5. The options included a limited amount of tourism to the socialist countries.

6. Baudilio Castellanos, "All the Resources for the People," an interview with Castellanos, the first president of INIT included in the special edition of Hosteltur, *Cuba, More Than 100 Years of Tourism*, April 2001.

7. Fidel Castro, "Speech on 26 July 1988," *Cuba Socialista* No. 35 (September/October 1988).

8. U.S. government policy toward foreign governments it wants to destabilize has often consisted of two tracks, official governmental measures and "unofficial" measures, those taken by groups or individuals that are not formally part of the government, although they might be government funded. These are often presented as "people-to-people" contacts. From the beginning of his presidency Clinton increased the use of the second track, beginning with the legislation to enact the Torricelli Act and escalating in particular in October 1995. The Cuban government reacted strongly and publicly, organizing many measures inside Cuba to oppose the U.S. "Track II" policy.

9. Throughout the Special Period much unemployment has been hidden through underemployment. Although underemployment played an important positive social role during the crisis, it is a barrier to the improved material standard of living that is the central focus of Cuba's economic policies at the present time, and Cuba has politically committed itself to dramatically reducing it in the near future.

10. F. Castro, presentation at the UN Conference on Environment and Development, Rio de Janeiro, June 12, 1992.

10

Tourism

Natural Product, Source of Exchange with the Outside World, and Ideological Challenge

ALFREDO GARCÍA JIMÉNEZ

Since the early 1990s, tourism has become a high-priority activity in the development strategy designed by the Cuban state and government. Its primary goal has been to secure foreign-exchange earnings in the short and medium terms which, given how Cuba's foreign exchange has historically constrained its growth and development, are necessary for the country's economic recovery from its post-1990 economic crisis. Beyond that is the need for Cuba to reinsert itself into the changed international economic markets in radically new ways. Tourism was the key sector for accomplishing this purpose in the 1990s, and it is still one important sector today.

Although Cuba has faced a foreign-exchange constraint on its growth and development since before the beginning of the Revolution, the events of the late 1980s and early 1990s transformed this problem from chronic to extremely acute, when Cuba's favorable external economic relations with the former USSR and Eastern Europe, which had existed for two decades, ended. Seemingly overnight, Cuba had to cope with the most difficult economic situation it had faced since the victory of the Revolution in 1959. Not only did it have to redirect 75 percent of its foreign trade, which in itself is a mammoth problem for any country, but it also faced an even more difficult problem: to radically adapt Cuba's entire economic model to make it compatible with the new necessity for much more extensive trade with the capitalist world economy. In addition to this fundamental structural problem, the U.S. economic blockade was strengthened even further by the adoption of the Torricelli and Helms-Burton Acts, increasing its already high yearly cost to Cuba.

Such a major disruption and additional interference in the external economic environment of a small, open, and dependent economy such as Cuba's had the potential to cause economic collapse. To avoid this, the Cuban state and government moved quickly to change the basic components of its economic development strategy. Being open and dependent, the Cuban economy needed external inputs in nearly all its productive processes. When its longstanding input sources from the socialist countries suddenly terminated, Cuba had to buy what inputs it could afford from the world capitalist markets. That, in turn, required it to earn a lot more convertible foreign exchange than before. Cuba's new survival strategy targeted the generation of external income based on maximal exploitation of two comparative advantages that it had not extensively commercialized before: scientific-technical capacity and tourism. Both of these had the potential to generate rapid returns on investments. On one front Cuba began to commercialize its human capital, especially in biotechnology and pharmaceuticals (see chapter 12). Even more remunerative in the very short term, Cuba radically increased the commercialization of its comparative advantage in particular types of natural conditions and resources, creating almost de novo an international tourism industry.

One particularly important aspect of tourism is its ability to earn very rapid foreign-exchange profits on investment. No medium or large economy can live off tourism alone, of course, and the revival of agriculture and industry, which also have potential to earn the foreign exchange required by the Island's open and dependent economy, is essential. But in 1990 it was clear that the revivals of those branches of the economy, which both had to be entirely redesigned, would be lengthy processes. Only tourism could generate the foreign exchange in the short term that would allow Cuba to survive long enough to carry out a medium-term recovery.

The rapid development of tourism had an immediate and major impact on Cuba's process of economic recovery. According to estimates, in just a decade and a half the tourism sector grew from being economically insignificant to accounting for nearly 7 percent of the GDP,[1] employing 6.3 percent of the total workforce, and providing 18 percent of the total export revenue. Currently, tourism is one of the most influential economic activities within the Cuban economy. Between 1990 and 2007 tourism export earnings (including the international transportation of passengers) contributed $27.1 billion to the country. This represented nearly one in three dollars earned through the export of goods and services in that period. In terms of the functioning of the entire Cuban economy, it has paid for approximately the same percentage of Cuba's necessary imports.

Currently Cuba—the largest island in the Caribbean with a population of more than eleven million inhabitants and a surface area of 110,860 square kilometers—continues to face the challenge of developing its tourist activities in the highly competitive Caribbean market in order to maintain that sector as a major contributor to the Cuban economy. This chapter considers three distinct but related aspects of the challenge Cuba faces. First is the challenge of "tourism itself," that is, its relation to and impact on nature. Second is the challenge of tourism's contribution to relaxing Cuba's always binding foreign-exchange constraint on its growth and development, that is, its foreign-exchange earnings. And, finally, the presence of a large body of privileged international tourists from wealthy capitalist countries presents a crucial ideological challenge to the socialist nature of Cuba's development strategy.

Tourism and Natural Resources

Three issues merit consideration concerning the relation of tourism to natural resources. In the first place, there is the basic issue of what sorts of natural resources can serve as the basis for a tourism industry in a given country. A second issue is the conservation of those natural resources, and hence the conservation of the tourist industry itself, given that tourism typically has a negative impact on the very natural resources it depends on if it is not carefully regulated. Finally, an issue that has just emerged in the last decade as important for tourist industries to consider is the medium- and even short-term effects of rapidly accelerating climate changes on a given tourist industry.

The Natural Resource Bases for Cuban Tourism

The best-known tourism resource of Cuba is, of course, its coastlines. Although Cuban tourism policy deliberately develops many of the country's other natural resources, its 300 beaches, 1,600 islets and keys, and coastal shelf still attract the largest number of tourists. Other important tourism resources include its remarkable biodiversity and rich flora (more than 6,370 botanical species) and fauna (more than 13,000 animal species); its moderately humid tropical climate; a number of picturesque mountain ranges and valleys; a cave system containing more than twenty-two significant caves, some of which contain pictographs; and a very large swamp system. Many of the non-beach natural attractions have been protected and promoted in a system of fourteen national and natural parks, sixteen biosphere reserves, eleven game reserves, and other related protected areas (see table 10.1).

According to surveys,[2] the tourists who choose to visit Cuba derive great enjoyment from its natural resources. Further, they report having attached a great deal of importance to this characteristic when selecting their destination. These attractions, along with the supporting institutional and commercial policies, drew 24.2 million tourists to Cuba from 1990 to 2007, capturing 23 percent of the increased number of tourists to Caribbean islands. This trans-

Table 10.1. Areas of natural interest in Cuba

Name	Type of reserve
Sierra del Rosario	Biosphere reserve
Valle de Viñales	National park
Península de Guanahacabibes	National park
Ciénaga de Zapata	National park
Los Indios	National park
Punta Francés	National park
Topes de Collantes	Protected natural landscape
Caguanes	National park
Cayo Guillermo—Santa María	National park
Desembarco del Granma	National park
Turquino	National park
Baconao	Biosphere reserve
La Gran Piedra	Natural park
Alejandro de Humboldt	Natural park
La Mensura	Natural park
Pico Cristal	Natural park
Jardines de la Reina	Natural park

Source: A. García, "Evolución del turismo en la década de los 90," *Cuba: Investigación Económica,* no. 3 (1998).

Table 10.2. Natural resources and tourist development potential

Tourist regions	Resorts	Places of interest	Beach area (kilometers)	Room potential (thousands)
Main regions	52	267	256	148.7
Other regions	29	174	40	21.4
Regions lacking infrastructure[a]	12	123	14	2.4
Total	93	564	310	172.5

[a]This includes the regions of Baracoa, Granma, and the northern part of Las Tunas, which have markedly less infrastructure to develop tourism than the other two regions in this table.
Source: A. García, "Evolución del turismo en la década de los 90," *Cuba: Investigación Económica,* no. 3 (1998).

lates into an annual growth rate of 11.6 percent, a higher rate of growth than was registered both worldwide and in the Caribbean for this period.

To gauge Cuba's potential for future tourism growth, multidisciplinary working groups overseen by the Cuban Ministry of Tourism conducted studies to identify places of touristic interest and to evaluate the prospective number of tourist rooms that would be appropriate for those sites. More than five hundred attractions were identified with a potential to support more than 172,000 rooms (see table 10.2).

Eight main regions have been targeted as priorities for immediate and midterm development: Havana, Varadero, the south-central coast, the Jardines del Rey archipelago, northern Camagüey, northern Holguín, Santiago de Cuba, and Canarreos archipelago, in particular Cayo Largo del Sur. Together these regions account for 56 percent of the total number of existing tourist resorts in the country, 47 percent of the places of interest, and 86 percent of the room potential (see table 10.2).

The diversity of Cuba's natural resources and attractions has enabled the country to offer a variety of different types of natural-resource-based tourist offerings. For example, nature tourism, water sports, and diving have experienced important growth recently. Nature tourism has been adopted on a basis of sustainability (discussed further later). Nature tourism is a broad-based concept comprising a variety of different activities associated with natural spaces. The national and nature parks, biosphere reserves, game reserves, and other protected areas serve as a base for much of this type of tourism. Different specific activities include ecotourism, nature-culture-history programs and tours, trekking, bird-watching, cycling tours, horseback riding, and excursions. For another segment of tourists, adventure tourist activities are available, such as Jeep safaris, spelunking, orienteering, mountaineering, river kayaking, and skydiving.

Significant potential exists for expansion in this market niche. Annually since 2000, Cuba has hosted the International Meeting on Nature Tourism to promote this type of tourism. This event brings together tour operators, businesspeople, scientists, and specialists.

The country's natural resources allow for numerous recreational and specialized nautical sports. The Island boasts twelve marinas with around five hundred berths, offering both tourist services and services required by foreign yachtsmen. Tourist services include excursions, chartered sport fishing, houseboat tours, and others. Recreational boaters come not only because the Cuban coasts and waters are a prime destination, but also to take part in the large variety of nautical events organized in Cuba every year. A large increase in boating is expected once the travel ban to Cuba for American citizens is lifted,[3] which is estimated to result in fifty thousand U.S. motorboats and yachts calling at Cuban marinas annually.

Several specialized publications from the World Tourism Organization and other sources rank Cuba as a prime destination for snorkeling and scuba diving, due to its crystal-clear waters and its beautiful seabed. A number of articles in scientific and specialized diving magazines report that the Cuban seabed is in excellent condition and has not suffered the degradation that has occurred in a number of other parts of the Caribbean in the last forty years.[4]

While natural-resource-based tourism has dominated Cuba's tourism over the last two decades, the Ministry of Tourism has simultaneously been implementing a policy of diversification by promoting several new types of tourism. Hence, it has been successfully increasing Cuba's health tourism, events tourism, and cultural tourism.

Tourism and Conservation

Tourist activities are largely based on the consumption of natural resources, and some authors, such as Jost Krippendorf, have even labeled tourism "the landscape eater."[5] Industrial activities also consume natural resources, but with an important qualitative difference: for tourism (and some industries, such as fishing) to continue, it is essential to balance the use of natural resources with their conservation.[6]

A related but slightly different way of considering the problem is to think of tourism as transforming natural resources as it uses them. If we take as an example so-called sun-and-beach tourism, it needs physical space to build infrastructure such as hotels, marinas, golf courses, urban developments, and so on; and to provide access via roads, parking spaces, and the like. At the same time, tourists need natural resources that have not been overexploited so that they can enjoy swimming in the ocean, traveling along the coast, visiting unique places, and so on. Clearly a tourist's satisfaction is related to the quality of the environment where the tourism takes place.

More specifically, what is involved here is a feedback mechanism in which overuse prevents the expansion, or even the continuation, of tourist activities, when natural resources essential for the continued development of tourist activities are degraded. Hence the environment, reflected in natural resources, is the core capital of a tourist industry, and therefore must be cared for and preserved. Extensive environmental exploitation, whether existing or planned, must be careful and precise.

From the beginning of the tourist industry's rapid expansion in the early 1990s, Cuba's tourism model targeted strategies that deliberately aimed to harmonize the development of tourism with the conservation and sustainable use of Cuba's natural, historical, and cultural resources. Speaking on this issue, Fidel Castro stated that "we are not going to develop just any kind of tourism, we have to develop quality tourism and, above all, tourism that is integrated into nature."[7]

The first comprehensive declaration of the Cuban government's commitment to environmental protection came long before international tourism became a significant issue in Cuba's environmental considerations. Act 33 for the Protection of the Environment and the Rational Use of Natural Resources was enacted in January 1981, leading shortly thereafter to the establishment of a master plan for the protection of nature. In 1994 environmental protection in Cuba took another big step forward with the founding of the Ministry of Science, Technology, and the Environment (CITMA). One of CITMA's many responsibilities since its inception during the initial rapid expansion of tourism in Cuba has been to monitor the development, construction, and operational phases of tourist infrastructure. To date it has been largely successful in ensuring minimal degradation of the ecosystem during the creation and subsequent operation of the infrastructure for tourism.

Tourism and Climate Change

One of the challenges currently facing the development of tourism internationally relates to climate change. The declaration at the October 2007 Davos Conference on Climate Change and Tourism stated that "climate is a key resource for tourism and the sector is highly sensitive to the impacts of climate change and global warming, many elements of which are already being felt."[8]

Cuba, as both a tourist destination and an archipelago, will be strongly affected by rapid global climate change. According to the climate predictions of specialists from the Meteorology Department and the Physical Planning Institute of the Ministry of Economy and Planning, by 2050 there will be notable tangible climate changes on the Island.[9] This study discusses many different consequences. Cuba's average temperature is expected to increase, with associated detrimental effects on agriculture. The eastern part of the Island, in particular, will suffer prolonged droughts. The frequency and the intensity of hurricanes will increase. These and other changes, beyond their numerous negative consequences for the population and the economy in general, will create problems for the tourist industry. But the biggest challenge for Cuban tourism, given the continued dominance of sun-and-beach tourism, will be the rise in the sea level due primarily to the melting polar ice caps.

The higher sea level will change the water depth all along Cuba's coastal shelf, thereby changing the local ecology. Flooding will increase, and some low-lying coastal areas will become permanently submerged, changing the morphology of the coast and especially the mouths of rivers. The sea level will rapidly rise above the level where vegetation now limits erosion, dramatically increasing coastal erosion, with associated negative impacts on the coastal shelf and on fishing. The study also forecasts the death of coral reefs due to the rise in ocean temperature as well as the rapid change in sea level, eliminating ecosystems that have evolved over thousands of years, disrupting fishing, and curtailing diving tourism.

Rising sea levels (and increased hurricane activity) will also disrupt or destroy much tourist infrastructure along the coasts and on the keys. These changes will affect twenty-one tourist regions, including fifty coastal tourist resorts. Of those, forty-two are on beaches, 55 percent on the mainland and 45 percent on keys. The remaining affected tourist developments consist mostly of seaside towns and fishing hamlets.

The most greatly affected aspects of tourism will be outdoor activities. Activities such as sea bathing (thalassotherapy) and sunbathing (heliotherapy) are directly related to both the state of the ocean and the levels of ultraviolet radiation. Greater ultraviolet radiation will increase the danger of sunburn and sunstroke, reducing the amount of time a tourist can spend each day in beach and ocean activities. Marine recreation such as diving, game fishing, sailing, speedboating, and water skiing will be curtailed by an increase in storms and hurricanes. Farther inland, various forms of nature tourism and ecotourism, such as hiking, bird-watching, wildflower photography, cycling, and mountaineering, will be harmed as climate change affects the archipelago's ecology.

Undeniably, in the medium term climate change will damage what has become an important pillar of the Cuban economy: tourist activities. Internationally, it is recognized not only that every tourist activity will need to adapt to the impending major climate changes, but further that whoever adapts most rapidly to the constantly changing situation will gain an important advantage in this highly competitive industry. In this regard, for the tourist industry to respond proactively to climate change demands both the informed participation of all relevant players and steadfast political leadership to achieve broad-based cooperation and consensus among them. Conducting more accurate environmental impact studies and promoting more sustainable use of resources by tourists are important for both informing the actors and building cooperation and consensus. Achieving sustainable development of tourism is an ongoing process requiring constant monitoring of impacts in order to introduce appropriate preventive or remedial measures as needed.

Cuban Tourism as a Source of Foreign Exchange

The Cuban economy is an extremely open economy, strongly dependent on foreign trade for the operation of its domestic economy. Over the last five decades it has typically run a significant deficit on its current account, caused by a negative balance of trade in goods. Together, these factors have meant that foreign-exchange earnings have been a chronic binding constraint on Cuba's growth and development.

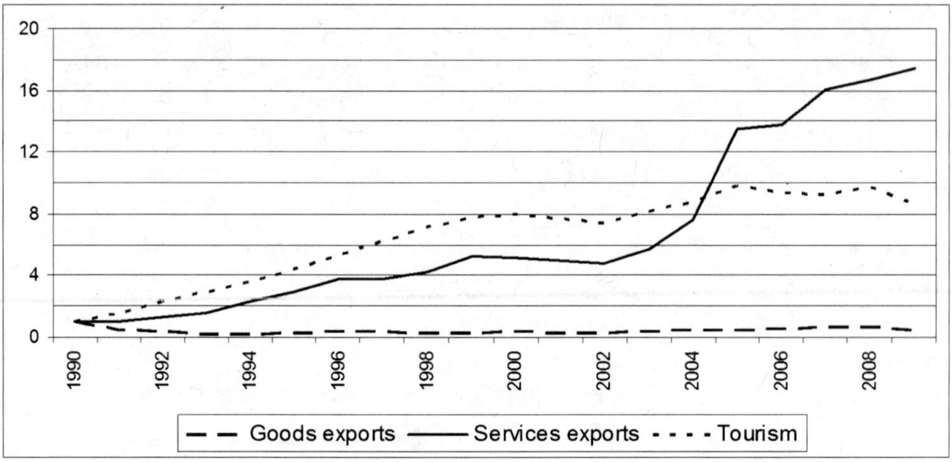

Figure 10.1. Growth trends in export variables, 1990–2009 (1990=1). *Sources:* Author's estimates based on ONE, *Anuario Estadístico de Cuba* (Havana: ONE, 1996, 2000, 2005, 2006, 2010).

Cuba's international tourist industry appeared as an economic sector in about 1990, almost out of nowhere. In the 1990s it played the central role, first in the survival and then in the early recovery of the economy. Direct job creation in the tourist industry was important in itself, but the foreign exchange it generated was essential to the survival and recovery of the whole economy. Tourism became the leading sector of the economy in the 1990s and remained a leading sector over the next decade, even as several other sectors recovered or grew, because it was the only sector that simultaneously met five conditions: (1) it earned foreign exchange, (2) it had a higher rate of growth than the overall average for the national economy, (3) it had the potential to operate on a relatively large scale, (4) it filled a significant unmet demand, and (5) it had potential linkages, and therefore potential spillover effects, to numerous parts of the domestic economy.

In the 1990s, tourism was clearly the most dynamic portion of the Cuban economy (see fig. 10.1). By 1999 other service exports had matched tourism's rate of growth, and after 2003 they surpassed it. Like tourism (since the Revolution), these other exports were nontraditional for Cuba, the most important being health and communication services. Given the size the tourist industry had achieved by that time, it has remained a central pillar of the Cuban economy into the twenty-first century.

In the first half of the 1990s tourism became Cuba's main source of foreign exchange, overtaking the sugar industry, which at the time was strongly depressed by both the drop in international prices and the lack of the technical and material requirements for production (see table 10.3). Currently, tourism

Table 10.3. Tourist earnings as a share of total exports (%)

Exports	1990	1994	2000	2006	2007	2009
Sugar	72.7	30.0	10.4	2.2	0.7	1.8
Alcoholic beverages	0.2	0.3	0.3	0.3	0.5	0.6
Tobacco	1.2	2.2	3.2	2.3	1.9	1.8
Nickel	6.5	7.9	13.3	14.1	17.5	7.3
Tourism	4.1	34.1	45.1	24.4	18.2	17.7
Other	15.3	25.5	27.7	56.7	61.2	70.8

Source: Author's estimates based on ONE, *Anuario Estadístico de Cuba* (Havana: ONE, 1996, 2000, 2005, 2006, 2010).

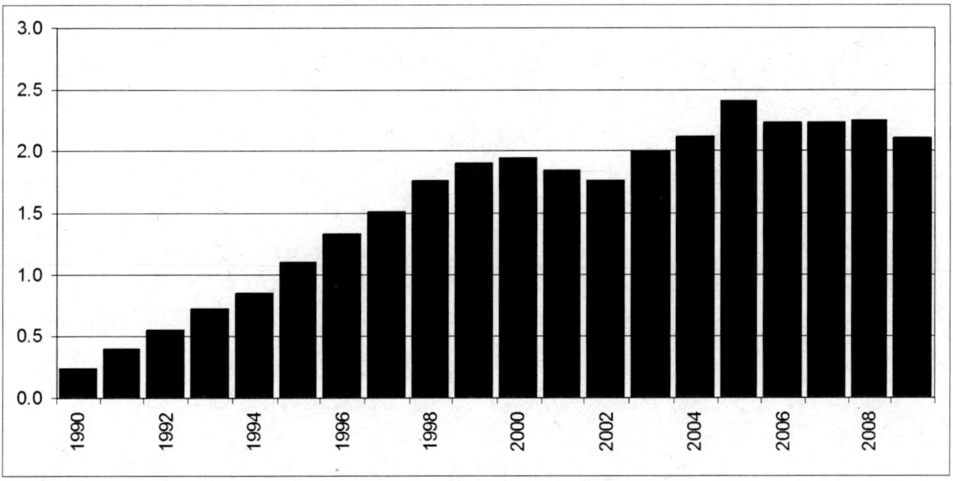

Figure 10.2. Tourism-related earnings, 1990–2009 (billions CUC). *Sources:* Author's estimates based on ONE, *Anuario Estadístico de Cuba* (Havana: ONE, 1996, 2000, 2005, 2006, 2010).

remains one of the country's main sources of foreign exchange, along with medical services[10] and nickel.

In absolute terms, in 1990 tourism-related earnings were 243 million CUCs,[11] accounting for 4 percent of income from the export of goods and services (see fig. 10.2 and table 10.3). By 2009, tourism-related earnings had increased to 2.1 billion CUCs, accounting for 17.7 percent of the country's income from exports. Figure 10.2 also shows, however, that tourism's phenomenal growth occurred in the 1990s, and it has expanded very little since 2000. From 1990 to 2000, absolute earnings from tourism increased eightfold, almost doubling every three years.

Figure 10.3 graphs the tourism dependence indexes over the evolution of the Cuban tourist industry, showing tourism's export earnings as percentages of exports of goods alone and of both goods and services (the latter category includes tourism). It clearly illustrates the points made in the opening of this chapter. Even though the tourism sector's absolute earnings only tripled from 1990 to 1993, it went from 4 percent to 62 percent of the value of goods exports. As the export (and even the production) of goods imploded, tourism served as a lifeline that offset a portion of the losses. By 1998 tourism earned 16 percent more than goods exports, and it stayed above goods through 2005 (except for a slight reversal in 2004). For almost a decade tourism was by far the major earner of the foreign exchange that was so vital for reviving the Cuban domestic economy.

As Cuban economists immediately recognized at the time, such heavy dependency on one product is never good for a national economy. In fact, after 2005 exports of a number of goods did expand. Nickel grew first, but when nickel prices fell after 2007, exports of biotechnology and pharmaceutical products, and to a lesser extent of medical products and in some years of certain agricultural goods like tobacco, prevented a return to anything like the tourism dependency ratios seen in 1998–2005. Tourism earnings did fall about 15 percent from 2005 to 2009, but the main cause of the declining tourism dependence index was the real increase in the exports of goods, reflecting an important diversification of the economy.

The tourism dependency index relative to all goods and services exports indicates the other important development after 2005. Both dependency indexes show similar patterns through about 2003. Because tourism was the only major

Figure 10.3. Tourism dependence indexes for Cuba, 1990–2009 (%). *Sources:* Author's estimates based on ONE, *Anuario Estadístico de Cuba* (Havana: ONE, 1996, 2000, 2005, 2006, 2010).

service export in the 1990s, the goods-and-services index peaked by 1998 and then leveled off. Both indexes began to drop in 2003, but unlike the goods-only index the goods-and-services index did not jump back up in 2005, even though tourist earnings reached their highest amount ever. The difference was that a major surge in the export of other services began in that year. Although expanded exports of goods were the primary factor accounting for the continuing drop of this tourism dependency index in 2006 and 2007, the index continued to decline even after goods exports fell off in 2008 and 2009, because exports of other services expanded, especially health and communication services. Tourism remains a pillar of the Cuban economy, and its export earnings are crucial, but both goods and services exports have diversified greatly since the late 1990s.

Figure 10.4 shows specifically the important diversification in service exports that began in the mid-2000s. The near doubling of absolute tourist earnings in 1991, just as the economy began its sharp contraction, took tourism to more than three-quarters of all service earnings. Tourism remained above 70 percent in all years except one until 2003. Then in 2005 the sharp increase in other service exports produced a sharp decline in tourism's earnings share, and the strong performance of other exports continued for the remainder of the decade (though tourist earnings declined slightly in 2009).

Table 10.4 brings together six indicators of tourism's role in Cuba's external sector. I have discussed the first three of these already. The remaining

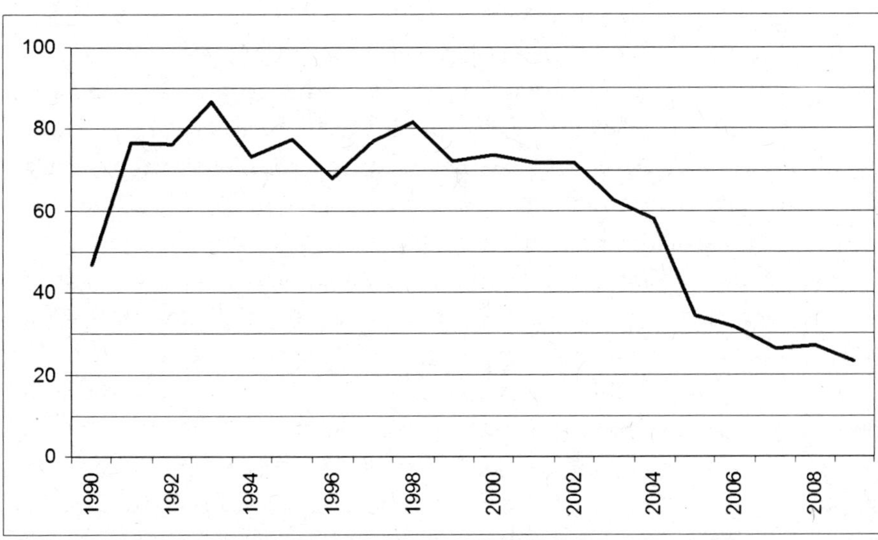

Figure 10.4. Tourism earnings as a share of exports of services, 1990–2009 (%). *Sources:* Author's estimates based on ONE, *Anuario Estadístico de Cuba* (Havana: ONE, 1996, 2000, 2005, 2006, 2010).

Table 10.4. The impact of tourism on the external economy, 1990–2009

Tourism measures	1990	1995	2000	2005	2007	2009
Tourism earnings (millions of CUCs)	243	1,100	1,948	2,399	2,236	2,106
Tourism dependency (incl. goods and services)	4.1	37.8	45.1	26.8	18.2	17.7
Tourism's share of service exports (%)	46.8	77.5	73.7	34.4	26.5	23.4
Deficit of commercial goods offset (%)	12.2	79.1	62.4	43.3	38.8	34.9
Imports paid for (%)	3.0	31.8	37.6	25.2	23.2	22.7
Contribution to current account (%)	n.d	30.9	38.5	27.9	23.7*	n.d

*Data for 2006.
Source: Author's estimates based on Oficina Nacional de Estadísticas, *Anuarios Estadísticos.*

three indicate, respectively, how much tourist earnings offset the chronic deficit in the balance of goods, how much of total imports tourism revenues paid for, and (always close to the previous figure) how much of the total current account spending they paid for. The two points I made earlier stand out clearly in this table: tourism has made a fundamental contribution to Cuba's external sector throughout the Special Period, and even though tourism remains a significant activity, economic recovery combined with some successes in diversification have significantly lessened its importance in the twenty-first century.

During the years of crisis and subsequent economic recovery in the Special Period, international tourism became an indispensable economic activity for Cuba. The Cuban government's decision at the very beginning of the 1990s to dramatically intensify tourism development as the primary short-term means to offset the devastating shortage of foreign exchange was a life-and-death gamble that paid off. For the near future it will be necessary to continue expanding the tourist sector in Cuba for two basic reasons. First, although diversification is proceeding and other export lines are contributing growing shares to the country's foreign-exchange earnings, tourism remains important. Cuba's natural resource advantages give tourism the potential to remain an important industry permanently, not just in the short run. Second, the tourism industry has potential links to many Cuban domestic industries. Cuba has the almost immediate potential to produce nearly all the inputs used by the tourist industry, which is not the case for some of the very-high-tech branches of production that are also developing. Thus, international tourism is a particularly large, still far from fully tapped, potential pull factor for the whole domestic Cuban economy. It is virtually impossible for any other sector or activity to take on all the multiple, essential roles of tourism in the Cuban economy in the short or even medium term.

The Ideological Challenge of Tourism

It would be naive to think that there is any specific form of tourism that does not represent, reinforce, and perpetuate some particular ideology or set of values.[12] Many tourist-receiving countries, mainly the underdeveloped ones, have adopted and fostered a tourism model similar in form and ideology to that of developed countries. Because these countries have lacked an endogenous long-term vision of tourism based in their own development goals and a prospective assessment of its future material and ideological impacts, the industry has brought various serious problems to many of these nations.

Many advocates of progressive tourism in Cuba and abroad argue that healthy tourism must fulfill two basic requirements. First, it must promote the host country's social development. Second, it must be aligned with that society's most fundamental social values. In Cuba, the government designed the international tourism industry to be consistent with socialism's social, political, and economic values and goals. In concrete terms, this meant, among other things, that

- the benefits obtained from tourist development must be used to ensure a permanent increase in the social well-being of the entire population, particularly for the maintenance and expansion of health care and education;
- tourist development would embody respect for Cuban identity and would contribute to maintaining the country's complete political and economic autonomy;
- there would be conscious efforts to minimize the harmful consequences associated with tourism—in particular, given the nature of Cuba's pre-Revolutionary tourism, that tourism would not include gambling or promote prostitution;
- tourist development must be based on both utilizing and increasing Cuba's human capital, implementing a precise strategy for the training and development of human resources; and
- sustainable tourist development must be achieved on the basis of an environmental policy that preserves the country's natural and cultural heritage.

The rapid development of tourist activities presented the risk of introducing a set of undesired aspects with deleterious effects on Cuban society. The following is a representative Cuban evaluation of the cost–social benefit trade-off of tourism after a decade of development: "The measures taken to gradually leave the crisis behind had a certain cost associated with emerging disparities in income. Certain patterns of behavior emerged that are not representative of our ethics and were, on some occasions, unseemly. But society as a whole has prepared itself to face these issues, and this is a permanent battle."[13]

On the organizational level the social benefits connected to tourism include, among others, the enhancement of cultural exchanges between Cubans and people from other societies. Many individual Cubans have formed friendships with foreign visitors, intensifying a sentiment of cross-national human solidarity. Tourism has also contributed to Cubans' sense of social solidarity in their own country through a movement called My Contribution to Life,[14] whereby employees in the tourist industry voluntarily donate a portion of their gratuities to the public-health sector, mainly to children's hospitals.

The development of tourism, however, also involves an important number of political and ideological social costs, whose complexity and magnitude must not be underestimated. Most significant are outcomes that hinder the continuous process of developing a socialist consciousness in Cuban society. The preceding quotation briefly referred to the two most important of these. The first is tourism's contribution to economic and hence social stratification in Cuba because workers in that industry gain both direct and indirect access to foreign-currency earnings. The second is the emergence of vice and unlawful activities, such as drug use and prostitution, which are inconsistent with both the ethical principles of the majority of Cubans and Cuba's socialist goals of an egalitarian society grounded in human dignity and both individual and collective human development.[15] At present, these activities have been minimized and there is active and constant vigilance to contain them.[16] To this end, in February 1999 the National Assembly of People's Power adopted Act No. 87, which modified the penal code to tighten the penalties for drug trafficking and production, prostitution, and sex with minors.

Given that achieving comprehensive and socially harmonious tourism development requires the understanding and participation of all of society, a central aspect in the sociological and ideological analysis of tourism is the degree of public acceptance of tourism policies. To determine popular support, a number of surveys and studies have been conducted periodically since tourist development began in 1990 and continue today. The results generally confirm support for the development of international tourism and a trend toward more positive attitudes over time, but they also reveal a number of concerns. The six main results of these surveys and investigations are as follows:

- The Cuban population for the most part has a favorable attitude toward international tourism.
- Of those polled, 72 percent believe that most of the population bene-

fits from this industry and that it promotes the nation's socioeconomic development.

- Whereas in 1990, 19 percent of respondents associated the word *tourism* with concepts of development, economy, exports, and foreign exchange, at present 64 percent of respondents make such associations.
- In the early years of international tourism development, respondents expressed some dissatisfaction over the corresponding reduction in domestic tourism services. At present the population accepts the need for this reduction, although they still wish for greater development of domestic tourism opportunities.
- The most frequently mentioned harmful effects of tourism are the increased economic and social differentiation of society and a loss of some important values.
- Of those polled, 60 percent claim to be fairly well informed about the performance and evolution of the country's tourist sector.

These results indicate that besides the two basic concerns of growing inequality and weakening of important social values, the other frequently mentioned concern was that international tourism has been developed at the expense of the domestic tourism that Cubans had enjoyed in the 1970s and especially in the 1980s. To address this issue, the state set aside limited resources for national tourism, under a policy of offering hotel accommodations to Cubans when available based on individuals' (usually work-related) merits or their performance of some social objective.[17] This policy did not fully satisfy the public's expectations and needs, so a series of measures have recently been adopted to allow Cubans access to all hotel facilities. Although this is an important step, the most important task is to continue working to create and implement a single tourist policy that integrates international and domestic tourism, in order to provide greater enjoyment for the Cuban population while continuing to derive essential economic benefits from international tourism.

For the future, the greatest tourism-related ideological challenge that Cuba faces is to continue minimizing the industry's ideological cost to Cuba's central project of building socialism. These costs are connected with the emergence and intensification of such problems as income inequality, gambling, prostitution, drugs, money trafficking and laundering, and corruption. Political-ideological education will play an important role in this effort, targeting not only workers in the industry but especially executives and senior managers who are responsible for making decisions concerning the nature of tourism that their enterprise attracts.[18] At the same time, the local population must derive greater advantages from the development of tourism. To that end, it will be necessary to promote, implement, and expand community-oriented tourist projects, whereby Cubans come to directly see and enjoy the benefits of tourism in their own region.

Notes

1. R. Quintana, M. Figuerola, M. Chirivella, D. Lima, M. Figueras, and A. García, *Efectos y futuro del turismo en la economía cubana* (Montevideo: Editorial Tradinco, S.A., 2005).

2. Survey by the Center for Tourist Studies of the University of Havana, July 2005.

3. The U.S. government prohibits most of its citizens from traveling to Cuba at all, and especially for tourism.

4. These include *Geography* (U.S.), *Shark Diver Magazine* (U.S.), *Diver* (Canada), *Diver* (UK), *Octupus* (France), and *Espacio Profundo* (Mexico).

5. J. Krippendorf, *Die Landshaftsfresser* (Bern: Hallwag, 1975).

6. R. Bosh, L. Pujol, J. Serra, and F. Vallespinos, *Turismo y medio ambiente* (Madrid: Editorial Centro de Estudios Ramón Areces, S.A., 2001).

7. F. Castro, "Palabras en la inauguración del Hotel Playa Pesquero, Holguín," *Granma*, January 21, 1993.

8. "Davos Declaration: Climate Change and Tourism. Responding to Global Challenges," October 2007, sdt.unwto.org/sites/all/files/docpdf/davosdeclaration.pdf (accessed January 31, 2010).

9. Instituto de Planificación Física and Instituto de Meteorología, *Diagnóstico del cambio climático en Cuba* (Havana: IPF, 2006).

10. Separate figures for medical services are not yet publicly published for political reasons related to U.S. aggression against the Cuban foreign medical aid and services program, so in table 10.3 they appear only as part of the rapidly growing "other" sector. The current and growing importance of medical services is, however, documented in data available to Cuban researchers, so it merits mention as one of the most important current sources of foreign exchange.

11. In addition to the non-convertible Cuban peso which is used internally, the Cuban government issues a convertible currency called CUC. The exchange rate between CUCs and foreign freely convertible currency is set by the Cuban government. Some items in Cuba are purchasable only in CUCs, and persons or entities that need to deal with foreign exchange keep their accounts in CUCs, converting funds to the relevant freely exchangeable foreign currencies through the Cuban Central Bank. The exchange rate in 2009 is $1.08 per CUC, so these tourist-related earnings are roughly equivalent to dollars.

12. S. Molina, *Conceptualización del turismo* (Mexico City: Editorial Limusa, 1991).

13. I. Ferradaz, "La espiral del turismo," *Revista Habanera* No. 21 (2001).

14. This contribution amounts to more than $3 million, set aside mainly for the purchase of drugs and equipment to fight cancer.

15. Quintana et al., *Efectos y futuro del turismo en la economía cubana.*

16. In underscoring the importance of fighting the risks of tourism, Fidel pointed out that by fighting vices we can develop our virtue. F. Castro, "Palabras en la inauguración del Hotel Cayo Coco en Ciego de Ávila," *Granma*, November 23, 1993.

17. Note that, particularly in light of the increasing economic inequality, hotel rooms were distributed through a social process and not via the market process of allocation to the richest.

18. Ortelio Soler, *El turismo en Cuba: Economía y estrategia sociopolítica* (Havana: Ediciones Balcón, Escuela de Altos Estudios de Hotelería y Turismo, 2004).

11

Agriculture

Historical Transformations and Future Directions

ÁNGEL BU WONG AND PABLO FERNÁNDEZ DOMÍNGUEZ

Agriculture has been a determinative sector in the economy of the Island ever since the European conquest. Although it has fallen as a share of GDP over the last twenty years, agriculture remains a crucial sector for the well-being of the Cuban population. In the short term, preventing the food supply from collapsing in the face of the economic difficulties of the Special Period has been vital for preserving the Revolution's gains in eliminating hunger, particularly rural hunger. But even with such a collapse averted, high food imports have combined with reduced agricultural exports to exacerbate Cuba's problems with its always binding foreign-exchange constraint. A series of new programs concerning ownership, management, and organization of agricultural land are being put in practice to address this issue immediately. In the medium and long term, Cuba needs to achieve food sovereignty (the ability to supply its own food needs) as an essential part of national sovereignty and sustainable development. In addition, the agricultural sector must develop export capacities in some additional crops in order to realize its potential to contribute to relaxing Cuba's foreign-exchange constraint. And all of this must be achieved with heightened ecological awareness, both for the immediate, direct well-being of the Cuban population and because, as experts worldwide are coming to recognize, ecologically sound agricultural practices are economically efficient in the medium and long run.

History of Agriculture's Role in the Cuban Economy

From the sixteenth through the early twentieth centuries, the main pillar of the Cuban economy was agro-business, as the country did not have significant mining capacity. The first agro-industry was cattle raising, to supply salted meat, grease, and hides to the Spanish fleets calling at Cuban ports in transit to conquer the American continent or on their way home to the peninsula. Next came a boom in the export of tobacco manufactures such as snuff, pipe tobacco, and rolled tobacco, the predecessor to the world-renowned Cuban cigar. Finally, after the Haitian Revolution disrupted agricultural production on Hispaniola at the end of the eighteenth century, Cuba concentrated on meeting international demands for sugar and coffee. These products were the main sources of both income and employment for Cuba in that period.[1]

From the beginning of the U.S. military occupation in 1898 until the proclamation of the pseudo-republic in 1902, the U.S. government laid the groundwork for subordination of the Cuban economy to the dictates of Washington. In particular, it threw open the main branches of the feeble Cuban economy to inflows of U.S. capital. Northern investors took tremendous advantage of the opportunities presented by Cuba's incipient neocolonialism. This process was to have great significance beyond Cuba. As José Martí warned, U.S. economic and political neocolonial domination subsequently replicated the Cuban experience throughout Latin America, from the Rio Grande to Patagonia.

During World War I sugar became the main commodity of world trade. In this context of high sugar profits and U.S. neocolonial domination, Cuba's sugar industry and its agrarian system of sugarcane plantations grew to unprecedented dimensions. American companies acquired large expanses of land, building sugar mills and refineries to supply the demands of U.S. and world markets.

Thus a property ownership structure was created in which landholding was extremely concentrated in the hands of large proprietors. According to records from the first half of the twentieth century, 7 percent of largest landowners held 49 percent of the country's total agricultural land. The next 17 percent of medium to large landowners held another 25 percent of agricultural land. Hence just 24 percent of landowners held 74 percent of the land in the form of moderate to large estates. These owners consisted of both foreign companies and native landowners belonging to a national oligarchy. In collusion with contemporary political leaders, and aligned with the dictates of Washington, they operated a regime of extreme agricultural exploitation that mixed capitalist methods with remnants of a semi-feudal system. Meanwhile, the remaining 76 percent of proprietors owned just 26 percent of the arable land, on the order of a little more than seven million hectares.

The severely skewed land distribution produced additional structural problems beyond the injustice of the concentration of ownership alone. No more than 35 percent of the land was farmed, mainly with sugarcane. Of the remaining land, nearly four million hectares were used for grazing, mostly in an unimproved state, and the rest was left idle. The result was a structural foreign dependence in which nearly 40 percent of food for domestic consumption was imported, mainly from the United States.

In its social aspects as well the model presented colossal inequities. Rural poverty prevailed among the large masses of peasants and agricultural workers. This was connected with illiteracy, chronic unemployment, a lack of health care, social insecurity, and the existence of systems of labor exploitation that were closer to a feudal regime than a capitalist model. Most agro-industrial earnings ended up in the hands of foreign companies and the national oligarchy. These were the main characteristics of Cuban agriculture until the victory of the Revolution in 1959.

Agriculture in the Revolutionary Period

In his well-known defense statement in 1953, "History Will Absolve Me," Fidel Castro summarized the state of Cuban agriculture on the eve of the Revolution:

> Eighty-five percent of Cuban small farmers are paying rent and living under the constant threat of eviction from their plots of land. More than half of the best farmland is in foreign hands. In Oriente, which is the biggest province, the stretches of land belonging to the United Fruit Company and the West Indies Company link the north coast with the south coast.
>
> There are 200,000 rural families that don't even have a small piece of land to plant roots and tubers for their hungry children. At the same time there are nearly 300,000 caballerías [about four million hectares] lying unfarmed in the hands of powerful interests. If Cuba is essentially an agricultural country, if its population is largely made up of peasants [back then, around 45 percent], if the city depends on the countryside, if the countryside fought for independence, if our nation's greatness and prosperity depend on healthy, vigorous peasants who love and know how to work the land of a state that protects and guides them, how can this state of affairs continue?[2]

Consequently, during the uprising period of 1957–58, the Rebel Army decreed Act 3 from its Sierra Maestra headquarters, granting ownership of the land to all those who farmed it in the areas liberated by the rebels. Then, immediately after the victory of the Revolution, the First Land Reform Act was enacted, eliminating from Cuba the dismal conditions in the countryside that Fidel had spoken out against.[3] Adopted on May 17, 1959, this act granted land to all those who farmed the land without owning it, thereby benefiting around 160,000 rural families. It also set the maximum amount of land that an individual could hold at around four hundred hectares, with any existing landholdings in excess of that amount to be turned over to the state. The state then used this land to fulfill its promise to give land to all the peasants who labored on but did not own the land, with any undistributed land becoming state property. The enactment of this law constituted a landmark in Cuba's history, ushering in the beginning of a non-capitalistic approach to economic development. The Second Land Reform Act, enacted in 1963, reduced the limit for individual landownership to sixty-seven hectares and made the state the main landowner in Cuba (see table 11.1).

These profound structural changes in ownership and use of agricultural land were instrumental in gradually transforming the quality of rural life. The transformation was carried out through diverse social and infrastructure-development programs whose priorities were to eliminate rural poverty and modernize the agricultural industry. These programs addressed basic services such as education, health care, housing construction, developing the communications infrastructure, and electrification.

A key decision made at the very beginning of the Revolution, as part of transforming the quality of rural life, was to create a mechanized and technically sophisticated agriculture. This entailed both the commitment of a large amount of material and financial resources and the development of the necessary scientific infrastructure. Specific objectives included improving the quality of the soil, protecting plants and animals from pests and diseases, increasing irrigation by creating reservoirs and irrigation systems, creating and modernizing the industry for processing agricultural raw materials, and developing new branches to supply agriculture, such as fertilizers and agricultural machinery.

As part of this process, a nationwide system of agricultural science and technology institutions was established. It consisted of more than twenty research centers specializing in various fields, plus a large number of experimental sta-

Table 11.1. Structure of landownership under the First and Second Land Reform Acts

	First Land Act		Second Land Act	
Sector	**Thousands of ha**	**Pct. of agricultural land**	**Thousands of ha**	**Pct. of agricultural land**
State sector	3,903	44	5,514	61
Private sector	5,174	56	3,563	39
Plots less than 67 ha	3,331	36	3,563	39
Plots more than 67 ha	1,863	20	0	0

Source: Guillermo Cayado, *Agricultura cubana: Estructuras organizativas y programas de desarrollo (1959–2007)*(Havana: Agroinfor, 2008).

tions. These eventually expanded and evolved into a network of more than forty agricultural research and development centers, a substantial increase from the four research centers in Cuba before 1959. A simultaneous priority was to establish a comprehensive program for training qualified staff at all levels, through expanding the scope of university technical courses in agricultural specialties throughout the country. A national network of seventy-four agricultural polytechnics was created for training intermediate-level technicians and qualified workers; in addition, provincial schools attached to the Ministry of Agriculture served to train workers.

Building on this progress in scientific-technical development and staff training, a number of productive programs were designed and implemented between 1965 and 1990. Their main objective was to diversify production in order to promote the dual goals of increasing the domestic food supply and exploiting Cuba's comparative advantages in agriculture to increase its exports and reduce certain of its agricultural imports. The following are key actions and technological adaptations in seven of the major programs.

Sugarcane

- Establishment of sugarcane cooperatives, subsequently turned into state farms
- Mechanization of some of the agricultural work, including tilling the land, loading and unloading the cut cane, and later mechanical harvesting
- Use of fertilizers and herbicides
- Use of irrigation
- Expansion of the capacity of the sugar industry

Cattle Raising

- Genetic improvement of the cattle stock in order to increase its potential milk production. Until that time, cattle had been raised primarily for meat.
- Development of a fodder base with a capacity to feed larger herds. This involved applying fertilizers to grazing land, introducing new varieties of fodder, and expanding irrigation.
- Complementing pastureland grazing with concentrated supplements, such as honey and various by-products of the sugar industry
- Directing large-scale investments to the construction of dairy farms, development centers, breeding centers, fattening centers, and other facilities[4]

Citrus Fruit

- Planning and implementation of a program designed to increase citrus exports as well as domestic consumption (occurring in 1966–68). To that end, more than 100,000 hectares of different species and varieties of citrus fruits (oranges, grapefruit, lemons, and tangerines) were planted.
- Building of several industrial complexes for processing these fruits

Rice

- Expansion of existing plantations and facilities
- Construction of dams and gravity irrigation systems to water some 140,000 hectares
- Introduction of new rice varieties
- Activation of a modern fleet of tractors and harvesters
- Construction and assembly of modern drying sheds and mills

Poultry Farming

Prior to 1959, poultry production (eggs and meat) was small scale and scattered, without industrial technology. A large portion of consumption relied on eggs and chickens imported from the United States. The following steps were taken to expand production:

- Launching in 1964 of a plan to reach a target figure of sixty million eggs per month
- Creation of the National Poultry Enterprise, a business entity for the development of intensive methods of poultry farming
- Development of a genetic program for light and heavy breeds, based on pure lines of fertile eggs imported from Canada
- Implementation of an investment program to expand existing and construct new animal feed plants and to build various types of poultry and egg farms
- Training of expert staff in the various phases of the productive process

Swine Production

- Development of a nationwide genetic improvement program that involved importing selected young breeders. These were introduced in the context of a policy of cross-breeding and selection for size of the swine stock.
- Investments in expanding swine-raising capacity, including centers for breeding, pre-fattening, fattening, and genetics

Forestry Resources

In 1959 forests covered only 13 percent of the national land area. By the end of 2007 Cuba had succeeded in increasing the forest coverage to 25 percent of the national land area.

- The First Land Reform Act made the state responsible for maintaining and developing the nation's forestry resources.
- A reforestation program was initiated at that time, mainly in mountainous areas and in the Zapata swamp. At the same time, sawmills were modernized and an infrastructure was developed for timber extraction.

Because the agricultural sector was a high priority in the development model implemented during the Revolution, the state provided the large majority of logistical support and investments. Between 1960 and 1990, investments in the agricultural sector accounted for 24 percent of the country's total investments. In addition, as noted earlier, the model called for a technological transformation of agriculture. To achieve its stated goal of transforming agricultural technology, the state built industrial plants to supply inputs, unfinished goods, equipment, and services for agriculture. Such products included fertilizers, disease- and pest-control products, animal feed, containers, and agricultural tools and implements, while the services included agricultural workshops and other educational and training activities.[5] A further dimension of the transformation of agriculture involved expansion and modernization of the processing industries for agricultural raw materials, such as sugar, dairy, dried meat, and fruits, through retrofitting existing factories and building new ones.

These efforts created a large, nationwide agro-industrial complex that contributed 35 percent of the GDP in the late 1980s and generated 80 percent of Cuba's hard-currency export earnings.[6] Such strong performance was enabled by the economic and financial relations Cuba established with the former socialist countries of Eastern Europe. CMEA accounted for 85 percent of Cuba's foreign trade and provided guaranteed markets for its exports, supplies of necessary productive inputs, favorable terms of trade, and requisite credit arrangements.

Some branches of agriculture experienced significant growth as a result of these policies. Others, however, showed unremarkable gains, despite being high priorities for expansion and receiving heavy technical-material support. Particularly problematic, most of the gains came only from extensive growth without increased efficiency. Despite the large-scale introduction of technology, especially in public-sector enterprises, productivity and hence yields remained below their potential.

The new relations of production in the emerging agricultural model were not matched by corresponding innovations in organization and management. This, in fact, became one of the main obstacles to achieving high productive efficiency and competitiveness. One of the organizational factors that produced the greatest inefficiency was the excessive size of state farms, which precluded effective management of their productive processes. The average size of state agricultural enterprises in 1989 was more than five thousand hectares, while cooperatives averaged around six hundred hectares. In regard to management, excessive administrative and centralized managerial mechanisms weakened the economic-financial mechanisms that normally provide incentives for social actors. This also contributed to the weak economic performance of the agricultural sector.

The overall result was a degree of stagnation of agricultural production in the late 1980s. This had two particularly important consequences. First, the model became increasingly dependent on imported supplies and machinery, and even on foodstuffs to feed the population. Second, there was a progressive increase in subsidies, primarily directed to public-sector enterprises.

Agriculture in the 1990s and the Challenges of the Current Millennium

The Cuban economy is, structurally speaking, an open economy. Because foreign trade is a determining factor for its domestic operation, its import capacity is a decisive vector in its matrix of economic relations. Thus, the demise of the socialist bloc in Eastern Europe in the late 1980s and early 1990s was devastating for Cuba. It plunged the Cuban economy into a profound crisis. Recovery required an abrupt, dramatic change in the Island's trading relations, which in turn required an extensive restructuring of Cuba's entire economy to make it compatible with prevailing world market trade conditions. This process, still under way, must also cope with the tightening of the U.S. economic blockade.

The total trade turnover, which averaged $12 billion per year between 1981 and 1990, plummeted as of 1991. It hit rock bottom in 1993 at just $3.2 billion, a mere 27 percent of the 1980s figures. Cuba's crucial imports similarly plummeted. From a total of around $8 billion in the late 1980s, they fell 75 percent to only $2 billion in 1993.

By 1994 it was possible to stop the economic free fall and begin a process of recovery based on a group of new economic measures. Several economic policies had been implemented as of 1993, all of which had strong effects on the agricultural sector as well as the rest of the economy. Principal among these policies are the following:[7]

- Opening the economy to foreign investment. This was much more than just a search for new sources of finance. It focused particularly on securing new export markets to replace those lost with the demise of the socialist community and on developing the competitive technology necessary to conduct trade.
- Eliminating the state monopoly on foreign trade, as external economic links were transformed
- Decriminalizing the ownership of hard currency within Cuba, as a means to enable the state to capture a portion of it to support its social programs and purchase necessary foreign inputs for its economic productive activities
- Attempting to attract some of the newly unemployed workers into agriculture, in order to simultaneously address the food shortage and the unemployment problem
- Authorizing and expanding of self-employment in order to alleviate unemployment[8]

Complementary changes were introduced into the planning system. Until then it had been based on the planning model that prevailed in the former socialist community, which had prioritized material aspects of the economy over financial ones. By the middle of the 1991–95 five-year period, the reproduction process was managed by means of financial instruments as the basic tools of the new planning system.

Since 1994 the Cuban economy has experienced continual recovery and growth. The GDP has grown every year, yielding, for example, 40 percent growth between 2001 and 2006.[9] With regard to the crucial capacity to import goods, including the agricultural imports that remain essential to the population's well-being, in 2006 goods imports reached $9.4 billion, surpassing the highest levels recorded prior to the economic crisis. Meanwhile, export earnings from goods have experienced more modest improvement, from $1.2 billion in 1993 to $2.8 billion in 2006.[10]

In recent years, funding for this essential high level of goods imports has been derived mainly from surpluses on the balance of services, typically somewhat over $6 billion in the early twenty-first century, before the worldwide Great Recession hit. A strong contributor to this surplus has been the significant increase in the export of high-value-added services, made possible by the human capital accumulated throughout the revolutionary period (see chapter 12); other income came from tourism (see chapters 9 and 10) and other services such as telecommunications and air transport. Until the onset of the Great Recession, the fifteen-year process of revitalization and expansion of a number of industrial and service-based activities made it possible to achieve domestic increases in household and government consumption while increasing accumulation.

The economic crisis of the early 1990s and the lengthy recovery from it had a highly adverse effect on the performance of all the country's main economic branches, but the agricultural sector was hit especially hard. Between 1990 and 1994 the country's GDP decreased by 33 percent while agricultural GDP declined by 50 percent. Through its guaranteed markets and supplies of essential inputs, favorable terms of trade, and necessary credit conditions, the socialist bloc had supported the strong technical-material base that Cuba had developed in agriculture. The disruption of all those relations was devastating, but there was a still deeper reason for the collapse of the agricultural sector: the prevailing agricultural model was exhausted. In retrospect, it was clear this had been the case for the preceding decade, but the crisis both exacerbated agriculture's collapse and exposed the model's weaknesses for all to see. For example, cattle production dropped by 60 percent as a direct result of the then-current agricultural model. Over several decades the stock-raising industry had become increasingly dependent on imported fodder as inputs for the processing of animal feed. Nearly two million tons of feed were consumed in 1989, but after the sources of external supplies evaporated, that amount dropped to only about some 700,000 tons in the 1990s.

Agriculture had an essential role to play in the critical process of economic recovery, but this required a new agricultural model. One necessary change was import substitution for many of the items in Cuba's still-massive food imports. A second was export promotion of both traditional and new agricultural products, including where possible those with high added value, which is often accomplished through processing. And most important, the entire system of agricultural production had to be fundamentally revamped and, above all, labor productivity increased.

Food is a disproportionate commodity in Cuba's overall import structure, comprising one-sixth of the Island's entire imports in 2009 (see table 11.2). Hence, an important step in promoting economic recovery is increased cultivation of food for domestic consumption, in order to reduce the financial burden of maintaining such large food imports.

The structure of Cuba's exports has changed significantly with the loss of the European socialist market. One important change is a dramatic drop in the sales of citrus fruits. But by far the most significant factor is the drop in revenues from sugar exports. This is a combined effect of the termination of the

Table 11.2. Cuba's import structure by product type, 1990 and 2009

	1990		2009	
	Value (million US$)	Pct.	Value (million US$)	Pct.
Food items and food raw materials, beverages, and tobacco	903.8	12.2	1,520.90	17
Fuels and lubricants	2,022.80	27.3	2,648.70	29.7
Machinery and transportation equipment	2,718.50	36.7	1,748.80	19.6
Other manufactured items and non-food raw materials	1,771.40	23.9	2,991.10	33.5
Total[a]	7,416.50	100	8,909.50	100

[a]At constant 1997 prices.
Sources: ONE, *Anuario Estadístico de Cuba* (Havana: ONE, 1998, 2010).

Table 11.3. Cuba's export structure by product type, 1990 and 2009

	1990		2009	
	Value (million US$)	Pct.	Value (million US$)	Pct.
All agricultural and fishing products	4,750.90	87.7	569.2	19.8
Sugar products	4,337.50	80.1	226.3	7.9
Tobacco products	114.4	2.1	212.3	7.4
Other agricultural products	183.9	3.4	14.5	0.5
Fishing products	101.9	1.9	46.5	1.6
Beverages	13.2	0.2	69.6	2.4
Mining products	398.2	7.3	841.4	29.2
Other products	265.8	5	1,468.40	51
Total[a]	5,414.90	100	2,879.00	100

[a]At constant 1997 prices.
Sources: ONE, *Anuario Estadístico de Cuba* (Havana: ONE, 1998, 2010).

preferential prices Cuba had obtained for its sugar in Eastern Europe and the declines in sugar production in recent years. Responding to these changes, the Cuban government decided soon after the millennium to restructure the sugar industry, reducing the number of industrial plants by more than 50 percent and converting 50 percent of sugarcane lands to other crops, cattle, and forestry. Currently, the primary efforts in the sugar industry are directed toward increasing agricultural efficiency and yields and toward diversifying industrial production toward bioenergy and higher-quality sugar (that is, higher-value-added products) for export.

These measures have brought about a profound structural transformation in the economy, especially in the agricultural sector. Agricultural and fishing products, which had constituted 88 percent of exports in 1990, declined dramatically to a 20 percent share by 2009. As table 11.3 shows, the massive reduction in sugar exports was the overwhelming cause of this drop.

Agricultural Efforts to Cope with the Demise of CMEA

The industrialization of Cuban agriculture rested on a high import factor that was enabled by the trading and financial relations between Cuba and the socialist countries of Eastern Europe in CMEA. Through becoming a member of CMEA in the early 1970s, Cuba was able to achieve a prominent position in Latin America in terms of agricultural mechanization, the area under irrigation, and the use of chemical fertilizers and pesticides. The demise of the European socialist community led to the dismantling of many of the industrial technologies that had predominated up to that time, particularly on state farms.

In that context it became necessary to adopt a number of structural adjustments in order first to stop and then to reverse the fall in agricultural production. Among other measures, it was essential to develop new technologies that were less dependent on external supplies of inputs. This step would bring imports in line with what is realistically possible for the Cuban economy, which, as mentioned, has always been characterized by a binding foreign-exchange constraint. Among the structural adjustment measures implemented as part of the aforementioned program of overall economic reforms are the following, each of which will be discussed in detail below:[11]

- Turning a portion of state farmlands into cooperatives, as part of a process of streamlining agricultural activities and as a formula to create incentives by giving producers collective ownership of the productive assets. Most importantly, this ties income to agricultural output.
- Conveying land in usufruct to individuals and families who will use it to produce export crops (tobacco and coffee) and food
- Reopening farmers' markets where prices are determined by supply and demand, again intended to increase the production of food
- Decentralizing the highly centralized state management by moving more decision making to the provincial or enterprise levels
- Implementing a program of urban agriculture

Structural Changes in the Relations of Ownership

The change in agricultural ownership that directly affected by far the most agricultural producers was the establishment of a new type of cooperative, the Basic Unit of Cooperative Production (UBPC). The majority of UBPC members are former agricultural workers from state farms. Each UBPC receives free of charge usufruct rights to a plot of land for its collective use, usually land formerly owned by a state farm, and is sold the rest of the assets (installations, machinery, cattle, and so on) on very soft credit terms.[12] In 2010 the 2,200 UBPCs farmed 37.5 percent of the agricultural surface area in Cuba. The entire nonstate agricultural sector—consisting of UBPCs, the roughly four thousand preexisting cooperatives (Credit and Service Cooperatives [CCSs] and Agricultural Production Cooperatives [CPAs]), and an increased number of individual farmers—together accounted for 79.3 percent of the total area (see table 11.4).

As table 11.4 shows, the ratio of landownership between the state and nonstate sectors has been inverted since 1992. The majority presence of nonstate social actors indicates a change in the dominant relations of production in Cuban agriculture. This not only transforms the obvious areas of methods of planning and management; it also extends beyond them to the whole socioeconomic environment. The state is no longer the main actor at the microeconomic level, and economic laws play a more active role in the regulation of production. Two immediate economic results of this movement away from state farms and toward UBPCs are the reduction of excessive labor forces in many places (hidden unemployment) and the closer connection between total remuneration (individual and collective) and the results the enterprise obtains.

As of the end of 2009 the greatest potential for agricultural growth lies in returning presently idle farmland to production. At present almost 20 percent of the country's farmland is idle, of which more than 50 percent is in the hands

Table 11.4. Landownership structure in Cuba since the Special Period

	Agricultural surface area owned (%)		
	1992	**2007**	**2010**
State sector	75.0	35.8	20.7
Nonstate sector	25.0	64.2	79.3
UBPCs	-	37.0	37.5
CPAs	10.0	8.8	8.8
CCSs and private owners	15.0	18.3	33.0

Sources: ONE, *Anuario Estadístico de Cuba* (Havana: ONE, 1994, 2008); preliminary estimates for 2010 by the authors.

of state enterprises. Around a quarter of the land lying fallow has only been idled in recent years due to the lack of both incentives for production and the necessary machinery. To address this problem the Cuban government enacted Decree-Law 259 in mid-2008, which conveys idle farmland in usufruct to individuals or groups who commit to return it to production. By the end of 2010, 1 million hectares have been turned over for cultivation to 108,000 individuals and 2,000 cooperatives. Table 11.4 shows the sharp increase in this sector since 2007.

The Supply-and-Demand Farmers' Markets

As one of the mechanisms to increase food production, the government decided to reopen farm produce markets where prices are set by supply and demand. This commercial structure had a precedent back in the early 1980s, but it was abandoned when certain consequences emerged that were considered to be contrary to the principles of the economic model at the time. A major problem was that the state sector dominated the nation's agricultural production but was not allowed to participate in the farmers' markets. Hence in practice the only suppliers were the relatively small sector of private agricultural producers, which generated a certain oligopolistic bias.[13]

In contrast, the new agricultural markets are open to all types of agricultural producers: state enterprises, cooperatives, and individuals. Once they meet their sales contracts to the state-run food collection agencies, they may elect to offer any surplus for sale in the farmers' markets. These markets have been in existence for more than a decade, maintaining a food supply that complements the food rations and other supply channels. Despite some operational problems and often unacceptably high prices in these markets, they have contributed to improving the food supply, not only quantitatively but also qualitatively. They also eliminated a black market in food that had emerged following the drastic contraction in the food the state supplied to the population as a result of the severe economic recession in the early 1990s. This black market was a serious problem not only because, as an illegal enterprise, prices in it were much higher than in the current farmers' markets, but also because it motivated a growing problem of theft from state production to sell in extralegal channels.

It is important to understand that even though free agricultural markets play an important and significant role today, they still only supplement the primary food supplies. The public receives a large amount of its food for consumption, particularly basic foodstuffs, in the form of rationed goods distributed at highly subsidized prices; limited amounts of other goods are available at prices set below the agricultural free-market levels; and most importantly, Cuba allocates supplies for social consumption in schools, hospitals, maternity homes, nursing homes, and other social assistance facilities. The population receives 60 percent of its calories, and 40 percent of its protein and fat intake, in subsidized consumption through the rationing system and the food supplied in hospitals, schools, and workplaces, among other venues. For several years the government has indicated its intention to reduce the proportion of total food consumption that is subsidized, and in particular to eliminate the ration card, once these steps become possible without harming the population.

The quantities of agricultural produce destined for the state-run collection agencies have also been increased via the incentive of raising the prices these agencies pay to producers. Milk and meat products have seen the most significant price increases, though they are not the only comestibles affected. State prices on other goods have been decentralized and are now set by the People's Administrative Councils in the provinces. These prices are usually set slightly lower than the prevailing prices in the farmers' markets and are adjusted periodically using the free-market prices as a reference. This pricing system now even includes products set aside for social purposes, which are funded from the state's budget. The food supply has also been improved by directly linking producers with some of the main consumption centers, with the goal of more accurately meeting actual demand and thereby reducing commercial losses.

Changes in Management Mechanisms

As the productive structure of agriculture has been transformed through changes in landownership and the emergence of new productive agents, management mechanisms have had to change as well. The former management system was characterized by a high degree of centralization in decision making about production, distribution of inputs and supplies, and marketing of end products. The management system has had to gradually adapt to the new structure of agriculture, which contains a much larger number of "legal persons" (enterprises) and "natural persons" (individual producers), and hence also a larger assortment of technologies and natural and human resources.

The most significant change in management has been a progressive decentralization that has brought the base units closer to the level where decisions are made regarding the structure of output, the use of resources, workers' income, and so forth. The institutional changes involved in the vertical decentralization of the main administrative apparatus of the Ministry of Agriculture have been particularly important. Municipal offices have been established and charged with being proactive. They have received power to draw up their own Regional Self-Supply Plans, in coordination with the local People's Power councils and other grassroots political organizations. The management of some lines of production was fundamentally changed by the introduction of a number of commercial networks for obtaining inputs and distributing outputs, rather than these all being specified in accordance with a fully centralized and quite detailed national plan. However, Cuba's ongoing structural problem of a binding external financial constraint has made it impossible to fully decentralize foreign-exchange-related issues in agriculture or any other part of the Cuban economy. These major decisions must still be made by central economic bodies.

Urban Agriculture

Urban agriculture is defined spatially as agriculture that occurs within a ten-kilometer radius around any provincial capital, a five-kilometer radius around any municipal capital, a two-kilometer radius around any urban center with more than ten thousand inhabitants, or locally in settlements of fewer than one thousand people. Such agriculture, which was almost nonexistent prior to the Special Period, is a new initiative designed to promote food self-sufficiency. Prior to the economic crisis, Cuba had some of the highest levels of per capita consumption of both calories and proteins in the third world, nearly on par with a number of first-world countries. With the onset of the crisis, however, food consumption dropped sharply, and many city residents took the initiative to grow food in their backyards, on idle plots, and on rooftops. Many even kept animals to ensure a supply of protein for their family.

In the mid-1990s urban agriculture started to shift from subsistence to larger-scale production, with growers marketing some of their output locally. The government strongly supported and promoted this change, through both a social campaign and resources and training. Given the extremely limited transportation resources in Cuba at that time, the most immediate objective was to reduce the need for transportation in supplying necessary agricultural inputs and in distributing agricultural products to the population. The primary target among the many goals the urban agriculture program adopted as it became formalized was to increase vegetable consumption to three hundred grams daily per inhabitant, the amount recommended by the UN Food and Agriculture Organization.

The following core principles define the objectives and organization of urban agriculture in Cuba:

- The program is to be uniformly distributed across the country, being developed in all urban areas.
- Food is produced locally and consumed by the urban population in that region.
- Food production is a top priority for all available land: to achieve high agricultural and livestock total yields without depending on imports.

- The food production potential of the workforce is maximized by raising the labor productivity of urban agriculturalists.
- Maximum synergy is achieved by integrating plant and animal production, whereby agricultural residues and by-products are recycled to nourish plants and animals. Two common examples are the use of otherwise discarded parts of food crops for animal feed and the use of animal waste to enrich compost.
- Organic matter is intensively used in place of chemical fertilizers to increase and preserve fertility.
- Pests are controlled with biological rather than chemical agents wherever possible.
- Cultivation is grounded on intensive application and multidisciplinary integration of science and technology.
- The population is guaranteed a supply of fresh, high-quality products.
- Concrete goals have been set for urban agricultural production, such as ensuring a minimum of three hundred grams daily of vegetables per person and corresponding amounts and varieties of animal protein.

Urban agriculture is organized and administered through twenty-eight subprograms that encompass all aspects of vegetable and animal production nationwide. These subprograms target, among other things, production of fresh vegetables, spices, fruits, rice, grains, animal feed and seeds and promote programs in beekeeping, cattle raising, aquaculture, soil conservation and treatment, use of organic matter, marketing, and operating cottage industries. While there is overall system-wide integration of the urban agriculture program, each subprogram is supervised separately, based on specific relevant factors and relying on specialized technical assistance.

Recent Trends in Agricultural Production

These general and specific measures have succeeded in stabilizing the food situation and, more broadly, beginning the recovery of agricultural production, albeit not to the level the country requires. External dependence on food supplies remains significant, despite Cuba's possession of natural resources (land, water), human capital, and technology that if used more intensively could greatly reduce and eventually eliminate that dependence.

Between 2003 and 2005 Cuba faced its worst drought in forty years. Table 11.5 illustrates the decline in agricultural GDP at the end of this period and in the following year, when the cumulative effect of the drought was the greatest. The upward trend in agricultural GDP resumed in 2007 and experienced only a minor dip in 2008 despite widespread destruction from the worst hurricane

Table 11.5. Evolution of national and agricultural GDP, 1994–2009

	Value in millions of pesos[a]						
	1994	2005	2006	2007	2008	2009	2009/1994
National GDP	21,010.4	39,167.9	44,063.8	43,883.3	45,774.0	46,352.0	2.20
Agricultural GDP	1,435.8	1,700.5	1,597.7	1,885.9	1,879.9	1,962.7	1.37
Agricultural as pct. of national GDP	6.8	4.3	3.6	4.3	4.1	4.2	0.62

[a] At 1997 prices.
Sources: ONE, *Anuario Estadístico de Cuba* (Havana: ONE, 1998, 2010).

Table 11.6. Cuban output of major agricultural products in 2009 as a percentage of 1993 levels

Product	2009 output (% of 1993 level)
Rice	186
Roots and tubers	182
Vegetables	482
Bananas	132
Corn	460
Beans	605
Citrus fruit	60
Other fruit	634
Tobacco	127
Beef	99
Pork	166
Poultry	67
Mutton and goat	197
Cow's milk	100
Eggs	152

Source: ONE, *Anuario Estadístico de Cuba* (Havana: ONE, 1998, 2010).

season on record. By 2009 the value in constant pesos of agricultural production was 37 percent above its low point in 1994. This is an important outcome for both exports and the domestic food supply, but it is still far short of both Cuba's agricultural potential and the contribution agriculture must make to the Cuban people's overall well-being.

In general, the technological patterns of food production have been adjusted to be much more sustainable. New systems maximize the use of local resources, both human and material, and hence are much less dependent on imported inputs. This is particularly relevant because absolute production levels of many agricultural products, such as tubers, roots, grains, and noncitrus fruit, are now higher than even in the pre-crisis 1980s. As table 11.6

shows, production levels of almost all products are significantly higher today than at the depth of the food crisis in 1994. Such is not the case for some livestock products, however, which have remained more dependent than the other branches of agriculture on external inputs. Their weak growth (or in some cases actual decline) from the 1994 overall food nadir has necessitated an increase in imports of proteins, mainly milk and meat, because the Cuban Revolution remains committed to providing a healthy minimum diet for all its citizens, despite the macroeconomic harm this causes to Cuba's balance of trade.

Other Issues Related to the Agricultural Sector

Rural poverty was eradicated at a very early stage of the Revolution, and despite the complex situation Cuba faced in the early 1990s, the new policies, reforms, and measures the state adopted in response to the crisis prevented its reappearance at that time (see chapter 6). Most significantly, the state decided to do everything possible during the economic crisis to maintain the social achievements in employment, health care, education, and social security accomplished over the course of the Revolution. Another important contribution to increasing Cuba's rural standard of living has been the expansion of basic infrastructure, such as access to housing, drinking water, electricity, and educational and public health facilities. These programs also have remained in place despite the intense financial constraints of the last two decades.[14]

Table 11.7 documents recent trends in employment and income in the agricultural sector. The recent dramatic rise in the average income per agricultural worker is one important result of the intensive programs to expand both agricultural production and employment that are in force as of 2010.

Table 11.7. Recent trends in agricultural employment and income, 2005–9

	2005	**2006**	**2007**	**2008**	**2009**
Agricultural workers (thousands)	956.3	951.6	912.3	919.1	945.6
Income by type of enterprise (millions of pesos)					
State farms	752.2	1,107.5	1,104.3	1,197.7	1,544.6
Cooperatives	914.4	988.6	1,137.8	1,372.7	1,489.6
Private farms	1,762.4	1,781.8	2,625.6	3,568.5	4,626.8
Total	3,429.0	3,877.9	4,867.7	6,138.9	7,663.0
Average income/worker (pesos)	3,585	4,075	5,336	6,679	8,104

Source: ONE, *Anuario Estadístico de Cuba* (Havana: ONE, 2010).

Final Considerations

As this chapter has documented, guaranteeing food security for the Cuban population and eradicating rural poverty have been central concerns of the Cuban state since very soon after the triumph of the Revolution. Public policies since then have targeted these goals, their successes have been significant, and they have been preserved even throughout the dramatic downturn in the Cuban economy in the early 1990s and the subsequent gradual recovery. Recent positive developments in the agricultural sector have included the restructuring of the sugar industry, the increase in domestic food production as a way to substitute for imports and enhance the people's diet, the diversification of agricultural exports, the reorganization of the productive apparatus, and the redesign of the roles of the state and the other economic actors.

Currently, progress continues on the design and application of the new agricultural policy. Several organizational formulas and models involving new management concepts are being studied and experimented with. Among these are strengthening incentives for producers through new pricing systems, establishing monetary and material bonuses, and prioritizing improvements in rural ways of life. The underlying objective of all these efforts is to achieve financial, technological, and environmental sustainability of the agricultural sector.

Cuba possesses sufficient human capital proficient in current agricultural technologies. The infrastructure is in place, and it remains strong despite the effects of the crisis. New forms of ownership characterized by smaller economic units and less centralized operational methods have been established. There is a strong, publicly expressed political will to support and prioritize agricultural development. To be sure, major subjective and objective problems remain to be resolved. However, Cuba is generating reasonably good responses to the strains on the capacity of its national agricultural system. Without denying or even downplaying the serious problems the agricultural sector must address, these strengths represent a solid base on which it can move forward.

The two most serious continuing challenges for Cuban agriculture are to heighten food security and to reduce the environmental costs of production. Two interrelated external problems have emerged as major concerns over the last half decade: high international fuel prices and the burden of food imports on Cuba's hard-currency balance. Given the binding nature of the hard-currency constraint on the Cuban economy over the entire Special Period, and particularly since the effects of the global Great Recession hit Cuba beginning in 2008, these two concerns are critical at this moment.

A final issue emerging at the present time concerns anti-neoliberal international cooperation in agriculture within the framework of ALBA. Within this forum since 2004, Cuba and Venezuela have launched agricultural cooperation programs for producing soybeans, rice, poultry, and dairy products with the goal of increasing the food security of both nations. As more countries join ALBA, the potential for international agricultural collaboration should increase, based on the principles of national sovereignty, cooperation, and integration of the goals of improving the diet and well-being of the population.

Looking forward, it is clear that agriculture will continue to be a strategic sector in the Cuban economy. Its contribution to national income, employment, and food consumption makes it very important macroeconomically. But more broadly, the policies Cuba has adopted as part of its new and evolving development strategy, just as in the various stages of Cuba's development strategy over the last five decades, will necessarily give agriculture a prominent role within the social and economic programs that concretize that strategy.

Notes

1. Julio Le Riverend, *Historia económica de Cuba* (Havana: Editora Revolucionaria, 1981).

2. Fidel Castro, *La historia me absolverá* (Havana: Oficina de Publicaciones del Consejo de Estado, 1993).

3. Guillermo Cayado, *Agricultura cubana: Estructuras organizativas y programas de desarrollo (1959–2007)* (Havana: Agroinfor, 2008).

4. Alfredo González, Pablo Fernández, and Ángel Bu, *La ganadería en Cuba: Desempeño y desafíos* (Montevideo: Universidad de Uruguay, 2004).

5. Alfredo González et al., *El sector agropecuario y las políticas agrícolas ante los nuevos retos* (Montevideo: Universidad de Uruguay, 2000).

6. Ángel Bu Wong and Pablo Fernández Domínguez, "La cadena agroalimentaria en Cuba y su reto," *Cuba: Investigación Económica* 10, nos. 3–4 (2004).

7. Alfredo González, "Economía y Sociedad: Los retos del modelo económico," *Cuba: Investigación Económica* 3, nos. 3–4 (1997).

8. Self-employment did reduce unemployment, but it also undermined efforts to get the unemployed to participate in agriculture, which were largely unsuccessful. The unemployed were almost all urban residents who had strong cultural prejudices against agricultural work, and the legalization of a broader range and greater quantity of self-employment in the cites gave them an alternative to the agricultural work they resisted.

9. ONE, *Anuario Estadístico de Cuba* (Havana: ONE, various years).

10. Ibid.

11. González et al., *El sector agropecuario y las políticas agrícolas ante los nuevos retos.*

12. Ángel Bu Wong and Pablo Fernández Domínguez, "Las UBPC y su necesario perfeccionamiento," *Cuba: Investigación Económica* 2, no. 2 (1996).

13. Alfredo González, Pablo Fernández Domínguez, and Ángel Bu Wong, "Mercado agropecuario: Apertura o limitación," *Cuba: Investigación Económica* 1, no. 4 (1995).

14. Ángela Ferriol, "Política social en el ajuste y su adecuación a las nuevas condiciones," *Cuba: Investigación Económica* 5, no. 1 (1999).

12

Expansion of Knowledge-Based Economic Sectors

The Advantages Socialism Offers for Cuba

VITO N. QUEVEDO RODRÍGUEZ

In ten years Cuba managed to more than double its GDP, from 25,366 million pesos in 1997 to 58,604 in 2007, despite an intensified U.S. blockade that has been very costly to the Cuban economy. This expansion has been possible because of the will and resilience of the Cuban people, the quality of its leadership, and in part, as this chapter addresses, the appropriate and intelligent management of knowledge. Cuba has made tremendous efforts over the last fifty years to access, generate, and implement knowledge that will promote sustainable development and the well-being of its citizens.

In the relatively short period since the victory of the Revolution in 1959, and starting from a relatively low baseline level, the Cuban state took decisive steps to promote the people's economic, social, and cultural development. Among the outcomes achieved are the internationally recognized illiteracy eradication program; an average educational level of eleventh grade; health indicators comparable to those in developed countries; full employment; a shift from sugar monoculture to diversified industrial and service production; world-class accomplishments in sports, culture, and science; military preparedness; civic safety; and the consolidation of a society free of drugs and other social scourges. In terms of human development, the country's indicators are similar to those of developed countries, making Cuba an example to the world of what can be accomplished even with limited resources, if the commitment exists. These successes have been achieved despite the ongoing U.S. blockade over almost the entire course of the Revolution, and its reinforcement over the last two decades; the severe consequences for the national economy of the collapse of the socialist bloc around 1990, particularly of the former USSR; and the costly internal errors, shortcomings, and insufficiencies that are unavoidable by-products of the process of building any new society. Many of these accomplishments have been possible because of Cuba's combination of patriotism, the people's confidence in their central leaders, social cohesion, and solidarity.

One aspect of Cuba's development paradigm is particularly important to understand: its goal is not economic growth that benefits only a minority of the population (usually hidden by reporting only figures for "the whole country"), but rather it includes a battle for equity and increased human well-being. This makes the task of building a new society much more complex and difficult. Yet Cuba has been very successful over the last five decades in harmonizing its economic development with the construction of an equitable society. Cuba is known for its degree of equity and the broad coverage of its social benefits and gains across the entire population, but there are still asymmetries and inequities that it can, must, and wants to address. Another crucial element of a development paradigm focused on human well-being is environmental sustainability. As I will discuss, over the last two decades Cuba has achieved international recognition for the many environmental protection programs and practices it has built into its new, still evolving, development paradigm.

These many tangible results demonstrate the improvement of the Cuban population's well-being over the last five decades. But although that development is ongoing and far from over, it remains markedly inadequate to meet the population's economic, social, and cultural needs. On one hand, many people ask how Cuba has been able to accomplish so much, especially with limited natural resources and in the face of costly, relentless aggression from the world's major power. On the other, some question whether Cuba could have done more if it had pursued various alternative courses in the past. The general consensus, however, is that today Cuba is pursuing a unique path for a third-world country in terms of its economic, social, and cultural development—in a word, its human development—and therefore merits careful study.

The new millennium has brought economic challenges related to neoliberal globalization and its consequences, such as increasing food shortages, profound and menacing climate changes, and serious energy and water crises. These issues demand that Cuba implement development strategies based on knowledge, technology, organization (management), and above all human resources.[1] Science, technology, and innovation have been a part of the broad-based process of transformation undertaken in Cuba in two basic ways: through generating more knowledge and through increasing the capacity to assimilate and adapt foreign technologies. In this regard Cuban society has made great progress over the last five decades. Once characterized by widespread illiteracy, Cuba now transfers technologies not only to the third world but to numerous organizations in the first world. Once technologically colonized, it is now designing and taking the initial steps to create a knowledge-based society.

And where there was once virtually no scientific activity, Cuban scientists are now outstanding in several high-tech sectors such as biotechnology, medical equipment, and the electricity industry. These are the types of tools that Cuba will need to continue to develop in order to facilitate and promote national and international development.

There have been errors, shortcomings, and limitations in this five-decade process of scientific-technical development. But only by considering these in conjunction with Cuba's many achievements can one really understand the errors and shortcomings, learn from them, and improve future performance. Much of the international media and many international organizations opposed to Cuba tend to focus only on the errors in this area, as they do in Cuba's broader social policies. Such an outlook serves no purpose other than to promote a falsely negative image of Cuba—which, of course, is their goal. The generation of scientific knowledge and technology has indeed contributed to the development of Cuba and the entire world, despite errors and shortcomings in the development process.

Cuba's progress in scientific fields is indisputably documented by internationally recognized results and contributions. Therefore, it is essential to consider what factors have contributed to a type of success that is very unusual for a third-world country. These factors include, among others,

- consistent political and material support from the government, which instituted practices to foster science over a period of fifty years;
- popularization of science, with opportunities for all citizens to participate, and establishment of a basic organizational structure from the national to the municipal levels;
- integration of human, financial, material, and organizational resources;
- large-scale training of human resources via a strong nationwide system designed specifically for that purpose;
- creation of a broad and diverse structure of research centers, universities, and entities in support of science, technology, and innovation; and
- establishment of the System of Science and Technological Innovation (SCIT), with strategies and plans for developing and managing both science and technology.

This chapter elaborates on the evolution and main aspects of science, technology, and innovation in Cuba since the triumph of the Revolution and reviews their current status. In particular, it emphasizes their increasingly direct connection with the economy. Following a general description of knowledge-based sectors in Cuba's current and prospective economy, the last third of the chapter is devoted to examining in detail four sectors that are particularly important to Cuba's contemporary economic development: biotechnology, information technology and communications, energy, and the environment.

The strengths and challenges in Cuba's policies and programs to develop knowledge-based sectors of the economy will be considered in the framework of Cuba's central goal of building a socialist society. On the one hand, the ability of a planned economy to channel resources toward, and mobilize the social forces necessary to develop, socially prioritized sectors is an important advantage. On the other hand, socialism's goals of equity, sustainable development, and a better quality of life for its citizens will always complicate the necessary interaction of Cuba's knowledge-based sectors with the capitalist-dominated world economy. This conflict has caused and will continue to cause forces in the capitalist world economy to carry out policies deliberately designed to isolate Cuba or even sabotage its efforts to commercialize its knowledge-based products.

Overview

The path the Revolution has traveled from the literacy campaign of the 1960s to today's incipient creation of a high-tech economic sector has been complex. Although it has not been without difficulties, barriers, and errors, it has achieved important successes. Today, the human potential for scientific research created over fifty years has allowed Cuba to produce a solid body of internationally significant scientific results. It has built a network of research centers, and recently it advanced these further with the creation of SCIT. The infrastructure for concrete scientific and technological innovation now exists at national, regional, sectoral, and grassroots levels. It thus transcends elitism and allows all interested citizens to participate in this important aspect of social development. Without downplaying the tremendous amount of work that remains to be done, one can say that important connections among science, society, and the economy have been forged. Knowledge-based sectors have already begun to contribute in important ways to the development of the national economy and society and to the internationally important issue of environmental protection. Like much of the third world today, Cuba began in 1959 with few scientific or endogenous technological resources. Its success is an example of the importance of unity, will, and a clearly defined strategy for fostering this economically, socially, and culturally necessary component of authentic development.

Prior to the victory of the Revolution in 1959, Cuba had about one million illiterate people, almost 20 percent of its population. There were no research centers and only four experimental stations with a total staff of fewer than one hundred. There were only three universities and no government funding available for research programs.[2] Cuba was dependent both on the import of technologies, essentially from the United States, and also on the hiring of foreign experts or advisers or the overseas training of Cuban professionals. Innovations important for Cuba's domestic industry, particularly in technological fields, were made outside the country and without Cuban participation. The most advanced technologies were owned by transnational corporations, and their products were intended to satisfy the culture of consumerism rather than the needs of society as a whole. All this not only had obvious, severe negative economic effects, but beyond that, it greatly dampened the creativity and "can-do spirit" of the Cuban people. Notwithstanding this adverse situation, a few outstanding Cubans did emerge who contributed to scientific knowledge on an international scale. Among them were Carlos J. Finlay, Pedro Kourí, and Tomás Romay.

The revolutionary victory ushered in a new stage of serious, sustained work promoting the development of science and technology in Cuba. In 1960, President Fidel Castro said, "Cuba's future must be a future of men of science, of men of thought." This simple proposition became the first, and has remained the most important, premise of Cuba's national scientific and technological policy. Based on it, in that year Castro outlined and started to implement Cuba's overall economic, social, and cultural—as well as scientific and technological—strategy of training human resources. Starting from the overall premise Castro expressed in 1960, Cuban scientific policy has been developed and organized around five pillars:

1. Support for the country's development
2. Development of its scientific potential
3. Generation of endogenous technologies
4. Assimilation of international knowledge and technologies
5. Integration (explained later)

Cuba's promotion of its scientific potential began with, and today still rests on, its general educational policies. Currently, essentially 100 percent of the Cuban population receives schooling. The country boasts more than sixty-five universities. Recently, a University Venues in the Municipalities program has been launched, greatly increasing higher education by making it available in all 169 of Cuba's municipalities, close to where people live and work. Cuba has more than 700,000 university graduates in its population of 11.2 million, and intense postgraduate training is continuously ongoing. The ratio of engineers and researchers in 2005 was 1.9 per 1,000 inhabitants. The Island had 8,500 doctors, more than 5,500 researchers, and nearly 80,000 people working in science and technology fields.[3] In line with the policy since the beginning of the Revolution, development of human resources is considered Cuba's main asset, both in taking on the challenges of national development and in fulfilling Cuba's commitment to international solidarity. In terms of infrastructure dedicated to scientific knowledge, today Cuba has more than 220 scientific entities, 115 of which are particularly prestigious and are recognized as scientific centers of excellence.

In line with the five aforementioned pillars, Cuba's Scientific and Technological Activity (ACT) has always been undertaken in parallel with the development priorities its citizens adopted as part of the socialist socioeconomic project. These priorities require the creation of endogenous scientific potential and technology, and simultaneously the assimilation and application of international scientific knowledge.[4] The latter is contingent on three factors: trends in the specific scientific field, the international situation, and existing international scientific cooperation agreements.

SCIT was created more than ten years ago, during the difficult economic situation known as the Special Period. It was established with the goal of enhancing the efficiency, effectiveness, and excellence of Cuba's forty years of achievements in science, technology, and innovation. SCIT's goal is systematically to increase the contributions that these areas make to the country's economic and social development within the shortest possible time, while enhancing protection of the natural environment.[5] The current national scientific and technological policy is founded on these principles and organizes research projects in a pyramidal hierarchy, whose origin, formation, and development will be discussed later.

Cuba has greatly increased its national scientific output in three very different dimensions: the number of scientific publications, patents, and applications of science to the economy and society. The last dimension is considered particularly important to national development, and so notwithstanding the recent achievements, Cuba is not resting on its laurels but is redoubling its efforts at expansion. In this regard, the importance of some aspects of ACT are being reevaluated according to a new criterion: the "impact" of scientific, technological, or innovative outcomes. The importance of a given scientific project is measured in part by its tangible contribution to the economy, to scientific knowledge, and to Cubans' standard of living. This assessment of impact is then combined with evaluation of the project's contribution to the fifth pillar of scientific policy, integration, referring to the concept of interaction, cooperation, and support among various specific programs. Integration is key for considering the extensive positive externalities or synergies that exist in science and technology. A secondary evaluation measure involves a comparison of Cuba's results with those of other developing countries or, when appropriate, with developed countries.[6]

As a result of the scientific, technological, and innovative work done in the country, particularly in the last twenty years, Cuba can now boast of internationally recognized accomplishments in several knowledge-based economic sectors. The most outstanding of these are biotechnology, information technologies, disaster management systems, modernization of meteorological systems, environmental protection, and, recently, the efficient generation and conservation of energy. Presently, scientific activity is beginning to address the international problem of conservation and rational use of water. But despite its increased attention to the impact factor, Cuba always keeps in mind the methodological issue that such impacts are only possible on the basis of efficient organization, promotion, and management (all of which require extensive and accurate statistical indicators) of science and technology.

In sum, it is clearly accurate and appropriate to say that "Cuban science is a genuine achievement of the Revolution."

Development Period: 1960–1990

The leaders of the Revolution recognized early on the essential connection between scientific and technological development and revolutionary Cuba's general social and economic goals. Therefore, scientific and technological education received strong support right from the beginning of Cuba's new universal and comprehensive system of education. This attention to technology and innovation was very soon given extra impetus by the beginning of U.S. aggression against the Revolution. The first phases of the U.S. blockade, the partial embargo of October 1960, and its escalation to a near-total embargo in February 1962 prevented Cuba from obtaining replacement parts to maintain its stock of machinery. To help address this serious economic attack, Commander Ernesto "Che" Guevara, then minister of industries, launched a campaign with the slogan "Worker, build your machinery." This was the first official innovation program in Cuba, and it led to the birth of the Association of Innovators in 1963, renamed the National Association of Innovators and Rationalizers (ANIR), on October 8, 1976. Part of the strategy of innovation was the creation and development of Quality Committees, a Cuban application of the international concept of Quality Circles.

In 1964 Commander in Chief Fidel Castro proposed the creation of a brigade of young people who, provided with particularly good working conditions, could promote the technical-material foundation for socialism in the country. Subsequently, the Technical Youth Brigades (BTJ) were launched with the main objective of channeling young people's creative initiative and constant drive to improve whatever they encounter.

By the first half of the 1980s the scientific and technological situation in Cuba had changed significantly from the 1960s. Yet although an important network of scientific centers and a considerable number of researchers existed, the nation still had not reached its full scientific and technological potential, particularly because research did not always mesh with the country's socioeconomic development needs. The matter of spare parts is a good example of the problem at this time. Purchasing parts presented a major cost to the economy, a problem that should have been resolvable given Cuba's existing scientific and technological capabilities. Hence in 1983 Castro initiated the formation of the Spare Parts Forums. This large-scale, politically and ideologically oriented movement, which served to increase unity among all producers in Cuba, was aimed at manufacturing and refurbishing spare parts, a factor of great importance to maintaining Cuba's productive processes. At the suggestion of Fidel himself, this movement was renamed the Science and Technology Forum (FCT) at its eleventh annual meeting. Drawing on the creativity, scientific knowledge, and innovative effort of the people, FCT went on to play a decisive and in particular an integrating role in the search for solutions to the many pressing problems related to Cuba's economic and social development. In particular, the FCT movement has become a bulwark for the dissemination, expansion, and generalization of proven, practical scientific-technical knowledge and a legitimate, organized movement promoting innovation.

A new element was added to this process in 1989 with the organization of Quality Committees on the national and provincial levels. Jointly sponsored by the CTC, ANIR, and BTJ, these committees operated under the auspices of the National Standardization Office. They have been instrumental in spreading innovations and in solving quality problems in production and services, with the direct involvement of the workers. Today, the FCT movement, ANIR, and BTJ are elements in SCIT, and they continue to energize it.

It is important to understand the essential difference between scientific and technical activities in the 1960–80 period versus those that came thereafter. The colossal effort just discussed was aimed primarily at solving the pressing problems of production. By the 1990s and especially in the twenty-first century, Cuba's ACT had been redirected to strategically projecting, and guaranteeing the competitiveness of, various productive sectors. This new stage in Cuba's scientific and technological activity is described next.

By the late 1980s Cuba could boast of good results in its ACT, creating a tremendous potential for scientific research. It suffered, however, from an insufficient capacity for direct interactions between the scientific sector and the sectors that produced goods and services. This limited the effective introduction and widespread dissemination of scientific findings into production, a limitation that has not been completely overcome to this day.

Current Period: 1990–2010

As noted, the 1990s opened with the collapse of the socialist community, especially the USSR, and the strengthening of the U.S. blockade. The following two decades, known in Cuba as the Special Period, have had two interacting key characteristics: popular resistance aimed at overcoming Cuba's worst economic difficulties since the Revolution and major transformations in the economy and social institutions. The result was that Cuba engineered a process of constant, gradual recovery from a collapse in production very similar in depth and length to the U.S. Great Depression of the early 1930s (but with the hardships shared much more equally across society). It is frequently noted that Cuba achieved this recovery without closing a single school or hospital, even in the worst of times, a notable contrast to the neoliberal recipe for responding to severe external shocks. Additionally, and pertinent to this chapter, not a single scientific institution was closed, Cuba's overall ACT was not reduced, and scientific production actually increased.

In 1991–92 scientific clusters began to emerge as an innovative concept for promoting systematic interactions among research activities, teaching, specialized production, and scientific-technical information. The first such cluster created was the Scientific Cluster of Western Havana, geared specifically toward accelerating development of biotechnology. The model of this and other scientific clusters in Havana was subsequently extended to the remaining provinces. Then in 1992 the creation of the Trade Union of Science Workers added an important new element to Cuba's strategy of integration. It joined the scientific clusters ANIR and BTJ, and FCT, another key institution in the promotion of science, technology, and innovation.

In parallel with the gradual economic recovery in Cuba, and as part of the country's vision of the role of science and technology in the new millennium and in the new economy, the process of consolidation, intensification, and enhancement of scientific, technological, and innovative activities has continued in the twenty-first century. These are now seen as indispensable tools for raising the efficiency of domestic enterprises and the competitiveness of those doing business internationally. Heightened efficiency and effectiveness are necessary to raise the standard of living of the Cuban population, achieve economically and environmentally sustainable development, and preserve and promote social equity.[7] Among the important developments in this respect are

- establishment of CITMA in 1994;
- implementation in 1994 of SCIT;
- enactment in 1997 of Law No. 81, the Law of the Environment; and
- nationwide implementation in the late 1990s of the process of enterprise improvement (perfeccionamiento empresarial).

The country's highest leaders and the many institutions participating in SCIT have achieved important results in key sectors of the economy and society through their efforts to promote scientific and technical development. For one, they accomplished their desired goals of increasing the number of high-value-added export products and the substitution of imports. Yet the overall conclusion was that scientific and technological activities, and particularly innovation, were still insufficient to promote the levels of economic dynamism and efficiency in the national economy, particularly in the productive sector, necessary to support the increased standard of living and the economically and environmentally sustainable development that Cuba is pursuing. This inadequacy led to the implementation of a program designed to solve the problems, with the following results:

- Delineation of strategies to develop science and technology in support of, and as contributions to, the regional development plans; the productive and service sectors; and large numbers of enterprises, entities, and communities
- Enhancement of ACT throughout all of Cuba, via a broad-based and popular movement promoting science, technology, and innovation
- Promotion of local development consistent with the economic, social, and environmental aspects of national development. Local development is considered a particularly important component of economically, socially, and environmentally sustainable development.
- Implementation of specific measures, such as the following:
    - Replacing process-based measures with impact-based measurement of results (as discussed)
    - Organizing research in a pyramidal hierarchy in accordance with economic development priorities. These priorities are expressed in strategies that are carried out via series of projects. The success of these strategies and priorities is measured by their impact on the nation's social, economic, or environmental activities (fig. 12.1).
    - Making each individual project the basic unit for the organization, funding, and execution of the large-scale research, development, and innovation activities undertaken in Cuba. These are grouped at the national, sector-specific, regional, or institutional levels.

- Introducing SCIT into the appropriate levels of all relevant organizations
- Preparing and implementing a legal framework to regulate the development, organization, execution, and monitoring of scientific and innovative activities, as well as those designed for technology transfer, training of human resources, and other related actions

The result of these developments over the two decades of the Special Period is that today an organizational structure is in place to organize, execute, and monitor the country's scientific and technological strategies and policies. This structure contains appropriate mechanisms for planning, management, transfer of knowledge and technologies, and performance evaluation, among other activities. It also provides various procedures, regulations, and guidelines that serve to facilitate, harmonize, and unify Cuba's standards for high-tech activities.

Cuba's science and technology system covers a vast area, ranging from the generation, assimilation, and accumulation of knowledge to the production and marketing of goods and services. It encompasses basic and applied research, technological development, vertical and horizontal technology transfer, development of related scientific-technical information and services, many aspects of social development, creation and assimilation of modern management techniques, study of synergies and assorted coordination activities, standards for quality and standardization, the definition of industrial property in a socialist context, and the development of effective marketing procedures. It is

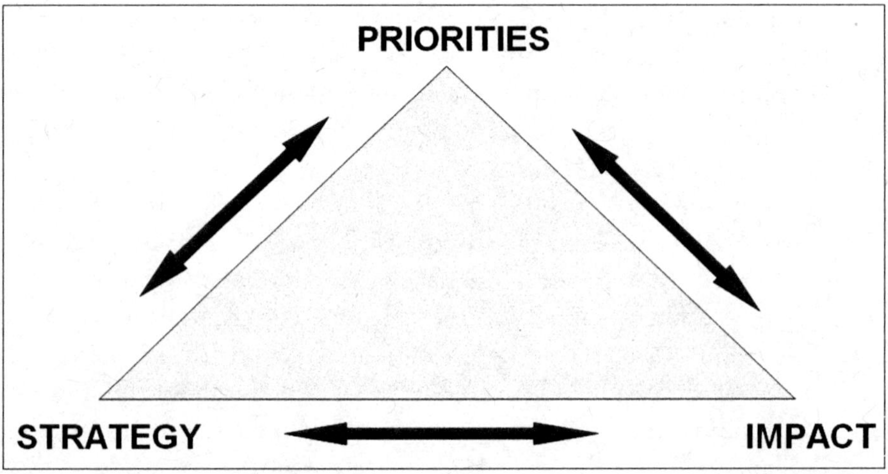

Figure 12.1. Pyramidal organizational structure of Cuban research.

composed of the organizations involved in planning, organizing, and managing SCIT; those directly involved in research and development; those directly involved in production; and those that coordinate and integrate various elements of SCIT. In addition, the legal regulations and methodological guidelines that control and standardize the operations of all these organizations are part of the system, as are the interrelations and interactions established among all these organizations.

Among the organizations that make up the scientific-technical system today are the scientific clusters, the FCT, ANIR, the BTJ, Cuba's Academy of Sciences, the scientific societies, and the associations of specialists, grouped by branch and region. In addition, the system includes enterprises and entities engaged in production and services, as well as banking and financial entities. The final components are the universities, research-and-development centers, scientific information centers, the Cuban Observatory of Science and Technology, and other similar organizations that investigate prospects for information and technology. The channels and modalities that connect scientific findings with the technological demands of productive systems are being expanded, although they remain seriously inadequate, and productive chains are being strengthened, particularly those with a strong basis in science. The fundamental focus for strengthening this connection is on well-defined problems that have concrete applications to production.[8]

The many social and economic gains that Cuba's science and technology policies have accomplished offer a broad indication of their success. The following are a few of the many indicators in which science and technology have played an important role. Cuba now boasts health indicators comparable to those in developed countries. Beyond health care, it has one of the highest HDIs of any third-world country, again comparable to some developed countries. Electricity and treated drinking water are available to 96 percent of its population. Cuba has developed vaccines otherwise manufactured only in highly developed countries. It has developed a high level of security and preparedness against natural disasters such as hurricanes. Cuba's international environmental and ecological prestige has increased, with its world-renowned urban agriculture program being one outstanding example. Many countries, particularly the poorest, have benefited from both Cuba's quick and efficient literacy method and Operation Miracle's proven technology to remedy certain common eye diseases.

The RAND report to the World Bank on the status of science and technology worldwide contains a more specific measure of Cuba's achievements.[9] This report listed a group of indicators relevant to the development of science and technology, such as available scientific potential, publications, patents, installed scientific capacity, spending on science and technology, and per capita GDP, which were then combined to generate a general index for each country. Based on the value of this index, countries were divided into three levels of scientific and technological development: (1) developed, (2) competent, and (3) backward. Cuba's general index of 0.11 placed it in the second group, outranking all other countries in the Caribbean and Latin America, and almost all third-world countries.

Although Cuba's SCIT is still functioning and is responsible for important achievements, it has not reached the desired levels of efficiency, harmony, and integration. To declare the existence of a system of scientific and technological innovation is not enough; it has to be built. There are organizational, financial, technological, and human barriers along this path, and overcoming these constraints is the key to realizing more fully SCIT's goals of maximizing science and technology's potential contribution to Cuba's development.

In this regard, the following ongoing needs constitute important challenges:

- To increase effective introduction and dissemination of scientific and technological advances in the country's economic and social realms
- To enhance the training, effective use, and constant requalification of human resources linked to Cuba's ACT
- To re-equip and refurbish the infrastructure of research-and-development facilities gradually and in accordance with Cuba's overall investment process
- To increase the efficiency and effectiveness of ACT planning and funding in the country, in both academic and productive sectors

In sum, albeit the application and generalization of Cuba's scientific-technical policy has been imperfect, it has still contributed decisively to enhancing the country's general development, the efficiency of its productive enterprises, and the quality of its service-based entities. The policy's success has had direct repercussions on the competitiveness of many of Cuba's important industries—such as nickel, software, and steel—and on its services—such as health care, education, and environmental protection. It has promoted national culture, developed strategic thinking, supported the training of human resources, created the necessary infrastructure of institutions and organizations, and promoted the application of science in the interest of national development, productive processes, and human well-being, while contributing to the defense of peace and international solidarity.

Knowledge-Based Sectors

The accelerated development of science and its increasing connection with the economy are unquestionably distinct features of the new millennium. Notable are the influential role of the management of knowledge in development, the significant weight of accumulated technological knowledge in economic performance, and the ever-increasing transformation of knowledge into an essential, direct factor of production. Most scholars currently accept that knowledge is becoming and will be the most dynamic element of, and the most important resource for, economic development, even more important than capital. It is no wonder that knowledge economy and knowledge society have become buzzwords today.

Over the last twenty years, the importance of knowledge-based productive sectors has risen, especially in developed countries. These sectors are a growing component of the total business activity in the European Union, Japan, and the United States, reaching 15 percent in some of these countries.[10] Knowledge-based production is more important in services than in goods sectors, because knowledge-based inputs tend to add higher value in the former.

The OECD has categorized all productive processes as high, medium, or low value-added according to the level of knowledge and technologies employed.[11] The following nine branches of production are listed in OECD's "high-tech" category: aeronautics, computers and office machines, electronics and telecommunications, pharmaceuticals, scientific instruments, electrical machinery, chemicals, non-electrical machinery, and armaments.

Cuba's support for ACT, its well-trained human resources, and its government's foresight and decision making have promoted the emergence of a knowledge-based sector that has begun to yield not only scientific results but also social and economic results. The strongest economic results to date are in biotechnology, information technology, energy, and the environment, although the effort is gradually extending to other goods and services industries as well. Services are believed to have the greatest potential for future development. The foreign-exchange earnings from knowledge-based goods and especially services have already contributed to relaxing Cuba's current main economic constraint, its negative balance of trade on goods (that is, foreign-exchange constraint). But the earnings come from a limited range of knowledge-based goods and services, because Cuba's research and investment into most knowledge-based sectors is best described as relatively small but important first steps. Yet knowledge is seen as the central axis of Cuba's future economic development.

The remainder of this chapter summarizes four significant knowledge-based sectors: biotechnology, information and communications technology, energy, and the environment. Due to the scope of this chapter and the complexity of these sectors, they cannot be evaluated according to highly specialized criteria. Nevertheless, the main activities and results in each sector are presented and discussed, along with its current and prospective contributions to the national economy and to the development of Cuban society.

Biotechnology

Pharmaceuticals constitute a powerful industry and one of the fastest-growing sectors in the modern world economy. Pharmaceutical production is concentrated in developed countries, where similarly more than 80 percent of total sales occur. Annual sales in the United States are on the order of $235 billion, nearly 35 percent of the worldwide market.

Biotechnology, one sector of the pharmaceutical industry, first appeared as a field of industrial interest and development in the 1970s. It is recognized as an industrial sector based on knowledge, rooted in scientific research, and characterized by products with a high density of value added from knowledge and technology. It is expected not only to become a major sector in the future world economy but, more importantly from a human point of view, to have tremendous impact on human health and food production.

Today, more than five thousand closely linked companies and research centers comprise the global biotechnology industry. Annual sales are more than $70 billion, of which more than 60 percent are in the United States. About 80 percent of the biotechnology sector is concentrated in the United States and Europe, with almost all of the remaining 20 percent in Japan.

Cuba is one of the few third-world countries with a biotechnology sector that is successful in terms not only of economic results but also social impact. Several factors contributed to this internationally recognized result:

- The foresight of the country's leaders
- The commitment and will of the government
- The training and the human and scientific quality of the human resources in the sector
- The support and cooperation of scientists, specialists, and technicians from other countries

Today Cuban biotechnology employs more than ten thousand workers, 50 percent of whom are university graduates. There are some 120 research centers, production units, commercial companies, medical products companies, and other facilities, many of which are part of the Western Scientific Cluster.

Cuba has shared its experience in biotechnological production with China, Brazil, India, and Spain, where there are production plants that operate on technology transferred from Cuba. In economic terms, Cuba's biotech sector has increased more than fivefold in the last ten years, with 2007 sales of nearly $230 million in roughly fifty countries. It has become the most dynamic export branch in Cuba's foreign trade, already making an important contribution to the country's total exports.

The original reason for the development of biotechnology in Cuba was, however, its social impact. To date its main social benefits have been in health care, not only for Cubans but also for people from other countries. This sector furnishes the Cuban health system with more than 160 medications. Using its own vaccines, Cuba managed to control a meningococcal meningitis outbreak and reduce hepatitis B to a very low incidence in the population. Cuba produces eight antigens used in the thirteen vaccines currently administered to infants and children, by which means nine diseases have been completely eradicated from the population.

A second social impact concerns food production. One important accomplishment is the development of vaccines used in fish and shrimp hatcheries. A bio-nematocide has been developed and is already being marketed to protect vegetables from parasitic worms. Although these products and a few others are being used nationwide and exported internationally, Cuba has but scratched the surface of applications of biotechnology to food production, an area with great potential rewards for popular well-being.

The result of Cuba's emphasis on developing its biotechnological and medical sector is a portfolio of products whose breadth is unique for a small third-world country. Cuba now produces fifty diagnostic products or systems and makes more than sixty generic drugs. Table 12.1 indicates the explosive growth of biotechnological products over the last two decades and lists many other advanced products that have entered production or are undergoing experimental research as of 2006. Cuba has filed for 1,500 international patents for processes, products, and equipment, 500 of which have been granted (the rest are pending). Of these patents, 170 are for products or equipment, categories that are particularly important for generating foreign-exchange earnings. Cuba is maintaining and enhancing its reputation for quality in this area by registering its products with the National Certification Center, which subjects them to rigorous quality standards.

The model for the Cuban biotechnology sector is unique, appropriate, rational, innovative, and effective. Besides its aforementioned organizational foundations, three features are important in producing its impressive results. The first is the application in all biotech centers of the principle of instituting

Table 12.1. Biotechnology products from Cuba's scientific clusters

1981–1990	1991–2000	2001–2006
BC anti-meningococcal vaccine	meningitis vaccine	vaccine against Haemophylus influenzae B
recombinant alpha Heberon	hepatitis B vaccine	combined vaccines (HB-Hib, DPT-Hib, DPT-HBb-Hib)
diagnostic kits	Heberkinasa	vaccine against meningitis B
	recombinant alpha Heberon	vaccine against hepatitis B
	Hebermin	vaccines and AcM for anti-cancer therapy
	Gavac	vaccine against meningococcal meningitis ACYW135
	SUMA system	vaccine against hepatitis B in Uniject
	DIRAMIC system	vaccine against leptospirosis
	Hebertrans	vaccine against salmonella
	culture of cells	EPO Erythropoietin (CIM, CIGB)
	policosanol	products and equipment for neurophysiology and neuroinformatics
	Trofin	new diagnostic systems
	natural products	Streptokinase (w/o HAS)
	neuro-diagnostic systems	neurological restoration/rehabilitation services
	anti-CD3 Monoclonal antibody	tetanic toxoid
	Surfacen	granulocyte colony stimulating factor (GCSF)
	generics	anti-allergenic
	placenta-derived products	regenerant trofin
	neurological restoration/ rehabilitation services	interferon (liquid, w/o HSA)
		interferon (lyophilized, w/o HSA)
		interferon + ribavirin
		recombinant gamma interferon
		Interleukin-2
		PPG-plus anti-thrombolytic
		humanized recipient antibody (anti EGF)
		SUMA diagnostic system
		agricultural biotech products (GAVAC, bionematicide)
		EGF (parenteral)
		human transfer factor
		culture of cells
		new advanced generics
		cytotoxic drugs
		technology transfer
		placenta-derived products

"a complete cycle" from research to production to marketing. The second is the constant study and incorporation of international "best practices in production." The third is the system of constantly training and requalifying its human resources.[12]

Cuba's biotech sector has proven sustainable in terms of its economic earnings, portfolio of products, and international prestige. However, we can never forget that it exists in a small country with a low industrial productive capacity, with a national economy that is limited by a hostile blockade and that has suffered severe decreases in investment and international trade over the last twenty years. All these factors pose risks for the sector's future. Externally, it faces trade barriers and insecure sources of inputs, many of which come from the United States. In order to be able to compete externally, Cuba needs to expand its internal productive capacity, consistently direct extensive resources into both research and training human resources, continually replace equipment (which becomes obsolete very fast in this field), and fully match its national regulatory system for medicines and equipment to international standards. All these tasks are constrained by the small size of Cuba's economy and its limited investment resources, particularly for those aspects requiring hard currency.

The existence and growth of the biotech sector in Cuba is an example of what can be done to incentivize local knowledge and technologies in third-world countries. For one thing, it demonstrates that cutting-edge science and technology can be as important to economic and social development there as in the developed world. But beyond that, it shows that third-world countries can not only transfer cutting-edge technology but can also innovate and develop it. Further, they can develop new or improved, high-value-added products by incorporating advanced science and technology into the production process. Notwithstanding third-world countries' much more limited resources, they can still strive for technological parity and hence compete internationally with developed countries if they focus on a limited number of sectors. However, when drawing lessons for other third-world countries from Cuba's successful development of knowledge-based sectors, we must keep in mind the unique factors that derive from Cuba's commitment to socialism, which does not privatize knowledge, promotes integration among all economic actors, centers attention on human development, and favors investments that benefit the majority of society.

Information Technology and Communication

Recognizing the international accumulation of electronics knowledge and products in the mid-1960s, Cuba's revolutionary leaders had the foresight to begin planning for, integrating people and institutions into, and promoting training, research, and production in this sector. Ernesto "Che" Guevara played an important part in this process. He asserted that electronics and chemistry had to be among the disciplines that undergirded Cuba's productive development, and he founded the still operational Center for Research on Sugarcane Byproducts. Ever since then Cuba has worked tirelessly to build the foundations of what is today its information technology (IT) sector.

In a little more than forty years, more than five thousand students have graduated as computer science specialists and information engineers. Recently, universities and polytechnics have expanded their capacity to educate students in IT fields. Computers have been integrated into all sectors of the country's economy, particularly in education at all levels and in health care. Cuba has created the material, scientific, and organizational base for a dynamic economic branch based on knowledge and technology that is important for today's global society and will remain so in the future.

An early milestone in this process came in 1970 when, after remarkable effort and with constant encouragement from President Fidel Castro, the first Cuban microcomputer (CID-201) was developed at the Center for Digital Research of the University of Havana. While this microcomputer was in itself an impressive success of Cuban engineering, it also demonstrated the creativity and can-do attitude of Cuban researchers, technicians, innovators, and decision makers. This attitude not only spread to other branches of science and technology but became the prelude to what the country had in store in this sector.

In the 1970s and 1980s, the University of Havana began training future cybernetics specialists. Meanwhile, the Universities of Villa Clara and Oriente incorporated computer science into their syllabi, later adding microelectronics, automation, and telecommunications, which were also taught at the José Antonio Echevarría Higher Polytechnic. This effort has multiplied over the years, and IT engineering is now offered at more than ten universities. The University for Computer Science opened its doors in the 2002–3 academic year,[13] and its first graduates are already employed. Cuba now possesses a strong educational infrastructure for training highly skilled human resources in computer science, automation, and electronics careers. There are a number of research centers, among which are the Central Institute for Digital Research, the National Center for Scientific Research, and the Neuroscience Center of Cuba. Each municipality in Cuba has recently established a Youth Computer Science and Electronics Club, creating an important new level of infrastructure. Other elements of the infrastructure are computer equipment factories, branch-related enterprises, the Electronics Group, and the current Ministry of Informatics and Communications.

The IT sector has already made important contributions to the Cuban economy and society through the production of software, medical equipment, solar panels, and electronic equipment, among other products. These products are currently exported to more than twenty countries, another example of the worldwide dissemination of Cuba's endogenously produced technology in a highly competitive knowledge-based field.

With regard specifically to medical equipment, Cuba's products are designed to combine current electronics technology with the most advanced level of Cuban medicine. Today, much of the medical equipment used throughout the national health system is domestically produced. Some of this equipment is also transported to a large number of countries when Cuban doctors go on their internationally renowned health-care missions. In addition, more than ten thousand pieces of medical equipment have been exported to eleven countries in Latin America and elsewhere. Medical equipment is already an export line of considerable importance in the Cuban balance of trade. Some of the medical and educational equipment designed and produced in Cuba is particularly high-tech; examples include magnetic resonance tomography equipment, brain-mapping equipment, and educational software. The last has been successfully used, in conjunction with modern pedagogical methods, to eradicate or reduce illiteracy in various places around the world.

The development of solar panels and systems for their operation is another line of electronics-related work that the Ministry of Informatics and Communications carries out. Solar panels have made it possible to provide some of the country's most remote areas with a renewable source of electricity. Panels have been installed in more than twenty-five hundred schools, so that the students and teachers in rural areas can access the same educational technology available in the country's capital. This development has an extremely important social impact, in that first-class education is ensured in classrooms located in remote areas where there are few students, in some instances only one. In addition, it has immediate economic results. Consider, for example, the cost savings this high-value-added, knowledge- and technology-based product offers for transportation, lodging, food, and the supply of energy given the current prices of oil and foodstuffs.

Automation is an important part of IT. Cuba boasts some important automation achievements in its biotechnological and pharmaceutical facilities. Automation systems have also been installed in tens of new hotels and large tourist facilities and in the large and midsized offices of Cuba's postal system.

These examples illustrate the many possible benefits for the Cuban economy from this high-value-added, knowledge- and technology-based sector.

Yet it has yet to be developed on a large scale. That will require continued and expanded investments, along with resolution of a number of important challenges. Seven major ones are

1. establishing an endogenous Cuban model for the development and application of IT;
2. qualitatively and quantitatively increasing human capital;
3. developing networks to support IT research and development;
4. protecting and institutionalizing knowledge generated on the Island;
5. increasing the procurement of knowledge from overseas;
6. developing high-tech enterprises tailored to Cuba's economic model; and
7. shifting progressively toward open informatics standards.

Energy

The provision of electricity to the population is one of the most significant accomplishments of the Cuban revolutionary government. Over the last fifty years, the National Electrical Energy System (NEES) has increased its generation capacity thirteen-fold, from 397.1 megawatts (MW) in 1959 to 5,429.4 MW in 2007. This growth has provided the electrical energy needed for the Revolution's large expansion of housing, social, and productive facilities. Currently, 96 percent of the Island's inhabitants have access to electricity. The remaining 4 percent live in remote or even inaccessible locations where it has not yet been possible to extend the power grid. They will gradually receive electricity through the use of renewable energy or self-generating units burning conventional fuels or, where possible, by the extension of the NEES.

Currently, the NEES has an installed capacity of 2,901.4 MW in thermal power plants (53 percent of the total); 1,513.0 MW in self-generating units (27 percent), of which 1,443.7 MW utilize new technologies; 426.7 MW in gas turbines (8 percent); 40.9 MW in hydroelectric power plants (less than 1 percent); and 546.5 MW in other sources of generation (10 percent). The annual gross generation of electricity in 2006 was 16,468.5 gigawatt-hours. Electricity generation consumes a great deal of fuel, costing Cuba more than 40 percent of its total spending per annum.

Besides setting up production, repair, and maintenance units and establishing channels for addressing people's complaints, many additional activities were necessary for the expansion of NEES's generating capacity. Two major knowledge-based tasks were the large-scale efforts to train skilled human resources and to develop capacities for research, technological development, and generation of new knowledge. For its research and development of electrical energy and associated branches of knowledge, Cuba relies on a network of research centers and universities located throughout almost all the provinces. Given the importance of this branch to society, every university offering technical sciences courses is part of this network. These universities and research centers conduct studies and develop technological innovations applicable to the implementation, operation, and automation of the NEES, efforts that have been internationally recognized. Other important topics of study relate to increasing energy efficiency and developing renewable sources of energy.

The sudden rupture of Cuba's source of imported petroleum when the socialist community collapsed in the early 1990s complicated the generation of electricity. The result was daily power cuts for long hours throughout the country. Although this problem is not uncommon in many third-world countries in times of economic crisis, or sometimes even as a matter of course, it had been nearly eliminated in almost all parts of Cuba for several decades. As the government launched many organizational, technological, and financial measures to overcome the problem, it was the social solidarity of the population that kept the country from falling into irreversible chaos, which would have made any government-organized social responses impossible.

In the midst of the complex circumstances that existed not only in the energy sector but throughout the entire economy during the Special Period, the government launched a process of modernization and transformation of the electricity-generating sector. A central effort initially was the difficult project of converting Cuba's power plants to operate on domestically produced Cuban crude oil, which, unlike the previous imports, is very viscous and has a high sulfur content. This project required many years and involved a large team of highly specialized research scientists, technicians, and staff. Two other knowledge-based programs launched in the first phase addressed incipient use of renewable energy sources and increased energy efficiency (which was a technological, organizational, and economic program) and construction of many new (smaller) productive units. Simultaneously, a nationwide social program sought to educate consumers on energy conservation.

The drastic reduction in petroleum imports also created a need to increase the extraction of Cuban crude oil, despite its poor quality. New processes and technologies were developed for efficiently extracting it, treating it prior to use (in addition to converting the power plants), and capturing the natural gas that often co-occurs with oil deposits, which otherwise is simply burned off in inefficient production technologies. In 1989, Cuba imported 94 percent of its oil supply and produced only 6 percent domestically. By 2005 those figures were 56 percent and 44 percent, respectively. Whereas in 1995 Cuba produced only 1.4 million tons of oil, by 2004 this figure had increased almost two and a half times, to 3.3 million tons. The capture of the accompanying natural gas, which had previously been essentially nonexistent, reached 198.8 million cubic meters in 2006.

The energy situation in Cuba generally improved over the first phase of the modernization program, although with some fluctuations. By a few years after the millennium, power cuts had been greatly reduced but still did occur, especially when some accident befell part of the national power grid. Secure energy supplies remained a high priority for the people. Therefore, building on the scientific and technological knowledge accumulated in the country, the government showed the political will to launch a second phase under its direct oversight. This phase, referred to as the Energy Revolution, began with an in-depth reanalysis aimed at identifying and planning for a lasting and stable solution to the energy problem. A particularly important concern was to establish new, more efficient and secure electricity-generation processes.

Given that so many of the most dynamic sectors of the Cuban economy are linked to export promotion, it is worth stressing that neither the petroleum production nor the electricity-generation sectors have any connection with exports. The driving forces have been the social well-being of the population and the defense of Cuba's political sovereignty. The energy sector clearly demonstrates that producing for export is not an end in itself but a means to achieve Cuba's central goals of social well-being and defense. Of course, all of Cuba's new knowledge-based development projects—be they pharmaceuticals, medical services, software, or even tourism—simultaneously increase the supply to the domestic market as they generate exports.

To date, the Energy Revolution has identified, evaluated, and initiated nine development programs with the primary objectives of enhancing energy savings, increasing energy efficiency, and creating a distributed generation structure. The two overarching goals are to generate power efficiently under normal conditions and to ensure a level of emergency generation sufficient to maintain critical functions under extreme situations, such as weather events. The program, fostered directly by Fidel Castro, has research and development as one of its main components. Accordingly, thirty-two scientific research centers, twenty-plus universities, and tens of enterprises and entities are currently connected with this project. A second component is the intensification and deepening of the first-phase programs that concern saving energy, using it rationally, and increasing the efficiency of its production.

A central characteristic of the new Cuban energy model has been to create a distributed generation system, with more, smaller generation units that are closer to the user, as compared to the previous system based around a few very large power plants. This structure not only produces large savings by minimizing energy losses in transmission from production to consumption points, but it is also much more stable. These smaller units can be designed with a greater percentage capacity for reserve generation than the larger plants. And even if an accident should stop production in one or several small units, it would not disrupt the entire system the way accidents did in the former large units. In addition, this distributed generation structure is compatible with greater incorporation of renewable energy sources, particularly wind energy, most of whose production units are intrinsically small-scale.

Environmental Protection

Cuba occupies a prominent place globally in terms of its success in implementing an environmental policy underpinned by sound and accurate environmental management. In the last two decades Cuba has received international recognition for combining environmental protection with its long-standing commitment to socially equitable economic growth. In recognition of its commitment to environmental protection, Havana was selected along with Turin, Italy, to cohost the UN-sponsored World Environment Day in 2001. In 2006 the "Live Planet" Annual Report of the World Wildlife Fund named Cuba as the only country making progress toward sustainable development based on the combined increase of its HDI and decrease of its ecological footprint.

The Island's accomplishments in the environmental field rest on three key elements. The first is the country's commitment to the environment and Fidel Castro's active role in promoting environmental protection programs. Throughout his political life Castro has demonstrated his commitment by his unceasing work to identify and denounce the terrible consequences for human survival of the current irrational patterns of consumption of fuel, water, and other resources, as well as of inadequate environmental management around the world. The second key element is the extensive and deep stock of knowledge in this area created through the scientific work carried out over more than thirty years at specialized research centers, universities, enterprises, and scientific-technical service centers. The creation of this knowledge base has been facilitated by extensive investments in scientific infrastructure and, as with all of Cuba's knowledge-based programs, human resources. This conceptual basis has enabled the third key element, namely, environmental management directed toward the most important and useful priorities for the country.

Cuba's commitment to environmental protection has produced several environmental research centers that tackle such important and complex issues as tropical geography, soils, harbors, coasts, geology, meteorology, seismology, geophysics, and forestry. This scientific research and innovation has been applied in scores of environmentally related programs and projects at national, branch-specific, and provincial levels. One example is that Cuba has reduced its CO_2 emissions to the extent that it is not a major contributor to the global problem. Important on a more localized level is the reduction of particulates and other local contaminants that have immediate effects on the population's health. Cuban meteorology has also made important advances and today operates effectively using current technology. The ability to forecast and track hurricanes, long a scourge to Cuba, has critical implications both for public safety and for minimizing economic losses. Cuban scientists have also done excellent recent work on earthquake prediction, always a major danger and vulnerability for an island nation.

Yet the significance of the environmental sector to Cuba extends even beyond economic development, health, and physical safety. There are also national security implications, in that, for example, the condition of the water and soil influence food production. Finally, it has even had broad cultural effects in changing the way Cubans understand their nature as human beings and their relationship with the environment. For example, rather than seeing themselves simply as consumers who maximize their immediate material acquisition of whatever they can take—an attitude that promotes generalized selfishness and lack of concern for others—environmentally conscious Cubans understand themselves as custodians of the world that all humans live in, as socially connected and therefore socially concerned beings committed to sustainability.

Through educating Cuban citizens on the environment, changing their environmental consciousness, and developing a national culture of environmental protection, Cuba has improved the overall condition of its natural environment. Nevertheless, a number of major environmental challenges loom in the immediate future. Some of these have national origins, whereas others are fundamentally global issues but nevertheless have serious effects on Cuba that must be addressed. Global warming and limited water supplies are two examples of global issues with immediately obvious effects on agriculture and hence the well-being of the Cuban population. These problems also have many other, more subtle associated effects in need of study, such as the apparent correlation of global warming with increased frequency and intensity of hurricanes. Other problems of national scope are inadequate forestry cover (which Cuba has been working to remediate for fifty years), soil degradation, various forms of air and water pollution, and loss of biodiversity. The keys to addressing all these issues will be continuing to deepen the stock of knowledge in this sector, to increase the human resources that embody it, and to improve the systems of management for translating the accumulated knowledge into practice.

The current complex and ever-changing world faces growing challenges that potentially threaten the existence of humanity itself. Many people have advocated for a paradigm of "sustainable development," which balances sustainability and equity with development. There is nearly universal consensus that applying new science and technology to the productive processes that humans rely on for their existence will be an important component of any movement toward sustainable development.

Conclusions

The analysis in this chapter has aimed at documenting how Cuba's science and technology policies over the course of the Revolution have been directed at developing knowledge-based sectors in conjunction with overall social and economic strategies. The success of these policies has rested on several key factors. Among the most important have been (1) consistent government support both politically and financially/materially; (2) a large investment in human capital via scientific and technical education; (3) creation of a diverse network of research centers, universities, and other entities that support science, technology, and innovation; (4) development of a pro-science, pro-innovation consciousness and participation throughout society; (5) development of effective systems of organization, management, and evaluation; (6) development of sound methodological and regulatory procedures for these activities; (7) integration of programs across disciplines; (8) integration of research with social and economic applications, particularly in increasing the value added during production; and (9) global scientific and technological interactions, not only effective inflows of information and technology, but also, for several decades now, effective outflows as part of Cuba's interactions with scientifically advanced countries and its overall aid to less-developed countries.

The biggest lesson for other countries is that the Cuban experience provides an example of what a small and relatively poor country can accomplish in knowledge-based sectors if the commitment is present. A feature that sets Cuba's achievements apart, however, is the connection between development of knowledge-based sectors and Cuba's central goal of building a more just and equitable socialist society, which yielded advantages that have facilitated Cuba's achievements.

Notes

1. CITMA, Documentos rectores de la ciencia y la innovación tecnológica (Havana: CITMA, 2001).

2. Vito Quevedo et al., Bases para el perfeccionamiento y desarrollo de la innovación (Havana: Ediciones Academia, 2003).

3. CITMA, Indicadores de ciencia y tecnología, 1996–2005 (Havana: CITMA, 2006).

4. CITMA, "Prioridades de la ciencia y la tecnología cubanas" (CITMA document, 2008).

5. Vito Quevedo, Jesús Chía and Armando Rodríguez Batista, "Midiendo el impacto," Ciencia, Innovación y Desarrollo 7, no. 1 (2002).

6. Sandra Brisolla, "Producción y difusión de indicadores de ciencia y tecnología: Su utilización en las esferas nacional y regional" (presented at the V Taller de indicadores de Ciencia y tecnología, RICYT, 2001).

7. Quevedo et al., Bases para el perfeccionamiento y desarrollo de la innovación.

8. Partido Comunista de Cuba, "Resolución económica del V Congreso del PCC" (1995).

9. RAND, "Colaboración en ciencia y tecnología: ¿Creando capacidades en los países en desarrollo?" (report prepared for the World Bank, March 2001).

10. Vito Quevedo, "La cooperación científico–técnica entre los países del sur, la propiedad intelectual y la transferencia de tecnología: Retos y oportunidades" (presented at the II Foro de Negocios de los Países No Alineados, November 2007).

11. OECD, Revisión de las clasificaciones de los sectores y de los productos de alta tecnología (Paris: OECD, 1997).

12. Agustín Lage Dávila, "Conectando ciencia a la economía: Las palancas del socialismo," Cuba Socialista No. 45 (2007).

13. Fidel Castro Díaz–Balart, Ciencia, tecnología y sociedad (Havana: Editorial Científico Técnica, 2004).

Contributors

Juan Carlos Alfonso Fraga is a researcher and director of the Center for Studies on Population and Development. He has directed and participated in many national and international studies about and related to fertility and aging. In 2002, he was national director of Cuba's last population and housing census.

Elena Álvarez González works for the Government Standing Commission for Implementation and Development responsible for implementing the new economic model unfolding in Cuba. She directed the National Institute for Economic Studies until 2005, when she became an adviser to the minister of economy and planning. Her writings on Cuba's external sector, its model of development, its policies during the 1990s crisis and recovery, and on its medium- and long-range planning have been published internationally. In 2003, she won the National Prize in Economics and later coauthored *Política social y reformas estructurales: Cuba a principios del siglo XXI.*

Ángel Bu Wong is director of research at the National Institute for Economic Studies and professor at the University of Havana. He has produced many works on agroindustry and agricultural cooperatives and coauthored *La ganadería en Cuba: Desempeño y desafíos*.

Al Campbell is professor emeritus of economics at the University of Utah. His research and publications have focused on the nature and performance of contemporary capitalism and the theoretical and empirical study of possible alternatives.

Rita Castiñeiras García is a researcher at the National Institute for Economic Studies and director there of the social policies section. A founding professor of the Department of Economics of the University of Havana, she has extensive experience in planning, social development, and social policy and has published widely on these themes.

Pablo Fernández Domínguez is professor at the University of Havana, consultant to the Food and Agricultural Organization, and adjunct researcher at the National Institute for Economic Studies. He has written many articles about Cuba's agricultural and livestock sector and coauthored *La ganadería en Cuba: Desempeño y desafíos*.

Dr. Ángela Ferriol (1953–2011) directed the National Institute for Economic Studies from 2005 to 2011. Coauthor of *Política social: El mundo contemporáneo y las experiencias de Cuba y Suecia*, she published works on Cuba's labor market and employment policy, inflation and real wages, food security, equity, poverty, income distribution, social policies, and the achievement of the Millennium Goals. For her research, Ferriol won the Annual Award of the Academy of Science in 1999, 2003, and 2004.

Miguel Alejandro Figueras is currently an adviser to the minister of tourism. He was formerly deputy minister of the Ministry of the Sugar Industry and the deputy first president of the Central Planning Board. He is professor in the Department of Economics at the University of Havana and the author of five books on the Cuban economy. He won the National Economics Prize in 2008.

Alfredo García Jiménez, professor at the University of Havana, currently directs the National Institute for Economic Studies. He has coauthored various books and published numerous articles on the development of tourism in Cuba. He won the Academy of Sciences Award in 2005.

Dr. Alfredo Morales Cartaya (1948–2010) focused his technical science education and his life's work on the situation and condition of working people in Cuba. Elected to the national secretariat of the Confederation of Cuban Workers at its fifteenth congress and later acting as its secretary general in Havana, he also served as minister of labor and social security of Cuba from 1999 to 2009. At the time of his death, he was president of the national commission of the Social Prevention and Care System.

Vito N. Quevedo Rodríguez is director of science, technology and innovation in the Ministry of Science, Technology and the Environment. A senior professor specializing in electric power, he has published widely on this subject and produced numerous national and international works on Cuba's policies for the development of science, technology, and innovation.

Nancy A. Quiñones Chang teaches in the Department of Macro-microeconomics at the University of Havana. A researcher at the National Institute for

Economic Studies from 1985 to 2011, she has focused her research since 1990 on the reinsertion of Cuba into the Caribbean, Latin American, and world economic and trade systems.

Dr. José Luis Rodríguez is an adviser at the Center for Studies of the World Economy in Havana. Minister of economy and planning of Cuba from 1998 to 2009, he has authored numerous books, articles, and studies on the Cuban economy and on socialist economic and political issues.

Oscar U-Echevarría Vallejo is a researcher at the National Institute for Economic Studies, specializing in studies related to planning and macroeconomics issues. A professor of advanced graduate and specialization courses at the University of Havana, he has published widely on macroeconomic planning.

Index

Page numbers in italics refer to figures and tables.

Contemporary Cuba

Edited by John M. Kirk

Afro-Cuban Voices: On Race and Identity in Contemporary Cuba, by Pedro Pérez-Sarduy and Jean Stubbs (2000)
Cuba, the United States, and the Helms-Burton Doctrine: International Reactions, by Joaquín Roy (2000)
Cuba Today and Tomorrow: Reinventing Socialism, by Max Azicri (2000)
Cuba's Foreign Relations in a Post-Soviet World, by H. Michael Erisman (2000)
Cuba's Sugar Industry, by José Alvarez and Lázaro Peña Castellanos (2001)
Culture and the Cuban Revolution: Conversations in Havana, by John M. Kirk and Leonardo Padura Fuentes (2001)
Looking at Cuba: Essays on Culture and Civil Society, by Rafael Hernández, translated by Dick Cluster (2003)
Santería Healing: A Journey into the Afro-Cuban World of Divinities, Spirits, and Sorcery, by Johan Wedel (2004)
Cuba's Agricultural Sector, by José Alvarez (2004)
Cuban Socialism in a New Century: Adversity, Survival, and Renewal, edited by Max Azicri and Elsie Deal (2004)
Cuba, the United States, and the Post-Cold War World: The International Dimensions of the Washington-Havana Relationship, edited by Morris Morley and Chris McGillion (2005)
Redefining Cuban Foreign Policy: The Impact of the "Special Period," edited by H. Michael Erisman and John M. Kirk (2006)
Gender and Democracy in Cuba, by Ilja A. Luciak (2007)
Ritual, Discourse, and Community in Cuban Santería: Speaking a Sacred World, by Kristina Wirtz (2007)
The "New Man" in Cuba: Culture and Identity in the Revolution, by Ana Serra (2007)
U.S.-Cuban Cooperation Past, Present, and Future, by Melanie M. Ziegler (2007)
Protestants, Revolution, and the Cuba-U.S. Bond, by Theron Corse (2007)
The Changing Dynamic of Cuban Civil Society, edited by Alexander I. Gray and Antoni Kapcia (2008)
Cuba in the Shadow of Change: Daily Life in the Twilight of the Revolution, by Amelia Rosenberg Weinreb (2009)
Failed Sanctions: Why the U.S. Embargo against Cuba Could Never Work, by Paolo Spadoni (2010)
Sustainable Urban Agriculture in Cuba, by Sinan Koont (2011)
Fifty Years of Revolution: Perspectives on Cuba, the United States, and the World, edited by Soraya M. Castro Mariño and Ronald W. Pruessen (2012)
Cuban Economists on the Cuban Economy, edited by Al Campbell (2013)
Cuban Revelations: Behind the Scenes in Havana, by Marc Frank (2013)
Cuba in a Global Context: International Relations, Internationalism, and Transnationalism, edited by Catherine Krull (2014)